Praise for *Advertising Creative*

Like the constantly morphing ad business itself, this book immerses students in the dynamic pace of an industry that demands smart, up-to-the-minute players. Using the 'power writing' style the book promotes, the authors tell what to do, and most importantly, what not to do in concepting, designing, writing and making full use of new media. Mimicking what good ads do, this text uniquely hooks and involves classes in interactive exercises where blogging and social media, totally within students' comfort zones, are used. Finally a book as exciting as the ad industry it writes about.

—Mary Loporcaro,
St. John Fisher College

Advertising is a science; if you have the conditions, you get the result. *Advertising Creative, Second Edition,* shows—in a refreshingly, accessible and casual style—how to get to results and is packed with well chosen, up-to-date insights and work samples. Its fundamentally holistic approach shows how now, more than ever, ideas need substance to work both, across all platforms and with truly global consciousness. And it shows the authors' true passion for advertising, a passion their readers will need.

—Thorsten Jux, Managing Partner,
Leagas Delaney, Prague

Advertising Creative shows students how to write ads, rather than preaching to them. It's written in a casual, conversational style that makes it easy and inviting to read. Sounds like the authors are just talking to the students. Geez, isn't that what we tell them to do when writing copy?

—Sheri J. Broyles,
University of North Texas

What I love about this book is that finally someone has had the guts to state what most great creatives already know—that it takes a bold and fresh strategy to give birth to great creative work. What Tom Altstiel and Jean Grow do is lay out a very clear, very simple process for getting to great work. Everything from branded storytelling to interpreting research to evaluating research is covered here—with contemporary campaigns to back it all up. . . . Bravo, I say, for creating a wonderful dual purpose resource that both inspires and instructs. Read it, absorb it, learn it—steal from it. I sure will.

—Josh Mayer, Executive Creative Director,
Peter A. Mayer Advertising

I found the "more how/less why" approach of *Advertising Creative* to be appropriately focused, businesslike, and approachable. The Ad Stories and Words of Wisdom are just about the right touch for "advice from on high."

—Greg Pabst,
University of San Francisco

Advertising Creative, Second Edition, is descriptive and fun to read. Using great examples—many that step beyond the general market—Altstiel and Grow inspire. They demonstrate that succeeding in advertising is as simple as learning your craft, paying attention to detail, and having an un-ending passion for the business. I, for one, was reminded of why I got into this crazy world almost 20 years ago.

—Leo Olper, SVP/Chief Operating Officer,
Lápiz

The time I most love working in advertising is when the brand promise is something that can really move the consumer to a better place. If the consumer is an advertising creative, then this book does just that. It doesn't promote mindless tactics to sell people more toilet paper and frozen pizza. It helps readers understand how to connect consumers with brands in ways that honestly benefit their lives.

—Donna Charlton-Perrin, Group Creative Director,
Ogilvy

This *Second Edition* of Altstiel and Grow's book provides golden nuggets of information that will help equip students in developing sound strategy and deploying solid tactics.

—Ginger Rosenkrans,
Pepperdine University

Advertising Creative, Second Edition, provides a wonderful orientation. The parallel paths of explanation, cases, personalities, and history create a 360-degree view that entertains as it informs. Full of experience and inspiration, it moves knowledge toward wisdom. . . . It feels fresh and creates natural appeal. Good to see something so modern.

—Lynda Pearson, Executive Creative Director,
Amazon Advertising

I'm a big fan of the book's "more how/less why" approach. . . . You can tell the authors have real-life experience, which is a plus. I think the WORDS OF WISDOM are great. By the nature of the layout of the book, the quotes are sure to be read, and there are some real gems here. They match the tone of the book and contain worthwhile perspectives.

—Lara Zwarun,
University of Missouri-St. Louis

An essential tool for all who teach creativity—anywhere—and for all who want to learn more about the business of ideas.

—David Roca, Professor,
Universidad Autònoma de Barcelona, Spain

Does *Advertising Creative* make a contribution? Definitely! The organization, examples, and tone of the work make it especially attractive to advertising educators.

—Jason Chambers,
University of Illinois at Urbana–Champaign

The *Second Edition* of *Advertising Creative* is well researched, written, and designed. But more importantly, the conclusions are bang up-to-date and entertainingly presented.

—Rob Morrice, Managing Director,
IAS B2b Marketing, London

Basic concept approaches are very straightforward and provide students a much more concrete place to begin than just "make an ad."

—Kendra L. Gale,
University of Colorado-Boulder

Advertising Creative is an amusing, witty, and enjoyable book that challenges you to create advertising that's anything but boring—don't miss this book!

—Michal Charvát, General Manager,
OgilvyAction, Prague

advertising
CREATIVE

SECOND EDITION

advertising CREATIVE

SECOND EDITION

STRATEGY, COPY + DESIGN

TOM **ALTSTIEL**

PKA Marketing

JEAN **GROW**

Marquette University

Los Angeles | London | New Delhi
Singapore | Washington DC

For information:

SAGE Publications, Inc.
2455 Teller Road
Thousand Oaks, California 91320
E-mail: order@sagepub.com

SAGE Publications Ltd.
1 Oliver's Yard
55 City Road
London EC1Y 1SP
United Kingdom

SAGE Publications India Pvt. Ltd.
B 1/I 1 Mohan Cooperative Industrial Area
Mathura Road, New Delhi 110 044
India

SAGE Publications Asia-Pacific
  Pte. Ltd.
33 Pekin Street #02-01
Far East Square
Singapore 048763

Printed in Canada

Library of Congress Cataloging-in-Publication Data

Altstiel, Tom.
Advertising creative: strategy, copy, and design/Tom Altstiel, Jean Grow. —2nd ed.
    p. cm.
Rev. ed. of: Advertising strategy. c2006.
Includes bibliographical references and index.
ISBN 978-1-4129-7491-2 (pbk.)
    1. Advertising. I. Grow, Jean. II. Altstiel, Tom. Advertising strategy. III. Title.

HF5823.A758 2010
659.1—dc22   2009015073

This book is printed on acid-free paper.

09 10 11 12 13 10 9 8 7 6 5 4 3 2 1

Acquisitions Editor:	Todd R. Armstrong
Assistant Editor:	Aja Baker
Editorial Assistant:	Nathan Davidson
Production Editor:	Brittany Bauhaus
Copy Editor:	Melinda Masson
Typesetter:	C&M Digitals (P) Ltd.
Proofreader:	Jenifer Kooiman
Indexer:	Diggs Publication Services, Inc.
Cover Designer:	Dan Augustine
Interior Designer:	Lennis Mathews
Marketing Manager:	Jennifer Reed Banando

Chapter 1. Copy, Design, and Creativity   1

Chapter 2. Before You Get Started   17

Chapter 3. Branding   29

Chapter 4. Strategy   43

Chapter 5. Issues in a Changing Marketplace   65

Chapter 6. Concepting   89

Chapter 7. Design   111

Chapter 8. Campaigns   133

Chapter 9. Headlines and Taglines   149

Chapter 10. Body Copy   171

Chapter 11. Print   191

Chapter 12. Electronic Media   211

Chapter 13. Digital   235

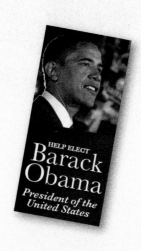

Chapter 14. Direct Marketing 255

Chapter 15. Beyond Media 271

Why a Second Edition of This Book?

When we began this process, we set out to write the *one* creative strategy and tactics book that would educate and motivate students and working professionals. We thought we came close with the first edition of *Advertising Strategy: Creative Tactics From the Outside/In*. The truth is there is no single book to cover all facets of the creative process, since our business has evolved into a seamless blend of concept, copy, design, promotions, and unrelenting technological advancements. The best we can do is cover some of the basics that will always apply to the creative process, as we adapt to the fast-changing nature of our industry. So along with the new title, you will see far more emphasis on strategy, concepts, design, and integration of media and technology, which more accurately reflects today's world of strategic communications.

As a working professional, Tom brings an outsider's point of view while working inside academia. Jean draws on her years of experience in the outside world in addition to the discipline and in-depth analysis that comes from years of research as she earned her PhD and tenure as an associate professor. Each of us brings a unique blend of real-world and academic perspectives. Our approach is to share what we've learned in this business, what has worked well for us in the classroom, and what we've observed from others who are far more talented and successful. The rest we've just borrowed from other authors (with every attempt to give credit where it's due).

This book has several other differences from traditional textbooks:

More how, less why: The focus here is on creative strategy and tactics. We skip most of the principles and history of advertising. Instead, we offer more tips and techniques, checklists, and how-to stuff. We recognize that creativity does not come from reading a list or following some formula, but the presentation of some concepts may help readers get organized or trigger a burst of creative thinking.

Strategically blending copy, design, and digital technology: The nature of our business calls for writers who understand design, designers who understand copy, and all creatives who understand the opportunities and challenges of online marketing. We focus on copy while stressing the synergy between copy and design. Above all, we wrote it with strategy top of mind.

Up-to-date examples: About 90% of the examples we present here were less than 2 years old at the date of publishing (about half were less than 6 months old when the manuscript was shipped). Older gems are used to illustrate key points, not to represent the latest trends. Best of all it's printed in color!

Student-created ads: Students, this is your competition. These examples not only illustrate particular points; they show the incredible untapped resources in our colleges and design schools.

Ad stories: We offer short case histories and anecdotes from some of the top creative people in this business.

Exercises: This time around we decided to provide some exercises to help bring some of the concepts to life in the classroom and beyond. Some work best as in-class exercises, while others can stretch to outside assignments. Most are adaptable to individual teaching styles.

Test bank: Teachers, once you've ordered our book, you'll have access to our test bank through SAGE. Just call 800-818-7143 and request our test bank on a CD.

Our blog: We wanted to extend this book into an ongoing dialogue. So we are blogging about teaching advertising creative, with students joining in the discussion. We'd love to have you join the conversation. You can find us at teachingadcreative.com.

We hope you like what we've done with the new edition. If you have ideas about how to improve the book and would like to contribute an exercise, we would love to hear from you. We like to think of this book as a work in process. Send any correspondence to jean.grow@marquette.edu or tom.altstiel@gmail.com.

If you learn nothing else from this book or from an advertising class, remember this: Never stop learning. Never stop growing.

Let's get started.

Ancillaries

An author-hosted interactive blog provides both instructors and students with a forum for an ongoing dialogue about teaching and learning *Advertising Creative*, posting work, and sharing assignments. For more information about teaching advertising, visit www.teachingadcreative.com and join the conversation today!

An instructors' test bank is available on the password-protected Web site, www.sagepub.com/altstiel2einstr. Qualified instructors may receive access to the site by contacting SAGE Customer Care at 1-800-818-SAGE (7243), 6am–5pm PT.

Acknowledgments

We are grateful to all those who contributed to this book. So many are unnamed, but their contributions have not gone unnoticed. However, we would like to acknowledge a few specific people. We begin with those who have shared their wisdom in the form of *Ad Stories* or *Exercises.* Each has added depth and insight, making this a richer book. Ileana Alémán-Rickenbach (BVK/MEKA), Michele Barker (The Martin Agency), Scott Bedbury (Brandstream), Jeanie Caggiano (Leo Burnett), Janet Champ (formerly of Wieden + Kennedy), Johnathan Crawford (DataDog Interactive Marketing), Jeff Ericksen (Ms. Coffmansen's Portfolio Finishing School), David Fowler (Ogilvy), Dave Hanneken (Laughlin Constable), Margaret Johnson (Goodby, Silverstein & Partners), Laurence Klinger (Lápiz), Michael Lebowitz (Big Spaceship), G. Andrew Meyer (Leo Burnett), Charlotte Moore (formerly of Wieden + Kennedy), Anna Morris (formerly of Burrell), Matt Nyquist (Olson), Jennifer Randolph (Saatchi & Saatchi), Dave Schiff (Crispin Porter + Bogusky), Maureen Shirreff (Ogilvy), and Brenna Whisney (Olson), we thank you for helping us bring *Ad Stories* to life. For our *Exercises* we gratefully acknowledge Sheri J. Broyles (University of North Texas); Mike Cissne (Bader Rutter); Jeff Ericksen (Ms. Coffmansen's Portfolio Finishing School); Kwangmi Ko Kim (Towson University); Sue Northey (Cramer-Krasselt); Dorothy Pisarski (Drake University); Kimberly A. Selber (University of Texas–Pan American); and Roy Winegar (Grand Valley State University). Thank you for providing strategic inspirations, often with a touch of whimsy.

No book of value makes its way to press without the enormous contribution of reviewers. The authors and SAGE thank our reviewers for their insightful wisdom, for they have made this a better book. For our first edition: Sheri J. Broyles (Department of Journalism, University of North Texas); Jason Chambers (Department of Advertising, University of Illinois–Urbana-Champaign); Cynthia M. Frisby (Department of Advertising, Missouri School of Journalism, University of Missouri–Columbia); Peggy J. Kreshel (Grady College of Journalism and Mass Communication, University of Georgia); Deb Merskin (School of Journalism and Communication, University of Oregon); and Greg Pabst (Department of Communication Studies, University of San Francisco). For our second edition: Olorundare E. Aworuwa (Department of Mass Communication, Jackson State University); Ruth E. Brown (Department of Advertising, University of Nebraska–Kearney); Tim Chandler (Department of Communication, Hardin-Simmons University); Brenda E. Innocenti (Department of Communication Design, Kutztown University of Pennsylvania); Mary Loporcaro (Department of Communication and Journalism, St. John Fisher College); Ginger Rosenkrans (Communication Division, Pepperdine University); Kimberly A. Selber (Department of Communication, The University of Texas–Pan American); L. Andrew Stanton (Department of Communication Studies, Fort Hays State University); and Nancy R. Tag (Department of Media & Communication Design, The City College of New York).

We also gratefully acknowledge the support and encouragement of our editor, Todd Armstrong, who went to bat for us at every turn. Along with Todd, a number of others at SAGE patiently guided and supported us. Aja Baker is editorial assistant extraordinaire. Claudia Hoffman, production manager, and Brittany Bauhaus, production editor, provided the skilled hands and patient spirits to make this a beautiful book. Melinda Masson, copy editor, came to see the English language through the lens of advertising, while Jenifer Kooiman provided thorough proofreading. We are grateful. Jennifer Reed Banando has provided enthusiastic promotional assistance. We thank you all.

Special thanks goes to Lennis Mathews, for her work on the book layout, and to Dan Augustine, for his cover design. Their design skills and patience made our words beautiful. And we are most grateful to our colleagues at Marquette, who have continued to support our work as writers.

Above all we thank our families and close friends. They have kept us going when we might otherwise have let exhaustion lead us astray. We'd like to give special thanks to Mary Altstiel. Her patience and sense of humor kept us going through some long nights. And her diligent proofreading—reading this book from cover to cover—was an exceptional contribution for which we are deeply grateful.

We close with a note of gratitude to our students, for it is you who inspire us to teach with passion and continually remind us that humility and good humor go a long way. Thank you.

Copy, Design, and Creativity

No one can teach you to be creative. But you may be surprised how creative you really are. You may not have been an A+ English student. But you may find you're an excellent copywriter. You may not be a great sketch artist. But you may discover you have a talent for logo design or ad layouts. If you're lucky, you'll take classes that allow you to discover a lot about creative strategy and tactics, and probably a lot about yourself. At the very least you should learn:

- The correct format for writing copy for each medium.

- The basic rules of copywriting and when to break them.

- How to put more sell into your copy.

- Design basics that apply to all media.

- How to connect the reader or viewer with the advertiser.

- How to keep continuity throughout a campaign.

- The importance of presenting your work.

Who Wants to Be a Creative?

At the beginning of each semester we ask students, "Who wants to be a copywriter?" We get a halfhearted response from about 1 in 6 at the beginning of the class. "Who wants to be an art director or designer?" Usually we get a few more people raising their hands, but not many. The truth is most students don't want to commit to any specific career path in the creative field. These are the most common reasons:

- "I think I want to be an account exec."

- "I might want to be an account planner."

- "I want to be a media director."

Words of Wisdom

"Properly practiced creativity can make one ad do the work of ten." [1]

—Bill Bernbach

- "Words are boring. I'm more of a picture person."

- "I'm not sure I can write."

- "I'm not sure I even want to be in advertising."

Those are legitimate reasons, but we can make a case for learning about creative strategy and tactics to answer every one of them. Account executives need to know how to evaluate creative work. Does it meet the objectives? What's the strategy? Why is it great or not so great? When account executives and account managers understand the creative process, they become more valuable to the client and their agency. Account planners have to understand consumers, their clients' products, market conditions, and many other factors that influence a brand preference or purchase. In essence they function as the voice of the consumer in strategy sessions. The skills required to develop creative strategy are key components in account planning.

Media folks need to recognize the creative possibilities of each medium. They need to understand tone, positioning, resonance, and the other basics pounded into copywriters. Their perspectives can also contribute to great strategies and tactics.

Designers, art directors, producers, and graphic artists should know how to write or at least how to defend their work. Why does it meet the strategies? Do the words and visuals work together? Does the font match the tone of the ad? Is the body copy too long? (It's *always* too long for art directors.) As we'll stress repeatedly through this book, writers also need to understand the basics of design. Design can't be separated from the concept. There is English, and there is advertising copy. You're not writing the Great American Novel or even a term paper. You are selling products and services with your ideas, which may or may not include your deathless prose. What you say is more important than how you write it. Ideas come first. Writing with style can follow.

Creativity is still useful outside of advertising. You can put the skills learned through developing creative strategy and tactics to work in more fields than advertising. The ability to gather information, process it, prioritize the most important facts, and develop a persuasive message is useful in almost every occupation.

Even if you don't aspire to be the next David Ogilvy, you might learn something about marketing, advertising, basic writing skills, and presenting your work. Who knows? You might even like it.

The Golden Age of Creativity

Every generation seems to have a Golden Age of something. Many people who are in their creative primes look back to the 1950s through the early 1970s as the Golden Age of Advertising. This so-called Creative Revolution was one of many uprisings during turbulent times. Unlike any other era before or since, the focus was on youth, freedom, antiestablishment thinking, and—let's face it—sex, drugs, and rock 'n' roll. So it's not surprising that some of the world's most recognized ads (some of which are included in this book) were created during this time.

What made these ads revolutionary?

- First, they began to shift focus to the brand, rather than the product. They developed a look, introduced memorable characters, and kept a consistent theme throughout years of long-running campaigns. All of these factors built brand awareness and acceptance.

- Second, they twisted conventional thinking. When most cars touted tailfins and chrome, VW told us to "Think Small." When Hertz was bragging about being top dog, Avis said they tried harder because they were number two. When Levy's advertised their Jewish rye bread, they used an Irish cop and a Native American as models.

- Third, they created new looks, using white space, asymmetrical layouts, minimal copy, and unique typography— all design elements that we take for granted in today's ads.

The driving forces of this revolution included such giants as Leo Burnett, David Ogilvy, Mary Wells Lawrence, Howard Gossage, and Bill Bernbach, all of whom are quoted heavily in this text. First and foremost, they were copywriters. But they were also creative partners with some of the most influential designers of their era, such as George Lois, Helmut Krone, and Paul Rand. Even though these top creative talents went on to lead mega-agencies, their first love was writing and design.

In this brave new world where the "Third Screen" will become our primary news and entertainment vehicle, we may be entering a new Golden Age. Who knows? Maybe *you* could become a leader in the next creative revolution.

Image 1.1

Dentyne's "Make Face Time" campaign puts the human back in communication. It's not only visually attractive; it also shows the benefit of using the product.

The Creative Team

Most copywriters do a lot more than just write ads. In fact, writing may only be a small part of their jobs. Although this section focuses on the copywriter, many of these functions are also handled by designers or art directors.

Co-captain of the creative team

Traditionally a creative team includes a copywriter and an art director, with participation by Web developers and broadcast producers. This team usually answers to a coach: the creative director.

Every player has his or her role, but in many cases, the copywriter drives the creative process. However, once the art director understands the creative

Image 1.2

When other automakers were crowing about being bigger, faster, and more luxurious, VW took the opposite position. VW's innovative campaigns not only established a very successful brand; they also ushered in a new age in creative advertising.

Image 1.3

This rough layout clearly shows the idea behind this ad, which conformed beautifully to the brand image of USA Today. The idea should always come first. Design and copy come later.

problem, he or she may be the idea leader. No matter who drives the process, the creative team needs to know the product frontward and backward, inside out. They have to understand who uses the product, how it compares to the competition, what's important to the consumer, and a million other facts. No one does it all. Sometimes art directors write the best headlines. Or writers come up with a killer visual. While someone on the team should drive the creative effort, he or she does not have to dominate it.

So, what else does a writer do?

In small shops, the writers wear so many hats, it's no wonder they develop big heads. Some of the responsibilities besides writing copy include:

- **Research**: Primary and secondary.

- **Client contact**: Getting the facts direct from the source rather than filtered through an account executive, presenting those ideas, and defending the work.

- **Broadcast producer**: Finding the right director, talent, music, and postproduction house to make your vision come to life.

- **New business**: Gathering data, organizing the creative, working on the pitch, and presenting the work.

- **Public relations**: Some copywriters also write the news releases, plan promotional events, and even contact editors.

- **Internet/interactive content**: The Internet has become an integral part of a total marketing communication effort. A lot of "traditional" media writers are now writing Web sites and interactive media.

- **Creative management**: Much has been written about whether copywriters or art directors make the best creative directors. The answer: yes.

Controlling the Creative Process

Step 1: Get the facts. If you have a research department and/or account planners, take advantage of their knowledge. But don't settle for someone else's opinion. Talk to people who use the product, as well as those who don't or won't even consider it. Talk to retailers who sell the product. Look at competitive advertising: What's good, and where is it vulnerable? In short, know as much as you can about the product, the competition, the market, and the people who buy it. Try to make the product part of your life.

Step 2: Brainstorming with a purpose. If you've done your homework, you should know the wants and needs of the target audience and how your product meets those needs. From that base, you can direct the free flow of creative ideas. Thanks to your knowledge, you can concentrate on finding a killer creative idea rather than floundering in a sea of pointless questions. But you must also be open to new ideas and independent thinking from your creative team members.

Step 3: Pick up a pencil before you reach for the mouse. This is critical, because it's all about the creative concept. Even if you can only draw stick people, that's OK. Where does the headline go? How much copy do you think you'll need? What's the main visual? How should the elements be arranged? Even though artists may ridicule your design, they will appreciate having the raw elements they can massage into a great-looking ad.

Step 4: Finding the reference/visuals. You may have a clear vision of the creative concept. Can you communicate that to your art director, creative director, account exec, or client? You can help your art director by finding photos, artwork, or design elements, not to rip off others' ideas but to make your point. The finished piece may not look anything like your original vision, but at least you can start with a point of reference. Browse the Web, stock photo books, and awards annuals. We can't emphasize this enough, especially for beginning writers: If you can't find what you want, browsing might trigger a new idea. The visual selection is a starting point, not the end game.

Step 5: Working with the rest of the team. For most creatives, the happiest and most productive years of their career are spent collaborating with others. When two creative minds click, the whole really is greater than the sum of the parts. A great creative partnership, like any relationship, needs to be nurtured and will have its ups and downs. While one person may want to drive the whole process, it's best not to run over other teammates. They may come up with some ideas that will make you look like a genius.

Step 6: Preselling the creative director and account executive. Chances are you will not be working directly with the client, and even if you are, you probably won't be the sole contact. That's why you need the people who interface with the client to buy into your ideas. Maintaining a good relationship with the creative director not only protects your job; it also gives you an ally when you pitch your ideas to the account executive and client. In many cases, the account executive represents the client in these discussions. He or she may try to poke holes in your logic or question your creative choices. That's why every creative choice must be backed with sound reasons. In the end, if the account executive is sold, you have a much better chance of convincing the client.

Image 1.4

The creative team helps develop the brand story and then must carry it through the campaign, which may last for years. The challenge is to stay true to the brand, which this ad does beautifully.

Step 7: Selling the client. As the person who developed the idea, you have to be prepared to defend your work, using logic rather than emotion. Many times your brilliant reasoning will fail since clients usually think with their wallets. Over time you'll know how far you can push a client. The trick is to know when to retreat so you can fight another day. Most clients don't mind being challenged creatively, as long as there are sound reasons for taking chances.

The three things you *never* want to hear from a client:

- "That looks just like the competitor's ads. I want our ads to stand out."

- "I was looking for something a lot more creative. Take some risks."

- "You obviously don't understand our product or our market."

You won't hear those things if you take care of Steps 1–6.

Step 8: Getting it right. OK, you've sold the client, so now what? You have to hand your creation to the production team, but your responsibilities don't end. Does the copy fit the way it should? If not, can you cut it? Can you change a word here and there to make it even better? Are the graphics what you envisioned? Your involvement is even more critical for broadcast. Did you have a specific talent in mind for voice or on-camera roles? Does the director understand and share your vision? Does the music fit?

If you remember nothing else, keep the following thought from the great Leo Burnett in mind and follow it through Step 10: *Nothing takes the guts out of a great idea like bad execution.*

Step 9: Maintaining continuity. Almost everyone can come up with a great idea. Once. The hard part is extending that great idea in other media and

Image 1.5

The creative team is responsible for maintaining continuity through a campaign. For Absolut vodka, the product has always been the star.

repeating it, only differently, in a campaign. Over time, elements of a campaign tend to drift away from the original idea. Clients usually get tired of a look before the consumer. Art directors may want to "enhance" the campaign with new elements. Someone on the creative team needs to continually monitor the elements of an ongoing campaign to make sure they are true to the original idea.

Step 10: Discover what worked and why. If the ad or series of ads in a campaign achieve their objectives, great! If they win awards but the client loses market share, look out. Keep monitoring the efficacy of the campaign. What are the readership scores? What do the client's salespeople and retailers think? How are sales? If you had to make any midcourse corrections, what would you do? If you never stop learning, you'll never miss an opportunity to make the next project or campaign even better.

Where Do I Go From Here?

A lot of entry-level copywriters and art directors set lofty career goals—most often the coveted title of creative director. However, many junior writers or designers don't consider the other exciting possibilities. We've listed a few to consider. You may actually take several of these paths in your career.

Copywriter/art director for life: It could happen. Many people are happy to hone their creative talents throughout their whole career. You can do it if you continue to improve and never stop growing.

Management/creative director: A great job with great responsibilities. It often involves more personnel management than creative talent, requiring the skills of a head coach, sales manager, and kindergarten teacher.

Account manager: Many writers are drawn to the "dark side." It makes sense, especially if you like working with clients and thoroughly understand the product, market, and consumers. In some small shops, the copy-contact system gives account execs an opportunity to create and creative types a reason to wear a suit. Art directors also work directly with clients and, in many cases, are the primary agency contact person.

Account planner: A natural for many writers who like research and enjoy being the conduit between the account manager, the creative team, and the consumer. It involves thorough knowledge of research, marketing, creative, and media and a lot of intuition. Most successful advertising copywriters already possess those skills.

Image 1.6

Talking babies are not the most original idea. However, when E*Trade combined a great adult male voice, realistic dialogue, and seamless lip sync editing, viewers had to take notice. The creative team develops the idea, but it takes a whole crew of professionals to make it work.

Image 1.7

The Barack Obama campaign was named "Marketer of the Year" by Advertising Age. *Although not officially commissioned by the Obama team, Will.i.am's "Yes We Can" music video was a media and viral sensation.* Adweek *named it the Best Ad of 2008, commenting, "Nothing else really came close."* [4]

Promotion director: Writers and art directors are idea people. So it makes sense to use that creativity to develop sales promotions, special events, sponsorships, specialty marketing programs, displays, and all the other marketing communication tools not included in "traditional advertising." This is a rapidly growing area with a lot of potential for creative people.

Public relations writer: Although most PR people won't admit it, it's easier to write a news release than an ad. Most advertising writers won't admit that editorial writing is usually more persuasive than advertising. PR writing involves much more than news releases, though. You may become an editor for a newsletter or an in-house magazine. You may produce video news releases or schedule events, press conferences, and any number of creative public relations efforts.

Internal advertising department: So far, we've outlined agency jobs, but other companies need talented creative people. In small companies, you may handle brochure writing or design, PR, trade shows, and media relations, in addition to advertising. In larger companies, you may handle promotional activities not covered by your ad agency. You may even write speeches for your CEO.

Web/interactive: The Web is so integrated into most marketing communication programs, it seems ridiculous to consider it nontraditional media. Any writer or designer today should be Web savvy. You should know the terminology and capabilities of the Internet—just as well as you understand magazines or television. You don't have to be a whiz at HTML, but having some technical expertise is a huge plus. As with any phase of advertising, creativity, not technology, is the most precious commodity.

Image 1.8

Copywriters and designers today need to think beyond traditional media to develop new ways to involve consumers with their brands. For example, this extension of Dove's campaign invites women in the United Kingdom to be part of Britain's biggest photo album.

Freelance writer/designer: A lot of people like a flexible schedule and a variety of clients. Being a successful freelancer requires tremendous discipline and endless self-promotion, plus the mental toughness to endure constant rejection, short deadlines, and long stretches between assignments.

Producer/director: Like to write broadcast? Maybe you have the knack for writing scripts, selecting talent, editing, and other elements of audio and video production. As with Web and interactive, creative talent and a logical mind are the keys. Technological expertise can be learned on the job.

Consultant: Too often it's another word for unemployed. A select few actually make a living as creative consultants. Sometimes they are no more than repackaged freelancers.

Sometimes they are "rainmakers" who help with a new business pitch. Still, a number of downsized companies and agencies will pay consultants for skills and contacts they don't have in-house. Keeping current and connected is the key to success.

Creativity and Online Media

While traditional media advertising usually rides up and down on the waves of economic conditions, many advertisers are shifting more money into social media, in good times and bad. According to the Forrester Research report, "Word of mouth, blogging and social networking will withstand tightened budgets . . . these findings stand in contrast to previous economic downturns, when spending on Internet advertising cratered as marketers turned to tried-and-true media."[5]

So what does this mean for the future of creative advertising? Many marketers will shift their emphasis to "middle of the funnel" social media applications such as discussion boards, in addition to paid search and e-mail marketing. Creatives will have to understand how to do business in the space and adapt at an increasingly faster pace to changes in technology, pop culture, and online viewing trends. That means you will have to know more than how to create a banner ad. You may have to develop entire online communities for very specific target audiences and find ways to keep them engaged . . . and oh, by the way, you still have to sell something.

What's in It for Me?

You've probably already discussed the role of advertising in society and explored ethical issues in other classes. You have reviewed theories of communication and might have even read about the great creative people of all time. That's all good, but let's be honest: If you want a creative career, you're only interested in three things: Fame, Fortune, and Fun—not necessarily in that order. Let's look at each one in a little more detail.

Fame: Everyone wants recognition. Since advertising is unsigned, there are only two ways—awards and having people say, "You're *really* the person who did that?" If they're judged good enough, writers and art directors are immortalized in *Communication Arts* annuals. Last time we looked, there are no books showcasing account execs or media buyers.

Fortune: Depending on experience, the economy, the results they generate, and a million other factors, creative people can make as

Image 1.9

The synergy of words and pictures can be developed by the copywriter, the art director, or even the account executive. This student-designed billboard is a great example of a simple idea where everything comes together (except the tools).

Image 1.10

The message: With no limits you can put all of Europe on your American Express card. How did the creative team communicate that? The copy starts (in Ireland) with "I want that . . . and that . . ." and continues all over the continent until it ends in the Greek isles with ". . . and two of those, please."

Image 1.11

Creative people tend to care about much more than promoting products. Whether they are projects for paying clients or pro bono projects, many important causes benefit from the talents of concerned professionals.

much or more money than any other people in advertising. Recent salary surveys show salaries for top creatives and top account supervisors are pretty much the same. But as a writer or an art director, you get to wear jeans, have a tattoo, pierce your nose, and spike your hair. But only if you want to.

Fun: You can be famous and rich and still be unhappy in any business. Even if you're not well known or a millionaire, you can still get a kick out of solving problems for clients. It's still a treat to work with other creatives, interact with musicians and actors, win presentations, and travel to exotic locales. No matter how much you're earning, when it stops being fun or if you lose your edge, you should probably consider getting out.

Knowing the rules and when to break them

We will not dwell on too many of the rules of advertising writing and design, but we will look at some accepted practices. These are the tips and techniques that have proven successful over time.

One "rule" will always be true. Advertising is a business—a business populated by a lot of crazy people, but still a business. Although the slogan "It's not creative unless it sells" has lost its impact, we still have to persuade someone to buy something. This reality leads to something we call "creative schizophrenia"—the internal conflict between the stuff you want to do and the stuff clients make you do. For example, if you want to get a job, you need really cool, cutting-edge stuff in your portfolio, which is usually not usable in the real world. When you land that job, you'll probably be forced to do a lot of boring stuff that sells products but looks terrible in your book. That's the nature of this business, and unless you can live with a split personality, it's hard to survive.

You don't have to be crazy, but it helps

Psychologists have spent years studying creativity. We know that creativity is not an isolated right-brained activity. Rather, it "reflects originality and appropriateness, intuition and logic. It requires both hemispheres."[6] The left side likes words, logic, and reasons. The right side likes pictures, emotions, and feelings. Bringing both hemispheres together in a mediated form is what Mihaly Csikszentmihaly calls "flow . . . a phenomenon constructed through an

Freelancing: Working for Multiple Bosses in Your PJs

Freelancing is not just about 'being your own boss.' Sure, there are those undeniable perks: choosing your own hours, working in your pajamas and showering as a 'personal choice.' But an often overlooked reality of freelancing is that you don't have a single boss, you have many: your prospective clients, your established clients, and your clients' clients. That means you have to bring more to the table than just creativity. You also need professionalism, reliability, flexibility, patience and diplomacy. You have to negotiate the demands of parties who, all too often, have varying and sometimes competing visions for the final product.

"In working with a new client, I found myself in the middle of a classic freelancing 'sticky situation.' My client was a small but well regarded local design firm who was working with a private all-girls' school. I was brought in to write the school's view book with the aim of boosting recruitment by creating a younger, hipper, more appealing image of the school. Through their research, the design firm had determined that the students made their own decisions about which school to attend. So I was directed to come up with concepts and copy that would speak to the average 14-year-old girl. So they had to be current, fun, and irreverent.

"I came up with some sample copy and ideas, which were run by the school administrators in a phone call. The design firm believed they were totally on board but I wasn't so convinced. So I was not surprised the first draft came back with deep edits and requests for rewrites on many of the sections. The tone was all wrong. The copy emphasized the wrong aspects of the school. Thankfully, I was granted a one-on-one phone conversation with an administrator at the school—my first. I was finally able to get an unscreened view of the image they wanted to project: that the school was academically rigorous and a life-changing experience. Then I created a new draft, one that hit the points that she emphasized, while also trying to contemporize the school's image. The final product was an in-between—not as bold as the design firm wanted, but much more inviting than what the school had been able to achieve. In the final equation, it was a beautiful piece of work.

"So life as a freelancer means being a juggler, a negotiator, sometimes a mind-reader, and a servant to many masters. Even if you are your own boss you seldom call the shots. But that 'working in your pajamas' thing? That's totally true. And it's pretty sweet."[7]

—Mia
Freelance copywriter, Chicago

interaction between producers and audience."[8] Flow requires flexibility and "the capacity to adapt to the advances, opportunities, technologies, and changes that are a part of day-to-day living."[9] Advertising creativity is the end product of balancing logic with irrationality, artistic freedom with the constraints of the creative problem, and divergent thinking with convergent thinking.[10] It's about making strategy come to life. What does that mean for you?

Daniel Pink, in his groundbreaking book, *A Whole New Mind: Why Right-Brainers Will Rule the Future,* argues that we are moving away from left-brain leadership toward the attributes associated with the right brain. Pink describes right-brain thinking as holistic, big picture, intuitive, and nonlinear. He states, "The Information Age we all prepared for is ending. Rising in its place is what I call the Conceptual Age, an era in which mastery of abilities that we've often overlooked and undervalued marks the fault line between who gets ahead and who falls behind."[11] So we are moving from high tech to high concept and high touch. The Information Age was about knowledge workers. *The Conceptual Age is about creators and empathizers—in other words, right-brain thinking.*

Who's Who?

In this and future chapters, you'll see some Words of Wisdom floating around. Who are these wise guys and gals? At the end of most chapters we'll provide a very brief bio of some of the best known voices in advertising, as well as other innovators whom we have cited in Words of Wisdom and Ad Stories.

Founder of the agency that still bears his name, **Leo Burnett** established a new creative style of advertising, along with many memorable characters that are still working today, including Tony the Tiger, the Jolly Green Giant, the Keebler Elves, the Marlboro Man, and the Pillsbury Doughboy. Burnett believed that creativity made an advertisement effective but, at the same time, that creativity required believability.

Perhaps the most well-known scholar on creativity, **Mihaly Csikszentmihaly** is a faculty member in the Department of Psychology at the University of Chicago. His work takes him far outside academics, where he has actually studied advertising creativity. His concept of "flow" is well known among those who study creativity. If you want to learn more, check out his book called *Flow.*

While CEO, chair, and president of the legendary Wells Rich Greene agency, **Mary Wells Lawrence** was the highest-paid, most well-known woman in American business. She was also the first female CEO of a *Fortune* 500 company. Her innovative campaigns for Braniff, Alka-Seltzer, Benson & Hedges, and American Motors brought a fresh new look to established brands. At age 40, she became the youngest person ever inducted into the Copywriters Hall of Fame.

Born Peretz Rosenbaum, **Paul Rand** was a very influential graphic designer best known for his corporate logo work in the 1950s and '60s, including IBM, UPS, and ABC. He was inducted into the New York Art Directors Club Hall of Fame in 1972.

Exercises

1. No More Wonder® Bread

Wonder® Bread is bland, white bread. Sorry to insult any Wonder® Bread lovers, but in advertising you can't be bland. You must have flavor. Back in the 1940s Wonder® Bread made the claim that it "built strong bodies in 12 ways." That's where we begin.

Below are 12 ways to build strong insights.

- Begin by keeping a journal, with an entry for each experience: who (alone or with friends), what (brief note on what the experience is—for instance, the title of a foreign film or the name of a club . . .), where (a no-brainer), when (another no-brainer), and why (your reaction, how it made you *feel*). Use your senses as you describe how each experience made you feel. That's where you'll find insights.

    1. Go to the local public market, where "slow" food is sold.

    2. Watch a subtitled foreign film.

    3. Hit the Latin dance floor.

    4. Catch the week's news on BBC online: http://www.bbc.co.uk/.

    5. Check out live jazz or blues at a neighborhood club.

    6. Attend an event sponsored a student organization for which you don't fit the demographic profile. Try the Gay-Straight Alliance, the Muslim Student Association, the Black Student Council, or an international student organization.

    7. Attend a local Rotary function.

    8. Dine on tofu.

    9. Settle in for an afternoon of NASCAR racing or World Wrestling Entertainment viewing.

    10. Experience a meeting of the College Republican/Democratic Student Association—and it has to be the opposite of your own political point of view.

    11. Join in the fun at a bingo gathering.

    12. Visit the local art museum and check out the current special exhibits.

2. Personal Branding Timeline

Now it's time to track brand consumption and loyalty across a consumer's lifespan—and you're the consumer.

- Create a map that moves across your life at 5-year increments, beginning with birth and ending with one's current age. The last increment might be less than a 5-year gap. For each 5 stage generate a list of the brands you associated with that time of your life.

- After each brand write two statements: 1) what that brand meant to you then, and 2) what it means to you now.

(Continued)

(Continued)

- Now extend your map forward by 10-year increments, 30, 40, 50, 60, 70, and 80. List brands five brands, which you think will be a part of your life, at each age. Now write a single statement about why you believe that brand will be relevant to you then.

- Discuss factors influencing your choices: familiarity, aspiration, current usage, personal or family associations, trends, and so forth.

- See if there are any brands that were constant over a long period of time. Discuss what makes those brands have traction over time. What inherited qualities and brand messages enable brand loyalty and why?

Notes

1. William Bernbach, *Bill Bernbach Said . . .* (New York: Doyle Dane Bernbach, 1989), p. 3.

2. Janet Kestin, interviewed by authors, June 2007.

3. Quote from University of Texas at Austin, Department of Advertising, http://advertising.utexas.edu/resources/quotes/ (accessed May 19, 2005).

4. Tim Nudd, "The Year on ADFREAK," *Adweek,* December 15, 2008, p. 14.

5. Brian Morrissey, "Social Media to Weather Recession" [Electronic version], *Adweek,* February 6, 2008, http://www.adweek.com/aw/content_display/news/digital/e3idcbc5d3b3d8cd77104f087d7ef56ffb7.htm (accessed December 2, 2008).

6. Wayne Weitten, *Psychology Themes and Variations* (Belmont, CA: Thomson Wadsworth, 2005), pp. 255–256.

7. Mia, Ad Story: *Freelancing: Working for Multiple Bosses in Your PJs,* February 2009.

8. Mihaly Csikszentmihalyi, "Implications for a Systems Perspective for the Study of Creativity," in *Handbook of Creativity* (Cambridge: Cambridge University Press, 1999), p. 314.

9. Mark Runco, "Creativity," *Annual Review of Psychology* 55 (2004), p. 659.

10. Mark Runco, "Creativity," p. 658.

11. Daniel Pink, *A Whole New Mind: Why Right-Brainers Will Rule the Future* (New York: Penguin, 2006), p. 3.

12. Quote from Born to Motivate Web site, http://www.borntomotivate.com/FamousQuoteCarlAlly.html (accessed May 19, 2005).

Chapter 2

Before You Get Started

Most texts will tell you that you just can't start creating an ad from scratch. Of course you can. And you just might get lucky the first time. But can you repeat that success? That's why we need to discuss the foundations of marketing communications. First, a few definitions.

Advertising, MarCom, IMC, or What?

Everyone knows what advertising is, right? George Orwell said it was "the rattling of a stick inside a swill bucket."[1] H. G. Wells claimed, "Advertising is legalized lying."[2] For a less cynical take, Professor Jef Richards of the University of Texas says, "Advertising is the 'wonder' in Wonder Bread."[3] You've probably learned that advertising is paid communication to promote a product, service, brand, or cause through the media. Is direct mail advertising? Well, if you consider mail a medium, yes. How about a brochure? Probably not; however, it can be mailed or inserted into a magazine as an ad. The Internet? Yes and no. A Web site by itself is not really advertising although a banner ad on that site is. Social networks? They can be a vehicle for ads, but they are even more effective when they influence consumer behavior without obvious advertising. Public relations? No, because the advertiser is not paying the editor to publish an article (at least not directly). Confused? Don't feel alone. Many marketing professionals can't make the distinction between advertising and other forms of promotion.

MarCom (Marketing Communications)

That's where the term *MarCom* arose. MarCom to some people takes in every form of marketing communication. Others describe MarCom as every form of promotion that's not traditional advertising. Traditional advertising usually covers print (newspapers, magazines), television, radio, and some forms of outdoor advertising. "Nontraditional" promotion includes direct marketing, sales promotion, point of sale, public relations, e-mail, online advertising, search engine marketing, mobile, social networks, guerilla marketing, viral/buzz, word of mouth, and

Words of Wisdom

"Marketing was really better called 'advertising.' Marketing is about communicating the values of a product after it had been developed." [4]

—Seth Godin

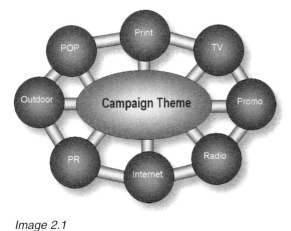

Image 2.1

In an Integrated Marketing Communications program, all elements work individually but must also work together to maximize exposure to the advertiser's message.

everything else you can attach a logo, slogan, or message to. These divisions evolved as large agencies discovered that they could make money beyond earning media commissions for "traditional" advertising. So they created MarCom units or separate interactive, direct, and sales promotion divisions. Sometimes these are set up as separate entities under the corporate umbrella of a large agency.

IMC (Integrated Marketing Communications)

IMC unites the MarCom elements into a single campaign. IMC has become a buzzword, especially for agencies that set up MarCom divisions. Actually, IMC is nothing new. Smaller full-service agencies and in-house ad departments have been doing it for years under the banner of "doing whatever it takes to get the job done." With limited budgets, companies need to get the most mileage from their promotional dollar with a variety of tools, including advertising.

Advertising's Role in the Marketing Process

The buying process for some products may take a couple of seconds, such as picking out a sandwich at the drive-through, or it may take years, as with buying a multimillion-dollar piece of industrial equipment. No matter what the time frame, there is a process that starts with awareness and ends with the sale. One of the best ways to describe the process is using the acronym AIDA. It's not the opera, but rather it stands for Attention, Interest, Desire, and Action. Understanding AIDA helps you as a creative person to guide a consumer from just recognizing your brand to demanding it. Here's how AIDA works in advertising:

1. **Attention:** How do you get someone who is bombarded with hundreds if not thousands of messages a day to look at your ad or commercial? If you're a writer, one way is to use powerful words, or if you're an art director, you need a picture that will catch a person's eye.

2. **Interest:** Once you capture a person's attention, he or she will give you a little more time to make your point, but you must stay focused on the reader or viewer's wants and needs. This means helping them to quickly sort out the messages that are relevant. In some cases, you might use bullets and subheadings to make your points stand out.

3. **Desire:** The Interest and Desire parts of AIDA work together. Once a person's interested, they need to really want the product. As you're building the reader's interest, you also need to help them understand how what you're offering can help them in a real way. The main way of doing this is by appealing to their personal needs and wants. Another component of Desire is Conviction—the willingness to buy when the opportunity is right. So even if your message does not result in an immediate sale, keeping the messages on track and on time could eventually trigger a sale.

Ad Story

honey, please don't go

Save the Honey Bees

"If your client is called to appear before Congress because of a campaign you've created for them, you know you've either done something really good or really bad. The client in the hot seat: Häagen-Dazs, makers of super-premium ice cream. In this case, it was something really good.

"In 2008, after two successive price increases, Häagen-Dazs came to us in dire need of an out-of-scale effect on a very small budget. Knowing that every piece of advertising that we created needed to be a creative media multiplier, using the power of PR to give the campaign the scale and reach that the modest budget could never accomplish with a standard media buy.

"We started by asking Häagen-Dazs to let go of its traditional product-focused approach. Once the client bought in to making a radical change in direction, my partner, Jim Elliott, and I challenged our group to forget about filming expensive shots of delicious high-end ice cream and instead focus on something much more negative yet much more profound: Colony Collapse Disorder, one of the great scientific puzzles of our time. Honeybees are disappearing, and nobody knows why. Without the bees to pollinate them, close to a third of the natural foods that humans eat will disappear, including many of the natural ingredients in Häagen-Dazs ice cream.

"First we launched the 'hd loves hb' (Häagen-Dazs loves honeybees) initiative by creating a new flavor, Vanilla Honey Bee, with proceeds to be donated to Penn State and UC Davis to help fund honeybee research. A print campaign for the new flavor let people know that they could help the cause simply by enjoying ice cream.

"To dramatize the plight of the bees, we brought to life their symbiotic relationship with flowers in an epic television commercial, a tragic tale of love and loss rendered in state-of-the-art CGI and set to a custom-commissioned, heart-rending operatic score.

"The Web site we created, helpthehoneybees.com, gave visitors an immersive space to learn about the problem, with the tools to donate to the research program and help spread the word.

"We shot a series of cheap, comical bee-dance videos and engineered their viral spread, bringing the problem to the attention of millions of earth-conscious YouTubers and eco-bloggers.

"We ran a magazine insert made of seed-infused paper that consumers could bury in the ground and grow wildflowers for honeybees to feed on. We handed out samples of Vanilla Honey Bee ice cream and millions of wildflower seeds at farmer's markets across the US. Community groups and schools joined in to help foster community gardens and farms.

"Soon, every major media channel in America picked up on the story and helped champion our cause. A week after launch, the campaign had generated over one hundred and twenty-five million PR impressions—our goal for the entire year.

"And in June of 2008, Häagen-Dazs, together with a national coalition of beekeepers, testified on the bees' behalf in front of Senator Hillary Clinton and the House Agricultural Sub-committee on Capitol Hill to urge Congress to allocate funding for additional honeybee research. I guess you could say we did something really good—for Häagen-Dazs and for honey bees."

—Margaret Johnson
Group Creative Director, *Goodby, Silverstein & Partners*, San Francisco

4. **Action:** OK, the reader's hooked. Now what do you want them to do? Visit a Web site? Take a test drive? Call for information? Plunk down some cash now? You should be very clear about what action you want your readers or viewers to take.

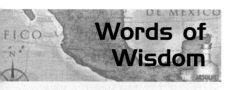
Knowing What Makes the Consumer Tick

Consumer behavior is the study of how people buy, what they buy, when they buy, and why they buy. It blends elements from psychology, sociology, and marketing, and quite a bit of insight. Marketers attempt to dissect the buyers' decision-making process, both for individuals and for groups. They study demographics, psychographics, and lifestyles to understand what people want and how they want to get it. Billions of dollars are spent on research to test new products and the consumer's willingness to buy. But many times the most successful marketing concepts spring from some crazy idea no research could predict. (Can you say Google?) We'll discuss some of the tools you can use to gauge consumer attitudes and opinions later in this book. However, at this point suffice it to say a successful creative practitioner writes and designs materials that appeal to a consumer's wants and needs.

Creating from the consumer's point of view

If you remember nothing else from this chapter, remember this:

People do not buy things. They buy satisfaction of their wants and needs.

You may have studied Maslow's theory of the hierarchy of needs. This model is usually depicted as a pyramid, ranging from the most basic needs to the most complex and sophisticated.

Image 2.2

When you travel, you keep memories of loved ones back home in your heart. That's the message in this ad for Iberia Airlines, which shows the connections from Madrid to Rio in very personal terms.

According to Maslow, the needs at each level must be met before one can progress to the next level. Maslow considered less than 1% of the population to be truly self-actualized.[6] Some communication theorists have expanded on Maslow's list. Some texts list more than 30 needs. To simplify matters, we can probably sum up wants and needs from a marketing communication standpoint as follows:

- Comfort (avoid pain and discomfort; convenience)
- Security (physical and financial)
- Stimulation (aesthetic, physical)
- Affiliation (esteem, respect)
- Fulfillment (self-satisfaction, status)

So how does all this talk about Maslow and wants and needs play in the ad business today? That's where account planning comes into play. The account planner is the connection between the business side and the creative side of a marketing campaign. The planner works with the account manager to understand what the client is looking for and then relate that to what the consumer wants. The planner also helps the creative team develop a more focused creative brief to lead them to that One Thing. Planners want to know what makes people tick—to bring the consumers' voice into the strategic process. They use that information to develop branding strategy for the campaign. It is the planner's job to take all this information, insight, and nuance and condense it into a form that the creative team can understand (preferably short sentences for the writers and pictures for the art directors). We provide more detail about account planning in Chapter 4.

But what exactly do we do with all this? Once you have discovered consumers' sweet spot, you have to communicate in a way that convinces them your brand can satisfy their wants and needs. One of the best explanations of a consumer's wants and needs can be found in this simple declaration: ***Don't tell me about your grass seed. Talk to me about my lawn.***

Think about that. People aren't really looking for seed. They need a play area for their kids. They want a calm green space for relaxing or a yard the neighbors will envy. Security. Comfort. Fulfillment. Wants and needs. A $50 Timex will probably tell the time just as well as a $3,000 Rolex. (Well, close enough for most folks.) So what wants and needs are satisfied by spending 60 times more? Hint: It's really not about telling time.

Good Taste, Good Sense, and Good Business

As you'll see in later chapters, the perception of ad messages can vary widely depending on the audience. You may find it's worth taking a creative risk to persuade one small group, knowing full well it will turn off most everyone else. You have to weigh the risks (which may include loss of overall sales, adverse

"If you can't turn yourself into your customer, you probably shouldn't be in the ad writing business at all."[7]

—Leo Burnett

Image 2.3

Don't tell me about your grass seed. Talk to me about my lawn. Here's a great example. The copy almost reads like poetry. For example, "Green says we're committed to something. Something the whole neighborhood believes in. Something good. Something the world, even in its best days, could use more of." While this ad isn't for grass seed, it's about a lot more than fertilizer.

publicity, and even lawsuits) against the benefits (higher sales to a select group, publicity, and creative recognition). We do not advocate doing anything creatively for the sake of shock value. Nor do we recommend using sexist, racist, or homophobic messages; sleazy gimmicks; or gutter humor to gain attention. Some of the examples in this book may go beyond the threshold of acceptable taste for many people. They are what they are, and even if we don't always agree with their content, they are part of the real world.

The American Association of Advertising Agencies provides this creative code of ethics for its members. Even if you're not a 4A member, it's good advice:

Knowing what *not* to do does not absolve you of responsibility. While you might not be able to change the world through advertising, you can certainly avoid adding to the current problems. We encourage you to find ways to include positive images of minorities and marginalized groups in mainstream advertising. Overall, the philosophy of "enlightened self-interest" works best. When you do good, you'll do well.

We the members of the American Association of Advertising Agencies, in addition to supporting and obeying the laws and legal regulations pertaining to advertising, undertake to extend and broaden the application of high ethical standards. Specifically, we will not knowingly create advertising that contains:

a) False or misleading statements or exaggerations, visual or verbal.

b) Testimonials that do not reflect the real opinion of the individual(s) involved.

c) Price claims that are misleading.

d) Claims insufficiently supported or that distort the true meaning or practicable application of statements made by professional or scientific authority.

e) Statements, suggestions or pictures offensive to public decency or minority segments of the population.

We recognize that there are areas that are subject to honestly different interpretations and judgment. Nevertheless, we agree not to recommend to any advertiser, and to discourage the use of, advertising that is in poor or questionable taste or that is deliberately irritating through aural or visual content or presentation.[8]

We hope we've got you thinking about some of the ethical issues involved in what you, as a creative person, actually do. How can you make a difference for you, for your client, and for society? It really does matter how you frame an issue, highlight a benefit, select an image, take on the competitor, or choose your words. It's about ethics, but it's also about legality because the law kicks in where ethics ends.

Legal concepts that really matter

Whole books have been written on the subject of the law and advertising. However, for this text we thought we'd like to very briefly focus on two aspects that we think really matter to copywriters: claims and copyright.

Stake your claim

Copywriters make all kinds of claims, and most of them are perfectly legal. Yet, it's worth briefly talking about what *legal* really means. All fact claims are viewed very seriously under the law. There can be no deception. However, advertisers have a fair amount of wiggle room found in the nonfact claims that advertisers routinely use: puffery and lifestyle claims. Most of us write claims that fall into one of these categories, and thus we escape the scrutiny of the law.

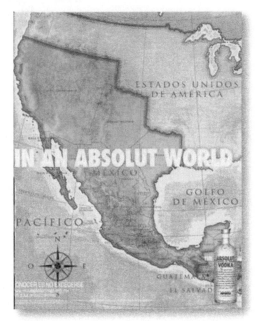

Image 2.4

The definition of good taste stems from a thorough understanding of the target market. Latinos may feel this ad speaks to their cultural pride. Many Anglo residents of the Southwest saw things totally differently.

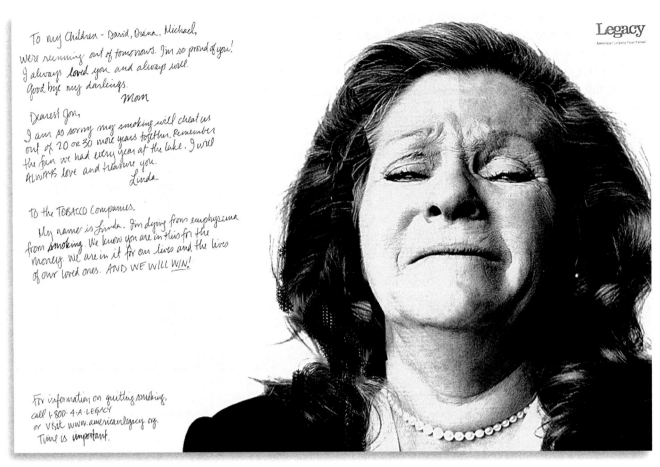

To my Children – David, Diana, Michael,
We're running out of tomorrows. I'm so proud of you!
I always loved you and always will.
Good bye my darlings.
                                    Mom

Dearest Jon,
I am so sorry my smoking will cheat us
out of 20 or 30 more years together. Remember
the fun we had every year at the lake. I will
ALWAYS love and treasure you.
                                    Linda

To the TOBACCO Companies.
My name is Linda. I'm dying from emphysema
from smoking. We know you are in this for the
money. We are in it for our lives and the lives
of our loved ones. AND WE WILL WIN!

For information on quitting smoking,
call 1-800-4-A-LEGACY
or visit www.americanlegacy.org.
Time is important.

Image 2.5

This woman is dying of emphysema. The unbearable pain of saying good-bye to her loved ones is etched on her face, and the reader can't turn away. The messages she leaves her family are even more poignant. You can state facts and figures about the effects of smoking, but if you understand consumer behavior you know it's far more effective to tell your story in personal terms.

Image 2.6

Bud Light claimed to offer everything you want in a beer . . . including the ability to fly. Since a reasonable person would know this is impossible (unless they drank too many Bud Lights), this is considered puffery and perfectly legal.

- **Puffery** is using superlatives or obvious falsity to tout the greatness of your brand—so consumers are bound to know it's an exaggeration. As one judge said, "The bigger the lie, the bigger the protection." For example, a commercial for Bud Light stated you would be able to fly if you drank their beer. It showed the comically disastrous results of this ability and closed by reneging on the claim. Any claims of ultimate superiority should be avoided unless you can be sure the audience will realize they are not measurable and not meant to be taken seriously. For example, stating you are the number-one hot dog brand in America should be backed by facts. However, saying that your product is "paradise on a bun" is puffery and acceptable.

- **Lifestyle claims** are claims that are subjective assumptions about how consumers feel about your product or its effects. Think of television spots for Viagra. They are making some big assumptions—and the claim is implied. They are also making some big assumptions that a bunch of guys with ED love to sit around the campfire and sing "Viva Viagra" with each other.

As long as your claims fall somewhere within the bounds of these two categories, you're probably safe.

Using celebrities

Public figures are protected from commercial use of their name or likeness without their permission. That includes dead celebrities. Whether it's Albert Einstein or The Three Stooges, you can't use an image of a recognizable person without gaining permission first. The cost will depend on how and where the image is used. You might wonder how paparazzi shots of celebrities can be plastered all over magazine covers. In this case, public figures have less protection than the general public because they are considered newsworthy.

Image 2.7

The headline (with the graphic completing the sentence) implies that low-sodium soup is heart-healthy, a claim that can be substantiated.

Copyrights and copywriting

A *copyright* is the exclusive right granted to authors, artists, and composers to protect their original work from being plagiarized, sold, or used without their permission. It's very important to understand and respect copyright law.

Most of you know that as students and instructors, under the *"fair use" doctrine*, you can reproduce nearly anything—just as long as it's for educational purposes. In fact, the ads in this book are being used for educational purposes and thus fall under the fair use doctrine.

When concepting ads, "fair use" also applies. Since the advent of the computer and the massive expansion of the Internet, art directors and copywriters have been borrowing images and pasting them into layouts. Actually they are using the images to illustrate concepts for their clients. The fact that they are not reproducing them for profit is what allows them the wiggle room. That's where "fair use" ends. After that they must either buy the image or re-create it in a manner that is substantially different so as not to be construed as copying the likeness of the image.

Trademarks

Most slogans and taglines are considered protected. So are brand names. A trademark, designated by ™ or ®, means the brand or slogan is registered with the federal government. When you are applying for a trademark, you will have a better chance of success if your brand has a unique spelling. The brand name

Words of Wisdom

"We operate in a symbolic economy. It's one where crass products and their meaningless material benefits can be transformed into living vessels of meaning." [9]

—Douglas Atkin

Häagen-Dazs was created to sound exotic, when in fact it is not related to any specific language. It was easy to register and easy to remember. Even if you pick a brand name that is already in use, you may be able to register it when it is used in a different market. For example, both Microsoft and Volunteers in Service to America can use the Vista brand.

Using someone else's slogan or tagline will get you into legal trouble, and it won't do much for your career. You need to do your homework in order to be sure that the brilliant tagline you just thought up is not already being used by another brand somewhere, somehow. When in doubt, run it by a colleague or do a word search and check online government resources such as TESS (Trademark Electronic Search System). If you're still in doubt, contact legal counsel. In short, don't make assumptions and do your homework.

Who's Who?

Jay Chiat teamed up with Guy Day to form Chiat\Day in 1962. Chiat later became the first notable American advertising executive to use account planning. It proved highly successful, and Chiat\Day went on to create many memorable advertising campaigns including Apple's "1984" campaign and the Energizer Bunny campaign. The agency was named U.S. Agency of the Decade in 1989. In 1999 Chiat was inducted into the American Advertising Federation Hall of Fame, and he died in 2002.

Nancy Hill is the first ever CEO of the American Association of Advertising Agencies (AAAA). Her career began in 1983 at the Doner agency in Baltimore and advanced with increased responsibilities. Prior to accepting the AAAA position, she served as CEO of Lowe Worldwide in New York. Her personal and professional interests have long focused on the high-tech sector, serving such clients as AOL, Cisco Systems, Sony, Motorola, and Verizon, among others. As CEO of the AAAA she is firmly committed to the "business case for diversity . . . whether we are talking about race/ethnicity, points of view/life experience, and skill sets . . ."[10]

Stanley Pollitt began his career in London at Pritchard Wood Partners. He later started his own agency, Boase Massimi Pollitt (BMP), where he launched account planning, which he viewed as facilitating a new account team role that combined research and planning to inform creative development with a focus on consumer insight. Though he lived to only 49, his impact on the advertising industry was tremendous.

One of the early leaders in account planning, **Jon Steel** is well known for his innovative approach to focus groups, in which he elicited opinions from people where they lived, worked, and shopped, rather than in sterile interview rooms. As head of Goodby, Silverstein, & Partners' planning department, Steel was named "West Coast Executive of the Year" by *Adweek* in 2000. He also finds time to share his depth of knowledge in the world of academia at Stanford University's School of Business as a regular lecturer. His first book, *Truth, Lies, and Advertising: The Art of Account Planning,* has become a must-read for anyone interested in account planning.

Exercises

1. AIDA in Action

Consider the buying process for the following product categories using the AIDA steps: hybrid cars, microbrews, running shoes, frozen vegetables, and cosmetics. Or create your own categories.

- Working in a group, create a list for each category based on the following questions. What gets your *attention?* What part of the brand messages within this category captures your *interest?* At what point and due to what circumstances do consumers feel a compelling *desire* for the product? What are common intended *actions* that might be relevant to this product category?

- Now find an ad for each category and discuss how the AIDA process works for that brand. How much influence do advertising and promotion have on the buying decision for that brand?

2. Supporting Your Claim

It's time to think like a lawyer. Analyze the following product claims and decide which would be legal and explain your opinion. If you feel the claim is not supportable, make suggestions on how to change it.

- Nobody makes a beer colder than Coors Light.

- With adult education classes at Bridgestone University, one night a week can change your life.

- The new Hyundai Genesis offers the luxury and performance of a BMW 5 Series for about half the sticker price.

- You can't survive in this climate without a Trane air conditioning system.

- The most dependable, reliable, and energy-efficient coffeemaker ever made.

3. Whose Ethics?

Get ready to test your ethical boundaries. Find six print ads you feel are "ethically questionable."

- Write up a one-page critique of each ad. Explain why you feel it is ethically questionable—focusing on the ad and not the product itself (i.e., not "drinking is bad and shouldn't be advertised," but "ads promoting alcohol should not target minors . . ."). Focus your comments on the target, placement, content, and so forth.

- Next write a short survey. Poll 10 people from various backgrounds on the ads you found ethically questionable, but add in two neutral ads (ads that are not "ethically questionable").

- Write a summary of the results. Begin with a quantitative summary. Move onto to a commentary considering the following questions: Did the people you polled feel like you? Did you notice any demographic (age, ethnicity, gender, or income) patterns? What did you find that was surprising? End with a short reflection asking yourself: What kind of socially responsible person do I want to be? What is the advertising industry's responsibility? What would I do if I was asked to work on something I felt was ethically wrong or simply bad for society at large?

Adapted from an exercise shared by Kimberly Selber, PhD, Associate Professor, University of Texas–Pan American.

Notes

1. Quote in Angela Partington, ed., *The Oxford Dictionary of Quotations* (New York: Oxford University Press, 1992), p. 501.

2. Quote in Michael Jackman, ed., *Crown's Book of Political Quotations* (New York: Crown Publishing Company, 1982), p. 2.

3. Quote from University of Texas at Austin, Department of Advertising, http://advertising.utexas.edu/resources/quotes/ (accessed May 19, 2005).

4. Seth Godin, *Purple Cow: Transform Your Business by Being Remarkable* (New York: Penguin, 2002), p. 96.

5. Quote from University of Texas at Austin, Department of Advertising, http://advertising.utexas.edu/resources/quotes/ (accessed May 19, 2005).

6. See "Maslow, Abraham Harold," in Microsoft Encarta Online Encyclopedia, 2005, http://www.encarta.com (accessed May 19, 2005).

7. Leo Burnett, *100 Leos: Wit and Wisdom From Leo Burnett* (Chicago: NTC Business Press, 1995), p. 47.

8. See the AAAA Web site at http://www.aaaa.org.

9. Douglas Atkin, *The Culting of Brands: When Consumers Become True Believers* (New York: Portfolio, 2004), p. 111.

10. Quoted in William Arens, Michael Weigold, and Christian Arens, *Contemporary Advertising,* 12th ed. (New York: McGraw-Hill Irwin, 2009), p. 132.

Chapter 3

Branding

Why the Obsession With Brands?

It seems we are firmly entrenched in the age of the brand or, as marketing guru Scott Bedbury calls it, "a new brand world." It's become fashionable to focus on brand image, brand character, brand values, brand management, integrated brand promotion, brand equity, and brand blah, blah, blah. Some ad agencies have even changed their identities to become brand consultants.

Some people theorize the proliferation of ad messages makes it impossible to remember detailed product information. People are lucky to remember a few select brand names. In addition, some people see a shift from information to images, so the brand symbol is more important than the product itself. Another explanation is that we've always stressed brand names, only now we're a lot more sophisticated in managing their deeper meaning for the consumer. In fact, Marty Neumeier says, "A brand is not what you say it is. It's what they say it is."[1] Enter the consumer. Today more than ever consumers' interactions with a brand are critical. And managing those interactions is at the heart of branding.

Before you start supporting a brand, you first have to understand what a brand is and what it does. Many authors have their own ideas about brands, and they're all good. We've summarized them into two main thoughts:

What it is: A brand is a promise. It's shorthand for all the product's attributes, good and bad.

What it does: A brand makes the promise personal by conveying the product's personality, which reflects on the people who buy the product. It's really all about relationships.

Luke Sullivan expands those thoughts when he says, "A brand isn't just a name on the box. It isn't the thing in the box either. A brand is the sum total of all the emotions, thoughts, images, history, possibilities and gossip that exist in the marketplace about a certain company."[3] If you think he's exaggerating a bit, consider the fact that brands (at least those with positive images) are assets, sometimes worth billions of dollars to a company. Some companies protect their brands like a

In Germany there are no getaway cars.

Porsche 911

Image 3.1

What's the most common adjective that's attached to Porsches? Fast. This clever use of synergy in this classic ad says it all.

momma bear guarding her cubs. Put yellow arches on a taco stand or an unlicensed Harley logo on a T-shirt and you'll quickly find out how sharp those claws can be.

Companies spend millions to establish and nurture a brand image. Brand image advertising (and promotion) sells the personality, the mystique, and the aura surrounding or emanating from the product, not the product itself. Think of the old cliché, "Sell the sizzle, not the steak."

Every product has a brand image. Some are stronger than others. Think of the brand image or brand character of well-known products. How does the brand image of BMW differ from that of Cadillac or Lexus? They all cost about the same, but all have different characters as do their customers. How did Apple differentiate itself from IBM? Not as a technically superior and more expensive computer, but rather as one with an easy-to-use operating system favored by right-brain types. IBM told people to "Think." Apple said, "Think Different." Luke Sullivan states, "Most of the time we're talking about going into a customer's brain and tacking on one adjective onto a client's brand. That's all. DeWalt tools are tough. Apple computers are easy to use . . . Volvos are safe. Porsches are fast. Jeeps are rugged. Boom. Where's the rocket science here?"[4] To support a brand's image, advertisers use simple, unique, and easily recognized visuals. Over time, the brand (and all its attributes, good and bad) comes to mind when a consumer catches even a glimpse of these visuals.

Branded Storytelling

Every brand has a story behind it. A marketer's job is to make sure it's a good story, one that can be told over and over again by satisfied customers. In the past, advertisers developed the Unique Selling Proposition. Today they're searching to create

Image 3.2

Logos are a major component of brand identity. Can you name these brands?

their Unique Story Proposition. Alain Thys writes, "Great brand stories stem from the reason a brand exists. *Apple* wanted to free creative spirits while slaying the Microsoft dragon. *Coco Chanel* set out to re-invent fashion and liberate women from tradition. *Pepsi* wants to be a catalyst for change for every generation. Dig into the history, people and promises of your brand to uncover its *Unique Story Proposition (USP)*. Make this the anchor for every story you tell."[5]

Stories are driven by emotions, and consumers are expressing these emotions through their consumption choices. Let's use Nike to explore how stories merge personal experiences with branded experiences. Think of how Nike has managed to direct all their communications toward one underlying message—the will to win. They have to do this through telling the story of individual athletic success, but always in the context of the athletic community—the Nike community. In the process consumers see themselves within these stories and thus within the Nike community. They too dream of winning, and Nike's stories represent their stories—or at least their mythological possibility. Nike's advertising provides the context for this mythology to grow. It also demonstrates how branding and the Unique Story Proposition shape consumers' experiences.

Identity and branding are inseparable. "In the postmodern world, people have multiple identities. Their identity is subject to modification as cultural tastes change. Most important, consumers living in the postmodern world, seek a narrative upon which to base their identities."[6] Just consider the brand narratives or stories shared among Harley Owners Groups (HOGs), the sexual narratives that surround Abercrombie & Fitch and are played out by its consumers, or the narratives shared over a grande latte at Starbucks. These stories are bound together by branded

Image 3.3

As the Mac-versus-PC campaign became even more effective, Microsoft became more desperate to counter this simple but brilliant approach to branding. When Microsoft launched their "I'm a PC" campaign, Apple countered by simply showing PC sliding more money into marketing instead of fixing the Vista operating system.

Image 3.4

What's the first brand that comes to mind? Bet you said "Harley." Actually this is a visual from a campaign for an insurance company. All these guys are real Allstate Insurance agents and real bikers.

Image 3.5

This ad from Mexico proves that "Just do it" works in any language, and you don't even have to say it. The ubiquitous swoosh precludes the need for any other brand support. The visual puzzle may take a few microseconds longer to process in the brain, but once that "aha!" moment comes, you remember it.

It's not a golf ball

Titleist
1

It's a story !

Telling that tall tale is never complete without a Titleist. More than offering the best performing golf ball on the market, Titleist lets you recreate those moments you love best! Whether it's smashing a 300 yard drive down the fairway or sinking that 15 foot birdie putt, you know Titleist will never let you down!

YOU TELL THE STORY, WE PROVIDE THE ENDING

Image 3.6

This student-designed ad for golf balls tells us the ad is not about the product; it's about the joy of golfing (presumably made even more joyful by Titleist balls).

belief systems that stimulate very specific emotions and prescribe equally specific behaviors. And these belief systems are not accidental. According to Laurence Vincent, "Advertising plays an important role in the development and sustenance of a brand's narrative, but once that narrative is established, it has the potential to take on a life of its own."[7]

This is where brand agents come into play. Consider the power of Martha Stewart, Phil Knight, and Barack Obama to shape their brands. It is their personal stories that provide the mythology that shapes and sustains their brands. Thought of in this way, myths give a brand an emotional context, which provides the platform from which consumers find a sense of identity and belonging. Remember Maslow? Think of brands as "the narrative of mankind. It's a story told with a collective voice and a shared point of view."[8] When brands are conceived in this manner, you can see how the brand story articulates the brand promise.

How do you establish a relevant brand? Some people would say saturate every advertising medium and slap it on anything that won't move. However, advertising funds are limited, even for huge companies, so a more sophisticated approach is required to make that brand stick in the minds of consumers. Two concepts, which started as theories, are now considered crucial to establishing a strong brand. These are *positioning* and *resonance*.

Assume the Position

Jack Trout and Al Ries revolutionized marketing in the late '70s and early '80s with their theory of positioning. Their book, *Positioning: The Battle for Your Mind,* introduced a new way of thinking about products and how they fit into the marketplace. This is the best definition of positioning we've found:

> ***Simply stated, positioning is the perception consumers have of your product, not unto itself, but relative to the competition.***[9]

The key to understanding and using positioning lies in the consumer's mind. The consumer files product considerations in two broad categories: garbage ("nothing there for me") and maybe-I'm-interested. In the second category, he uses subcategories for different products, often aligning those positions with heavily promoted brand images. For example, BMWs are fast. Volvos are safe. Jeeps are rugged. And so on. So if you asked most consumers to "position" or rank those brands in various categories, you'd probably find some resistance to the idea that a BMW is as safe as a Volvo, a Jeep can be as fast as a BMW, or a Volvo can be as rugged as a Jeep. All true in some cases, but not universally believed. Once a position is established, it takes a lot of effort to change it.

Before you develop the position of your client's product, you have to ask:

- What is the current position?
- What is the competitor's position?
- Where do you want to be?
- How are you going to get there? (That's strategy.)

Writing the positioning statement

Your clients may have the positioning statement figured out. Chances are it's more of a vague wish to be successful than an honest appraisal of where they are and where they need to go. The following is an actual attempt at a client's positioning statement and a good example of what *not* to do:

Superbrand [not the real name] will become the world's most respected supplier of water equipment for the residential market as we are in commercial, agricultural, and industrial applications.

This is some CEO's dream of world domination and probably not accurate or even possible to achieve. A better way to do it might be:

Superbrand will leverage our positive image in commercial applications to become known to contractors and consumers as a reliable provider of water treatment, transport, and disposal technology for the residential market.

Image 3.7

Two great brands on one billboard—Absolut and IKEA. After you've furnished your apartment with all new stuff, you might be in need of a drink.

Image 3.8

In what was one of the most expensive and shortest-lived branding campaigns for Microsoft, Jerry Seinfeld teamed up with company founder Bill Gates. The 90-second spot was basically about "nothing" like the Seinfeld show and, as a result, left most viewers shaking their heads, saying, "What's up with that?" Within weeks, the creative shifted to the "I'm a PC" campaign.

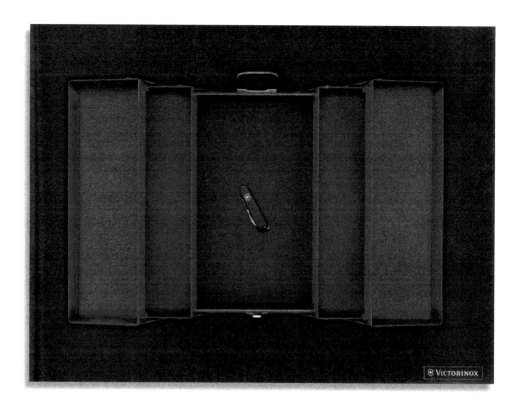

Image 3.9

The positioning of Victorinox is clear: the all-in-one tool kit. Its multitasking portability is reinforced by its placement at the bottom of the huge toolbox. The layers of red simply reinforce the inherent branded power of Victorinox. An uncomplicated positioning beautifully executed.

Image 3.10

Rolling Stone repositioned their magazine to media planners as the choice of a new generation of young upscale professionals rather than maintaining the hippie image it had a decade earlier.

The positioning statement identifies where you are, where you want to go, and if possible how you're going to get there. It does not have to be sexy. Save that for the tagline (which can be based on a positioning statement, such as "When you think water, think Superbrand").

Repositioning and rebranding

If you don't like your product's position, you may want to change it from what you have to one you want. Here are three examples:

Your grandfather bought **Old Spice** aftershave for its manly seafaring image in print and TV. Today, 18- to 24-year-olds have made it the top brand for deodorants and antiperspirants. Procter & Gamble launched splashy marketing campaigns for Old Spice High Endurance deodorants and Old Spice Red Zone antiperspirant and teamed up with video-game maker Electronic Arts to create a gaming tie-in. The hook? A football video game featured a "Red Zone" theme with a tagline, "When performance matters most." Procter & Gamble extended the Old Spice brand to include Swagger, also aimed at young men.

Rolling Stone magazine gained wide acceptance as the first mass-market counterculture publication. The Woodstock Nation grew up in the 1980s, cleaned up, and found that Wall Street was cooler than Haight-Ashbury. Yet they still read *Rolling Stone.* However, advertisers were still stuck in the '60s. *RS* needed mainstream advertisers, not smoke shops and Earth Shoes. Fallon McElligott Rice (the precursor of today's Fallon) did the trick with their famous "Perception/Reality" campaign. By using icons for the perceived image of *RS* readers next to a symbol of the real readers, *RS* attracted big-buck advertisers. This not only kept the magazine in business; it helped make it slicker and ultimately pushed it into the mainstream.

Corona beer was discovered in the 1980s by college kids on spring break who were looking for a light, inexpensive, yet slightly exotic brew (at least more exotic than Milwaukee's Best). Corona soon became a cult brand, known as the tropical party beer, especially when guzzled with a slice of lime. But as the spring breakers grew up, they moved on to more sophisticated beers and Corona sales suffered . . . until a new ad agency repositioned the brand as the one to relax with. Ads invoked images of lazy days in a hammock rather than wet T-shirt contests. The "Change Your Latitude" campaign put Corona back on the map, and sales soared. After all, no matter how hard you partied in college, you can always dream about relaxing on the beach.

Positioning redux

While Trout and Ries opened a lot of minds to a new way of thinking, a lot of writers take issue with their premise that creativity makes no difference. Sometimes it's the only difference. Creativity can develop the position or reposition the product. Another caveat is that they analyzed successful campaigns from the past and made them fit their theory. Did the 7UP creative team really think about positioning when they launched the Uncola campaign, or did they just want to do great advertising? Often the creative is the only thing that makes a brand memorable. Remembering that brand's position usually happens over time.

Image 3.11

Before he used Old Spice Swagger, LL Cool J was, uh, let's just say something less than Cool. This campaign featured the fictionalized early days of well-known guys in print, on TV, and online.

Words of Wisdom

"I believe brands have karma. If brand awareness was once a standard measure of brand strength, and brand resonance and relevance are the new yardsticks, I suspect that brand karma will be the ultimate definition of brand strength some day." [10]

—Scott Bedbury

From the Bean to the Experience: How Starbucks Became a Megabrand

Scott Bedbury was instrumental in helping Starbucks move from a local coffee bean merchant to a global brand. This is what he told us about the transformation.

"Originally, Starbucks would have spent their marketing money on coffee—the bean. We shifted that to the experience. The experience goes way beyond the cup. So originally the Starbucks story was all about roasting the beans. The big moment for me came when I was hiking up the side of this volcano in East Java with Dave Olsen (no relation to Mrs. Olsen of Folgers). Dave and I are out there and it's predawn in this amazing place and I say to Dave, 'What do you say will be the biggest opportunity for us?' Now remember, this guy lives for coffee. He's been with Starbucks 15 years and he literally worships the beans. He turns to me and says, 'Everything matters. It's not just about coffee. It's a whole story about the place, the store, the people, the employees, the sound, the music—it's everything.' It was a turning point in the collective mind of management. There was something much richer here than just the coffee cherry. 'Let's really pull the stops and make the most amazing experience possible.' After this only half went to the beans. The other half went to experience."[11]

—Scott Bedbury
CEO, *Brandstream;*
Former Chief Marketing Officer,
Starbucks and *Nike,* Seattle

Words of Wisdom

"*Each commercial, branded entertainment program or promo is a 'mini-story' within the overall framework of your brand. It should always connect to your Unique Story Proposition.*"[13]

—Alain Thys

Resonance: Did You Just Feel Something?

When you achieve resonance, your external message connects with internal values and feelings. Tony Schwartz notes, "Resonance takes place when the stimuli put into our communication evoke meaning in a listener or viewer . . . the meaning of our communication is what a listener or viewer gets out of his experience with the communicator's stimuli."[12]

Resonance requires a connection with feelings that are inside the consumer's mind. You don't have to put in a new emotion; just find a way to tap what's already there. In other words, to get your idea to resonate in the consumer's mind, your communication must trigger some internal experience and connect it with your message. Your brand story must be relevant. Relevance leads to resonance, which will strengthen awareness, begin building comprehension, and lead to conviction and possibly action. How's that for connecting multiple streams of psychobabble?

Want an even simpler explanation?

$$1 + 1 = 3$$

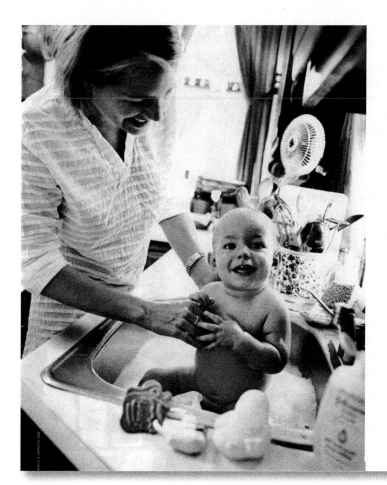

Who'd have ever thought the love of your life would be short and bald?

You always went for the tall, dark, mysterious types. You fell in love with one, married him and started a family. Then when the baby was born, an amazing new feeling hit you. And now, as much as you'll always love your husband, this new little man just takes your breath away. **Having a baby changes everything.**

Johnson & Johnson

Image 3.12

What's more appealing than a little baby? Johnson & Johnson knew that making the baby the star of this ad would resonate much stronger with moms than featuring the package. The tagline—"Having a baby changes everything"—also makes a strong connection with any parent.

Resonance is connected to branding because a brand can make a consumer feel something—sometimes it's something good; sometimes it's bad. A harried vacationer with a carload of hungry kids sees those Golden Arches and thinks, "At last—familiar food, Happy Meals for the kids, and clean restrooms." The next driver turns up her nose and thinks, "Ugh—greasy food, indifferent service, and a restaurant full of kids demanding Happy Meals." There's resonance, but for the mom looking for Happy Meals and clean bathrooms, there's also relevance.

Extending Your Brand

David Aaker, brand consultant and author of more than 14 books, suggests that the value of a brand is often rooted in the parent brand. Subbrands are the value brands. Marriott is the parent brand, while Courtyard by Marriott is a value-based subbrand. Aaker suggests there are three types of relationships between parent brands and subbrands: endorser, co-driver, and driver brands. Let's use Nike to walk you through.

Nearly every extension of the Nike brand, from Nike Golf to NIKEiD to **LIVESTRONG** (its philanthropic venture with Lance Armstrong), carries with it the cachet of the parent brand. Now let's see how it plays out.

- Endorser Brand: This brand is endorsed by the Nike parent brand—Nike+ (running gadgets).

- Co-Driver Brand: This brand is equal to the parent brand in terms of its influence with consumers and sometimes appears as a competitor—Adidas.

- Driver Brand: With this brand the parent maintains primary influence as driver and the subbrand acts as a descriptor, telling consumers that the parent company is offering a slight variation on the product or service they have come to know and trust—Nike Women.

- Next come line extensions. Robert Sprung, partner of a major branding services company, says, "A good line extension takes a brand with a solid core of values and applies it to an area where the brand has permission to go."[16] Staying with Nike, think of the various sports as line extensions: Nike basketball, Nike running, and so forth. Marketers for strong brands naturally want to leverage that strength whenever possible.

The Branding Strategy Insider Web site lists some guidelines for successful brand extension:

- Have you identified what your brand owns in the consumer's mind? [In other words, what is your brand's position?]

- Have you identified all the areas in which the consumer gives your brand position to operate?

- Have you identified all the ways your brand and others in its category have made compromises with the consumer?

- Have you found ways to redefine your business to break those compromises?

- Have you explored ways to make your brand more relevant to the next generation of consumers?

- Do you have a way to screen all new brand extension proposals for their congruence with the brand promise and impact on brand equity? [A fancy way of asking if you've done your homework.][17]

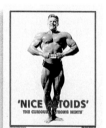

Image 3.13

Altoids' quirky advertising propelled them to the top of the mint category. But they didn't stop there. Curiously Strong sours, strips, small mints, and gum followed, all with distinctive campaigns.

Who's Who?

David Aaker is a brand consultant, CEO of Prophet Consultancy, and author of more than 14 books, including *Managing Brand Equity, Building Strong Brands, Brand Leadership, Brand Portfolio Strategy,* and *Spanning Silos: The New CMO Imperative.* Professor Emeritus at the Haas School of Business, University of California, Berkeley, he has been awarded four career awards including the 1996 Paul D. Converse Award for outstanding contributions to the development of marketing.

Scott Bedbury helped make Nike and Starbucks two of the most successful brand stories of all time. Now one of the world's most sought-after brand consultants and speakers, Bedbury brings to his clients and audiences brand development practices that can help any enterprise strengthen its business. He contends that a powerful brand has to transcend the features of a product and create a personal and more lasting relationship with consumers. Bedbury wrote the modern guide to brand strategy, *A New Brand World: 8 Principles for Achieving Brand Leadership in the 21st Century.*

Marty Neumeier is president of Neutron LLC, a San Francisco–based firm specializing in brand collaboration. Before launching Neutron in 2002, Neumeier was editor and publisher of *Critique,* the "magazine of graphic design thinking," which had quickly become the leading forum for improving design effectiveness. In editing *Critique,* Neumeier joined the conversation about how to bridge the gap between strategy and design, which led directly to the formation of Neutron and the ideas in his book, *The Brand Gap.*

Al Ries is a legendary marketing strategist and the best-selling author or coauthor of 11 books on marketing including *Positioning: The Battle for Your Mind, Marketing Warfare, Focus, The 22 Immutable Laws of Branding, The Fall of Advertising & the Rise of PR,* and *The Origin of Brands.* Before founding his own advertising agency in New York City, Ries worked in the advertising department of General Electric. Ries founded Ries & Ries in 1994 with his daughter Laura. The two work in tandem and consult with *Fortune* 500 companies, write books, and give seminars across the globe.

Tony Schwartz was a prolific advertising innovator and early guru of electronic media who predicted the decline of print media decades before the Internet came into force. He was a master of recording and editing ambient sound and used it to create thousands of sound-dominated commercials. He's been credited for the first use of children's real voices in radio commercials (previously children had been portrayed by specially trained adults). He shifted from commercial advertising to political work, including the controversial "Daisy" commercial for the 1964 Lyndon Johnson campaign.

Jack Trout is an owner of Trout & Partners, a marketing consulting firm. Along with Al Ries he is considered one of the founders and pioneers of positioning and marketing warfare theory. The 1981 classic book, *Positioning,* by Trout and Ries changed the language and practice of marketing strategy. In the more than 2 decades since then, Trout has authored or coauthored some of the best-selling marketing books of all time, including *Marketing Warfare, Bottom-Up Marketing, The 22 Immutable Laws of Marketing,* and *Trout on Strategy.*

Exercises

1. Brand Stretching

This is your chance to see how brands can extend their reach.

- Generate a list of five brands, each one from a different product category. Now, generate a list of brand extensions for each product. Consider what areas the parent brand already owns and in which areas of the brand they find growth opportunities.

- Next pick one brand. Post their brand and list of potential brand extensions for the class to see. Explain the rationale for each brand extension choice.

- Ask the class to help you generate other possible brand extensions.

2. Tagging the Heart of a Brand

This is your chance to see how personification works in the branding process.

- Working as a class choose four brands. Brainstorm a list of words that personify the heart of each brand—words that embody the emotional meaning inherent in that brand.

- Now break into groups of four or five, with one brand per group. Based on the words generated, write a positioning statement.

- Go to brandtags.net. Click "whatever it is they say a brand is." Now, find your brand. Discuss how your word list and positioning matches up to the Brand Tags list.

- Next click on "try guessing the brand . . ." and see how many of the first 10 brands that pop up your group can guess correctly. If you guess the brand, one can be pretty sure the brand positioning is strongly articulated and maintained.

- Now come back to the whole class and share your results and in the process learn which brands have strong positioning and why.

Notes

1. Marty Neumeier, *The Brand Gap: How to Bridge the Distance Between Business Strategy and Design* (Berkeley, CA: New Riders, 2005), pp. 2–3.

2. Seth Godin, *Purple Cow: Transform Your Business by Being Remarkable* (New York: Penguin, 2003), p. 87.

3. Quoted in Luke Sullivan, *Hey Whipple, Squeeze This: A Guide to Creating Great Ads* (New York: John Wiley, 1998), p. 28.

4. Sullivan, *Hey Whipple, Squeeze This*, p. 28.

5. Quoted in Alain Thys, "The Ten Truths of Branded Storytelling," *Future Lab,* July 26, 2006, http://blog.futurelab.net/2006/07/the_ten_truths_of_branded_stor.html (accessed December 9, 2008).

6. Laurence Vincent, *Legendary Brands: Unleashing the Power of Storytelling to Create a Winning Market Strategy* (Chicago: Dearborn, 2002), p. 9.

7. Ibid, p. 65.

8. Ibid, p. 70.

9. George Felton, *Advertising: Concept and Copy* (Englewood Cliffs, NJ: Prentice Hall, 1994), p. 60.

10. Scott Bedbury, *A New Brand World: 8 Principles for Achieving Brand Leadership in the 21st Century* (New York: Viking, 2002), p. 20.

11. Scott Bedbury, Ad Story: *From the Bean to the Experience: How Starbucks Became a Megabrand,* December 2004.

12. Quoted in Bruce Bendinger, *The Copy Workbook* (Chicago: The Copy Workshop, 2002), p. 105.

13. Thys, "The Ten Truths of Branded Storytelling."

14. Douglas Atkin, *The Culting of Brands: When Customers Become True Believers* (New York: Portfolio, 2004), p. 95.

15. Vincent, *Legendary Brands,* p. 101.

16. Quoted in Stefan Stroe, "Best & Worst Brand US Extensions. . . . But What About Romanian Ones?" May 7, 2007, www.stefanstroe.ro/2007/03/07best-and-worst-brand-US-extensions-but-what-about-romainian-ones/ (accessed December 8, 2008).

17. Quoted in Branding Strategy Insider, "The Brand Management Checklist-Advanced," July 15, 2007, http://www.brandingstrategyinsider.com/2007/07/the-brand-manage.html (accessed December 8, 2008).

4

Strategy

Creative Strategy in the Marketing Mix

Congratulations! Your agency was invited to pitch the Garlowe Gizmo account to introduce their new line of gizmos. Your job is to develop a creative strategy and build a marketing communication campaign that will knock the socks off the Garlowe management. You really need this account, because if you don't win, half of your agency will be laid off, including you. Right now, you know nothing about the company, their products, their customers, their competition, or their market. By the way, you've got 2 weeks until the presentation. Once again, congratulations!

The above scenario happens every day somewhere. The good news is you're invited to the dance. But there are very few "gimmes" when it comes to new business, and if you're lucky enough to win an account, the euphoria quickly dissolves into the daily grind of keeping the business.

Mad Men versus reality

In *Mad Men*, the award-winning TV program about 1960s advertising, Don Draper, the head creative director at the fictional Sterling Cooper agency, usually saves the day by (a) ignoring all research, (b) threatening to resign the account, and (c) delivering brilliant insight just as the client gets up to leave. His coworkers are envious, the client is impressed, his boss gives him another big raise, and everybody meets back in his office for martinis and cigarettes. It's great fun to watch, but it doesn't happen that way in today's advertising game . . . if it ever did. So, at the risk of destroying the myths of the Golden Age of Advertising, the following sections deal with the hard work of looking brilliant.

Strategy and tactics

The difference between strategy and tactics stumps a lot of clients and their agencies. They usually mix them up and throw in a few goals and objectives for good measure. Typically the net result is a rather random laundry list of what they'd like to happen—about as specific and realistic as wishing for world peace.

Words of Wisdom

"Brilliant creative isn't enough. You must be creative and effective. It's a time for the strategic thinker, not just the creative rebel." [1]

—Helayne Spivak

Other than drafting a mission statement by committee, listing strategy and tactics can be the most confusing and worthless task in marketing.

Don't get us wrong. A creative person needs to follow a strategy. Otherwise you're working for the sake of creativity rather than solving a problem. If your objective is to visit mid-America, think of strategy development as picking the destination, such as "I want to go to Cleveland." The strategy is to make the trip. The tactics are how you get there. If I drive, which roads do I take? Should I fly? If so, which airlines have the best rates? Where will I stay? How long will I be there? And a bunch of other questions that deal with specific actions you must take to get to Cleveland and back.

Account Planning: Solving the Client's Problem

Strategy often deals in long-term solutions such as building brand share. Strategy is concerned with continuity, growth, and return on investment (ROI). It should be very specific, measurable, and it begins with account planning.

If you were working on the Garlowe Gizmo account, where would *you* start? The first thing to do is ask, "What's the problem?" All clients have one. Otherwise they wouldn't need to promote their products. Some clients state the problem as a broad objective, such as sell more Gizmos in the next fiscal year. That's not the problem. The problem is what's going to make it difficult to sell more Gizmos and how those difficulties can be overcome. The client may tell you, but these may not be the only problems. Often clients don't have an in-depth understanding of their target audience. An even more challenging situation emerges when a client can't even identify the problem.

Account planning is how agencies come up with the solutions that solve a client's problem. So, even before you get to the strategies and tactics, account planning lays the foundation. All strategy documents and the subsequent strategies and tactics emerge from account planning.

TABLE 4.1   *Strategy Versus Tactics*

Strategy	Tactics
Increase awareness and comprehension of new arthritis medicine in 50- to 80-year-old women from 5% to 20% in 12 months.	Four-color full-page magazine ads in *AARP, Arthritis Today,* and *Arthritis Self-Management.* Create Web site to discuss trends in arthritis, treatments, and results.
Expand database of potential lawn mower buyers in top 25 DMAs from 50,000 to 200,000 names by January 31, 2006.	Sweepstakes to win a free lawn mower. Incentive to send in direct mail questionnaire. Promote sweepstakes on radio, TV, point of sale in stores.
Encourage 50,000 20- to 30-year-olds to test drive the new Honda Fit from April 1 through June 30.	Offer free backpack for test drive. Promote with network and cable TV, spot radio, and magazine ads in *Maxim, Cosmopolitan,* and *Rolling Stone.*

Here's a little background on planning. It developed in Britain in the late 1960s and was based on the desire to create an environment where creativity flourished but where the consumer's voice was a key part of strategic development. Coming into existence on the heels of the creative revolution of the 1960s, it's not surprising that planning also sought a modern, creative approach to research replacing irrelevant, inappropriate, and outmoded methodologies. Prior to the introduction of account planning, advertising research was highly marketing-oriented, often detached from both the creative team and the consumer. At the heart of account planning is the need to understand consumers—to bring their voice into the strategic process—to find the key insight.

Stanley Pollitt, of London's Boase Massimi Pollitt, is credited with developing account planning. His goal was to put a trained researcher, representing the voice of the consumer, alongside every account person. Many consider his groundbreaking work to be as innovative as Bill Bernbach's concept of teaming up art directors and copywriters beginning in the late 1950s. In the 1980s Jay Chiat, of the original Chiat\Day in Los Angeles, brought account planning to North America. He used account planning to launch Apple Computer and countless other campaigns. Planning in North America moved from West to East but has always been strongest in West Coast ad agencies. Jon Steel, of Goodby Silverstein in San Francisco and a noted author on account planning, calls account planning an essential strategy tool. By the mid-1990s account planning was common practice in many ad agencies across North America.

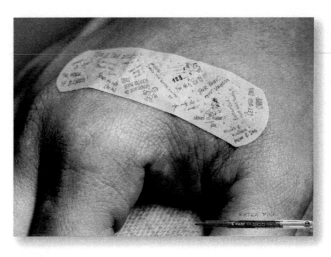

Image 4.1

The One Thing? This fine-point pen writes really small. You don't expect this ad to be for a pen. That's stopping power. And once you're drawn in, the feature (extra-fine tip) and benefit are demonstrated with wit and charm. That makes it memorable.

Get the Facts

The first step in planning for any type of research is gathering and organizing information. You have to answer the following basic questions:

TABLE 4.2   *Getting the Facts*

Marketing Task	What It Means
Define the target audience.	Who are we talking to?
Identify features and benefits.	What makes this product better?
Clarify the current position.	What do people think about the product?
Align wants and needs with the product.	Why should people buy it?
Determine the call to action.	What do we want people to do?

Ad Story

A Curiously Strong Approach (Just Don't Tell the Boss)
Andrew Meyer had a dream assignment—working on Leo Burnett's incredibly successful Altoids account. However, sometimes it's hard to convince others in the agency that you can make a good thing even better. Here's his solution to solving a client's problem (that the agency management didn't know existed).

"When I began working on the Altoids campaign, the original print and outdoor work had already been established as a perennially award-winning campaign. But as an outsider, it seemed apparent to me that there was a missed opportunity to bring the brand into other media. My partner, Art Director Noel Haan, agreed. Creative management at the time, however, was skeptical. The net result: We had no money, and no permission from the powers that be to pursue new work along these lines. Of course, that didn' stop us. Noel and I secretly wrote scripts and lined up a director and production company willing to foot the bill and shoot spec film for us. Management "didn't want to know a thing about it"—until we surprised our client with a finished educational film parody campaign for Altoids Sours. And they loved it. They gave us more money to create more and better spots, and ran them on TV, the Web and cinema. Sometimes, risk does equal reward."[3]

—G. Andrew Meye
Senior Copywriter, *Leo Burnett, Chicag*

Notice the above creative development questions include some of the basic journalism questions, such as who, what, and why. Where and when are media questions, which may also influence your creative strategy. For example, an ad in the *Sports Illustrated* swimsuit edition may inspire a far different look than an ad in the regular edition.

Where to look for information

Research can be divided into two basic categories: primary, where you gather the facts directly, and secondary, where you assemble research done by others. We'll look at secondary research first, because that's usually more accessible.

Secondary research

You can find a wealth of information about markets, products, and consumers. A lot of it is available for free on the Internet. However, most of the really good stuff comes from subscription services. Most university libraries offer the same information that costs companies thousands of dollars, although it is usually slightly out of date. Buying current data is often prohibitively expensive.

Primary research

Most people think of formal types of research such as focus groups or mail surveys, but primary research can be very informal and personal. Ethnography is common, as are other forms of fieldwork. The idea is to immerse yourself in the world of the consumer. The following are just a few forms of primary research:

- Visit a store and see how your product is displayed. Check out the competitive products. How does the shelf appeal of your product compare?

- Talk to the salespeople, retailers, and others who sell your product. What do they tell customers about it? Where do they place the product in the marketplace?

- Sometimes it's helpful to take a factory tour. However, you're usually getting the manufacturer's view instead of the consumer's. Take the tour, but also see where and how the product is used.

- Review ads and other promotional material for your product. Check out the competition. Study their visual structure and symbolism. Study their claims. Where are they weaker or stronger compared to your product?

- Read the publications your media department is considering. Watch the TV shows they recommend for your product.

- Talk to the people who buy your product. Why did they buy it? Would they buy it again? If not, why not?

- Talk to people who considered buying but did not buy your product. Why not? What would make them change their mind?

You can find subjects to interview in a number of places—stores, malls, sporting events, trade shows, basically any place where members of your target audience may gather. You can conduct more formal research with focus groups of members of the target audience. These groups, moderated by professionals, can explore attitudes and opinions in depth. Other types of research may involve mass mailings of questionnaires and telephone surveys.

Interpreting research findings

Funny thing about research—if it confirms the client's opinions, it wasn't really needed; if it contradicts the client's opinions, it's flawed. While the "facts" may be gathered and presented objectively, the interpretation is highly subjective.

Words of Wisdom

"Our job is to bring dead facts to life." [4]

—William Bernbach

Image 4.2

Research showed that many Latinos live in two cultures. This Web site mixes English and Spanish just as most Latinos do in the workplace and home.

Sometimes research reveals information about something you're not even measuring. For example, a survey for a business-to-business client revealed a strong negative opinion of the brand in the Southeast. Why did people love them in Ohio but hate them in Georgia? The client considered running some image ads in the South to build a more favorable opinion. Further investigation revealed the problem was not with the brand but with the person selling it. In this case, no amount of brilliant advertising could solve the problem. A quick realignment of the sales force did. Another observation we've seen from years of gathering information and testing concepts: Clients focus on verbatim comments rather than numbers. They pay attention to a few video interviews rather than a mountain of statistics. Clients, like consumers, want to see and hear real people. They may analyze all the facts and figures, but a few memorable quotes usually help them form an opinion. Knowing how clients respond to research can put the agency in the driver's seat.

Who is the target audience?

Whom are you talking to? Your client may tell you. Your account planner should tell you. Your secondary and primary research will tell you. If you're lucky, marketing objectives will be very specific, such as 35- to 65-year-old married men, living in the top 10 markets, earning $100,000 or more. Usually, though, a client tells the creative team about the product. Period. It's up to the agency to find out who is most likely to buy it and why. Unless you know who's buying the product and why, your creative strategy will be a classic example of "ready-fire-aim" planning.

Image 4.3

A nice play on words, but unfortunately a group of needlepointers took issue with being called "old bats." The billboard was modified so it would not offend, even though those ladies were not the intended target audience.

Features and Benefits

The object of your effort may not be a tangible product at all. It may be something you can't hold in your hand, like the local bus company, an art museum, or a government agency. It may be about corporate image—a campaign that promotes the integrity or strength of a company but doesn't highlight products. Good examples are utility and telephone companies and multinational megafirms like General Electric. You could also develop creative for an organization such as the American Cancer Society or Amnesty International. For the sake of simplicity, we will call the object of promotion the "product" no matter what it may really be.

From the inside: Features

Products have characteristics and personality traits just like people. By themselves these features are not good or bad. They're just there. That's why listing product features without putting them in the context of a benefit to the customer usually wastes time and space. Sometimes the benefit is so obvious the reader or viewer will make an instant connection. But other times, writers just include a list of features and hope someone will figure out why they're important. On a luxury car, for example, features can be technical, like a global positioning system; functional, like side curtain air bags; or aesthetic, like brushed aluminum console trim. In most cases, the more technical and abstract the feature, the greater the need to tie it to a benefit to the consumer.

From the outside: Benefits

Not all products have features you can promote, but all have benefits. A benefit leads to the satisfaction of a consumer's wants and needs. "Cool, crisp taste" is a benefit (it quenches thirst and tastes good). "Firm, smooth ride" is a benefit (it pleases the senses and gives peace of mind). "Kills 99.9% of household germs" is a benefit (you're protecting your family).

Anyone can write a feature ad. All you need is a spec list. As a writer, you have to translate those features into benefits that resonate within the customer. Sometimes it's as simple as listing a feature and lining up a benefit. That's the old FAB (Features-Advantages-Benefits) approach used for years in industrial brochures. However, we encourage you to think of more subtle and clever ways to promote the benefits. Edward de Bono, a cognitive expert, suggests that marketers pay close attention to "UBS" or the Unique Buying State of consumers. So, when you're thinking about how to leverage a benefit, consider the UBS.

As we'll discuss shortly, you should think in terms of an overriding benefit. Remember the adjective you need to tack onto the brand name. If that adjective is positive, such as *economical, stylish, effective, safe,* or *powerful,* you've established an overall benefit. And, don't be afraid to work with the account planners to connect your key benefit to the UBS. You might also consider the fact that many of the choices consumers make today are based on symbolic product attributes. So don't discount the intangible. Finally, when spinning your benefits, think back to your brand—to its promise. Can your benefit engender trust? If so, you have leveraged the feature to its maximum potential, creating great strategic advantage. Now let's get to work.

Images 4.4, 4.5

Old English has a story to tell, but no copy is necessary. The strategy is to differentiate itself as the polish that keeps wood alive. What better way to demonstrate that than to visually bring the tagline to life?

Image 4.6

The brand promise is expressed as a metaphor embedded in women's everyday life experiences. The elegantly simple layout creates an extendable campaign so benefit specific that no copy is needed.

TABLE 4.3 *The Relationship Between Features and Benefits*

Features	Benefits	Wants and Needs
Contains fluoride	Prevents tooth decay	Saves money, saves time
Automatic shutoff	Shuts off unit if you forget	Safety, saves money, convenience
Electronic ignition	Easier start in cold weather	Convenience
Slow release of nutrients	Greener plants, more flowers	Aesthetically pleasing, convenient

Assembling the Facts

You've gathered a lot of information. Now it's time to organize it into something you can use. We'll describe three basic ways to organize information: copy platform, creative brief, and consumer profile.

Copy Platform

The Copy Platform is also known as a Creative Strategy Statement and several other names. It can be as simple or as detailed as you'd like. No matter what you call it and how complicated it can be, a good Copy Platform should cover the product features/benefits, competitive advantages/weaknesses, information about the target audience, the tone of the message, and a simple, overriding statement about the product. We call this the One Thing. It can also be called the Central Truth, the Big Idea, or the Positioning Statement.

In Chapter 3 we discussed attaching an adjective to a brand. The best way to develop that connection is to ask this question:

"If you could say just ONE THING about this product it would be _____."

It's not an easy sentence to complete. When we begin working with new clients, we sometimes ask them to complete that statement. You'd be surprised how many times they struggle with an answer. The most common response is "Gee. Nobody really asked that before. It's really so many things. I can't think of just one." Then they provide a laundry list of features. No wonder they needed a new agency!

You'll find an example of the Copy Platform in the Appendix. It's a compilation of several forms used by different agencies. Each firm will have its own way to organize information, but this one will do a pretty good job most of the time.

To summarize, we use Copy Platforms for the following reasons:

- **Provide a framework for your ad:** You have all the basic facts about the target, the product, the competition, and the marketplace. If you have some blank lines, you know you need more information.

- **Identify the One Thing that's most important:** You could use a position statement. Or the single adjective to attach to the brand. Or it could be a long sentence that describes what you want the consumer to believe about this product.

- **Support that One Thing with believable information:** This could be features and benefits that support product claims. In the case of a copy-free ad, only the visual supports that overriding image of the product.

- **Connect people with the product:** In your Copy Platform you should ask: What do you want the reader/viewer/listener to do? What is the desired Conviction and Action step? Do you want people to take a test drive? Ask for more information? Visit a Web site? Or do nothing?

- **Organize the client's thoughts:** A good Copy Platform is a collaborative effort between client and agency. The client can provide a lot of information, and together you can clarify and prioritize it. This should not be done by a large committee—at least not by a committee larger than one or two people per client and agency. When completed, both the agency and the client have the same road map for creative strategy.

- **Justify your creative decisions:** If the client signed off on the Copy Platform, he or she will be less likely to criticize your creative efforts if you can prove you're on strategy. If the client says you're off target, you can ask where and why, based on your collaboration on the Copy Platform.

Creative Brief

Creative Briefs may be prepared from a Copy Platform or directly from the assembled information. The Creative Brief is a more linear progression from where we are to where we want to be and how we will get there. The strategy is more clearly defined than in most Copy Platforms. One of the best Creative Brief formats we've seen is used by the Virginia Commonwealth University Brandcenter. The questions are very simple, but if they are answered correctly, you've got just about everything you need to know to start concepting an ad.

- What do we want to accomplish? (objective)

- Whom are we talking to? (target audience)

- What do they think now? (current position)

- What do we want them to think? (reinforce position or reposition)

- Why should they think this? (features/benefits)

- What is our message? (the One Thing and how you say it and show it—the tone)

The following is a sample Creative Brief written by a student for Q-tips:

What do we want to accomplish?

The main objective of my campaign will be to introduce Q-tips Cotton Swabs to the next generation of adults, showing them the many uses as well as the quality that distinguishes Q-tips Cotton Swabs over the generic competition.

Whom are we talking to?

We are speaking to people who value a good product and want the best. More important, we are targeting the emerging 20-something crowd to sway their future buying habits.

What do they think now?

The majority of our new audience is indifferent to Q-tips Cotton Swabs. They consider this a very menial purchase and usually pick the cheapest package on the rack. They have always depended on others to pick up this item, so this will be a brand new purchase for them.

What do we want them to think?

We want to instill a brand image into their minds, when they walk into a grocery store for personal care products; we want them to think Q-tips. We want them to pass over the generic products and choose Q-tips because Q-tips are a personal product as well as a practical one.

Why should they think this?

Because Q-tips will be presented in a very edgy and fun way, we will be able to connect to our audience. This will carry over to the point of purchase and influence their buying habits. We want them to realize the importance of taking care of themselves with the highest quality of cotton swabs.

What is our message?

Q-tips Cotton Swabs are a personal item with practical applications.

Images 4.7, 4.8

Lipton was a classic brand looking for a way to reassert itself in a rapidly expanding category. Meshing its strong brand equity with an elegant expression of the benefits inherent in its new line of herbal teas was strategically brilliant and graphically delicious.

Consumer Profile

The Consumer Profile takes the Copy Platform and Creative Brief a step further by putting a human face on the target audience. Think of journalism's Five Ws in terms of the consumers: Who are they? What are their wants and needs; their buying intentions; their attitudes toward the product and competitors? What do they do for a living? What are their hobbies? Where do they live and work, and how does that affect their buying patterns? When are they planning to buy? When do they watch TV or use other types of media? Why should they consider your product or competitors?

Based on the demographic, psychographic, lifestyles and values, and other research, a Consumer Profile puts some flesh on the bare bones of the Copy Platform. You might consider summarizing the demographics in the first paragraph and include the psychographics in the second paragraph, while you weave the lifestyles and values through the whole profile.

The "Meet Maria" box on page 55 was written by a student to describe the ideal prospect for Excedrin Migraine.

You can see how by focusing on demographics and psychographics you can create a personal portrait of the ideal person within the target audience. From this profile, thanks to attention to her media habits, we know that an advertiser can reach Maria through radio (drive time), billboards (along her commute), direct mail, television, and in a more limited way newspapers and magazines. Through demographics and psychographics we know our approach must be intelligent (she's smart and successful) and to the point (she doesn't have a lot of spare time). The benefit of a nonprescription remedy that could relieve her symptoms without taking time out for a doctor's visit may be the main selling point.

Meet Maria

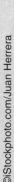

Maria Sanchez is a modern 35-year-old working mom with a husband and two children, aged 10 and 3. She graduated from the University of Illinois with a degree in management, which helped her get a job in the human resources department of a large insurance company in Chicago. She has steadily advanced to become assistant department manager. She earns $65,000 annually and expects to continue moving up the corporate ladder. Her husband Carlos is a sales representative for a large manufacturing firm. His income varies greatly from year to year, so Maria's large and stable income is extremely important to their family. Maria and Carlos live in a four-bedroom home in Hoffman Estates, which is a 45-minute commute one way (when traffic is moving). Maria loves her job, but the stresses of caring for a family, commuting, and the usual pressures of a human resources department can sometimes trigger a migraine headache. With her busy schedule, Maria can't take time off from work and family when she has a migraine. The increased frequency of her migraines creates even more stress, but she doesn't have time to visit a doctor or make an extra trip to the pharmacy.

In her spare time, Maria likes to ride her bicycle, play tennis, and shop. She and Carlos enjoy traveling, with and without the kids. They try to set aside at least one weekend a month as "date night" to recharge their marriage. After work and dinner at home with the family, Maria usually reads the mail and watches her favorite TV programs—*CSI*, *The Office*, and old movies on TCM. Occasionally, she will watch Telemundo when her mother visits. She rarely has time to read the newspaper, except on weekends when she relaxes with the Sunday *Chicago Tribune.* Maria and Carlos subscribe to *Time, Chicago,* and *Midwest Living,* but they seldom read every issue.

In the end, you have to use judgment. The ad will not write itself based on a compilation of facts. Sometimes a great creative idea stems from a minor benefit and blooms into a powerful image that drives a whole campaign. Our advice: Get the facts and use them, but don't be a slave to data.

So What?

When you see a feature or even a rather vague benefit, be sure to ask, "So what?" What does that feature do for the consumer? Keep asking, "So what?" until you get to the benefit that satisfies a basic want or need. Think about the questions you'd ask if you were buying something. You may not always get something you'd include in the body copy, but if you keep probing, you might get an idea for a whole campaign.

Images 4.9, 4.10

One product, but two different target audiences. The ad on the left appeared in Shape *magazine with the headline "Wow, my tush looks amazing." The other ad in* Maxim *stated, "She's totally checking me out."*

For example:

Dove soap is one quarter cleansing cream.

So what?

It's creamier, less harsh to the skin.

So what?

Your skin looks younger, less dry.

So what?

You feel better about yourself.

Now you've got a hook. Don't tell her about your soap; talk to her about feeling young, beautiful, free, and sexy.

Put yourself in the target customer's shoes. Luke Sullivan says, "Ask yourself what would make you want to buy the product? Find the central truth about the product . . . hair coloring isn't about looking younger. It's about self esteem. Cameras aren't about pictures. They're about stopping time and holding life as the sands run out." [9]

Finding Your Voice

You know what you want to say; now you have to figure out how to say it. Whether you create a formal tone statement or just think about it, you really do

The Only Crime He Ever Committed

Was Loving His Owners Too Much

Casey was always there for his owners. Every time they would have a bad day, he would give them his full love and attention. How did his owners show their appreciation? They threw him out on the streets to fend for himself.

Over 2 million dogs like Casey are subjected to living in shelters and over 97,000 dogs are euthanized because of limited space. To learn how you can help dogs like Casey log onto www.hsus.org for more information.

THE HUMANE SOCIETY
OF THE UNITED STATES

Image 4.11

What dog lover could resist this appeal? If you're in that target audience, you'd want to rush down to the shelter and save this dog. Or at least write a check to the Humane Society to help them save other pets.

need to define the tone of your creative effort. Another way to think about it is finding your voice: Is it loud and obnoxious; soft and sexy; logical and persuasive; fun and carefree; melodramatic; or some other characteristic? For example, if you did ads for a hospital, you wouldn't make jokes about kids with cancer. You'd be hopeful, respectful, empathetic, and maybe emotional. On the other hand, if you advertised an amusement park, you wouldn't feature a serious discussion about the benefits of a roller coaster. You'd be wild and screaming with excitement.

The tone or voice of an ad or a commercial is more than the concept. It's reflected in the selection of talent, music, editing, art direction, and voice inflection. For example, a TV commercial for Cheerios features baby boomers "lamenting" the fact they have to eat healthy food to reduce their cholesterol. The words are serious, but their facial expressions and the fact they are actually enjoying their Cheerios provide a totally different voice than if you just looked at the script.

As with everything else, know the target audience. Then find the right tone to communicate your message.

Ad Story

The child comes first.

Children's Hospital Foundation™

The Gift of Song

"A few years ago we were approached by Children's Hospital of Milwaukee. They wanted to launch a capital campaign and raise 75 million dollars. And, they wanted to raise the money in 5 years.

"Raising money is a lot different than just selling an item or service. Every organization or individual has one, or several, particular institutions or causes that they hold near and dear. To ask for money means that you have to either be in their circle of consideration, or find a way to become part of that circle.

"We conducted research on awareness and attitudes people had with the hospital. While most people were aware of its existence, they had no clear picture or emotional connection. To move them into the circle of consideration we had to create a campaign that emotionally bonded the hospital with the community.

"So we did something rather unusual: We wrote and produced an original song called 'Who comes first?' The song never mentions the hospital . . . until the end.

"'Who in this world do you love, more than you love yourself? Who is worth all the sacrifice, when the need is there, you never think twice . . . Who comes first? Who comes first . . . '

"We used this as the background for television, and two-minute and one-minute versions for radio. In fact, the song was requested so much, radio stations started placing the full-length version of the song in their rotations.

"The campaign worked wonderfully. In fact, the money was raised in less than four years. But we learned something even more from this effort.

"Since money could be donated from anyone, we needed something that resonated with everyone. That meant that our effort had to connect with men and women of all ages. From the numerous letters I received thanking us for 'the gift of a song,' all from women, we realized how connecting strongly with the female allowed us to also connect with the male. Music can be a powerful common denominator . . . when done right.

"Since then we have done quite a bit of proprietary research on 'dual audience decisions.' In a nutshell, if you find a way to reach the female, you can reach the male. However, if you find a way to reach the male, chances are you missed the female by a mile."[11]

—Tom Jordan
Chairman, Chief Creative Officer,
Hoffman York, Milwaukee

Call to action—what do you want them to do?

Remember AIDA? The Action component is the finish line of your advertising. If you can get the reader or viewer to contact the advertiser, most of your work is done. Although you will continue to reinforce the brand and encourage future sales to consumers who take action, your primary job is to connect buyers to sellers. It's up to them to close the deal.

The main idea is to connect the reader, viewer, or listener with the advertiser. Make it easy to get more information if it's needed. If personal selling is critical to a purchase, find a way to connect the prospect with the salesperson. These connections can take the following forms:

- Web site address

- E-mail address

- Reply card

- Toll-free number in ad

- Online or paper coupon

- Visit to the store/retailer

- Test drive

Think about the many ways customers can take action; then make it easy to connect them with the advertiser.

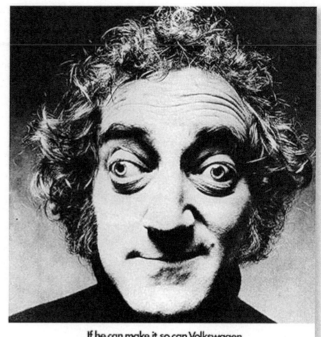

If he can make it, so can Volkswagen.

Image 4.12

The creative team was sure this shot of British comic Marty Feldman would catch the reader's eye. But where's the car? The copy explains that VWs are also small and not exactly beautiful but, like Marty, fun and successful. You have to give this client a lot of credit for having faith in their agency's intuition.

Putting It All Together

You've done your homework on the audience, the product, and the competition. Now you're ready to talk to a prospective customer. You're ready to be an account planner—or at least rely on one. It's your job to give voice to the consumer. Imagine you're talking to a neighbor over the fence, instead of writing an ad or a TV spot. Could you tell him or her the One Thing to know about your product? Could you give reasons to support that One Thing? Do you have answers to objections or misconceptions about your product? Could you convince that neighbor to seek more information, visit a store to compare, or just buy the product? It's all about making a personal connection. Think like a planner, but write like a creative.

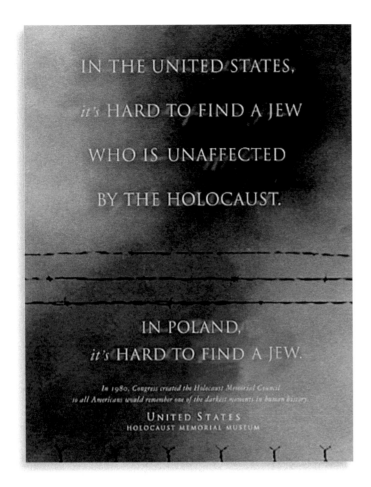

IN THE UNITED STATES,
it's HARD TO FIND A JEW
WHO IS UNAFFECTED
BY THE HOLOCAUST.

IN POLAND,
it's HARD TO FIND A JEW.

In 1980, Congress created the Holocaust Memorial Council
so all Americans would remember one of the darkest moments in human history.

UNITED STATES
HOLOCAUST MEMORIAL MUSEUM

Image 4.13

There's nothing light or clever about the Holocaust. So the tone of this ad matches the subject matter: somber.

Words of Wisdom

"Making the simple complicated is commonplace. Making the complicated simple, awesomely simple, that's creativity." [12]

—Charles Mingus

Here are a few samples:

Objective: Introduce new hybrid crossover utility vehicle

Type of Product: Considered purchase, high-involvement durable good

Target Audience: 20- to 30-year-old women in top 25 markets, $25K–$50K income

Possible Creative Strategy: Lots of pictures to show features and styling, with captions to explain benefits (environmentally friendly, dependable, lots of space, mileage)

Tone: Convey fun, independence, adventure, and social responsibility

Objective: Encourage contributions to animal rights group

Type of Product: Emotional issue, high involvement for select few

Target Audience: 18- to 64-year-old women

Possible Creative Strategy: Show animal suffering in lab tests; long copy tells story of animal and how you can help

Tone: Emotional, urgent, call to action (send money)

Objective: Introduce new style of brace for arthritic knees

Type of Product: Considered purchase, high involvement

Target Audience: 45- to 80-year-old men and women with arthritis

Possible Creative Strategy: Position as alternative to surgery and drugs; show active seniors, possible testimonials or before/after photos

Tone: Create peace of mind (postpone surgery, relieve pain, resume active lifestyle)

Who's Who?

Although he was the third name in Doyle Dane Bernbach, there was no doubt who was in charge of the creative process. **William Bernbach** revolutionized advertising from the late 1950s and through the 1970s, suggesting advertising was an art and not a science, with groundbreaking campaigns for Volkswagen, Alka-Seltzer, Polaroid, Avis, Orbach's, and many others. His simple yet sophisticated commercials generated huge sales for his clients as they wove their way firmly into the popular culture. Doyle Dane Bernbach not only changed advertising forever; it also spawned many of the creative superstars of the 1970s, '80s, and '90s who formed their own shops.

G. Andrew Meyer has created advertising campaigns that have been recognized by the Kelly Awards, the ANDYs, the Art Directors Club, *Communication Arts Advertising Annual*, The One Show, British Design & Art Direction, the CLIOs, and the OBIEs, among others. Meyer came into advertising as a designer and an art director, eventually morphing into a copywriter and an executive creative director at Leo Burnett in Chicago.

As chairman of the Ted Bates agency, **Rosser Reeves** originated the Unique Selling Proposition, which dominated advertising strategy until the Creative Revolution of the 1960s. His no-nonsense technique of hammering a single message home was very effective in turning features into benefits that consumers could easily understand.

Exercises

1. Competing Voices

Sometimes it's hard to determine the brand voice—a way to articulate a brand's personality. Here's one way to help understand how one brand's voice might stack up to its competition.

- Pick two competing brands—for example: Apple and Dell.

- Now select one student to draw two stick people on the board. Call one Apple and one Dell. Next generate a list of bulleted profile attributes next to each. Focus on demographics and psychographics (where they live, what they do, kids, income, hobbies . . . you know the drill). The idea is to sketch out who Apple or Dell would be, if each was a person.

- Next draw a speech bubble by each. Apple and Dell have just run into each other on the street. They know each other but are not friends. What might they say to each other? Fill in the bubble.

- Now for the interesting part. Give each one a think bubble. What are Apple and Dell thinking about each other—and can't or won't say? That's where you really get a picture of the brand as a person. This is a great way to make a brand real and get at brand personality. Fill in this bubble.

- Compare and contrast how each brand has its own personality.

Adapted from an exercise shared by Sue Northey, Vice President, Planning, Cramer-Krasselt, Milwaukee, WI.

2. What's the Big Idea, Buddy?

This exercise is all about finding the One Thing or the Big Idea and linking it to strategy.

- You'll be given three campaigns, each with at least three print ads.

- Write a Creative Brief for each campaign. As always, end with one sentence describing the overarching concept in the campaign—the One Thing.

- Now, as a class, compare how each student interpreted the message. If the messaging is tight, the briefs should be similar.

Adapted from an exercise shared by Kimberly Selber, PhD, Associate Professor, University of Texas–Pan American. (She suggests using *Archive* magazine for this assignment; the online version is great, because you can easily grab all the ads together.)

3. Strategies and Tactics

Strategies and tactics can often be confusing. This is designed to help you understand the difference.

- Review the following statements and determine which are strategies and which are tactics. Then discuss as a group or class and see if there is agreement.

  o Create a traveling mini first-class section for Virgin Airlines.

  o Make a virtual connection with all college-bound high school juniors.

  o Ensure that all new mothers have a personal experience with Purell hand sanitizer.

  o Demonstrate the strength of Master Locks.

- Having determined which are strategies, brainstorm at least five tactics to bring each strategy to life.

- Next draft rough thumbnail executions for each tactics.

- If you're really adventurous, try to write an objective that you think would have been the genesis for each strategy. Try to make it measurable.

4. Talking Products

Here's a way to really empathize with a product. You may realize that one product can have several benefits, depending on the target and behavioral situations.

- As a class brainstorm five occasions when someone might select a Hershey's chocolate bar from all the other snacks available at a point-of-purchase display.

- Now to come up with five more occasions or opportunities where a consumer might, select a Hershey's chocolate bar from all the other snacks available

Examples:

a) on a long road trip when paying for gas inside the convenience store

b) before a camping trip, in anticipation of making s'mores

c) when someone needs a not-too-serious Valentine's gift

- Now switch places. You're the chocolate bar! For each purchase occasion complete the sentence "You won't regret buying me because _____."

Examples:

a) I'll sweeten up your trip and make the miles go by more happily.

b) authentic Hershey's quality is needed for the best tasting s'mores.

c) no Valentine can resist the aroma and flavor of a Hershey's chocolate bar.

Adapted from an exercise shared by Dorothy Pisarski, PhD, Assistant Professor, Drake University.

Notes

1. Quote from the CLIO Awards Web site, http://www.clioawards.com/html/wsj/spivak.html (accessed January 10, 2005).

2. Mary Wells Lawrence, quoted in *Vogue,* February 15, 1972.

3. G. Andrew Meyer, Ad Story: *A Curiously Strong Approach (Just Don't Tell the Boss),* 2005.

4. William Bernbach, *Bill Bernbach Said . . .* (New York: DDB Needham Worldwide, 1989), p. 12.

5. Scott Bedbury, interviewed by authors, December 3, 2004.

6. Quote from the CLIO Awards Web site, http://clioawards.com/html/wsj/dusenberrry.html (accessed December 20, 2004).

7. Quote from the CLIO Awards Web site, http://clioawards.com/html/wsj/chiat.html (accessed December 20, 2004).

8. David Ogilvy, *Ogilvy on Advertising* (New York: Random House, 1985), p. 166.

9. Luke Sullivan, *Hey Whipple, Squeeze This: A Guide to Creating Great Ads* (New York: John Wiley, 1998), p. 35.

10. Quoted in Denis Higgins, *The Art of Writing Advertising: Conversations With Masters of the Craft: William Bernbach, George Gribbin, Rosser Reeves, David Ogilvy, Leo Burnett* (New York: McGraw-Hill, 2003), p. 125.

11. Tom Jordan, Ad Story: *The Gift of Song,* February 2009.

12. Quoted in Nancy Vonk and Janet Kestin, *Pick Me: Breaking Into Advertising and Staying There: Hundreds of Lessons You Can't Learn in School* (Hoboken, NJ: John Wiley, 2005), p. 15.

Chapter 5

Issues in a Changing Marketplace

We're All the Same...Only Different

Look around. Does everyone look like you? Until the late 1960s, advertisers must have thought everyone in the United States was a straight, uptight, well-dressed, white suburbanite. Because that's all they showed in their ads. It took time, but marketers finally discovered that African Americans own homes. Women buy cars. Gays and lesbians like vacations. Arab Americans are not terrorists. People who don't speak English as their primary language still know that money talks. Integrating advertising is not only the right thing; it is the smart thing.

While the advertising industry has belatedly addressed diversity of the marketplace, it still has a long way to go when it comes to hiring minorities and women. This book is not the forum for solving this problem, but as we've done throughout this book—we tell it like it is. And, if you look at the changing face of America, we'd suggest the industry get moving a bit quicker because having a diverse workforce, one that reflects all consumers, is in everyone's best interest. For now, let's get down to the business of understanding our changing marketplace.

As of 2007, 1 in every 3 Americans is a person of color, and that's a trend that will only increase. Ethnic identities and demographics are changing. "In fact in the last U.S. census more than half of the people who identified themselves as 'black in combination with at least one other race' were under 18 years old."[1] This points to the shifting ethnic identities, but it also suggests changes in age demographics. America is aging in huge numbers. The generation that created the youth culture of the 1960s is shifting not so gracefully into retirement. Women make up 51% of the total population, with 40- to 64-year-old women representing the single largest U.S. market segment.[2] And whether or not women are the end user, they make over 80% of the consumption choices. Now check this out: These specialty markets (African Americans, Hispanics, Asians, and women) make up 84% of the population.[4] No, your eyes did not deceive you—it did say 84%! Trust us; this chapter is worth reading.

Words of Wisdom

"You know why Madison Avenue advertising has never done well in Harlem? We're the only ones who know what it means to be Brand X."[3]

—Dick Gregory

Today, it's not a question of whether to appeal to multicultural audiences and specialty markets. It's more a question of how to do it. How do we show people of color and specialty markets in our ads without using stereotypes? If we avoid the obvious, do we deny their identities? Can we keep it real without alienating other audiences? Creating ads for today's marketplace presents a multiplicity of unique challenges.

Advertisers need to be responsive to a cultural shift that suggests many people see themselves as multiethnic or multicultural. Maybe as this takes root, the work of multicultural and general market agencies will begin to blend. Maybe not. As we've said, more than half of the people who identified themselves as "black in combination with at least one other race" were under 18 years old.[5] So being on the cutting edge of trends and understanding the shifting lines of cultural identity are imperative. Some of the hottest models today have an indefinable ethnic look, and they may also no longer be size zero. Tiger Woods is a great example of a celebrity who chooses to define himself as multiethnic, refusing to be categorized as African American or Thai or Asian American, ethnicities that define his parents. Woods embraces his multicultural heritage and fully expects advertisers who hire him to do the same. New magazines such as *Fader* celebrate cultural diversity. But the real growth is in social media, where culture is celebrated and the consumer is in control. Check out Web sites like mavinmag.com, blackvoices.com, and hiphop.com. Celebrating diversity is not just a trend. It's a way of life that advertisers must embrace. How will postmodern conceptions of culture and identity influence the way you define and speak to your target audience?

It's All There in Black and White

When advertising began to integrate in the late 1960s, the trend was to make African Americans look like "dark-skinned white people." While some African Americans were happy to finally be represented in mainstream advertising, others resented the lack of realistic models and situations and the limited media placements.

Ad professionals such as Thomas Burrell, founder of Burrell Communications, the largest African American ad agency in the United States, and Al Anderson, founder of Anderson Communications, Inc., have long argued "blacks aren't dark-skinned whites."[6] Forty years ago, before minority-owned agencies existed, the industry really lacked for messages that reflected cultural experiences beyond a white world. Today, according to Anderson, the *multi* in multicultural marketing has gotten a bit blurred: "Last time I checked, all marketing is targeted at somebody. Now how you construct this young, black, Latino, Asian person, I don't know. I've never met one of these folks."[7] Reaching multicultural audiences means creating connectivity between the message and the audience and using all avenues of integrated marketing to deliver that message. For Burrell and Anderson, success has come by tapping

The new Timberland PRO® TITAN® workboot features a lightweight titanium alloy safety toe and our exclusive PowerFit® comfort system. Because your workload is heavy enough.

WHAT TO WEAR WHEN YOUR WORKLOAD IS MEASURED IN METRIC TONS.

Timberland
PRO SERIES

Image 5.1

To some people this ad might represent a stereotype of African Americans as blue-collar laborers. To others, it's just another hardworking guy who needs a good pair of work boots. What do you think?

into the unique cultural experiences of African Americans and slipping that message into channels that resonate with their audience. But their success as owners of African American ad agencies also highlights the fact that general market agencies seem to be unable or unwilling to give voice to multicultural consumers. Thus today we see most work targeting multicultural audiences done by agencies that specialize in a particular demographic. The problem persists, but we hope to do our small part by at least putting the topic on the table.

How do they look today?

Just how much are African Americans represented in advertising today? Of all ethnic groups, other than whites, African Americans have the highest representation in mainstream magazine ads. Yet only 14% of the ads in mainstream magazines feature diverse groups of people.[8] So it's hard to say the advertising industry really embraces the diversity reflected in American culture. Although some brands including Skechers, Toyota, and CoverGirl have been at the forefront of multiethnic marketing trends, this is not necessarily the norm. When it comes to television, African Americans make up more than a third of the models in spots running during prime time.[9] Not long ago, African American endorsements went mainly to athletes. What's interesting is to see how African American endorsements have begun to move beyond sports figures. Queen Latifah had three major endorsement deals in 2007 alone including her CoverGirl Queen Collection, which invites women of color to enjoy their brown-skinned beauty while expanding cultural notions of beauty. Beyoncé has racked up deals with American Express, Pepsi, Samsung, DIRECTV, Armani Diamonds perfume, Disney, and L'Oréal. Usher came out with dual fragrances, He and She, and a deal with Macy's.[10] Seeing the diversity of product categories and range of celebrities suggests things may be changing.

Image 5.2

Until the 1960s, the best African Americans could expect from mainstream advertising was to be portrayed as happy servants.

Image 5.3

You can call Tiger Woods an incredibly gifted golfer, a multimillionaire product endorser, or a very savvy businessman. But don't call him an African-Asian-American, because he doesn't accept the labels that might define his parents.

Tapping into the African American market

It's sometimes hard to talk about a target market without sounding stereotypical. However, there are some cultural commonalities, and for an advertiser they are worth paying attention to. Community involvement is a huge part of African American life, and women play a very prominent role in family life. Don't underestimate

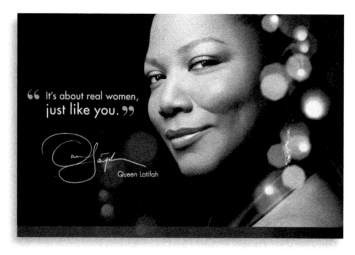

CoverGirl has brilliantly extended its line beyond the general market as the brand for "real women." Once the brand for straight, skinny, pale-faced models, CoverGirl has redefined itself through spokeswomen like Queen Latifah and Ellen DeGeneres.

African American women's influence or their buying power. They have the highest spending power among women of color. Knowing these facts, an integrated campaign that reaches into community life is essential when trying to reach African Americans. As you can also see by the list of endorsements from cars to fashion and beauty, personal expression is significant. At the same time, African Americans' preferences, habits, and attitudes reflect a broad range of sensibilities. In most cases, it's best to avoid using slang. If you aren't really part of the culture, it can be embarrassing at best and often insulting. We also know that media matter. Eight out of 10 African Americans are heavy magazine readers, and that's more than the U.S. average.[11] Both television and social media are big parts of their lives. And music is a huge cultural influence and form of expression. So it's no surprise to see music merge across multiple media.

Hip-hop goes mainstream

Hip-hop is just one of the ways we see African American culture merging into general market advertising. It has crossed over into the cultural mainstream thanks, in part, to Spike Lee and Nike's early collaborations. But what sets it apart is how pervasive and lucrative it has become. Now even big brands are comfortable spending millions of dollars using hip-hop in general market advertising, and that's because many niches within mainstream culture not only understand hip-hop; they embrace it. Today we see advertisers using hip-hop as a statement demonstrating their cultural cachet. Consider how Gatorade has embraced hip-hop culture with its new G campaigns by TBWA\Chiat\Day, adding an edge by deleting the Gatorade logo. Or look at how the hip-hop tradition is again embraced by Nike with the LeBron James *Powder* commercial by Wieden + Kennedy. Of course, as with any cultural trend, controversy or polarizing effects remain possible. The needle moves with 50 Cent for Coca-Cola's VitaminWater, but for other brands he is still too controversial.

¿Cómo Se Dice *Diversity* en Español?

In our discussions with Ileana Alémán-Rickenbach, a creative working at BVK/MEKA in Miami, we discovered that the debate over what to call Latin Americans is still raging. She told us that a recent poll indicated about 65% prefer to call themselves *Hispanic,* which is how the business world identifies the target audience. She said *Hispanic* is accepted primarily by older, more established residents in the United

Image 5.5

This "aptitude test" by hip-hop clothing company Akademiks resonates with urban youth. What do you think when you see a young African American man dressed like this?

States. Younger, more liberal types prefer *Latino* or *Latina,* which is less corporate and more personal. Her comments back up our anecdotal information. However, what's really interesting and what marketers need to pay attention to is the fact that people prefer to identify themselves by their country of origin. They are more likely to be proud of being *Chicano* or *Argentino* or *Cubana* than of being "Hispanic."[12] In this text we'll use *Hispanic* and *Latino* interchangeably, just to keep everyone happy . . . or annoyed.

Today nearly 50 million Latinos live in the United States, representing Mexico, Cuba, Puerto Rico, the Caribbean, and Central and South America, not to mention the blended Anglo-Latino cultures along the border from California to Florida.[13] That's more than a 20% increase from 3 years ago. About 1 of every 2 people added to the U.S. population during the previous year was Hispanic. Since 2007, Latinos have outnumbered African Americans. And they're young. The median age of Latinos is 27, and 1 in 3 is under age 18.[14] Consider this: Hispanic households have twice as many children under 18 as non-Hispanic households.[15] According to Leo Olper, chief operating officer for Lápiz, the fifth largest Hispanic ad agency in the United States, if we think about American Hispanics as a world economy, they would be number 13.[16] Hispanic advertising is outpacing all other sectors, growing four times faster. It's now a $5 billion industry.[17] Those are impressive numbers as a whole, but don't think there is one monolithic Hispanic culture. If you consider the differences between the English spoken in the United Kingdom, the United States, and Australia, think about the 19 countries in the world where Spanish is the primary language. You can't treat this market as one group.

Now, let's consider how language works, or doesn't, across cultures. An exterminator in Mexico will remove your *bichos* (bugs), but the same word in Puerto Rico refers to a man's private parts. You have to do more than just find the right slang. You have to understand the culture. Here are some examples:[18]

- A Coca-Cola ad may use the slogan *"y su comida favorita"* ("and your favorite food"), but for Miami Cubans the ad shows pork loin, for South Texas Mexicans it's tacos, and for New York Puerto Ricans they use chicken and rice.

- When McDonald's first developed a series of "Hispanic ads," they considered all Hispanics the same until they received complaints from Puerto Rico that the ads were "too Mexican."

Image 5.6

Dominion, an energy company in Virginia, tapped into their Hispanic customer base with the headline that reads (in English), "For Danny Segura, Spanish is not a second language. It's a cultural heritage."

Image 5.7

Dedication to family is a common thread that cuts across all Latino communities. So when the CDC needed to increase vaccinations of small children, appealing to family values was the right approach. The headline (en englés): "Love them. Protect them. Vaccinate them."

- A telephone company tried to market its products to Latinos by showing a commercial in which a Latina wife tells her husband to call a friend and tell her they would be late for dinner. The commercial bombed since Latina women generally do not give orders to their husbands, and their cultural concept of time would not require a call about being late.

- When translated literally into Spanish, the famous "Got Milk?" slogan means "Are you lactating?" Fortunately, the California Milk Advisory Board realized this before it was launched. The new slogan, "Familia. Amor. Leche" ("Family. Love. Milk"), not only avoids the problems of the literal translation; it also fits the culture better. Although Anglos might find the concept of milk deprivation funny, a Latino audience would consider it insulting.

Language takes another interesting twist if we think of how it's used. Nearly 90% of Hispanics learned Spanish before they learned English, and two thirds of them are more comfortable speaking Spanish and speak it at home.[19] Bilingual Latinos are influenced more by advertising in Spanish than by advertising in English.[20] Needless to say, when it comes to Latinos' private lives Spanish language media are *caliente.* However, when they head to work that changes dramatically. In the workplace two thirds of Latinos speak English.[21] When we also consider their acculturation (how much they embrace American culture), we see that one quarter are unacculturated and just over 10% are

Ad Story

McReality

"For many years, I was creative director at the world's largest African American agency, where McDonald's was one of our major clients. In the late 1980s, when McDonald's was changing its theme line, yet again, I decided to jump into the 'here and now.' I asked my creative group to come up with something that reflected modern reality. The result was two spots that pushed the envelope. 'Momma's Date' addressed a divorced (or widowed) mother who was getting back into the social swim, much to her young son's chagrin. He was totally disapproving until the gentleman caller treated them

to a visit to McDonald's, where the son ran into his classmates, including a little cutie pie. (I had to respond to a letter that accused us of promoting juvenile sexual promiscuity. Go figure.)

"The other spot, 'Second Chance,' introduced Calvin, an ex–juvenile delinquent. In his walk through the neighborhood, a voice-over conversation pointed out the noticeable changes in his personality and behavior. At the end it is revealed that he has been employed by the Golden Arches. Some members of McDonald's Marketing Department tried to kill it (too street), but the big kahuna loved it. Calvin was an immediate hit with consumers, as well as the owners and

operators of McDonald's, so we did a series of commercials with him as the hero. When we finally bid good riddance to Calvin, we thought he was history.

"Two decades later, Calvin resurfaced on *Chappelle's Show.* In a devastating send-up, Calvin [played by Dave Chappelle] gets a job at 'WacArnold's.' At first he is the pride of the neighborhood, but things rapidly go downhill. Chappelle's series of spoofs mirrored the original Calvin's progression, so it had to have made an impression on him. (I wonder if he got turned down for the role.)"[22]

—Anna Morris
Freelance Creative; Instructor,
Columbia College, Chicago

Image 5.8

The language of love transcends cultures and so do these ads for Docol showerheads. The benefit is visually merged with the product with words of a classic love song strategically pouring from the showerhead. ¡Bésame mucho!

highly acculturated.[23] That means that about two thirds of Hispanics consider themselves partially acculturated, which means they comfortably float between mainstream American culture and Latino culture. But by no means will they shed their Latino identity any time soon. For marketers that means it's time to learn about and embrace the diversity of Hispanic cultures and how those cultural nuances merge with mainstream American culture.

Has there been a paradigm shift when it comes to merging music trends into general marketer advertising? We think so. You can see this trend expanding with the use of Latin music now beginning to be woven in some mainstream advertising. When we say "Latin" we are talking about music from all over North, South, and Central America and the Caribbean. In fact, Univision, the largest Hispanic broadcast service, just launched a Latin music microsite, *En Directo,* specifically aimed at featuring the hippest new Latin voices. Toyota is already embracing this trend with a push for its new Corolla.[24]

Dígame más (tell me more)

Latinos tend to live in urban areas, but you'll find small communities popping up in unexpected places. The top three markets are Los Angeles, New York, and Chicago, with Miami and Houston close behind.[25] Your messages in each will be very different because their cultural experiences and incomes are very different. As with African Americans, advertising to Hispanics tends to come through multicultural ad agencies. Latinos are huge consumers of television and radio, and most of it is in Spanish. Univision and Telemundo are the top two Spanish-language networks.[26] Procter & Gamble, Sears, and General Motors are the top advertisers within the Hispanic market.[27] But when it comes to creativity, Special K and its agency Lápiz are big winners. Why? Because Special K found a way to reach across the cultural divide and share a consistent brand message with Hispanic women. In 2007 Grupo Gallegos struck gold at *Advertising Age*'s ninth annual Hispanic Creative Advertising Awards, with its California Milk Processor Board campaign.[28]

Tapping into the Latino market

As with other groups, we need to balance cultural commonality with stereotypes. That said, there are some things that are fairly typical within Hispanic culture and which tend to transcend individual national origin. Family-focused activities are a central element of Latino life, and it's not uncommon for multiple generations to share the same household. For Latinos, familial concerns often trump individual needs. Compared to some other cultures, everyday life can be a bit slower paced within the Latino community. Family-centered obligations often supersede outside commitments. Music is a big part of Latino life, and it often blends mainstream American culture with a multitude of Latino sensibilities. Consider the fact that *American Idol* is the top English-language TV program among Hispanics.[29] While the majority of Hispanic television originates in Mexico, Latino culture is far more diverse. Considering the specific heritage of your Latino audience will make for a more resonant campaign. Finally, Latinos are Web savvy. You might consider how to leverage Spanish language on the Web and stand out.

Words of Wisdom

"The challenge is to keep the flame burning, the flame of communicating to the Hispanic market in the language of their heart." [31]

—Tere Zubizarreta

Women in Advertising: Have We Really Come a Long Way, Baby?

Women hold 53% of the jobs within our industry, yet they account for only 28% of the top management positions.[30] Women have made great inroads into account management, account planning, and media, where they equal or outnumber men in similar positions. However, women are underrepresented on the creative side, holding only about a quarter of the creative jobs.[32] It surely can't be that women are not as creative as men. Perhaps the more compelling question for us to consider here is: Have we moved away from the stereotyping of women in advertising?

Rob Walker, who writes the "Ad Report Card" column in *Slate* online magazine, has commented on the trend for advertisers to have it both ways when they portray women—titillating images and noble intentions. "Typically, when advertisers do something that they suspect will offend a portion of the audience, they claim that they aren't actually *committing* the offense, they are *critiquing* the offense."[33] All you have to do is consider the huge public relations disaster created by Taxi, New York, with its Motrin ads calling the slings mothers use to carry their babies "fashion accessories." In less than 24 hours Johnson & Johnson's vice president of marketing issued a public apology, and all the offending ads were pulled.[34]

Women as other

It seems ironic to us that women are so often considered a specialty market when they make up 51% of the U.S. population and influence 85% of all purchases.[35] Yet women do view the world through a unique lens. "You have to attract a woman with honesty, humanity or something that sincerely piques her interest."[36] Reaching women requires doing your homework and not making assumptions.

Women take brands seriously, but be careful—they tend not to bond with brands they perceive as aggressively targeting them. The best way to reach women is to consider the unexpected and to pay attention to details because women do. Even the subtlest nuance can mean a lot. Consider that three quarters of all women in the United States work full-time and women over 40 have some of the highest spending power in the nation.[37] They're buying, so give them time to make their decisions. Now think about multicultural women. In the U.S., there are over 30 million women of color, and they have over $700 billion in purchasing power.[38] While there may be a lot of similarities along the gender lines, various cultural groups have their own distinct buying patterns. The really interesting thing is that most women of color embrace their American culture while holding fast to their ethnic identity.

Life doesn't have to be this hard.

The **must read** is now a **must watch**.

REAL SIMPLE.
R E A L   L I F E.

Get ready to simplify your life.

FRIDAYS 8/7c

A Discovery Company

realsimplereallife.com

Image 5.9

For years, advertisers showed "superwomen" who could do it all. Today, acknowledging the strains of balancing working outside the home with managing a household resonates with modern women.

Ad Story

Hispanic Hyperreality

Ileana Alémán-Richenbach at BVK/MEKA, a Hispanic advertising agency in Miami, explains that there is no single Hispanic culture but rather a "hyperreality" that blurs the difference between the symbolic and the real:

"*Hispanic* is really just a marketing term coined by the advertising industry in the U.S. This hyperreal market lumps together people of Latin American and Spanish heritage under one 'ethnic' classification, when in fact the 19 Latin groups under the Hispanic umbrella can be drastically different from one another.

"One of our clients, a top telecom, was launching a new international calling plan for mobile phones. Another opportunity to practice those hyperreal Hispanic Spanish skills, right?

"I started by asking Sandra, a Mexican coworker, 'How do you answer the phone?' We say, '*¿Bueno?*' (by the way, *bueno* literally means 'good'). Nereyda said Cubans answer '*Oigo*' ('I hear'). The Venezuelans told me they say, '*Aló*' (which has no meaning). Puerto Ricans say, 'Hello' (pronounced '*jel-ó*'). The Argentine said she had the only legitimate, polite, correct, and perfect phone greeting: '*Hola.*' From there on everyone had a say; visiting clients opined . . . '*Buenas,*' '*Dígame,*' '*Sí.*' It was Babel.

"A little later, the client called to 'remind' us that we should use the proper Mexican 'dialect' for the West Coast and 'generic' Spanish for the rest. That's exactly what we did. We created a pun for the West Coast version where one character answered the phone by saying '*¿Bueno?*' ('Good') and the caller replied, '*Bueno no, buenísimo*' ('Not only good, but very good'). We sent a creative rationale explaining that literally *bueno* means good, but that in context it really means hello. That it was a play on words to introduce the retail message (great prices), etc., etc. . . . of course. She never got it. The cultural divide was insurmountable. On the other hand, we never found a Pan-Latin way of saying hello. The hyperreal had turned surreal.

"We ended up creating a funny, clever, and very effective campaign where people call their countries of origin, but no one answers the phone by saying hello. We just started the spots midway through the calls. In the world of Hispanic Hyperreality, definitely less is more."[39]

—Ileana Alémán-Rickenbach, Chief Creative Officer, *BVK-MEKA*, Miami

If there's one thing we can say about all women, it's that they want and deserve respect. Women are also considered the leading indicators of social change. It's not just Hispanic or African American women who feel strong ties to family—it's women in general, and that often makes them very socially conscious. To reach them, we must understand the meaning, significance, and direction of large social changes. Now think of how that plays out in the work world. Women have a high preference for personal networking, and they prefer dispersed or shared authority. This makes them strong mentors. And they thrive on conceptual thinking, consensus building, and flexible work and lifestyles. In a nutshell, they want respect, autonomy, and flexibility. Don't talk down to them and don't assume you know everything about them. Respect them and their differences, and you'll earn their loyalty.

Tapping into the women's market

Here are some basic tips when it comes to women—at least women as consumers. Before you start talking to a woman, listen to her. She's got a lot to say—most of which you won't be expecting. Give her details. She'll respect you, and respect translates into loyalty. Talk to her as you'd speak to a friend, and she'll be your friend. Testimonials can have real power because they are real. Move past stereotypes. She has. If you think she's one-dimensional, you're wrong. Women juggle a lot. Target your brand to her lifestyle, and you just might reach her. Tell the truth. She'll catch you if you don't. She'll hold you accountable for your actions. Be a good corporate citizen.

Myths and myth busters for marketing to women

In her book, *Marketing to Women,* Marti Barletta explores eight myths, and we think she's right on the money:[40]

Myth 1: Marketing to women may be appropriate because it supports diversity; but with our limited resources, we need to stay focused on the business.

Myth Buster: Marketing to women is not about diversity—it's about sales, share, and profits.

Myth 2: We need to keep our marketing focus on our core customers—men.

Myth Buster: If you're always looking back, how do you expect to move forward?

Myth 3: Average income for women is lower than for men. It doesn't make sense to go after a low-income market.

Myth Buster: Be careful to look beyond the averages.

Myth 4: Marketing to women will require us to double our budget or, worse, split it in half.

Myth Buster: Marketing to women takes the same budget and delivers more bang for your buck.

Myth 5: With women, marketing is all about relationships.

Myth Buster: Don't buy into the simplistic assertions that with women, it's all about relationships.

Words of Wisdom

"The consumer isn't a moron. She is your wife." [41]

—David Ogilvy

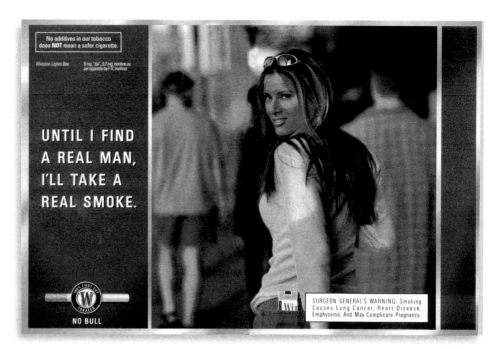

Image 5.10

As part of their "No Bull" campaign, Winston targeted independent women with high standards. Until Mr. Right comes along, they'll settle for a cigarette ("real men" must love secondhand smoke). With tobacco products now under FDA regulation, we may not be seeing many more cigarette ads. Bull or no bull.

Myth 6: The best way to focus on marketing to women is to undertake a dedicated initiative within our Emerging Markets group.

Myth Buster: Don't single it out—build it in.

Myth 7: We believe in gender-neutral marketing—it's what women want.

Myth Buster: Gender-neutral marketing is not how you put your sales into overdrive.

Myth 8: I've heard of companies that did women-specific advertising, and nothing happened or it backfired. Gender-specific marketing doesn't work.

Myth Buster: Bad gender-specific marketing doesn't work.

Don't Ask, Don't Tell, Just Sell

Depending on the survey, anywhere from 6% to 10% of the American population identifies as gay, lesbian, or bisexual. Smart marketers know they can't ignore 20 million to 32 million people. Aside from the sheer numbers, the gay and lesbian segment offers marketers other advantages: They tend to have more money than other Americans, and they spend it. They look fondly on products and services advertised in gay, lesbian, bisexual, and transgender (GLBT)

publications. Generally, GLBT households tend to be brand-loyal and seek out product upgrades at higher rates than their non-gay counterparts.[43]

Just do it

Back in the mid-1990s Nike ran an ad, "Canoeists," featuring two lesbians as a part of the "Just do it" campaign for the women's brand. Ironically, no one at Nike knew they were lesbians. That fact was not lost on the creative team, who consciously chose the two women because they felt they epitomized the empowerment theme and spoke to an often-ignored audience—not to mention it silently pushed a few buttons at Nike.[44] Today using lesbians in an ad doesn't have to be a silent response. In fact, some brands such as Pottery Barn, Absolut Vodka, Subaru, and Ikea benefit greatly from their gay-oriented positioning. It's all about knowing your target and its tolerance threshold. American Express also courted the gay and lesbian target when it began highlighting Ellen DeGeneres as a cardholder in its "My Life. My Card" campaign. It worked well because the campaign's One Thing originally focused on celebrities, so DeGeneres fit perfectly and slipped under the radar—but not to this community. Members of this group notice brands that speak to them, and they reward them. Just remember that backlash is always a possibility. Have a backup plan and be sure you know what's in the best interest of your brand. This will help you weigh opportunities against possible negative consequences.

To learn more about advertising to the gay and lesbian market, check out the GLAAD Advertising Media Program Web site at commercialcloset.org.

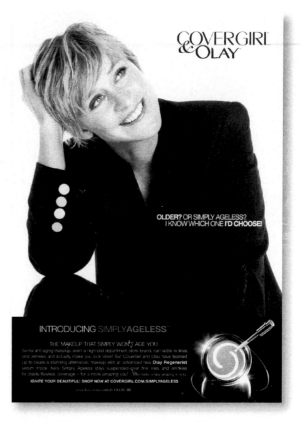

Image 5.11

Whether they are gay or straight, millions of women know and respect Ellen DeGeneres. So even though she is an outspoken lesbian, several international brands have employed her as a spokeswoman, including American Express and CoverGirl, demonstrating that the right celebrity can transcend formerly closed boundaries.

Tapping into the gay/lesbian market

If your assignment is to reinforce brand preference among gays and lesbians, you have several options, but one of them is not stereotyping. While gays and lesbians may identify themselves by sexual preference, they also tend to strongly identify as mainstream consumers. You might run your general market campaigns in mainstream media that also have a high gay/lesbian concentration. You don't change the creative, but the media selection indicates that you're interested in their business. Running in straight and gay media demonstrates your commitment to their community. They will notice and thank you at the checkout. Then, using visuals, copy, or both, incorporate gay themes and run those in gay publications. Reviewing gay and lesbian media, you'll notice that they tend to have the ability to laugh at themselves and the

Image 5.12

Levi's produced two commercials for their 501 jeans for the straight and gay markets. The concept was identical—a young man pulls up his jeans and his dream date magically appears. The only difference was the ending. The spots that ran on Logo, MTV's gay network, showed the young man with another guy instead of the young woman.

world; just be careful not to fall victim to stereotypical images. Another approach is to integrate gay-themed ads across the entire campaign. Ikea, for example, has used gay themes in television commercials that also reach the straight market. This demonstrates that you believe your brand is for all consumers and you're willing to risk a possible backlash. You might also consider keeping your mass-media advertising mainstream, or gender neutral, and focus on promotional and public relations programs that target gays and lesbians, such as sponsorship of an AIDS benefit or movie trailers at movies that appeal to this demographic. Just remember that it's all about context, and respect rules the day.

You're Never Too Old to Buy Something

If it's true that mature Americans tend to think of themselves as 10 to 15 years younger than they really are, does it make sense to turn off a huge potential market by showing a bunch of wacky geezers in your ads? Plain and simple, it doesn't. So how do you address the growing mature market, with baby boomers coming on board in droves? Two distinct groups emerge within the mature market. One is the *65-plus group.* These individuals remember World War II. They have a strong work ethic, and they are self-sacrificing, tolerant of authority, comfortable with conformity, loyal, and patriotic; they'll happily spend what they've earned and appreciate a good value. On the other hand, the 55–65 group, the *baby boomers,* are well educated, hedonistic, focused on self-improvement, and nonconformist. They believe work should be fulfilling, feel a sense of entitlement, tolerate differences, and seek adventure and new experiences. Despite their differences, people nearing or in retirement have a lot in common.

Mature consumers are a more dynamic group than you might think. They've also got a lot of money to spend. According to J. Walter Thompson's Mature Market Group, this segment controls 75% of our nation's assets as well as 70% of the nation's net worth.[45] However, much of that money comes from investments, which for the short term can have wild fluctuations in value. They travel a lot too—both domestically and overseas. And this might surprise you: Mature Americans represent the fastest-growing segment of Internet users in the United States. They actually spend more time online than college students, and they buy a lot more online. Most own cell phones, but unlike college students, you won't find them texting. They still prefer e-mail. Speaking of which, baby boomers are big on relationship marketing, especially in the online world, so use the Internet wisely.

These folks live full, active, and adventurous lives. They tend to consider themselves young at heart. Although this demographic skews heavily female, mature Americans have varying interests, education levels, and life experiences. Most own their own homes, and most of them are mortgage-free.[46] In short, they have time and money to spend. But, they are looking for ways to spend their money that stretch their dollars and fulfill their personal aspirations. With this diverse market with money to spend, you've got your work cut out for you.

Tapping into the mature market

Never make assumptions. Get to know the mature market, just as you would any other audience. This group tends to respond very positively to relationships—so build them. Consider using life-stage marketing because the mature market responds strongly to the life-changing events, especially those that are personal. Make these events the defining moments of your campaign. Not surprisingly, members of this group value personal relationships. Consider testimonials and use research and endorsements to back up your claims. Give them facts. Be clear and straightforward. Let them know the benefits; consider demonstrating your credibility. Education will engender loyalty. They want to trust you, so give them a chance. Above all, don't pressure them. They will take their time to make their decision. Once they've decided your brand is the one, they will be very loyal. From a tonal perspective, celebrate the joys of retirement and by all means avoid scare tactics. Scare tactics generally don't work anyway. The bottom line: Don't call them names. If there's one word they hate, it's *senior*. *Old* and *elderly* won't get you very far either. The single word that seems to have the most positive benefits is *grandparent*.

Connecting with the mature market

Now that you have an overview of your grandparents, or perhaps parents, here are a few specific things to consider related to various media, courtesy of AgeVenture News Service:[47]

- **Design with their eyes in mind:** Make your ads visually accessible; use 11- or 12-point type, plenty of white space, bold headlines, and clear subheads, and break your copy into columns.

- **Business cards:** Is the print legible? Is the type large enough?

- **Brochures:** Avoid glossy stock because it glares. Remember to use larger type and go for high contrast.

- **Newsletters:** Mature Americans take the time to read them cover to cover as long as the topics interest them.

- **Print ads:** Keep it simple and avoid clutter. They respond well to "how-to" copy.

- **Radio:** Keep background music to a minimum and remember they are heavy early-morning listeners.

Image 5.13

Perhaps believing their Gecko looked too much like their older customers, GEICO appealed to seniors with a nostalgic look at the way they were. Going back to the age of "sex, drugs, and rock 'n' roll" still resonates with many boomers.

Image 5.14

This banner ad targets active seniors, at least those active enough to consider a romantic evening at a Ramada Inn.

- *Television:* Nobody watches the news like they do (notice all the mature market products advertised during the national network news programs?). Watch the background music and keep titles on the screen just a bit longer.

- *Direct mail:* They like getting mail. It's not all junk mail to them.

- *Promotion:* If something can save them money and the offer doesn't expire too soon, they'll participate.

It's a Global Marketplace

Multinational companies demand global campaigns from their advertising agencies. While they tend to stress conformity in branding, there are two approaches to consider: the standardized approach and the globalized approach. The *globalized approach* takes the view that consistent branding supersedes most cultural differences. With the exception of language, campaigns are virtually identical from country to country. The *standardized approach* suggests consistency, but only to a point. Brands that adopt a more standardized branding approach internationally keep their logos and other branding elements consistent, but they make other changes to accommodate local cultures. While the globalized approach focuses on maintaining brand consistency to a much higher degree, neither approach can afford to completely ignore local customs and cultures. Regardless of which approach works for your brand, you must understand local laws and regulations, as they vary greatly from country to country.

In the global marketplace, advertisers usually think in terms of four levels:

1. *Local:* A local brand is advertised within a single location. Retail commonly uses a local approach, and from a global perspective *local* means country.

2. *Regional:* A regional brand is advertised within a specific geographic area, such as North America, Scandinavia, or Southeast Asia.

3. *International:* International brands are advertised across the globe but tend to use the standardized approach to advertising and thus make changes that reflect local culture.

4. *Global:* Global brands are those that embrace the globalized approach, described above, as they stretch their brand names worldwide. But these brands stress conformity in brand names and advertising images. McDonald's and Marlboro are great examples of global brands.

Global growth

As we move deeper into the 21st century, the global marketplace offers advertisers ever-increasing potential. For now, the growth is slow, similar to ad spending in the United States. Global brands look to the international marketplace for strategic growth, but not to the exclusion of the U.S. market, which still accounts for 45% of advertising spending.[48]

Companies such as Procter & Gamble, Unilever, and General Motors have been aggressive players on the global stage for years. For instance, Unilever—think Axe, Slim-Fast, Dove, and Ben & Jerry's—buys media in 72 of the 78 countries.[49] Yet, across the board, advertising media spending has been down while spending on sales promotion, sponsorship, interactive, and PR increases.[50] This trend will continue for the next few years as the global marketplace continues to struggle. Global brands, more than ever, need to look for new ways to expand their markets. Advertisers need to improve their measurement of advertising's effectiveness and efficiency as well as continue to be respectful global corporate citizens. As the global marketplace grows more competitive, Integrated Marketing Communications will rule, and traditional advertising will continue to compete against the other forms of marketing communication—and it had better do so effectively, efficiently, and with global consciousness.

Tapping into global audiences

There are entire books on this subject, and we certainly aren't trying to compete with them. But we do want you to consider just how fast the world marketplace is converging. Moriarty, Mitchell, and Wells offer a few tips for globalized and standardized advertising that we think are good—plus we've added a few of our own ideas.[51]

GLOBALIZED

- You can save money with economies of scale.
- Ensure that your advertising messages are complementary and consistent.
- The company can maintain control over its advertising image.
- Global media create more opportunities for global marketing.
- Converging buyers' wants and needs across the globe can increase desire for the same product.

Image 5.15

Global ads are designed so the concept can be understood in every language or culture. In this ad designed for the Asian market, the no U-turn symbol is universally recognized . . . but it takes on a different meaning when paired with the Viagra pill.

- There is limited competition in many foreign markets.

- Graphics and visual approaches can (sometimes) overcome cultural differences.

STANDARDIZED

- There's a better fit with the local marketplace, and advertising will be less likely to overlook variations in buyer behavior.

- Involve a local professional in the decision-making process to enhance local acceptance.

- Any cost increases resulting from a more culturally specific approach are often offset by off-target ads.

- Culturally respectful and strategically bound advertising can often be highly successful.

- The chances of cultural blunders decreases.

- Honoring local customs can lead to good PR.

When advertising a global brand, you can't afford to ignore the multitude of possible pitfalls. But you can and should be a conscientious and forward-thinking global corporate citizen.

Did We Miss Anyone? You'd Better Believe It

What about Asian Americans? While there are some cultural similarities, you can't use the same tactics for Chinese, Japanese, Korean, Indian, Pakistani, Thai, and the dozens of other Asian American ethnicities. And remember, Asian Americans may be a small market segment, but in general they are also a well-educated and highly affluent segment.

What about Arab Americans? Not all Arabs are Muslim. Not all Muslims are Arabs. How do we address them while not alienating other groups of Americans? American Muslims have $170 billion in purchasing power.[53] Hallmark, Wal-Mart, and 20th Century Fox have begun to take notice.

We've come a long way from using the most offensive stereotypes, but we still have a long way to go to integrate everyone into the mainstream. The same is true for disabled people. Every disability presents different wants and needs. Like African Americans before the 1970s, disabled people are nearly invisible in today's advertising.

Then there are children and teens. Teens speak a language anyone over 30 can't possibly comprehend. So how do you write ads to reach them? Children might well be the most interesting and perhaps the most controversial market segment to discuss. There just isn't enough time or space. In the spirit of the dance of relevance and respect, we can offer a few tips that apply to most situations:

- Don't make assumptions.

- Do your homework.

- Always remember that even within a market segment there can be huge variation.

- Market segments, like subcultures, are culturally bound.

- Social context matters.

- We'll steal an old slogan: "Act globally and think locally."

- Humility goes a long way.

- Above all, be respectful.

This last point needs some more discussion. John Kuraoka, a freelance copywriter, offers some advice regarding diversity and copywriting:

Racism, sexism, and other us-against-them motifs are not funny. It is no more acceptable to poke fun at a middle-aged white man than it is to poke fun at a young black lesbian. It makes no difference that you, personally, are either a middle-aged white man or a young black lesbian. On reflection, it's questionable whether poking fun at anybody helps sell anything.[55]

On the other hand, don't let political correctness overrule common sense. Kuraoka has some good advice on this, too: "*There is a difference between race and racism, sex and sexism.* It is foolish, for example, to make a pantyhose ad gender-neutral. Be aware of cases in which neutering the character of your copy will degrade its effectiveness."[56]

A final note: In preparing to write this chapter, we talked with a diverse group of advertising practitioners and also conducted extensive secondary research. We tried to be sensitive and unbiased regarding the various issues discussed here. Yet, some people may take issue with our content or the tone. Some might say we wrote too much on one issue and not enough on another or that we totally missed the point on others. The best we can do is to bring these issues out in the open and encourage you to be sensitive to them. How you handle them depends on your own perception and sensitivity.

"To be sure, men and women approach things differently. . . . But I'm not sure those differences create barriers. In advertising, the issue isn't who did it, but how good is it."[54]

—Helayne Spivak

Who's Who?

Al Anderson began his career working for the black-owned Citizens Trust Bank, where one of his first decisions was to reject an outside advertising pitch because it just didn't speak to his customers. The rejection changed his career and led him into the agency world. Today, he is CEO of Anderson Communications, Inc., in Atlanta, the second-oldest African American–owned ad agency. Anderson's clients include Chevrolet, Kraft Foods, Pillsbury, Procter & Gamble, and Reebok. He is perhaps best known for what he and Thomas Burrell preached during the 1970s: "Black people aren't dark-skinned whites."[57]

Marti Barletta is a recognized thought leader on marketing to women and the author of *PrimeTime Women: How to Win the Hearts, Minds, and Business of Boomer Big Spenders*. She's also author of *Marketing to Women*; CEO of the TrendSight Group, a think tank specializing in marketing to women; and founding member of the Women Gurus Network.

After starting in the mailroom of a Chicago agency, **Thomas Burrell** was promoted to copywriter in 1961. During the 1960s, as the race issue gained significance on Madison Avenue, Burrell became a leader in addressing race in advertising. He eventually opened his own agency, Burrell Communications, the first African American ad agency. By 1980, Burrell had become the largest African American agency in the United States, stressing the unique experiences of African Americans. Burrell's client list includes Coca-Cola, McDonald's, Procter & Gamble, and Sears, Roebuck & Co. and surpassed $168 million in billing in 1998.[58] Burrell has since retired, leaving a legacy that continues to inspire innovative young advertising professionals.

Charles Hall graduated from Marquette University. He joined VCU Brandcenter after 18 years of creating provocative, award-winning, and culturally relevant communications for Wieden + Kennedy, Ogilvy, SpikeDDB, TBWA\Chiat\Day, and Berlin Cameron. On Valentine's Day 2003 he launched Fat Daddy Loves You Bath Couture. He directed and co-produced *Are You Cinderella?*, a film documenting violence against women, which won Best Short Film at Urbanworld 2000 among a multitude of other awards. He is also the brand architect behind Jazz at Lincoln Center's "When Jazz is Killin'" and RadioJogaBonito.com.

Anna Morris is an award-winning creative who began her career with Burrell Communications, where she specialized in targeted radio and television commercials for clients such as Procter & Gamble, Coca-Cola, and McDonald's. Morris later founded an independent production company that specializes in television, targeting African American audiences. In addition to her evolving role as a producer, Morris is a part-time instructor in the marketing department at Columbia College in Chicago.

A Cuban-born entrepreneur, **Tere Zubizarreta** spent the first 12 years of her career working for mainstream ad agencies. After her experiences in the late 1960s and early 1970s, she came to believe that mainstream agencies didn't understand how to speak with resonance to Latino consumers. It was clear to her that taking an English spot and dubbing it was just not enough. In 1976, she established her own agency, Zubi Advertising. As of 2003, Zubi had gross billings of $147 million; the agency counts American Airlines, Ford, S. C. Johnson, and Wachovia Bank among its clients.

Exercises

1. **Different Voices**

   Head back to Chapter 4 and review the *Competing Voices* exercise. This time use the same product, but change the demographic group.

   - Pick one brand—for example: Swiffer.

   - This time your two stick people are from two different demographic groups. As a group work the profile bullet lists.

   - Next draw a speech bubble by each stick person. Consider how they would greet each other.

   - Now give each a think bubble. Consider if the two stick people might think differently about each other. This is the interesting part, because it gets to an exploration of demographic, cultural, and social differences. You might even begin to get at some of the deeper ethical issues, which are often hard to discuss.

2. **Brands as Global Personalities**

   How do some brands more successfully move across the globe then other brands? Why do some take a globalized approach and others a standardized approach?

   Begin by thinking of brands as people and be prepared to trace their personalities across cultures.

   - Generate a list of 10 of the most influential people on the globe.

   - Discussion on why each of these people is influential: What about their actions, personality, country of origin/current residence, profession/title, associations, and so on makes them influential?

   - From the previously generated list consider the qualities inherent in each person. Now, link a brand to each person.

   - Discuss why each of the brands exemplifies that individual.

   - Now write a brand personality statement for each brand. Consider how much this statement reflects the person associated with the brand.

   - Finally, discuss how these brands move across the globe based on their brand personality and cultural variations. Consider if a standardized or globalized approach is used and why.

Notes

1. Census Bureau, http://factfinder.census.gov/serlet/ (accessed January 12, 2004).

2. Marti Barletta, *PrimeTime Women* (Chicago: Kaplan, 2007), p. 10.

3. This 1962 quote from comedian and civil rights activist Gregory comes from Stephen Donadio, ed., *The New York Public Library Book of Twentieth-Century American Quotations* (New York: Stonesong, 1992), p. 70.

4. Marti Barletta, "Marti Barletta: Maddened by 'Mad Men': Decades Later, Markets Are Finally Coming to Understand Women's Buying Power," *Advertising Age,* July 28, 2008.

5. Stone Brown, "African Americans Aren't Dark-Skinned Whites," *DiversityInc.com,* http://www.diversityinc.com (accessed December 6, 2004).

6. Ibid.

7. Quoted in ibid.

8. See "Diversity," Magazine Publishers of America (MPA) Web site, http://www.magazine.org/diversity (accessed May 25, 2005).

9. Ibid.

10. Alex Stodghill, "Top 11 Black Celebrity Endorsers, *BlackVoices.com,* http://www.blackvoices.com/blogs/2007/12/18/top-11-black-celebrity-endorsers/U.S., (accessed December 31, 2008).

11. Mediamark, fall 2002.

12. Ileana Aléman-Rickenbach, e-mail correspondence, July 13, 2004.

13. Leo Olper, presentation, Milwaukee, WI, October 4, 2008.

14. "Hispanic purchasing power is expected to hit $992 billion in 2009."

15. Leo Olper, presentation, Milwaukee, WI, October 4, 2008.

16. Ibid.

17. "Hispanic purchasing power is expected to hit $992 billion in 2009."

18. http://css.edu./user/dswenson, October 8, 2001 (accessed June 1, 2005).

19. "Hispanic purchasing power is expected to hit $992 billion in 2009."

20. Ibid.

21. Leo Olper, presentation, Milwaukee, WI, October 4, 2008.

22. Anna Morris, Ad Story: *McReality,* July 6, 2004.

23. Ibid.

24. "Hispanic purchasing power is expected to hit $992 billion in 2009," *Association of Hispanic Adverting Agencies,* http://www.ahaa.org/media/Finalfacts04.htm (accessed December 31, 2008).

25. Leo Olper, presentation, Milwaukee, WI, October 4, 2008.

26. "Hispanic Fact Pack," *Advertising Age* (suppl.), June 21, 2004, p. 36.

27. Ibid.

28. Laurel Wentz, "Grupo Gallegos Scores On ComCast Triple Play Laughs Galore," in "Hispanic Creativity" (special report), *Advertising Age,* November 5, 2007, p. S-1.

29. Richard Kaplan, "Hispanic Viewers Again Crown 'American Idol' as Most Popular Show, Followed by 'CSI,' 'The Mentalist,'" *Hispanic Business.com,* http://www.hispanicbusiness.com/entertainment/2009/1/22/hispanic_viewers_ again_crown_american_idol.htm (accessed January, 31, 2009).

30. Barletta, *PrimeTime Women.*

31. Quoted in Peter Ortiz, "Calling the Shots—in Spanish," *DiversityInc,* December 13, 2004.

32. Sheri J. Broyles and Jean M. Grow, "Creative Women in Advertising Agencies: Why So Few 'Babes in Boyland,'" *Journal of Consumer Marketing,* 15, no. 1 (2008), pp. 4–6.

33. Rob Walker, "The Return of Hilarious Old People: Ads That Make Fun of the Elderly," *Slate,* May 26, 2003, http://www.slate.com/id/2083463 (accessed May 25, 2005).

34. "Taxi agency ensnared in Motrin viral ad controversy," *FP Posted, http://network.nationalpost.com/np/blogs/fpposted/archive/2008/11/18/taxi-agency-ensnared-in-motrin-viral-ad-controversy.aspx* (accessed December 31, 2008).

35. Barletta, *PrimeTime Women.*

36. Thomas Jordan, *Re-Render the Gender* (New York: Booksurge, 2009), p. 73.

37. Marti Barletta, *Marketing to Women: How to Increase Your Share of the World's Largest Market* (Chicago: Kaplan, 2006).

38. Ibid.

39. Ileana Alémán-Rickenbach, Ad Story: *Hispanic Hyperreality,* 2004.

40. Barletta, *Marketing to Women,* pp. xxvi–xxix.

41. David Ogilvy, *Confessions of an Advertising Man* (New York: Ballantine, 1971), p. 84.

42. Jeanie Caggiano, interviewed by authors, July 2007.

43. Gay Consumers Brand Loyalty Linked to Corporate Philanthropy and Advertising, Witeck-Combs Communications/Harris Interactive, http://www.witeckcombs.com/news/releases/20020722_loyalty.pdf (accessed July 20, 2009).

44. Jean Grow, "The Gender of Branding: Antenarrative Resistance in Early Nike Women's Advertising," *Women's Studies in Communication,* 31, no. 3 (2008), pp. 310–343.

45. Frank Kaiser, "Secrets of Successfully Advertising to Seniors," http://www.kaisercom.com/advertiseseniors .html (accessed May 25, 2005).

46. Ibid.

47. List adapted from http://www.eamet.com.

48. Laurel Wentz and Mercedes M. Cardona, "Robust Ad Spending Growth Forecast for U.S. Next Year," *Advertising Age,* December 8, 2003, p. 8.

49. "Global Marketing Expenditure," *Brand Strategy,* February 2004, p. 38.

50. Craig Endicott, "Top Marketers Spend $74 Billion," *Advertising Age,* November 10, 2003, p. 26.

51. Sandra Moriarty, Nancy Mitchell, and William Wells, *Advertising: Principles and Practices* (New York: Pearson Prentice Hall, 2009).

52. Quote from University of Texas at Austin, Department of Advertising, http://advertising.utexas.edu/resources/quotes/ (accessed May 24, 2005).

53. Michael Hastings-Black, "Marketers Must Engage the Muslim Consumer," *Advertising Age,* November 10, 2008.

54. Quote from the CLIO Awards Web site, http://www.clioawards.com/html/wsj/spovak/html (accessed January 10, 2005).

55. John Kuraoka, "How to Write Better Ads," http://www.kuraoka.com/how-to-write-better-ads.html (accessed May 25, 2005).

56. Ibid.

57. Brown, "African Americans Aren't Dark-Skinned Whites."

58. Ibid.

Chapter 6

Concepting

What's the Big Idea?

The word *concepting* usually trips up spell checkers. Usually they try to replace it with *conception*. We suppose in many ways it's similar to creating new life. Another way to say it is "ideation" and "the creative process." In this book we'll define concepting as the development of the Big Idea. If you have a central thought, that One Thing you can say about the product, how do you say it, and how do you show it? Concepting is the bridge between strategy and tactics, taking you from gathering facts and getting organized to creating words and pictures. At this stage in your career, you don't have to be a great writer or an accomplished art director. But you should start working on becoming a great idea person.

How to Be Creative (Concepting Strategies)

You can find many theories and recommendations on how to be creative. However, it's not a nice, neat linear process. That killer idea may pop up in the shower. On the drive into work. When you're watching TV. Or in a dream. No one can tell you when and how to think it. Concepting a single ad or a whole campaign is like making sausage. The end result can be delicious, but the outside world doesn't want to see how it's done.

While there is no single process that works for everyone, most people rely on two basic methods:

1. **Adapt the strategy to the creative.**

2. **Make the creative fit the strategy.**

Words of Wisdom

"Too many young creative teams look at pedestrian advertising and say, 'Hey, I could do that crap.' Then they get into the business and they do that crap." [1]

—Helayne Spivak

Image 6.1

It clearly highlights the product's benefit: The car's sophisticated brakes can sense what's in front of them, halting when something unexpected runs in front of you—like a child.

Working backwards. There's got to be a strategy in there somewhere. We've all done it. In a sudden fit of inspiration, you come up with a great headline or find a really cool photo. Now, how can you use it? There's got to be some client this will work for. Maybe it's so great it doesn't matter if it solves the client's problem. Any of that annoying problem-solving stuff can be handled in the body copy. Heck, you can throw in a subhead to explain it. After it's done, you can always go back and rationalize a strategy. Who knows? It might even be on target when you work backwards.

This approach is usually used in the following scenarios:

- Pitching new business ("We don't know much about your product but we can do wacky stuff.")

- Portfolio padding ("The ad looks great, and no one will know if it really didn't sell anything.")

- Awards competition (see above)

- Advertising class work ("This was the only decent picture I could find, so I had to build my ad around it.")

Concepting by the book

Great concepts begin with great strategy and great research. Garbage in/garbage out. Before you start scribbling, make sure you have the answers to the following questions:

- What is the client's real problem?

- Can I solve the problem creatively with marketing communications?

- Do I know the target audience?

- Do I know how they feel about my product?

- Do I know the product features/benefits?

- What is the One Thing I can say or show about this product?

- How much do I need to say or show? (Do I even need a headline?)

- Where is this product positioned? Where do we want it to be positioned?

- Do I know the competition's strengths and weaknesses?

- What should the tone be?

Depending on the product and target audience, some of the answers to the above questions may be "not applicable." For a mature package good, such as deodorant, you really don't need an in-depth analysis. But you do need to understand the target audience and find the right tone to reach them.

Concepting Approaches

As we mentioned, developing creative ideas is not a neat, orderly process. Many texts will provide formulas for concepts, which usually work great to describe a completed ad but don't help to develop a new one. At the risk of falling into the same trap, we offer several simplified approaches to concepting:

1. **Show the product**—establish or reinforce brand identity. Period.

2. **Show the benefit**—what happens when you use it; what does it do for you?

3. **Show the alternative**—what happens when you don't use it or use the competition?

4. **Comparison**—to other products or as a metaphor.

5. **Borrowed interest**—introduce something seemingly unrelated.

6. **Testimonial/case history**—an endorsement or a description of what it's done for someone else. It could be a celebrity or an ordinary person.

Show the product

It sounds boring, but some of the most innovative ads just show the product or logo. The benefit may be buried in the copy, implied in a tagline, or missing entirely. The main purpose is to establish a brand image or reinforce that image. For example, with most package goods, it's probably better to show the package or label rather than describe it in a headline. After all, it's what the consumer sees on the grocery store shelf. Sometimes you can set up a concept in a modified "question/answer" format, where the question (or problem) is stated and the product/package/logo is the answer (solution).

Show the benefit

In many cases this involves a straightforward declarative sentence proclaiming the main benefit. Usually the reader does not have to think too hard to get the concept. Sometimes this is the first thing you think of. From here you move on to more creative approaches. However, it may be exactly what's required, especially if you can pair your straightforward headline with a compelling, attention-getting graphic. For a soft drink, for example, you may not have any headline, but you show the can or bottle and people having fun. The benefit is implied—your product is connected with good times.

Show the alternative

This can be a lot of fun. One extreme example is a campaign for Terminix that shows outrageous ways people keep insects out of their homes—turning their living rooms into an ice-covered deep freeze, for one. That's a lot more interesting than showing a clean, bug-free house.

Auto-leveling. To the rescue.

Because nothing good can ever come from eyeballing it, Black & Decker created the BullsEye.™
Use it to find studs then hang it on your wall and follow the automatically level laser line to hang shelves or pictures evenly.
See our family of lasers at www.BlackandDecker.com.

BLACK&DECKER

BULLS·EYE™

Image 6.2

A headline that definitively states the benefit with a visual that demonstrates the alternative. Now that's setting things straight.

Image 6.3

Here's another way to show the alternative. The headline for Clorox Bleach Pen states, "There's an easier way to save white."

When you go back to basic wants and needs of the target audience, it becomes easier to visualize the alternative concept. In most cases, you think of the opposite of basic wants and needs—hunger, thirst, embarrassment, loneliness, illness, pain, and so on. You can probably think of several extreme images for each of these that are far more interesting than their positive counterparts.

Comparison

You can compare your product to a competitor or, by using a metaphor, compare it to just about anything.

Competitive/comparison concepts: When you go head-to-head against the competition, keep these factors in mind:

If you are the market leader, don't compare yourself to number two.

When you compare product claims, make sure you are correct.

A few examples:

Avis claimed they were number two so they had to try harder than Hertz to win your business. 7UP (the Uncola) is crisp, clear, and citrus-based versus brown cola-nut sodas. Both claims were true. Both claims were made by a competitor hoping to gain market share from the leader.

Pepsi has always been runner-up to Coke and from time to time has pursued a very aggressive series of campaigns that involved taste tests, celebrity talent, catchy jingles, cutting-edge concepts, elaborate sales promotions, and take-no-prisoners marketing tactics. While Pepsi has won the hearts and minds of ad critics with their creativity, they are still number two—probably because the consumer still can't perceive a real difference between Pepsi and Coke. Other direct comparisons have pitted Subway sandwiches against their high-calorie rivals from McDonald's and Burger King.

In the above examples, the rival products are basically the same price, except one is presented as superior. Other comparisons involve comparing a lower-priced product to a higher-priced premium brand. For example, the Hyundai Genesis was compared to a BMW in quality, luxury, and performance, even though it costs thousands less. While all that is true, many people buy BMWs for the emotional satisfaction the brand provides rather than the actual product features.

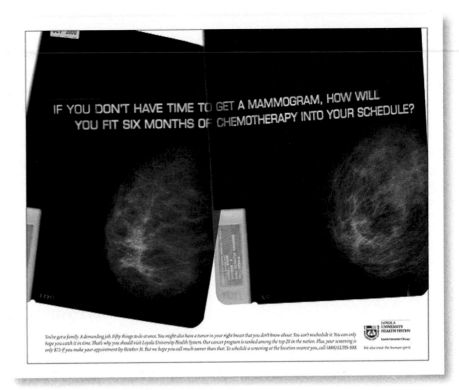

Image 6.4

Showing the alternative. "If you don't have time to get a mammogram, how will you fit six months of chemotherapy into your schedule?" This simple question clearly outlines the choices a woman can make.

Here are some tips for comparison advertising:

1. Make sure that your claims are as factually bulletproof as possible.
2. Try to collect hard evidence in advance to support your factual assertions (your lawyer will thank you).
3. Consider the risk-reward ratio—how much incremental benefit will you get from making the specific comparison versus how much additional risk you court by doing so.
4. Consider including a footnote with additional factual data, perhaps including (a) the applicable version numbers of the products in question and (b) the date of your data.[3]

Metaphors

Favorites of English teachers and awards judges. Since grade school, you've been instructed to use metaphors to spice up your compositions. Use what you know about metaphors and apply them visually to your ad concepts. Visual metaphors can be very direct, such as a grumpy bear morphing into a normal-looking guy

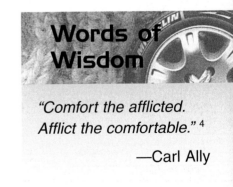

Words of Wisdom

"Comfort the afflicted. Afflict the comfortable." [4]

—Carl Ally

Image 6.5

Jenny Craig invited readers to compare 330-calorie meals. The company's side looks like more than one person can eat, and the alternative is barely an appetizer. Notice the urgency in the direct benefit headline.

after his first cup of coffee in the morning. Or they can be more subtle. Some are very obscure and require a few mental leaps to connect the visual with a product. Sometimes readers appreciate the minor challenge of making that connection themselves. They know the advertiser gives them some credit for having a brain.

Judging by recent awards programs, the greater the distance from visual to benefit or brand value, the higher the ranking, especially if you dispense with headlines or copy to sell anything. Even though you may lose many readers with obscure visual puzzles, sometimes you'll really hook the committed few who take time to study and understand your ads. You need to know if enough members of your target audience can solve your visual puzzle (unless your only goal is to pad your portfolio).

Borrowed interest

Sometimes you can use something seemingly unrelated to make a point. Like the visual puzzle, using borrowed interest relies on the visual for the bulk of the message, but unlike a metaphor, there's no obvious direct connection to the product name or benefit. Usually this approach involves some kind of attention-getting graphic and/or headline that snags the reader. Once they're hooked, the body copy reels 'em in. Sometimes, the only objective is brand recognition, and no copy is needed. Some texts call this the "indirect approach" versus a direct benefit. Whatever you call it, it can work very well as long as the reader gets your intended message and remembers the brand favorably.

Image 6.6

Visual metaphors work for business ads too, especially when you're discussing rather complicated subjects, such as improving data processing speed.

Images 6.7, 6.8, 6.9

This series of ads uses visual metaphors to show the benefit. The tire becomes a button, making the idea that Michelin tires keep you safe increasingly personal.

Testimonials/case histories

Years ago celebrities not only allowed products to attach a name to their fame; they actively pitched the product. Today, testimonials, celebrity and otherwise, are still a popular concept. To be effective, they must have credibility—sort of like an editorial feature.

The Concepting Process

Now comes the fun part. Time is running out. Your assignment is due tomorrow morning. You're still sitting in front of a pile of white paper, and your mind is as blank as the first sheet on the stack.

If you're not blessed with a sudden bolt of creativity, how do you get started? One of the best pieces of advice comes from Luke Sullivan: "Say it straight, then say it great."[5] In other words, try a straightforward approach just to get the facts organized and trigger more ideas. You can start with "This ad is about. . . ." Then you can toss that and move on to a more creative way to say it and show it.

This is also a great way to test the strategy internally. Work up a number of straightforward concepts that look like ads. Then review them with the account team. The objective is to get the group to say, "Yeah. That's the main idea. Now how do we make it better?" This not only makes for better concepts; it helps build good relationships with your team. Take their input, and then really go to work to do something great.

Words of Wisdom

"If a picture is worth a thousand words, a metaphor is worth a thousand pictures." [6]

—Daniel Pink

Image 6.10

This student-designed visual puzzle says Oxydol gets any smell out of clothes. Look closely and you'll see the "skunk" is actually a pile of dirty clothes.

You may want to start scribbling down product features or other attributes of a product and keep asking, "So what?" Those questions may lead to something that's interesting.

Brainstorming

Here's the recipe for a great concept: Combine two creative people, preferably a writer and an art director; add stacks of blank paper, Sharpies, pencils, and layout pads; mix in copies of *CA*, stock photo books, and popular magazines; turn up the heat with tight deadlines and client demands; let it simmer or boil over occasionally; if cooking process takes longer, add pizza, junk food, and beer; allow thoughts to cook until a number of rough ideas develop or one of the creative people has killed the other.

From our experience, we've found brainstorming works best with two people. Usually, the dynamic duo is the copywriter/art director team. But it may be two writers or two art directors. Or an art director/illustrator or writer/producer team. Sometimes a third or fourth party gets involved, but it's usually better to bring in those people to validate ideas rather than develop them.

"...I'm a St. Louis boy, and my wife is a St. Louis girl. I raised my family there and worked at a car plant thirty miles out.

I enjoyed what I was doing, but you reach a point in your life when you look at the future and decide to do something for no other reason than just believing it's right.

For me, Saturn was the chance to make a difference. To prove I have a mind, that I'm more than just a pair of hands.

I wouldn't have moved my family four hundred miles just to fail. Then have to pack them up and move again.

My wife had to leave a house she loved. A nice three-bedroom with a full basement and a patio in the back.

My 16-year-old was convinced we were

© 1990 Saturn Corporation

ruining her life. Her first serious romance, and all. I wouldn't have made the move unless the whole family said 'Let's go for it,' and my daughter knew it. So she decided to try. You know, I'm really proud of her for that.

Funny story. When I first heard about Saturn, I came home and we started hauling out the maps, looking for Spring Hill. 'Where's Spring Hill?' Sure enough, it's right in the middle of the fold and we couldn't find it.

Now, can you imagine trying to talk a couple of teenagers into moving to a town that's smaller than their high school?..."

A DIFFERENT KIND *of* COMPANY. A DIFFERENT KIND *of* CAR.

If you'd like to know more about Saturn, and our new sedans and coupe, please call us at 1-800-522-5000.

Image 6.11

Although the Saturn brand has fallen on hard times lately, when they introduced their brand, they didn't show cars. They told stories—about the families who moved to the new factory in Tennessee and how they believed in the promise of the new company. Notice the lack of headline and the boldface copy in the middle of the ad that states the central idea.

Images 6.12, 6.13

This visual metaphor clearly articulates Ziploc's benefit. Contrast is formed using white space and shadows, strategically allowing the food to float and thus accentuating the freshness factor.

Creating by committee is usually a bad idea, especially if a client is involved early in the process. Sometimes a creative team needs to really rip on the product or brand to get the silliness out of the way and/or really address some marketing problems. That's hard to do with a client in the same room. It's always better to ask a client, "What do you think of this idea?" instead of "What do you think we should do?" The process often isn't pretty. Most times you really don't want to know how it's done as long as the finished product turns out great.

Idea starters

Sometimes you don't have the luxury of brainstorming with another creative person. Your only companion is a blank sheet of paper, mocking every lame idea that pops into your fevered brain.

In this case, don't wait for the perfect concept to develop. Just start scribbling. Write down anything. Even the stupid stuff. Jot down key word. Doodle different visuals. Write out headlines or taglines. Just keep working, and eventually you'll have a stack of ideas. Most of them will be junk. But there just may be a few keepers. Show these to the art director. He or she may be able to work some magic. Or he or she may twist your idea into one that's even better.

Image 6.14

Long popular in Europe, the fuel-efficient Honda Fit was launched in the United States with a campaign that uses a playful visual metaphor to drive home the benefit. The symmetrical layout also demonstrates a strategic use of color while providing visual balance.

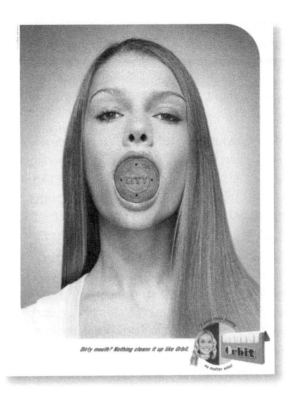

Image 6.15

Look closely. That's a manhole cover, not a cookie, in her mouth. Can you think of a stronger metaphor for bad breath?

Image 6.16

This student used white space inside and around his main visual to make a dramatic point about memory loss.

10 TIPS FOR BETTER CONCEPTS

Through years of trial and error (more of the latter), we've developed a few recommendations for developing creative ideas.

1. **Just do it:** Scribble down everything. Key word. Sketches. Stick people. At this stage, there are no stupid ideas. One key word or visual could trigger an entire award-winning campaign.

2. **Write, don't talk:** Keep scribbling. If something works, then describe it to your partner. If you can't explain it in a few well-chosen words, go back to scribbling.

3. **Throw it all on the wall and see what sticks:** Tack your ideas on a wall and stare at them for a while. If you have the luxury of time, come back the next day and see if they still look good. Invite a couple other people to look at them and ask for feedback.

4. **If you're on a roll, don't stop:** Once the creative juices get flowing, keep tossing out ideas. If you're lucky, you and your partner will get on a streak and come up with not only a killer theme but enough concepts for a whole campaign.

Words of Wisdom

"I have learned to respect ideas, wherever they come from. Often they come from clients. Account executives often have big creative ideas, regardless of what some writers think." [9]

—Leo Burnett

5. **Does this look funny?** During your concept development you'll come up with a lot of silly ideas. Some may make you fall down laughing, either because they're so funny or you're totally sleep deprived. Humor is a powerful force, so if your idea still makes you and others chuckle a couple days later, find some way to use it. With that said, don't set out to be funny. Try to be interesting.

6. **Show it, don't tell it:** One picture may be worth a thousand sales. Find an image that grabs a reader. Then develop a tagline or headline that works in synergy with that image, rather than just describing it. Luke Sullivan says, "Try to solve the problems visually if you can. As larger brands become globally marketed, visual solutions will become even more important. Visuals translate better than words."[10]

7. **Don't be different just to be different:** To paraphrase Bill Bernbach, don't show a man standing on his head unless the ad sells something to keep things in his pockets. Sometimes an art director will go crazy with backgrounds, weird typography, and other bells and whistles that satisfy his or her creative muse. But if they don't add anything to the concept, don't do it.

Ad Story

Clients Say the Darndest Things

"Coming up with a good idea is hard work. Whether it's a TV spot, radio commercial, a print or banner ad, a billboard, or even an infomercial, the concept has to be honest, creative, and strategically sound. But sometimes coming up with the idea isn't the hardest part—selling it to the client is. And even the simplest of concepts can be focus-grouped and overanalyzed to death. And I mean that literally. Many a good idea was killed due to filtration systems so opaque even microscopic concepts couldn't sneak past the watchful eye of a client who likes to second-guess everything.

"Some of my favorite examples:

- "I once produced a radio commercial for a state lottery in which the main character was slapping at mosquitoes the entire time while he sold the virtues of a new scratch game. (Mosquito bites make you scratch, get it?) The performance was terrific, and despite all the slapping sounds, the message came across loud and clear. At least I thought so. The client killed it before it could air because he felt we were promoting 'self-mutilation.'

- "I was producing a TV spot in which there were a group of guys playing darts in a bar. The main character was so bad at the game that he not only missed the bull's-eye each time he threw a dart, he missed the entire dartboard. Midway through the shoot, the client changed his mind because he suddenly felt that we were making fun of blind people. I told him that if any blind person *who watches television* called to complain, I would personally pay for the production of the spot. No luck. We had to rewrite the spot on the spot. What a mess.

- "A print ad for the Milwaukee Brewers baseball team showed three players in a visiting team's dugout. Only the photo was cropped showing the players from the waist down. When you looked closely, you could see that one player had a wooden peg leg. The headline read: 'BREWERS vs. PIRATES.' The client agreed to produce the ad, but later got cold feet (pardon the pun). He actually said that he was afraid to get complaints 'from pirates.' That comment shivered me timbers."[11]

—Dave Hanneken,
Vice President, Creative Director,
Laughlin/Constable, Milwaukee

8. **Keep it simple:** Don't lose sight of the main idea. You've got the concept burned in your brain, but does a casual reader get it? If not, adding subheads to explain the idea or cramming in extra inset photos won't help. Simple ideas break through the clutter; they are easier to remember, and sometimes they clarify the strategy.

9. **Don't second-guess the client:** Develop concepts that get attention and sell the product. Then worry about selling them to the client. Don't handcuff your creativity by worrying about what the client will like before you begin. The client hired you to be creative. Otherwise, they'd be doing their own ads.

10. **Build a "maybe" file:** Most of your ideas won't work, but don't throw them all away. File the better ones. They may be the answer for the next assignment. Keep a file of the scrap-stock photos, competitor ads, articles, and other stuff that trigger some great ideas.

Concept Testing

You should test your concepts at three stages, starting with yourself.

Self-evaluation

You've narrowed your stack of rough ideas down to a single concept that you love. But before you start asking the creative director for a raise, make sure you do a little internal evaluation of your ideas.

Level 1: Gut check. The first level of testing begins with you. Ask yourself, "Does this concept feel right?" If you have the luxury of time, put it aside for a few days and ask the same question. This means don't start thinking about it the night before it's due.

Level 2: Two quick tests. The first is the "matchbook test." Can you put your idea on the cover of a matchbook and still convey the one thing about your product? Another quick test is the "billboard test." If you have written copy and laid out the ad, cover up the body copy so you only see the headline and main graphic. Would it make a good billboard? If so, your creative idea communicates quickly and effectively. If not, maybe you need to come up with some new ideas.

Level 3: Honest evaluation. Your idea looks good and feels good. But it still has to meet some objectives. Remember strategy? So before you fall in love with your idea, ask yourself . . .

- **Is this concept doable?** Can you pull this off within the budget constraints? Can you execute it correctly? Do you have the talent? Props? Locations? All the other things required that make this idea work?

- **Is it on target for this audience?** You love it, but will the intended buyer? You might want to try it out on a few people in the target audience . . . but don't rule it out if all of them don't get it.

- **Does it have legs?** Will this idea work in an extended campaign? Is it a one-hit wonder, or can you expand this concept for use in other media?

- **Can you sell this to the client?** Is this idea so far out of the box the client will have a heart attack? Can you justify this concept with sound logic?

Level 4: Consumer interplay. OK, you're confident your idea is on strategy. You're not in love with it, though you love it. Now the questions are: Will consumers love it—or not? And, how will they interact with it? You want consumer interaction; you don't want consumer control. This is your baby.

Ad Story

Freaking With the King
"The Whopper. It's America's most beloved burger, and it has been for the past 50 years.

"But how do you prove love? In 2007, to commemorate the Whopper's 50th birthday, Burger King decided to take the Whopper off the menu for one day in one town to see what would happen.

"What happened was, people freaked.

"A town with just one Burger King was chosen as the location for this day of deprivation. The restaurant was rigged with hidden cameras inside and out, and trained actors, posing as BK employees, explained this new reality to unsuspecting patrons. A roving reporter, armed with a fake newspaper corroborating the story, was hired to capture people's candid reactions to the discontinuation of the Whopper.

"To push the experiment further, we substituted McDonald's Big Macs and Wendy's burgers for the Whopper. Would this elaborate two-pronged experiment prove that people really loved the Whopper, or would it just piss them off? As it turned out, it did a little of both.

"Video was cut into 15- and 30-second television spots, and drive-thru audio was turned into radio spots. All of which led people to a Web site, whopperfreakout .com, where a comprehensive 8-minute documentary of the experiment could be found.

"It is said that absence makes the heart grow fonder. But as Whopper Freakout proved, if you love something enough, absence makes you freak out."

Epilogue

"The Whopper disappeared from the menu for only a single day, but sales of the Whopper rose by double digits in the month after Whopper Freakout debuted. Apparently, just the notion of the Whopper being discontinued forever whetted a lot of people's appetites."[13]

—Bill Wright
Creative Director,
Crispin Porter + Bogusky, Boulder

- **Why will they love it?** OK, you've tried it out on a few people; now probe deeper. Why do they love it? What specially resonates with them? How can you take their reactions and extend them?

- **Once they fall in love—or not—what will they do?** This is the deal killer in today's media world, where consumers exert a lot of control. How will they interact with it? Will my ads become viral? Are they ripe for parody? If so, do I have a plan of how to leverage consumer-generated media? Do I have a plan to address possible negative reaction across social media?

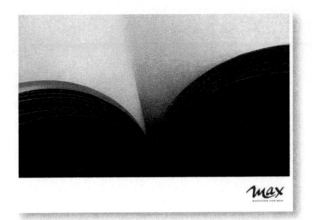

Image 6.17

What do you see first—pages in a book or something that's more in keeping with the tone set by Germany's Max *magazine?*

Client evaluation

Clients are fond of telling their agencies to think outside the box. What is this "box" anyway? Typically, clients confine the box to features and benefits. Some engineering-oriented companies think in terms of specifications. Marketing-driven companies think in terms of solving problems for customers. Your box should be much larger. Once you start working within your bigger box, look for ways to step outside of it. It's always better to have a bunch of crazy ideas you can pull back into the box than having the client tell you to be more creative.

Do the Twist

Not to be confused with a dance from the '60s, a twist is an unexpected element of an ad or a commercial. A TV commercial for Jimmy John's features a fun twist. In a gritty and very intense bank robbery, all the bank customers are ordered to lie flat on the floor. One heroic hostage secretly pulls out his cell phone and calls—you guessed it—Jimmy John's to deliver lunch. You never see it coming. Here's another TV twist: A prosperous-looking retired couple relaxes on their sailboat in the Caribbean. It looks like an ad for a mutual fund or an insurance company. The twist? It's actually a commercial about paper shredders. It seems that this sweet old couple stole your credit card number and they're now living the high life because you didn't shred your credit card receipts.

Words of Wisdom

"If you can't solve a problem, it's because you're playing by the rules." [14]

—Paul Arden

Finding the edge

It's starting to become a cliché, but people are still looking for an edge—some kind of creative device to separate their advertising from the rest of the pack. "Edgy" ads take risks. They may *push the envelope* (another overused term) to the breaking point. In summary, creatives who work on the edge:

- Risk offending general audience to appeal to target audience.
- Shock the reader/viewer into noticing.
- Drive a wedge between "our customers" and everyone else (us vs. them).

"Advertising needs to have a bit of an edge, whether it's aimed at the neighborhood or the world." [15]

—Phil Dusenberry

FUR?
I'd rather go naked

—Eva Mendes for PETA *PETA.org*

Image 6.18

PETA feels they need to get your attention before they can tell their story. But is portraying naked celebrities more effective than showing suffering animals?

Going for the edge may seem like the perfect approach. If you are willing to offend or confuse a large share of the total audience to make a stronger connection to a highly defined target audience, it might be OK. However, never forget the risks of pushing the envelope too far. Before you cross that line, you should review Chapter 5 and reconsider.

Before you get edgy

- Understand the tolerances of the total audience.
- Really understand how far you can push your target audience.
- Consider the risks (legal, ethical, business).
- Check your personal moral compass. Are you proud of the work?
- Be able to defend your idea logically, not just because you think it's cool.
- Have a backup idea.
- Don't try to be different just to be different.
- Get paid before the client goes bankrupt.

Image 6.19

One of a series of Nike ads supporting disabled athletes.
The campaign uses what could be seen as disturbing
photos and matches them to positive copy. The net result is
you don't feel sorry for these people; you admire them.

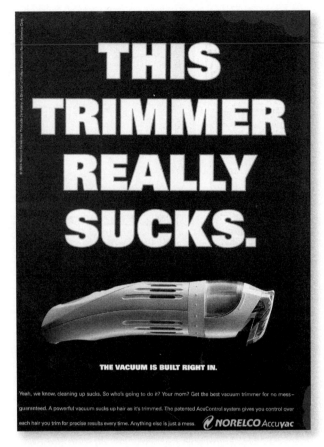

Image 6.20

Sure, it's a play on words for a vacuum trimmer, but does
the vulgar slang grab your target audience or just seem like
you're pandering to them?

What to Do When You're Stuck

Everybody develops writer's block. Sometimes the slump lasts a few hours,
sometimes a lot longer. Novelists have the option of waiting weeks and months
for inspiration. Copywriters don't. So what happens when that blank sheet of
paper becomes your worst enemy? We offer the following suggestions:

- **Back up:** Find out where you are, and you might know why you're stuck.
  Do you understand the product, the market, the target audience, the
  competition, and the tone? Did you miss something? Do you have enough
  information to "say it straight"? If so, you are very close to finding ways to
  "say it great."

- **Go back to the books:** Dig out the old issues of *Communication Arts*
  and *CMYK*. Check out new Web sites that feature award winners. Leaf
  through the stock photo books.

Words of Wisdom

*"Rarely have I seen any
really good advertising
created without a certain
amount of confusion,
throw-aways, bent
noses, irritation and
downright
cursedness."* [16]

—Leo Burnett

- **Talk about it:** Find a sympathetic ear and state your problem. Don't ask for ideas. Just explain what you know about the assignment and where you're stuck. You might find that by explaining it out loud, you'll find the solution yourself. Sometimes you'll mention an idea that seems kind of lame to you, and another person loves it. He or she might give you just enough encouragement to turn it into a great idea.

- **Take a break:** See a movie. Watch TV. Play basketball. Dig in your garden. Do something totally unrelated to work. This will unclog your mind and may allow some fresh ideas to sneak in. Taking a break is fine, but don't let it extend to an hour before your assignment is due.

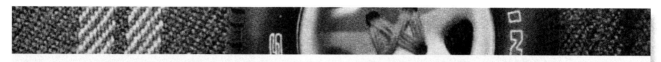

Who's Who?

Carl Ally, cofounder of Ally & Gargano, is known for cutting-edge and risky advertising that spoke very bold truths. Some of his breakthrough advertising included work for FedEx, Hertz, Dunkin' Donuts, Volvo, Fiat, Saab, MCI Communications, Polaroid, IBM, Pan Am, Piper Aircraft, and several others. He was the man responsible for winning a change in television rules against mentioning the competition in commercials. He was not afraid to take on corporate underdogs, and he changed many unknown companies into household names. He enjoyed taking on accounts that were new or troubled, and he built brands up from almost nothing.[17]

Jerry Della Femina, founder of Della Femina Travisano & Partners, is one of the most creative and irreverent talents in the business. He worked on such accounts as Isuzu (Joe Isuzu), Meow Mix (singing cat), Beck's beer, Blue Nun wine, Chemical Bank, Dow Brands (Fingerman), and Pan Am. He sold his agency, became a successful restaurant owner, and formed a new agency that later merged with Ketchum. He wrote *From Those Wonderful Folks Who Gave You Pearl Harbor* and tons of award-winning, hard-selling ads.

Phillip Dusenberry joined BBDO as a copywriter in 1962 and developed into one of the world's most influential creative forces as he rose to vice chairman at BBDO Worldwide. His impact came chiefly from memorable General Electric and Pepsi-Cola campaigns (including a megamillion-dollar deal with Michael Jackson). Dusenberry also played a major role with advertising's volunteer Tuesday Team, whose "Morning in America" commercials helped reelect Ronald Reagan. As a screenwriter, Dusenberry's credits include *The Natural*, starring Robert Redford.

Charlotte Moore was born in Chattanooga, Tennessee, and educated in Virginia, but the Southerner found a spiritual and professional home on the West Coast when she began to work for the creative hot shop Wieden + Kennedy. Over the course of almost 8 years, she worked as art director and, eventually, group creative director on accounts including Nike, Microsoft, and Coke. She did her most exceptional work with her partner of many years, Janet Champ, on Nike's print advertising for women. She left the agency in the fall of 1995 but returned as co–creative director of its European headquarters in Amsterdam. Ambition was interrupted by love, however, and she followed her heart to Italy, where she currently lives with her husband and children and pursues creative projects sometimes for money but more often for personal reasons. Along the way, she has been recognized by *CA*, One Show, and *McCall's* Advertising Women of the Year and has received four nominations and two back-to-back wins in Magazine Publishers of America's Kelly Awards for best, most effective print advertising.

Exercises

1. Failing Fast Is Fun

Whether it's an advertising copywriter struggling to nail that one perfect headline or a software developer searching for the next killer ap, there can be a method to the madness of creation. Like a jazz musician or an improvisational comic, this technique allows you to build off of ideas or themes and spin them into completely new directions. One thought leads to three. Those new three each lead to another three. And so on and so on. The trick is to not stop too soon. There will be time to edit, rationalize, and flesh out later.

- Your teacher will introduce a brand and note the objective at hand.

- Working in pairs or small tams, grab a stack of Post-it notes.

- Jot one idea down per Post-it note. Time is limited. You've got 15 minutes to post as many ideas as possible. Unlimit your thoughts.

- Review your Post-its and cluster them by concept. Pick your top ideas, using them as jumping-off points, and repeat.

- Repeat. Repeat. Repeat.

- One you've got three or four killer ideas, see which ones have legs using the same Post-it note technique to extend each idea.

- Repeat. Repeat. Repeat.

Adapted from an exercise shared by Jeff Ericksen, Founder and Instructor, Ms. Coffmansen's Portfolio Finishing School.

2. Spite Can Be Right

Most kids have the wonderful inclination to do exactly the opposite of what you tell them to do. Then you reach adulthood, and there's a fine line between smart and smart aleck. We're talking simply about going in the exact opposite direction of where everyone else is headed to find a solution to a problem. Conventional wisdom would tell you that when starting a company and asking investors for their trust, one should take their names very seriously. Tell that to Google. In the late '90s and early 2000s, bigger was better on American highways. Take that Mini Cooper. So here's how we put not doing what we're expected to do to work.

- Generate a list of issues in the marketplace at hand in as few words as possible. (something like: People want fuel efficient cars.)

- Now, write down the exact opposite next to each issue.

- Next, brainstorm around the opposite solution for a few minutes. How could you express the opposite idea in a way that works? Maybe use the Failing Fast Is Fun exercise.

- Rephrase your issue in a different way and write it down.

- Revisit each opposite issues and brainstorm.

Adapted from an exercise shared by Jeff Ericksen, Founder and Instructor, Ms. Coffmansen's Portfolio Finishing School.

(Continued)

(Continued)

3. Thinking Outside the Box

This exercise is designed to help you immerse yourself in a product. The specific objective is to help bring all of your senses into play. You'll begin working with a partner and eventually work on your own in this three-step exercise.

Step 1

- Send your teacher to a dollar store to buy as many products as there are students. Have he or she put them all into a covered box and bring them to class.

- Working in pairs, one person (explorer) will explore a product with the help of his or her partner (scribe). The scribe is in charge of taking notes based on the explorer's sensorial responses to the product. Then reverse the process.

- Without looking, the scribe reaches into the box and selects a product.

- The explorer keeps his or her eyes closed throughout the entire process. Trust your partner!

- The scribe places the product (still packaged) in the hands of the explorer.

- The explorer slowly, and with specific focus on each sense, explores the product—smell it, listen to it, touch it, taste it, see it (last). The scribe writes down his or her words. Explorers you'll need to trust your their partner as he or she guides you.

- Explorers describe the product's "features" with words and phrases rooted in your sensorial experience. Be as expressive and emotional as possible. Nothing is "wrong."

- Now reverse roles. Select a new product from within the box. Do not return the first product to the box.

- Begin generating word lists. It could be a list of all the words and images from the product's category. You could also focus on the competitor with a few "suffering points" to show the alternative if your product isn't used. Or you could do the "twist." There's also the possibility of playing with metaphors. Then again you might be so inspired that you'll think of ideas that aren't even ads and go nontraditional. The idea is to brainstorm ideas. The goal—to selectively amass a benefits list.

Step 2

- Next consider who the target is and write a consumer profile for the product you explored.

- Spin features into benefits and prioritize them.

- Now write a positioning statement.

Step 3

- Write 50 headlines and be ready to share 3 with the class. No headline may be more than eight words. Try using the Creative Tree to generate headline options.

- Select the most resonant headline and execute it in a font and color that strategically speaks to the positioning of your brand.

- Present your finished headline and discuss your rationale. Why is it was the best of the three? How does it reflect the positioning? Why does it speaks to the target with resonance?

Notes

1. Quote from the CLIO Awards Web site, http://www.clioawards.com/html/wsj/spivak.html, 1996 (accessed January 10, 2005).

2. Quote from the CLIO Awards Web site, http://www.clioawards.com/html/wsj/goodby.html, 1996 (accessed January 10, 2005).

3. See "Allegedly Out-of-Date Comparative Advertising Triggers Lawsuit," August 14, 2003, on the By No Other Web site, http://www.bynoother.com/2003/08/comparative_adv.html (accessed June 3, 2005).

4. Quoted in Christin Burton, "The Life and Career of Carl Ally," March 31, 2004, http://www.ciadvertising.org/sa/spring_04/adv382j/cristin44/home.html, 2004 (accessed June 3, 2005).

5. Luke Sullivan, *Hey Whipple, Squeeze This: A Guide to Creating Great Advertising* (New York: John Wiley & Sons, 1998), p. 52.

6. Daniel Pink, *A Whole New Mind: Why Right-Brainers Will Rule the Future* (New York: Riverhead Books, 2005), p. 50.

7. Morris Hite, *Adman: Morris Hite's Methods for Winning the Ad Game* (Dallas, TX: E-Heart Press, 1988), p. 165.

8. Paul Arden, *It's Not How Good You Are, It's How Good You Want to Be* (London: Phaidon, 2003), p. 80.

9. Leo Burnett, *100 LEO's: Wit & Wisdom From Leo Burnett* (Chicago: NTC Business Press, 1995), p. 52.

10. Sullivan, *Hey Whipple, Squeeze This*, p. 37.

11. Dave Hanneken, Ad Story: *Clients Say the Darndest Things,* February 2009.

12. Maureen Shirreff, interviewed by authors, February 2009.

13. Bill Wright, Ad Story: *Freaking With the King,* February 2009.

14. Paul Arden, *It's Not How Good You Are, It's How Good You Want to Be,* p. 49.

15. Quoted from CLIO Awards Web site, http://www.ciadvertising.org/sa/spring_04/adv382j/cristin44/home.html, 2004 (accessed December 20, 2004).

16. Burnett, *100 LEO's: Wit & Wisdom From Leo Burnett,* p. 7.

17. Quoted in Christin Burton, "The Life and Career of Carl Ally," March 31, 2004, http://www.ciadvertising.org/sa/spring_04/adv382j/cristin44/home.html, 2004 (accessed June 3, 2005).

Chapter 7

Design

Why me?

I'm not a designer.

Ah! But your eye went right to what you hoped would be the answer. By the end of this chapter, you'll understand and appreciate why your eye traveled as it did and be able to answer the question, Why me?

Why Every Creative Needs to Be a Designer

Or at least understand design. Whether your talents lie with the written word or visual expression, if you want to get a job, an internship in the creative department, or even a foot in the door, you'd better learn how to put your concepts into visually interesting layouts. Copy doesn't exist in a vacuum. You need to marry copy with design in an engaging layout. Mind you, we didn't say *perfect*—we said *interesting* and *engaging*.

Just what makes a layout interesting? We'll get to that a bit later. First, let's consider why all creatives need to understand design basics and, for that matter, why everyone on the advertising team should. We begin with a discussion that centers around two-dimensional design or print, but the same principles generally apply across all media. They have nuances depending upon the medium, but good design is good design.

- Words and visuals do not exist in isolation.

- Design visually expresses the Big Idea and sells the product.

- Good creative should engage the audience visually and verbally.

- Portfolios are important, and presentation matters.

- Multiple skills increase your value.

- Knowledge is power.

This last one deserves a little more discussion, even if you're never going to be a creative. Fine. Now, imagine yourself as an account executive who speaks the language of creative and clearly articulates design concepts to the client. Think you'll climb the ladder quicker?

Words of Wisdom

"Start your layout knowing that it's a problem to be solved as an integral idea. Treat it as an advantage, not a problem." [1]

—Paul Arden

Or buy a Volkswagen.

Image 7.1

Simple concept. Simple design. This art director's sketch became one of the most popular in a long line of groundbreaking VW ads.

So you want to be an art director

Art directors don't create in a vacuum. Great ideas, including most great advertising, emerge from collaboration. That's why brainstorming is so important. It gets your creative juices flowing, but it also helps ideas evolve collaboratively. As an art director you will have to find ways to visually convey the meaning in your copywriter's headline. You'll have to make body copy engaging and readable. Your layout will have to sign strategy. But above all you must learn how to attract attention, create interest, and stimulate action. In short, art directors share the same responsibility as writers—create artwork that sells an idea or a product.

Of course, as an art director, you need to understand the basic principles of design and execute them with skill and sensitivity. You should also have a mastery of the latest software. Most of all, you'll need the patience to develop multiple concepts *before* you sit down at the computer. The truth is many art directors are not masters of software. For art direction the key lies in the idea. That said, a good art director should still be conversant with software programs, especially early in your career when you are building your portfolio. At bigger agencies, art directors are often able to hand their rough concepts off to a production artist, who is adept on software and can quickly interpret the rough sketches of the art directors. Whether your career path takes you to the copy or art side of the creative business, the key is developing and communicating concepts. Advertising is an ideas business.

Don't Throw Away Your Pencil

We know most of you love computers and would rather be playing on your computer than reading this textbook. But creating ads involves ideas, and ideas don't live in computers. You need to start with a pencil. Believe it or not, the pencil is a design tool. Design starts in your head, flows onto paper or napkins or backs of folders or inside book covers via your pencil, and is executed using your computer. Yes, you'll use a computer, but it all begins in your head.

Use technology wisely. If you're seriously thinking about going into art direction, design, or production, you'll need to be competent in the programs that are the current industry standards. For art directors, that means knowing InDesign, Illustrator, and Photoshop very well and being conversant in Flash, iMovie, and maybe a few others. At the very least, learn the basics and keep practicing. But never, never use the computer to go shopping for concepts or visuals before you have your concept nailed down. Perusing the Internet can stimulate creativity, but your ideas—the concepts—should begin as thumbnail sketches. Remember the order: head, paper, computer. You're the genius, not the computer.

Basic Design Principles

Artists define design principles in their own way, and there are many books out there on design. All those opinions might seem confusing, but in reality it's a

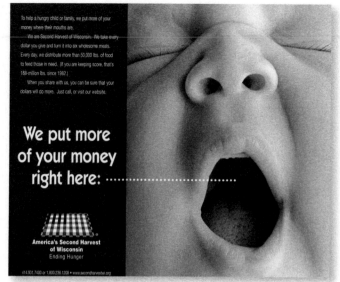

Images 7.2, 7.3

Do your planning on paper; then build it on the computer.

matter of perception and preference. We think Robin Williams does a great job. Her book, *The Non-Designer's Design Book: Design and Typographic Principles for the Visual Novice,* is terrific. She's clear headed and succinct. We are taking her lead and are focusing on the following *Four Principles of Design*:[3]

1. Proximity

2. Alignment

3. Repetition

4. Contrast

Before we begin, recognize that the concept of unity underpins these four principles. No matter what you are trying to accomplish and no matter how you execute one, or all, of the design principles, how the layout hangs together—unity—is what matters in the final analysis. For copywriters, a good way to think about unity is to consider thematic qualities in writing. You don't change the subject midsentence, so don't change your design theme midlayout. Use each principle consistently throughout your layout. Carry your visual concept all the way through your ad—from top to bottom, left to right, and page 1 to page 100.

Proximity

The principle of proximity suggests that you group related elements together. You can move them physically closer so the related elements are seen as one cohesive group, or you can move them farther apart, suggesting a less important relationship. And how you align them (the next principles) will help the viewer make sense of your visual story. All the elements have a relationship, and proximity helps viewers understand that relationship. Another

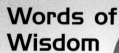

Words of Wisdom

"I can't just write an ad. I care how it looks as well as what it says." [4]

—Hal Riney

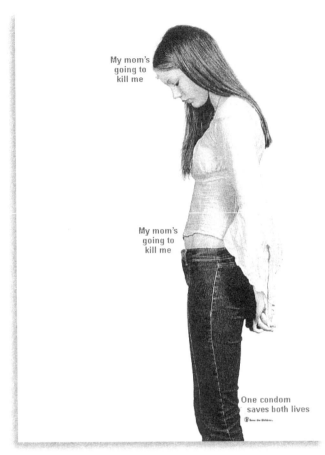

Image 7.4

Proximity is critical to the effectiveness of this ad. Both headlines say the same thing, but their position makes all the difference.

way to think about it is this: Think of grouping those elements while considering the target's needs and wants (emotions) and your strategy. See, you really can use the Creative Brief. If you tap into the target's emotion, if you find viewers' sweet spot, you've hooked them.

The basic purpose of proximity is to help designers and art directors (we'll use these words interchangeably) organize the elements of the layout in a way that brings the strategic concept to life. So what are the elements of a layout? They vary, but the basic ones are headline, subhead, body copy, tagline, visual(s), and logo. *Visuals* are the images that support the copy. They are almost always either photographs or illustrations. Avoid using the word *picture.* It tends to connote a photograph, which can confuse people or lock you into an unintended concept.

Alignment

Consider alignment as expressing what is rhetorically important. Each element should have a visual connection to another element and flow from a central point. Nothing should be placed arbitrarily. Nothing should hang alone. If your alignment is cohesive, then when you decide to break the alignment (occasionally) it won't look like a mistake. It will scream strategy. Consider alignment as the design principle that makes you a visual storyteller. Think of how a writer connects one sentence to the next, one paragraph to the next, one chapter to the next. Alignment is all about *making the verbal visual.*

Think of the principle of alignment as offering you invisible lines to direct a reader through a layout. Alignment is a system of organization. Organization or unity is central to this principle. How elements are aligned tells the reader that no matter where an element is placed it has a relationship to something else on that page.

The two key points to remember with the principle of alignment are visual flow and lines. Visual flow refers to how readers' eyes follow the layout, how they flow. The art director is in charge of the visual flow based on strategic objectives. Some novice designers start by centering the headline or the visual and everything that follows. That's a center-justified layout. We are not suggesting that you never center-justify anything, because sometimes a centered layout is perfectly on strategy and quite interesting. Rather than following a formula, it's better to let the strategic message, the Big Idea, guide your alignment. A common visual flow

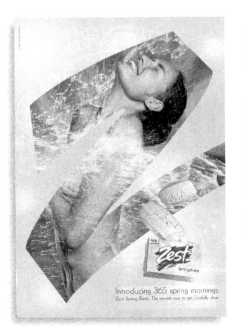

Image 7.5

Even an account exec could find a Z pattern in this ad.

Image 7.6

Drink. Textured lines with clearly strategic messages and perfectly aligned compel readers to not drive if they drink. The design is so elegant, yet powerful—the ideal combination for this type of message.

pattern and a good standard for beginners to rely on is the *Z* or backward *S* pattern. In Western cultures, our eyes tend to begin reading at the upper left and then naturally flow to the right, just like when we read a book (hence justifying the foundation for alignment). Then our eyes travel down, moving from upper right to lower left. Can you imagine the *Z* or backward *S* configuration? This classic pattern is the reason you so often see the logo anchoring the lower right corner of a layout, as we previously suggested. The bottom line is you are in charge of how the viewers interact with your layout.

Lines are the second key element of alignment, and they are central to visual flow. Lines can be the edges of visuals, the ends of lines of copy, the edges of blocks of copy, or actual lines. Robin Williams explains how lines work: "In any well-designed piece, you can draw lines to the aligned objects, even if the overall presentation is a wild collection of odd things with lots of energy."[5] Sometimes those lines are invisible, and sometimes they are literal.

Repetition

The principle of repetition is predicated on—well, repetition. Repeating some design element throughout your layout is essential. It might be shape, color, lines, texture, bullets, or a particular font. It can be anything, but it needs to be visually recognizable and strategically relevant. Think of this principle as the principle of consistency. Repetition does not have to be boring. In fact, it can be downright adventurous. Every ad in your campaign should have a visual repetitious theme. Every page in your brochure should

Image 7.7

The careful alignment of elements makes these oranges look like something else you might see squeezed in Brazil.

Images 7.8, 7.9, 7.10

Bet you had to search for the headline in these ads! In this case, that's the brilliance of the campaign. The art director began with an immense amount of respect for the curiosity and intelligence of the consumer and then brilliantly embedded the message directly within the product itself. "Have More Fun." And create a bit of buzz while you're at it.

repeat similar visual elements. Every screen on your Web site should have the same visual familiarity, if for no other reason than to promote ease of navigation. Repetition is what unifies your brand message.

Two main things to avoid when considering repetition are being annoying and overwhelming the viewer. Consider how contrast can work in combination with repetition. We'll cover that shortly. Chances are if your repeated elements are annoying, they are also overwhelming. Once you've overwhelmed or annoyed your target audience, you've lost them.

Contrast

The two main points to consider when working with the principle of contrast are optical weight and white space (negative space). Optical weight is a huge part of providing contrast. Every element in a layout has optical weight. Thin type seems light to our eyes, and we respond emotionally to that lightness. Conversely, a thick, dark line (rule) looks and feels emotionally heavy. Optical weight can play a significant role in how viewers respond to the contrasting elements in your layout. Make it a strategic role. White space also has optical weight. It is more than just the unused portion of the layout, and it's more than just the background. In fact, white space isn't even always white. White space is the negative space surrounding elements

Image 7.11

Here's a great use of repetition in design and a metaphor in concept. This student-designed ad clearly shows the protection levels of various SPF levels of Coppertone.

Image 7.12

Check the visual flow of this ad. Your eye tracks from the benefit headline, through the copy, and to the product and finally lands on the logo.

Image 7.13

Two ways to use white space. Banana Boat sunblock keeps you from turning red. Get it?

Image 7.14

Negative space doesn't always have to be white. Here the sillhoutte defined the brand (the Hartford elk) while the color choices drew the reader's eye to the headline.

within the layout, and it provides the backdrop for many other elements of contrast. Why use white space? Our eyes sometimes need a rest. White space offers that. It can also frame elements or form a base on which an element can visually rest or float. White space can draw attention to a headline, copy block, or visual. Respect white space. It's an art director's and a copywriter's friend.

As far as we are concerned, there's only one thing to avoid when it comes to the principle of contrast—as Robin Williams says, "Don't Be a Wimp." To test the effectiveness of your contrast, consider *mirroring.* Try to reflect the opposite weight, shape, or size in another part of your layout. Once you've mastered how to contrast visual elements and see how their weight balances the overall layout and works strategically, your design skills will improve.

Some Essentials

Like many of the design choices you'll make, the selection of type and color goes a long way to enhancing awareness and building strategic comprehension.

Typography

Serif/sans serif. Serif typefaces have little tails (serifs) at the ends of the strokes. Sans serif fonts do not. Probably the most important thing to remember about serif versus sans serif is that the serifs tend to make the type appear more flowing and easier to read. Conversely, sans serif type tends to be more stiff or edgy and perhaps a bit more dramatic.

Weight. When we speak of the weight of type we mean optical weight, just like when we discussed contrast. One font may be much heavier than another. That is, the strokes are much more substantive, making each letter visually heavier.

Size. In the graphics world, point size refers to the height of type. Interestingly, many styles of type vary slightly in height even if the point size is the same. The main objective is to go beyond legibility and make your copy inviting to read.

Reverse and Over Printing.

This has nothing to do with reading backwards. Reverse type refers to type that is white (actually colorless) because it "reverses" out of a block of color. Beware of using reverse type on low-quality paper. It will tend to bleed and you may not be able to clearly read your copy. For new designers we suggest using this technique sparingly.

Over printing is just the opposite. It simply means the type (usually black) is printed over a lightened (ghosted) image, texture, or tone.

Match font to tone. Type plays a big role in creating resonance in the reader. For example, which of the following best matches the brand image of a Chevy truck?

AN AMERICAN REVOLUTION

an American Revolution

Leave enough margin. We suggest half-inch margins and that you remember white space. White space will draw your eye in. Don't run your copy edge to edge and don't cram in so much copy that it becomes intimidating to read. Honor your margins.

TABLE 7.1   Leading

12/10	12/16
The lines become more compact.	The lines become farther apart.

TABLE 7.2   Justification

Center justified simply means the type is centered.
Right justified (as in Arabic literature) means the type lines up on the right side of the page and is "ragged" on the left.
Left justified (as in Western literature) means the type lines up on the left side of the page and is "ragged" on the right.
Justified means that the type is spread evenly across the page, column, or copy block and forms smooth edges both right and left no matter how many characters there are per line (as you would see in most daily newspaper columns.)

Color

Starting with the basics, think of colors as primary or secondary, warm or cool, and complementary or contrasting. From a designer's point of view, here are two key points:

- The human eye is most comfortable looking at warm colors.

- Complementary and contrasting colors should work to visually enhance your strategy.

Whether you're using warm or cool colors or engaging complementary or contrasting colors, you also need to keep in mind the social and cultural connotations attached to each color. Just as with words, colors can have multiple meanings. Think of the social and cultural meanings of each color. Then weigh those meanings against the brand, the colors associated with the brand, and its competitors. Also consider your audience's sensibilities when making color choices. Finally, remember color may be applied to many elements of a layout: type, line, and backgrounds. Visual images too have an expressed color palette.

Make wise strategic choices that you can justify. Some questions to help you select color:

- How will color enhance the Big Idea/that One Thing?
- Are your color choices in keeping with the strategy?
- Does the color support the brand?
- Will the audience relate positively to the colors?
- What are the cultural connotations of your color choice?
- What is your justification for each color choice?

This chapter deals mostly with print graphics. But when you design for television and online media, you can't separate the visual from the audio. They should work together in the same kind of synergy as visuals and text. This story describes how the Dove pro•age campaign searched for audio to match the look and feel of the graphics.

Better Layouts

Robin Williams offers a simple yet effective approach to nurturing the creative process and developing better layouts: "See it. Say it. Sketch it."[6]

- *See it.* Start keeping a file, scrapbook, or morgue—in other words, a collection of ads that you like. Learn to file anything that strikes you. Your scrapbook will be a great resource for ideas. Use it before you start concepting. Or when you're stuck. It's bound to trigger some fresh ideas.

- *Say it.* Write down why you like the ads you've selected. What makes them sing? Which of the four design principles are strongest? What made each one stand out? What caught your eye? If you can articulate why you like a certain ad, you are well on the way to defending your own ideas.

- *Sketch it.* Sometimes the most dreadful ads inspire great new ads. Cut schlocky ads apart and rearrange them. Or take a piece of tissue paper and draw over it. Make it better. This process may just inspire a great design for your next ad. The point is to put something on paper. You may be tempted to jump on the computer before you have a concept. Don't. Scribble something down first. Try some alternatives. When you're happy with your rough, then turn on your computer. And if you're allergic to paper or you just won't turn off your computer, be sure that you treat each thumbnail document as a sketch. Don't overwork them and don't fall in love with the first one.

Ad Story

What Does Antiaging Sound Like?
"We had great clients on Dove Pro-age. We shot the print with Annie Leibovitz and the TV with Lars Knorrn. The productions were smooth and drama free. We finished all the ads and they were beautiful. We put what we thought was an amazing sound to the TV: an original flamenco guitar piece by Pepe Romero. We felt that sound captured the heartbeats of our women. Our women in the spots and all our women consumers."

"The brand decided to put the launch on hold for a year. (For good reasons; they wanted to spend the appropriate amount of money on the launch.) So the finished ads and spots were in the can and we had to play watchdogs. What can happen is that folks want to tinker with the work. They call it enhancing or adding value to the work. I call it a potential nightmare. One of the clients began to entertain the idea of having a more well-known piece of music against

the pictures of our nude 50-year-old women. We had to do a deep negotiation with the following: Jimi Hendrix for 'Foxy Lady' and Joe Cocker for 'You Are So Beautiful (to Me).' As a creative I have to say: It was an interesting exercise. But I was sad. Isn't originality a good thing? Do I always have to 'dress up' an ad in a piece of celebrity to get it to be noticed?

"In the end, the Hendrix folks wanted gazillions of dollars so the effort went away. We went with our original. The timing of the launch worked out great . . . the delay presented us with the opportunity to launch on *The Oprah Winfrey Show*. Even if I had the money to spend, I feel our choice was the right one and the right sound."[7]

—Maureen Shirreff
North American Chief Creative
Officer, *Ogilvy*, Chicago

Layout patterns

There are two common organizational layout systems or patterns: grids and chaotic. Each of these layout systems can be experimented with by using that wonderful design tool—the pencil. We will explain each system. But the idea is to quickly rough out four or five thumbnails, sketching in squares or rectangle boxes for copy blocks, squiggles for display copy, and solid block shapes for visuals. Armed with boxes, squiggles, and blocks and using either the grid or the chaotic system as a jumping-off point, you'll be on your way.

Grids (also known as Mondrian layouts) are simply a systematic way of dividing up space using geometric patterns beginning with the basic rectangle, which makes up your page. Grids allow us to see how elements of a layout might be organized. Consider how many elements you have in your layout. That will help you decide how many blocks you'll need to create within your grid.

Don't think of a grid layout as a stack of blocks or a boring "checkerboard" where you have to fill in all the squares. You have a lot more creative latitude.

Images 7.15, 7.16

Denture wearers won't forget these ads or the benefits of Polident. A beautiful articulation of alignment and proximity, with readers' eyes being directed seamlessly from brand to benefit.

Image 7.17

Talk about headline and visual forming the perfect partnership. This use of a simple and perfectly aligned visual metaphor, combined with strategic color choices, speaks volumes about the environmental impact of light bulbs.

The grid simply provides a system. You use the four principles of design to arrange and rearrange your boxes, squiggles, and blocks. From a practical standpoint, grids are easier to build for print ads, Web ads, and Web sites—which are really a collection of interconnected tables or grids. Columns are much like grids. In fact, sometimes the terms are used interchangeably.

Chaotic layouts (sometimes called circus or field-of-tension layouts) are usually not as crazy as they sound. Generally, the organizing principle that pulls chaotic layouts together is alignment. Thus, the use of lines can bring organization to a chaotic layout. Proximity is another principle that brings order. The seemingly random placement of visuals can be organized, for example, by placing captions nearby or using lines (rules) to connect elements or using repetition to create unity. Use your boxes, squiggles, and blocks to play with the layout. Some chaotic layouts, especially from novice designers, are just that—a visual train wreck. Unless you have a well-defined design strategy and use some organization principles, we suggest you stick to something simpler.

Building your layout—boxes, squiggles, and blocks

Layout systems and thumbnails are the foundation to building your layouts. Use your boxes, squiggles, and blocks to decide where all the elements of your layout go, as well as the general proportion of each element. Once that's done, you can select your font. We encourage you to think of your copy,

Image 7.18

No copy needed here. A visual twist employs alignment, while emphasizing the product benefit and demonstrating visual flow.

particularly your display copy, as a graphic element. Overall, use the various principles discussed earlier in this chapter to guide you. When you figure it all out, it's time to use the computer.

The Design Process

In a nutshell, the process begins with your creative strategy. Work from your brief all the way through. Once you have a clear idea about what needs to be conveyed and a darned good idea about how many elements might be in your layout, start sketching or collaging. If you're more comfortable with sketching, draw thumbnails until you run out of paper. It you're more hands-on, try collaging. Remember our boxes, squiggles, and shapes—use those and move them around within the confines of your layout. Or combine both techniques. The bottom line is good design takes a lot of work. When you brainstorm a headline, you may create 50 or even 100 ideas. Most of which will be schlock. The same process holds true with layout design. Scribble and scratch or cut and paste 50 or even 100 ideas. In the process, you'll come to see what works best for your specific project. One last bit of advice that bears repeating: Don't start shopping for visual images until you've nailed down your Big Idea. We cannot stress enough how much your preliminary work—off the computer—will make or break the quality of your layout.

Selecting your visuals

As you'll see in later chapters, certain words in headlines and copy pull in more readers. The same is true with visual elements—in print or on the Web and television. As with "proven" headline words, don't use cliché visual choices just because they've generated results over the last 50 years. Try to find a new approach that gets noticed. Some of the visual choices that attract readers and viewers include:

People, not things. Given a choice, people like to see other people. It's all about satisfying those wants and needs. Is that person in the ad benefiting from the product? Is that person suffering because he or she's not using the product? Will I look like that handsome/beautiful person in the ad if I use that product? If asked, any reader would say, "Nah, I don't look at people in ads." But they do. And so do you. The choice of showing the product or people using the product depends a lot on the product category. For example, showing a medium-long shot of a sexy sports car racing through the night could be the most effective image for that vehicle. But showing a mom with her kids and a lot of stuff to carry may be the best image for a minivan.

Image 7.19

A classic grid pattern. Mondrian would be proud.

Image 7.20

Chaotic layouts really do have a purpose. In this case, the parts of the motorcycle flip the headline, building a picture of the consumer. Now that's something every Harley rider can relate to.

More visual, less copy. You need to know how to write copy. But you also need to know when to leave it out. While people will read long copy if they're interested, for many consumer ads, you just don't need it. It's better to use a visual to capture their attention than a mass of intimidating text. Once again, the choice depends on the target audience and type of product. Soft drinks and chewing gum don't need 200 words of copy. A business-to-business product might.

Illustration versus photography

Years ago illustration was much more common. Now with Photoshop, photo manipulation creates amazing effects that were only available with illustration. However, illustration is a valid option for a lot of reasons:

You can't show it any other way. Cutaway drawings, blueprints, overlays, ghosted images, and many other graphic treatments are executed as artwork instead of photography and sometimes in a combination of the two.

Create mood. Illustrations create resonance too. Sometimes you need a painting or drawing to elicit an emotion you can't get from a photo.

Dramatic effect. Illustration can be used to exaggerate a feature, make a problem look bigger than it really is, or enhance a benefit. These visual overstatements are more accepted as artwork than realistic photography.

Finding your visuals

One of the biggest problems faced by students (and most professionals) is where to get the visuals. Searching the Web for that perfect image often turns into a shopping trip. You might find something that looks cool but doesn't fit your concept. Try to stay true to your creative strategy, even if you can't find the perfect photo. Fortunately, with stock photo Web sites, your odds are greatly improved, even if the image is plastered with watermarks.

Web sites. You can find just about any image you might need using Google; however, the quality is usually not usable for anything other than a rough reference. When searching for images, try to limit your search to Extra Large, if you plan to put them in a layout. Another good source is iStock, which has a great library of still photos, videos, illustrations, and Flash animations. You'll have to pay for them, but the cost is nominal.

Magazines and other print material. If you need an image of a glamorous model in an evening gown, start looking at some fashion magazines. Remember you are assembling images for a layout, not a real ad.

Words of Wisdom

"Advertising is not a f—ing science! Advertising is an art. No question about it." [8]

—George Lois

Images 7.21, 7.22

Illustration can make a concept come to life in the viewer's imagination. The split heads use a twist that plays off the language of popular culture. Now, all viewers have a chance to engage with the ads based on their own travel plans.

Digital photos. Need a picture of a college student eating a pizza? Don't waste your time browsing stock photos. Just shoot your roommate (photographically, that is). With a little planning you can create all kinds of professional images on your own. This tactic also works very well to create photo storyboards for television commercials.

Draw it. If you can't find it and can't photograph it, try drawing it. Don't worry; you don't have to be a great illustrator. The agency will hire one. You just need to express your idea.

Design and campaign continuity

Design elements, along with great copy, tie a campaign together. The use of lines, type, color, and layout style, in particular, provide a certain look that is carried across a campaign. Pay special attention to logo treatment and taglines. They may have to work with a wide variety of executions in different media. It takes discipline to maintain graphic continuity in a long-running campaign, especially when new ads are developed halfway through the campaign's run. This is when you really have to understand how the various elements interact to form a unified whole. Without that understanding, a campaign can visually fall apart.

Digital Design: OK, Now You Can Put Your Pencils Down

Software makes design and layout faster and cheaper but not necessarily better. In many ways, the digital revolution has helped create a rapidly expanding plague of terrible design. People who used to depend on professionals can now play around with stale templates or lame clip art or develop their own masterpieces that violate every suggestion for good design listed previously in this chapter. Why? Because they can.

Here are a few tips on design for the Web, with one caveat. If you are serious about learning Web design, buy a different book! This book focuses on creative strategy and the creative process. This chapter focuses on design basics. When it comes to design, the basics are rooted in print. Now that we've provided our disclaimer, you're free to continue reading.

Designing for the Web

Considering the four design principles, when it comes to the Web one stands out: repetition. On the Web nothing is more important. Repetition lets visitors to your Web site know that they are still on the same site, no matter how deep into your site they travel. Repetition also allows you to create a clean graphic style, and a clean graphic style means smoother and, most likely, faster navigation. To accomplish a clean graphic style, repeat color schemes and use the same fonts. Repeat the same button styles and use similar graphic elements in similar places on each page. Simplicity ensures fast loading, which is essential if you want to keep viewers on your Web site.

When it comes to choosing fonts, choose wisely. You want fonts that will transfer no matter what platform your viewers are using. We suggest Verdana because it's found on all operating systems. You might also consider Helvetica or Arial. Times and Times New Roman are also pretty safe bets. Whatever you choose, make sure you lay it out in a readable style. Never, ever run your copy across the entire width of the Web page. Online, type is most easily read when it is framed within a textbox or table. In general, shorten the length of your copy within each textbox or table. Yet despite shorter blocks of copy, on the Web you can actually provide more information than you can in print. In fact, most people go to the Web to find more detailed information. So, when providing more detailed information, simply use shorter blocks of copy but more of them.

Whatever you do in terms of designing for the Web, nothing matters more than consistency. Repeat. Repeat. Repeat.

Thoughts on software

You can build an ad in Microsoft Word, Excel, or even PowerPoint. In fact, any program that allows you to import an image and manipulate text can be used to create an ad.

Words of Wisdom

"'Maximum message, minimum means' means every message is best communicated with simplicity and a core concept that is manifested in a compelling manner and a degree of clarity that makes it easily understood."[9]

—Woody Pirtle

Image 7.23

There's no mistaking the Coca-Cola brand anywhere in the world. Nobody does global branding better; however, world dominance can sometimes trigger local resentment.

But whether you're an aspiring writer or an art director, we *strongly* suggest that you get proper training as early as possible in the following programs: Adobe InDesign (or QuarkXPress) for desktop publishing; Adobe Photoshop for photo retouching; Adobe Illustrator for creating vector images; Adobe Flash for developing animations that can be used on the Web; Microsoft PowerPoint or Adobe Flash for slide presentations (try to experiment beyond the standard templates and backgrounds provided if you're using PowerPoint); and Microsoft FrontPage, iWeb, or some other basic Web page design program. The only way to become proficient is to practice. So try to execute your pencil layouts as you scribbled them but also experiment with other ideas. How would a headline look in a different font? Should the body copy be in two columns or one? Do you have room for an inset photo of the product? Can you make the margins wider, the logo smaller, and the copy more readable? Once you have the basic elements of your concept in place, you can start playing around with how they should be arranged on the page.

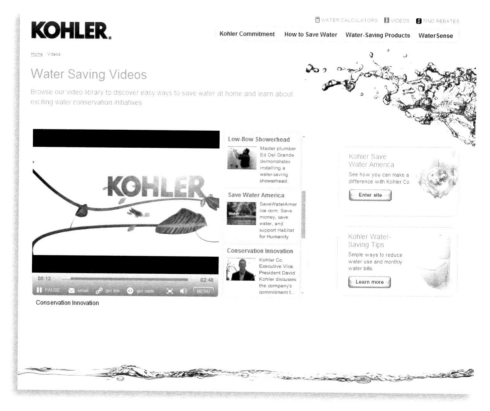

Image 7.24

This microsite for Kohler deals with the company's dedication to water conservation. The design is clean, the type easy to read, and the navigation logically laid out.

Putting It All Together

If you really want to become an art director or a designer, you must take design classes, preferably taught by working professionals who deal with real clients every day. Learn the rules and when you can break them. Above all, there is no substitute for experience, even if most of that experience is trial and error. Practice. Practice. Practice.

Writers can be designers and vice versa. Even if you become an account exec or a media director or can only draw a stick person, you should be able to evaluate design and have some good reasons for your opinions—and they should always be tied to strategy.

The following is a brief checklist of design tips and techniques. Use this to evaluate your work and the work of others. You may not follow every "rule" listed here. But if you don't, you should have a sound creative reason why you didn't.

Conceptual Considerations

- Does your layout convey the big idea?

- Did you design with your audience in mind?

- Did you prioritize elements? (The most important should be the most prominent.)

- Do your visuals and headlines work together?

- Overall, does your design catch the reader's eye?

- Did you keep it simple? (Less is more.)

Layout Considerations

- Did you consider alternatives? (You can never have too many thumbnails.)

- Did you consider the Four Principles of Design? (p. 111)

- Did you use white space effectively?

- Does you layout have a pleasing and logical visual flow?

- Did you choose a display font that match matches the tone of the ad?

- Is the body copy inviting to read—the right size and proportion?

- Did you honor the margins—allow enough space around critical elements?

- Did you keep it simple? (Less is more.)

If you remember nothing else about this chapter, remember this:

Keep it simple. Don't add so many elements, styles, and fonts that no one can figure out what you're trying to say. Another way to say it is, "Less is more." Keeping it simple doesn't mean you can only put one element in an ad. It means you need to unify multiple elements into a cohesive design—so the reader is impressed by your idea, not your technique. Another cardinal rule:

If you emphasize everything, you emphasize nothing. A cluttered, confused, truly chaotic layout repels readers. No one wants to take the time to figure out your message. Once again, "Less is more."

Who's Who?

Helmut Krone developed a clean, uncluttered look in the 1950s that still sets the standards for modern advertising design. Working with copywriter Julian Koenig, Krone created witty, tasteful, intelligent masterpieces for Volkswagen and other Doyle Dane Bernbach clients. Krone sweated print details and advanced professionalism among creatives in his relentless pursuit of perfection. He was elected to the Art Directors Club Hall of Fame and has been a perennial award winner as he revolutionized advertising's "look."[11]

George Lois gained fame and major awards with bold, clean work for Doyle Dane Bernbach, Papert Koenig Lois, and Lois Holland. He also became the youngest inductee into the Art Directors Club Hall of Fame. Lois's ads for Wolfschmidt Vodka, Xerox, Allerest, MTV, Maypo, Wheatena, and Edwards & Hanly and his *Esquire* covers reflected his "loosey-goosey" style and exemplified his idiosyncratic

"stun 'em and cause outrage" philosophy. Never an "establishment" model citizen, Lois is defined by his powerful early work.[12]

Woody Pirtle began a very successful career in graphic design as an art director at Stan Richards and Associates, which later became the Richards Group, one of the leading agencies in the Southwest. Under Pirtle's direction, "single reactive projects would become well-conceived programs where design was pervasive and execution was critical." After his stint at Richards, Pirtle founded Pirtle Design in Dallas and later became a director at Pentagram, one of New York's top design firms.[13]

Robin Patricia Williams is best known for her style manuals, such as *The Mac Is Not a Typewriter* and *The Non-Designer's Design Book*, as well as numerous manuals for various Macintosh operating systems and applications, including *The Little Mac Book*.

Exercises

1. Endless Possibilities

The idea here is to internalize the idea that there is an enormous range of opportunities when it comes to approaches to creative executions. There are endless possibilities.

- Pick a brand. Not a classic brand, but a new and somewhat hot brand. Something like Netflix.

- As a class brainstorm—just shout out anything that you think of when you hear the word *Netflix*. Anything. Now you have list of strange and wonderful possibilities.

- Take each item on that list and walk through the variety of possible points of association. Let's say the word is *couch*. Here is a list of options. What colors do you think of when you think of "couch"? What sounds do you associate with "couch"? What shapes to you think of when you think of "couch"? What do "couches" feel like? Where do you find "couches"? Who should you share your "couch" with? And so on. Ask the same questions of each item on the brand association list.

- Now everyone picks one word. With its multiple points of association create three thumbnails. Use the principles of design to guide your work.

- Everyone shares their thumbnails and provides constructive feedback. Along the way you'll begin to see the possibilities that brainstorming can unlock.

- You could take this to the next step and write a consumer profile and create a comped layout from each thumbnail. Then spin that into a mini campaign. Imagine the tactical opportunities you've generated!

2. Celebrity Fonts

This is a good exercise to become familiar with the program's font choices and finding personalities that work with font choices.

- As a class, list of the top 20 celebrities that you know.

- After creating the list, pick five celebrities and typeset their names, choosing the fonts and colors that work appropriately with that celebrities' present image.

Adapted from an exercise shared by Mike Cissne, Group Leader, Production, Bader Rutter.

3. Five Lines

This exercise is teacher driven and designed to help you experience how lines work as a design element.

- Take out a sheet of paper, draw five lines on it, and then sign your name and submit the sheet for review.

- Your teacher will lead a discussion, using the lines you drew, to demonstrate how many details and decisions could be involved to complete any task and that a designer should be aware of all of the choices.

- Now, generate a list all the questions that could be asked before completing a design project that involves liens: Should the lines be thick? Should the lines be thin? Should the lines symbolize something? Should the lines touch each other? Should a ruler be used? Should the lines be short? Should the lines be long? Should the lines be parallel? How much pressure should be used when drawing the lines? Do the lines need to be seen up close or far away? What color paper should be used? What size of paper should be used? What utensil should be used? Where should the name go in relationship to the lines? And many more . . .

- Discuss how we mostly take for granted these decisions but a good designer runs through all of these thoughts and many more before doing anything.

Adapted from an exercise shared by Mike Cissne, Group Leader, Production, Bader Rutter.

Notes

1. Paul Arden, *It's Not How Good You Are, It's How Good You Want to Be* (London: Phaidon, 2003), p. 78.

2. Quote from the CLIO Awards Web site, http://www.clioawards.com/html/wsj/krone.html (accessed December 20, 2004).

3. Robin Williams, *The Non-Designer's Design Book: Design and Typographic Principles for the Visual Novice* (Berkeley, CA: Peachpit, 2004).

4. Quote from the CLIO Awards Web site, http://www.clioawards.com/html/wsj/riney.html (accessed December 20, 2004).

5. Williams, *The Non-Designer's Design Book*, p. 35.

6. Ibid. p. 71.

7. Maureen Shirreff, Ad Story: *What Does Antiaging Sound Like?,* May 20, 2008.

8. Quote from the CLIO Awards Web site, http://www.clioawards.com/html/wsj/lois.html (accessed December 20, 2004).

9. Woody Pirtle, contribution to *Graphic Design: Inspirations and Innovations*, ed. Diana Martin (Cincinnati, OH: North Light, 1998), p. 50.

10. Quote from the CLIO Awards Web site, http://www.clioawards.com/html/wsj/spivak.html (accessed December 20, 2004).

11. "Top 100 People of the Century," *Advertising Age*, March 29, 1999, http://www.adage.com/century/people.html (accessed June 3, 2005).

12. Ibid.

13. Jack H. Summerford, "Woody Pirtle: Completing the Circle," 2003, on the AIGA Web site, http://www.aiga.org/content.cfm/content?ContentAlias=woodypirtle (accessed June 3, 2005).

Chapter 8

Campaigns

What Is a Campaign?

Before you can create a campaign, you need to define it. From a copywriting standpoint, we prefer Maxine Paetro's simpler description:

A campaign is a series of ads for a product (or service or company) that work individually and cumulatively to communicate the advertiser's message to the consumer.[1]

In other words, each element of a campaign has to be effective on its own, because that may be the first and only exposure. All the elements also need to work together to build a cumulative image. With a well-executed multielement campaign, the whole is greater than the sum of its parts. What makes a collection of marketing communication projects a campaign? In some cases a campaign can include the complete MarCom arsenal, or it can be as simple as a series of three fractional page ads, as long as they meet all of the following criteria:

Common objective: Well-defined target audience; awareness, comprehension, conviction, and action goals within a given time frame. In other words, there should be a campaign strategy.

Unified theme: Whether it's a tagline, graphic design, or copy message, a campaign needs to convey a single message so the consumer can connect that one adjective to the brand. This does not mean every ad has to look the same—but the overall message should.

Coordinated rollout: Depending on the time frame, all elements can appear at once in a blitz, or new elements can be added depending on changing marketing environments, such as seasonality and competitive response. This involves media and promotion planning, but it certainly affects creative strategy.

Overall, if you remember nothing else about campaigns, know this:

The primary purpose of a campaign is to support the brand.

From the client's point of view, a campaign is a more effective, more profitable, and more stable situation for establishing a brand name.[3]

Campaigns and IMC

In Chapter 2 we outlined a few elements of Integrated Marketing Communications. In a campaign, the operative word is *integrated*—elements have to work together in a planned approach. Campaign strategy can involve the whole marketing communication toolbox, including public relations and media planning; however, we'll limit our thinking to creative elements.

Campaign components

Think about any recent soda or fast food restaurant campaign. Where did you first notice it? Probably on television. But you also heard the radio commercials, saw the billboards, checked the coupons in the Sunday paper, got annoyed by the pop-up ads on the Web, and probably glanced at a display in a store or restaurant. Each individual component conveyed the message, and collectively they pounded it into your brain. So when you see that soda on the grocer's shelf or in a vending machine, you buy it, probably without realizing how many times you've been bombarded with different messages in the various media. What made you pull into the drive-thru to try that new sandwich? Maybe it was the ad on your car radio or the billboard you just passed. Again, you probably don't realize how many campaign components were working together to influence you.

Here are a few of the components that can be part of an integrated campaign:

Advertising: Consumer magazines, trade magazines and professional magazines, broadcast television, cable/satellite television, radio, local newspapers, national and trade newspapers, billboards, transit.

Promotion: Short-term sales contests, special offers, discounts, rebates, incentives, sweepstakes, cross-promotion with other products, publicity, and advertising of the promotion.

Public relations: Event planning, publicity of events, print news releases, newsletters, video news releases.

Internet marketing: Web sites, Internet advertising, permission-based marketing, search engine marketing, customer relationship marketing, and online and CD-ROM interactive programs.

Social media: While social media live on the Web, they're a different animal than Internet marketing—blogs, social networking sites, bookmarking services, photo and video sharing, and mashups.

Direct marketing: Database development, direct mailers (letters, cards, dimensional mailers), fulfillment (mailing information or merchandise).

Mobile: The Third Screen, your cell phone, and games and more that will evolve before this goes to press.

Images 8.1, 8.2, 8.3

This student-designed campaign uses primary colors and a playful tone that matches the target audience perfectly. The body copy also tracks nicely from the headline to hold the whole ad together.

If all of the aforementioned components are part of a campaign, they all have to work together yet stand alone as individual selling tools.

How to Enhance Continuity

Continuity does not mean conformity

The biggest difference between a single-shot ad and a campaign is continuity. Continuity within a campaign means the various components of the campaign have enough commonality that the reader/viewer/listener should perceive a common theme and unified message.

Continuity doesn't require that the TV spot use the same dialogue as the radio commercial or the billboards have the exact same graphics as the print ads. While it's nearly impossible to give you one set of guidelines that works for every campaign, remember this:

> **Don't repeat the same idea in every part of the campaign—repeat the creative strategy with different executions.[5]**

Extendability

To create an effective campaign, you need to think in two dimensions—*extending* the creative strategy across the various media and *repeating* that strategy within each medium. The first dimension—extendability—means you use the same

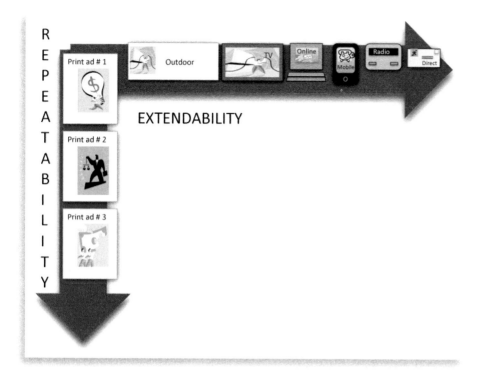

EXTENDABILITY

Image 8.4

Extendability spreads your campaign concept across various media. Repeatability replicates the campaign look and feel within each medium.

theme and common elements in two or more media. For example, can you carry that creative message from print to TV? Will the direct mailers look like they came from the same company as the billboards? Does the advertising support the promotion theme? Does the point of purchase material tie in with the campaign?

Repeatability

Repeatability is a little different from repetition. It does not mean rerunning the same ad or commercial until everyone is so sick of it they ignore it. That's a media decision. In a creative context, repeatability means using common elements to create a series of ads or commercials.

Image 8.5

We can't think of a better illustration of repeatability in a campaign. For years the "got milk?" campaign has featured the stars of the day (and days past). If you want to check out the origin of this long-running campaign, read Jon Steel's Truth, Lies, and Advertising: The Art of Account Planning.

They are not identical, but they are related—being able to stand alone but also working cumulatively to convey a campaign theme.

How to maximize extendability and repeatability

We've already covered some of the creative tools you can use to provide continuity to a campaign. You can use one or all of them to help hold your campaign together.

Music: When people can't remember the words of a commercial but can sing the jingle, you know your campaign's music is holding it together. Music is far more memorable than any other commercial element. For example, you'd have a hard time finding anyone over 30 who doesn't know the Oscar Mayer wiener song. You have as many ways to use music in your campaign as there are songs—probably more, with today's sampling and mixing technology.

Voice talent: Using the same announcer throughout your TV and radio campaigns helps establish a common sound. Here are a few examples:

- **Celebrity on camera:** Just have the celebrity appear in the spots and say something. In this case, the visual of the celebrity is probably more memorable than the sound of his or her voice.

- **Celebrity voice-over:** A lot of very famous people provide voice-overs for commercials without identifying themselves, such as George Clooney (Budweiser), Queen Latifah (Pizza Hut), Christian Slater (Panasonic), Julia Roberts (AOL), Gene Hackman (Lowe's), and Jeff Bridges (Duracell), to name a few. Using famous actors may be expensive, but they often have a distinctive voice that connects with the viewers or listeners. New research reveals that television commercials featuring celebrity voice-overs are most influential when consumers can't identify which actor it belongs to.[7]

- **Character voices:** People are used to hearing smooth announcers. So a distinctive voice treatment can shock them into listening. Gilbert Gottfried's jarring "Aflac" quack is a prime example.

- **Announcers:** Using the same announcer, even if he or she is not a celebrity, can provide continuity. Be careful to maintain the tone and delivery style, even though the copy changes from spot to spot.

Animated characters/animals

For years the Leo Burnett agency was known for its "critters"— those memorable animated characters that have been the common thread of many of its long-running campaigns. Before you dismiss these mascots as throwbacks to the 1950s, consider that they've been around for a long, long time. That means the agency has created long-term brand value and, in doing so, has retained clients much longer than most of its competitors.

Images 8.6, 8.7, 8.8

Animated brand mascots not only contribute to campaign continuity; they also never grow old, get arrested, or go into rehab.

Some characters, such as Tony the Tiger, the Jolly Green Giant, and the Keebler Elves, are inseparable from the product.

Celebrities/spokespersons

Celebrities: Back in the day when brands were the sole sponsor of radio and television programs, the star of the show was the brand spokesperson in his or her prime. Michael Jordan was one of the top commercial spokespersons, starting with Coke and then Nike before branching off to McDonald's, Hanes, and many others. His celebrity transcended his sports fame. Tiger Woods became the symbol of Nike golf products and Buick, among others. Beyoncé has stacked up endorsement deals with American Express, Samsung, Armani Diamonds perfume, Disney, and L'Oréal. George Foreman is better known for his cookware than as the former heavyweight-boxing champ.

As we discussed in Chapter 6, using a celebrity works best when he or she has some reasonable connection with the product. Whether your celebrity is from the world of sports, show business, politics, or any other public venue, the main considerations should be:

- Can we afford this person?
- Any skeletons in the closet—any future potential for embarrassing the client?
- Will he or she connect with the consumers?
- Will this person enhance the brand image?

Spokespersons/symbols: You can create spokespersons, and if things go right, they become celebrities. One of the most successful is Jared Fogle, who lost a ton of weight eating healthy food at Subway. He's still their spokesperson 10 years later, thanks to the brilliant foresight of a local Subway franchise owner who saw Jared's story, "Crazy Diets That Work," in *Men's Health*. Another "nobody" who has been a long-term spokesperson is the Verizon guy. He started years ago asking, "Can you hear me now?" and remains a symbol for Verizon even though the emphasis changed to the strength of their network.

Story lines/situations

Story lines: Some advertisers use testimonials or case histories, all with a common theme, to convey their message. Hospitals, for example, typically feature inspirational stories of survivors who owe their lives to the advanced technology and caring doctors of a given institution. Insurance companies also use this approach with the emphasis on caring for victims of some catastrophic event.

Situations: These are recurring themes or vignettes that involve (a) the same characters or (b) the same premise. Over the years Budweiser has featured their iconic Clydesdales in Super Bowl commercials. Another beer company, Coors, produced a long-running series of commercials that mated footage of actual coach interviews with lame questions from a fake audience. For several years GEICO insurance has run a campaign saying their online signup is so easy a caveman can do it, much to the disgust of surprisingly sophisticated modern cavemen. The commercials became so popular they were spun off into an ill-fated sitcom. It seems that one joke is all that's needed for a 30-second commercial, but it can't sustain a whole program.

Image 8.9

Using celebrity endorsements adds continuity to a campaign. In this case, Citizen uses several celebrities from the world of sports. Other companies use one spokesperson, such as Michael Jordan or Tiger Woods, to speak for their brand.

Design and tagline

As we discussed in Chapter 7, design elements can unify a campaign. Maybe it's a color, like the brown of UPS. They even built a slogan, "What can brown do for you?" around their distinctive color. It could be a layout style, a type style, or another graphic element that's the common thread. Once a look is established in the consumer's mind, extending it becomes a lot easier—until it stops getting attention. As we'll cover in Chapter 9, a slogan can also hold a campaign together.

Concurrent campaign strategies

While we strongly suggest keeping the theme simple and consistent, some advertisers have been very successful by running multiple campaigns, each with a very different look and feel. The most obvious is GEICO insurance, which offered three campaigns at once: (a) cavemen, (b) the talking gecko, and

With the Network,
you can work in more spots than just hotspots.

With Wi-Fi, you're trapped. Confined to hotspots. Get BroadbandAccess for your Mac or PC from Verizon Wireless and work in more spots than just hotspots. Simply click to connect and start working on the go, all on America's most reliable wireless broadband network.

UM 150 USB wireless modem
for your Mac or PC

To learn more about our mobile broadband solutions, get in touch with a dedicated business representative.

Call 1.800.VZW.4BIZ   Click verizonwireless.com/bba   Visit your local Verizon Wireless Store

Image 8.10

The Verizon guy used to wander around alone asking, "Can you hear me now?" Later he starred in TV and print ads as the front man for a huge army of support people who represent the strength of the Verizon network.

(c) celebrity spokespersons paired with ordinary customers. Each one was a strong campaign promoting convenience and saving money. Ad critic Seth Stevenson explains why this approach works: "Car insurance has perhaps the broadest target audience of any product. Who is Geico selling to? Pretty much everyone—man or woman, gay or straight, black or white, hip or hick. . . . As a result, Geico needs to air a range of spots that will appeal to many different people. Some ads are straightforward and tame (aimed at older drivers), while some are absurd (the kids seem to like this). All for a single product."[8]

Consumer-Generated Campaigns

As social media merged with marketing, advertisers used the Internet to give consumers an unprecedented opportunity to buy into their brands. Technically, anyone with a cell phone camera or a camcorder and a computer (or smart phone) can create consumer-generated media (CGM). Encouraging consumers to create their own commercials involves them in the brand far beyond being a loyal customer. Major corporations such as Kodak, American Express, and General Electric have sponsored consumer-generated campaigns. And we're pretty sure you haven't forgotten the Doritos spots that ran during the Super Bowl. Despite the current trend, it's important to remember that most consumer-generated media are short lived, very specific in scope, limited to a single product or brand extension, and not meant to replace the corporate or brand campaign. In many cases they could be considered a sales promotion that is supported by other media. Time will tell if CGM will remain a major force in brand support or whether it will be an intriguing bit of marketing fluff.

If you're planning to use CGM as the main focus or even part of your campaign, keep these tips in mind:

1. Don't separate your CGM from the main objectives for the brand or company—integrate it. Determine how your CGM will support your brand, not detract from the brand message.

2. Be honest about your intentions. You want people to create ads. Don't call it something else. Too many CGM programs have crashed because they weren't transparent.

3. Encourage participation—not just from entrants but also from people who can vote on the best submission. It's like Chicago politics—get them to vote early and often.

4. Facilitate syndication. Use viral seeding to get the videos out to a wider audience. Empower syndication by making it simple to upload and embed in blogs.

5. Consider long-term implications and opportunities. Can your CGM be leveraged into a longer-running campaign? Can it be mainstreamed into your primary branding campaign?

Integrated Digital Campaigns

As we'll see in chapters discussing online marketing and sales promotion, the Web has become the hub of many advertising campaigns. While consumers may not want to read a 100-word print ad, they might read 500 words on a Web site. In many ways, the purpose of a multichannel ad campaign is to direct people to a single landing page, which gives them the option to explore multiple methods of interacting with the advertiser. The Tide to Go campaign is a good example. Ads during the Super Bowl featured a "talking stain" on a job applicant's shirt that drowned out the person's voice with annoying gibberish. The TV ads directed viewers to click on a microsite to learn more. On the site, you could rerun the commercial, as well as create your own talking stain using your own picture, so you could "be the stain." There was also a CGM component where people could send in their own spoof commercials for Tide to Go, which were voted on by visitors to the site and could be shared with others. So the TV commercial was funny, but the Web site did the hard work of entertaining, motivating, and selling.

Knowing the Audience

Who uses a Mac? Design professionals who actually benefit from the superior functionality of using a Mac? Right-brain types? People who want others to think they're right-brainers? Hipsters who want the coolest-looking toys? Apple, in a brilliant brand positioning campaign, personified their computers by using a young, confident, relaxed, hip (but not too hip) guy named Mac. The guy named PC was older, wore a suit and nerdy glasses, and was insecure, flustered by technology, and openly hostile to the easygoing Mac. In every spot it seemed as if PC was having a meltdown while cool, confident Mac was either sympathetic or unfazed, without hyping the

Images 8.11, 8.12, 8.13

This campaign extends the spirit of the Nike brand as a champion of female athletes. The ads celebrate women's bodies with copy that visually conforms to the curves of each body part and words that celebrate an athlete's strength.

benefits of the Macintosh. So, if you're watching these ads, who do *you* want to be? We thought so.

The campaign was so successful, Microsoft ran a countercampaign showing a number of people—quirky, ethnically and culturally diverse, young, old, male, female—in essence every kind of person imaginable, and they all said, "I'm a PC." Did they change people's minds about who uses a Mac and who has a PC? Or did they just reinforce the cool image of Apple products to people who are already Mac fans?

NSAC: Like the Real Thing, Only More Fun

The National Student Advertising Competition, sponsored by the American Advertising Federation, provides an opportunity for college students to develop and present a professional advertising campaign for a real client. Some call it the World Series of college advertising. Each fall, teams begin work for the same client and compete in the spring at regional and

Ad Story

Start It Up and Say Goodbye: Sometimes You Can't Go Home Again

At Wieden + Kennedy, Charlotte Moore was part of the creative team that helped win scores of prestigious awards for Nike and other clients. After a sabbatical, she returned to W + K where she was assigned to their newest client, Microsoft.

"I had a creative person's pie-in-the-sky notions. I was exceedingly romantic about the possibilities, and why shouldn't I have been? What could lend itself to a wider and deeper (in fact, bottomless) dialogue than the world of communication, business, exchange, technology, creation? After all, isn't that what software really is? It's a tool, yes, but it's a tool that invisibly and, if well designed, intuitively serves our most basic human expressions. I was ready to delve into it.

"I was not prepared for the client, for the phalanxes of 'software people' who responded analytically, but utterly

unemotionally, to creative work. I was appalled that the people who made the very tools I was so excited about could see only the 'toolishness' of the tools, and not what they actually made possible on the bigger scale. I was frustrated that exciting work that addressed the big issues of communication and creativity and productivity was routinely shot down in favor of stuff that was more blandly corporate or features-oriented. And ultimately, I was incapable of accepting the results which were (to me) un-Wieden + Kennedy-like to the extreme. Not radical. Not interesting. Not moving. Not what I wanted to be responsible for.

"The final indignity was the production of a spot for the launch of Windows '95, which featured—in fact, was based on—the Rolling Stones' song, 'Start it Up' because it was linked, obviously enough, to the Microsoft Windows 'start button' feature. My partner had suggested it. (I don't blame him; it was a solution in a tight

squeeze, and perhaps from some point of view it was the right thing to do.) But I hated the cheapening of a rock classic. I hated the fact that the spot had no idea of its own, other than to throw mediocre visuals of people using computers against a 3 million-dollar soundtrack. And I hated the fact that in some way I was responsible, though I couldn't for the life of me figure out how.

"So I resigned. It seemed that where the agency wanted to go was not where I wanted to go. And no one asked me to reconsider. I did go back to the agency a year later as the co-creative director in Amsterdam. I've since moved on. But it's still the agency I consider my workplace, and my professional home. suppose it's no wonder that I've chosen, in its wake, to remain a free agent, taking projects here and there, but with no deep commitment."[9]

—Charlotte Moore
Former Creative Director
Wieden & Kennedy, Amsterdam

national competitions. For most college students, this is the closest thing to a real-world new business pitch. They work with real objectives and a real budget with real guidelines, both from the client and from NSAC. Some schools make participation part of their advertising curricula; others participate as Ad Club members.

NSAC consists of two main components: a plans book and a presentation. The plans book is the road map for a campaign. It includes an Executive Summary, Situation Analysis, Research, Media Strategy and Tactics, Creative Strategy and Tactics, and sometimes Promotion Strategy and Tactics. It also includes a Budget, which makes the plan real, not just a creative exercise. Also important is the Evaluation: What do you measure, how do you measure it, and when do you measure it?

How important is a plans book? In the NSAC competition, it's sometimes given greater weight than the

Images 8.14, 8.15, 8.16

Now here's a new twist on an old classic. This student campaign brings salt to life through the voice of its partner, pepper. And, it's a wonderful example of repeatability. The beautiful illustrations cast a strategic shadow over the brilliantly executed copy, as it walks you right to the brand. Now, how smart is that?

actual presentation. Some judges are more interested in how you think than how you present your thoughts.

The NSAC presentation is the fun part. Four or five presenters introduce their team, walk through their recommendations, show the creative work, and if they're smart, ask for the business. Following the 20-minute show-and-tell is a grueling 10-minute question-and answer session. This is where the judges really test the presenters. It can make or break the whole presentation.

If you have the opportunity to participate in NSAC, do it! It's a great experience to develop a plan, execute the various campaign elements, and then sell it to a real client. It's also a great opportunity to see other college teams in action. What's more, NSAC participation looks great on your résumé, especially if you win.

Putting It All Together

Creative strategy for campaigns begins with marketing objectives. As always, you have to ask, "What do you want to accomplish?" The more specific the goals, the better your plan. When the objective is to introduce and reinforce a brand, start thinking campaigns.

Don't limit your thinking to repetition of the concept or even to how it will work in other media. Look at the big picture. The most famous one-shot ad of all time—Apple's *1984*—was actually part of a campaign that involved a huge amount of publicity and public relations. The commercial was shown many times—for free—after its one and only appearance at the Super Bowl, and the buzz put Macintosh on the map. It's interesting to note that the client was so nervous about the approach before the Super Bowl that the agency sold off their time for a scheduled second airing.

Campaign tips

We've offered a lot of ways to improve the continuity and thus the effectiveness of campaigns. Here's some more good advice from Jim Albright:

- A campaign is a series of planned actions. Think big about a wide, multipronged attack on the marketplace.

- When assigned to write a one-time ad, check to see if the client has an ongoing look and sound and slogan. If so, make the point of the ad under the umbrella of the ongoing look, sound, and slogan.

- If the client has no continuity in its advertising, write the one-time ad so that it could be extended into a campaign, if necessary.

Words of Wisdom

"The greatest advertising isn't great for moving merchandise any more than the greatest literature is great for compelling plots. Somehow—in the service of carmakers and brassiere manufacturers and car rental agencies— these campaigns have discovered our humanity."[10]

—Bob Garfield

TOGETHER

University of Minnesota
NSAC

It's All About Connections

Hundreds of students from the nation's top advertising programs compete every year in NSAC, sponsored by the AAF. While it's a rewarding experience for all, here is only one winner. Here's the story of how the University of Minnesota team won the regional and ultimately national championship.

"There we were. Hearts pounding. Hair standing on end. And the biggest damn grins we've ever worn. We were the 2007 NSAC champions. Dozens of late nights, gallons of Red Bull and plenty of spirited debates had paid off.

"Ten months before, we were presented with a daunting task: Take the most ubiquitous brand in existence and increase brand health and brand consumption by 3% each among 13–24-year-olds (Millennials) living in the United States. We had to once again

make Coke relevant, while battling deep-rooted perceptions, an increasingly competitive category, and a fickle audience. To start, we knew we needed to learn about Coca-Cola and Millennials to identify where they intersect.

"To get smart, we took a trip to interview MTV, a brand with their finger on the pulse of this generation. We ran focus groups. We had Millennials make collages and yearbook entries. We had Millennials create Facebook profiles for the Coca-Cola brand as if it were a person, to help articulate brand qualities in an outlet that they understand. We administered over 1,000 surveys nationwide. We interviewed anyone who would talk to us. . . . and some who wouldn't. We learned Millennials desire social connection above anything else. While these learnings were vital, we couldn't ignore everyday truths.

"When you sit down with friends for pizza and order pitchers of soda for the group, inevitably someone says, 'Is Coke OK?' There is a collective acceptance. This is telling in and of itself. But dig deeper. Think about the context of a pitcher of Coke sitting in the middle of the table, surrounded by friends. It is metaphorically and literally a component and facilitator of the best social situations.

"Coke helps people connect and our targets' lives revolve around their social

experiences—YAHTZEE! The articulation of this idea served as the foundation for our creative strategy: Coke is an uplifting part of your favorite, shared experiences. This idea was so central to our campaign, not only was it the focus of all messaging, it informed the vehicles for messaging as well.

"We created an iPhone application that used GPS technology to brand maps and show the location of your friends and Coke vending/retail locations. Our TV ads made Coke the hero by creating a connection between people that wouldn't have been possible without the brand. We created a program with Coke as the exclusive sponsor where youth could support Tolerance Centers, places aimed at fostering education and tolerance of different races, religions, and cultures. Plus countless events and promotions all intended to place Coca-Cola in the center of our target's shared experiences.

"Will this campaign work? Our research said we were 'right on.'

"Did it work? Well, not only did we win the NSAC national competition, but Coca-Cola's leading marketing judge said, 'We could run your campaign tomorrow!'"[11]

—Matt Nyquist and Brenna Whisney
2007 NSAC Championship team
members, Minneapolis

- When writing an advertising campaign, don't repeat the same plot in different media. Repeat the creative strategy with different executions.

- Think extendability from the beginning. Sometimes a strategy is so narrow that only one or two good commercials or ads can be written under that strategy. Think ahead to all the different ways you can execute advertising under your creative strategy. You may have to write a song or have T-shirts printed.[12]

Who's Who?

A brilliant strategic thinker, **Charlotte Beers** became the world's highest-ranked woman in advertising. The Texas native joined J. Walter Thompson Co. in 1969. In 1979, Beers became the COO, then CEO, of Tatham-Laird & Kudner. She tripled billings and merged with Europe's RSCG to create what is now Euro RSCG Tatham. Her performance led WPP Group to name her chairman-CEO of Ogilvy & Mather Worldwide and, later, chairman of JWT. She served a brief stint as Under Secretary for Public Diplomacy and Public Affairs to improve America's image in Muslim countries.

Marie-Catherine Dupuy is a third-generation ad agency exec. Her grandfather founded one of the first French advertising agencies (which later became Saatchi & Saatchi in 1986). Dupuy joined Dupuy-Compton as a copywriter in 1970. In 1984 she became a founding partner and executive creative director at Boulet Dru Dupuy Petit (later to become part of TBWA). As writer and creative director, she has won more than 200 awards in the international competition for clients such as Virgin, BMW, McDonald's, TAG Heuer, Sony, and Bic.

Jeff Goodby was freelancing with partners Andy Berlin and Rich Silverstein while working as a copywriter at Hal Riney. Their freelance client eventually became Electronic Arts and got so big they decided to create their own agency with EA as their first account. It wasn't their last. Their creative risk taking led to breakthrough campaigns for the California Milk Processor Board ("got milk?"), Budweiser (Louie and Frank the lizards and the Wassup campaign), Nike, E*TRADE, and the Winter Olympics. That campaign, among others, helped the once tiny agency gain significant recognition, including multiple CLIO and Cannes awards. Goodby has been named by *AdWeek* as Agency of the Year and grew steadily with the addition of Unilever, Cracker Jack, Intel, and *The Wall Street Journal*.

Tom Monahan has helped thousands of people master creative thinking with his popular creative workshops. Through his consulting company, Before & After, he has worked with clients such as Capital One, Frito-Lay, AT&T, and Virgin Atlantic. He is also author of one of the top business-oriented books on creative thinking—*The Do-It-Yourself Lobotomy: Open Your Mind to Greater Creative Thinking*.

Exercises

1. Brand Stories

Here's a chance to learn about how personal stories influence branding.

- Pick a brand and find six people who use the brand.

- Interview each person, asking them to tell a story about their experience with the brand. Try to elicit from each person his or her emotional connection to the brand and record their conversations.

- Transcribe and review each interview. Using the stories, generate a positioning statement that personified the essence of the consumers' experiences with the brand.

- Next write three short branded stories, with a headline, that embodies the essence of the positioning and reflects the stories you heard. Limit your stories to 300 words.

- You might even consider who would be the perfect spokesperson for a branded campaign. Write a rationale explaining why.

2. Next Ones

This exercise works to help you understand the concepts of *extendability* and *repeatability.*

- Choose several campaigns across various categories.

- Working in teams, with one campaign per team, write a Creative Brief based on what you see in the existing campaign.

- Then, working with the concept of *repeatability,* concept one or two new ads that could seamlessly work with the existing campaign. You can do this with tissue roughs, using the existing layouts, or new full-blown creative executions.

- Next, working with *extendability,* generate two or three new media placements or touch points for the campaign. Consider the executional opportunities for these new placements.

- Finally, present your work in class, with a rationale for each execution and placement.

Adapted from an exercise shared by Kimberly Selber, PhD, Associate Professor, University of Texas–Pan American.

3. Endure the Pain and Enjoy the Gain

All writers must suffer for their art, right? Now, we're not talking about pursuing bad relationships, living on the streets, or abusing alcohol. Although some of those things will make for more interesting conversations at dinner parties. We're talking about soldiering through the painful part—writing body copy for the first ad of a campaign. One way is to start way outside the box.

- Start by writing the copy before coming up with the concept or headline. Imagine describing the client's brand, sale, or issue to their grandpa in an e-mail. Keep it clear and simple . . . you know how Grandpa gets confused.

- When you've finished this exercise you've accomplished a few things. You've stated their case in a manner any consumer will understand, and you are no longer staring at a blank page. Perhaps your mind also opened up to seeing that there could be several ways to solve the problem.

- Now consider the subject header of their e-mail. Maybe that's a headline?

- You might consider writing e-mails to the whole family. Who knows? Maybe you'll end up with an entire campaign.

Adapted from an exercise shared by Jeff Ericksen, Instructor and Founder, Ms. Coffmansen's Portfolio Finishing School.

Notes

1. Maxine Paetro, *How to Put Your Book Together and Get a Job in Advertising* (Chicago: The Copy Workshop, 2002), p. 7.

2. Laurence Vincent, *Legendary Brands: Unleashing the Power of Storytelling to Create a Winning Market Strategy* (Chicago: Dearborn Trade Publishing, 2002).

3. Thomas O'Guinn, Chris Allen, and Richard Semenik, *Advertising and Integrated Brand Promotion* (Mason, OH: South-Western, 2003), p. 50.

4. Quote from the CLIO Awards Web site, http://www.clioawards.com/html/wsj/dupuy.htm, 1996 (accessed December 20, 2004).

5. Jim Albright, *Creating the Advertising Message* (Mountain View, CA: Mayfield, 1992), p. 49.

6. Tom Monahan, "When an Ad is Not a Campaign," *Communication Arts*, May/June 2000, http://www.comarts.com/ca/colad/tomM_.31.html (accessed May 27, 2005).

7. See Nancy Gardner, "Celebrity Voice-Overs: That Not-Too Familiar Voice Could Be Selling You Something," Foster School of Business News Web site, December 20, 2005, http://bschool.washington.edu/new/full_stories/voice-overs.html (accessed December 10, 2008).

8. See Seth Stevenson, "The Best Ad on Television," *Slate* Web site, July 25, 2005, http://www.slate.com/id/21232851/ (accessed December 12, 2008).

9. Charlotte Moore, Ad Story: *Start It Up and Say Goodbye: Sometimes You Can't Go Home Again,* 2005.

10. Bob Garfield, "Top 100 Advertising Campaigns of the Century," *Advertising Age*, March 29, 1999, http://www.adage.com/century/campaigns.html (accessed May 27, 2005).

11. Matt Nyquist and Brenna Whisney, Ad Story: *It's All About Connections,* February 2009.

12. Albright, *Creating the Advertising Message*, p. 49.

Chapter 9

Headlines and Taglines

We can show you the easy way to get an A in this class.

Got your attention, right?

That's what a headline is supposed to do. It appeals to your self-interest. It can promise a reward. It makes you want to know more. It can draw you into the ad.

Why Have a Headline?

All forms of marketing communications use headlines, even when we don't call them headlines. In television it's the start of the commercial. In radio, it's the first few words of copy. In a letter, it may be a title or the first paragraph. David Ogilvy stated that the headline is the "ticket on the meat,"[1] which sounds rather simplistic for someone who wrote,

> **"At 60 miles an hour the loudest noise in this new Rolls-Royce comes from the electric clock."**

He found a benefit (exceptionally quiet ride), included specifics (60 miles per hour), and twisted it with an unexpected comparison to an electric clock, probably the last thing you'd think about when buying a Rolls-Royce. At 18 words, it's very long by today's standards, but still memorable.

Not all print ads have headlines, especially visual puzzles. However, it's important to know how to write a good headline first. Then you can decide if you need it. Some texts dissect and analyze headlines in great detail, but we'll boil their functions down to four primary points. A *good* headline does one or more of the following:

- Gain immediate attention (the old fishhook in the brain).

- Select the right prospect (appeal to self-interest).

- Lead readers into the text (they want to know more).

- Complete the creative equation (synergy with visuals).

Types of Headlines

Categorizing headlines is usually more helpful in describing completed work than helping you develop new concepts. Philip Ward Burton developed a list of categories that we like.[3] We modified his list a bit and kept the descriptions brief.

Proven styles of headlines

Additional research has shown that certain styles of headlines tend to pull better. Once again, it is far more important to write a headline that achieves one or more of its purposes than to have some empty bit of fluff that fits some formula.

The three proven styles are:

- Question

- How to

- Quote

The first two are effective because they involve the reader. If you ask a question (and the reader is interested), you stimulate involvement. The same is true with a "how to" headline, but you have to finish the sentence with something

TABLE 9.1   Types of Headlines

Type of Headline	Use this when...
News	. . . you want to introduce a new product, new brand, or new feature.
Direct benefit	. . . you want to promise a reward or highlight the prime benefit in the headline.
Curiosity	. . . you want to intrigue the reader into finding the main idea in the body copy.
Emotional	. . . you want to sell the image and/or invoke resonance in the reader.
Directive (command)	. . . you want the reader to do something.
Hornblowing	. . . you want to impress the reader by being the biggest, the fastest, the first, etc.
Comparison	. . . you want to differentiate your brand from the competitor or use a metaphor to describe your product.
Label	. . . you want to focus on the brand name, product name, or campaign tagline rather than discuss features/benefits.

Image 9.1

This comparison headline works because the contrast between the people is shocking. It creates a synergy that draws you in. You want to know more.

Image 9.2

This ad, in an arthritis magazine, uses the target audience (seniors) to spell out a benefit headline.

Image 9.3

Now here's an emotional headline with resonance. Using the product itself, Scrabble is reintroduced to a new generation of consumers in a way they just might remember.

Image 9.4

This directive headline challenges readers to conduct their own product demonstration of fire-resistant paper. The copy is directive too: "Hold this advertisement over an ashtray. Put a match or a lighter to it. Remove the flame, and the page stops burning."

that interests the reader. Quotations can be effective because they are usually connected to a person . . . and people are interested in other people, be they celebrities or ordinary Joes or Janes. A quotation hints at a story, which, if it interests the reader, fosters involvement. See Table 9.2 for some examples.

Creating headlines from product information

First start with a positioning statement, a description, or that One Thing you can say about the product. This is not a headline, but it will give you some idea starters to build one or several. The image below shows how the process starts using what we call a Creative Tree. You can keep adding more branches as you think of them. As with all creative writing, if you're on a roll, don't quit. Keep writing headlines even if 99% of them are awful. A real stinker may trigger a winner. You may end up with something that has no direct relationship to a specific product feature, but if it attracts readers and pulls them into the ad, you've done your job.

Writing Headlines With Style

If you work on it, you can try to add a little spice to your list of headlines. The following are a few suggestions. Try to work some of them into your long list and see if they lead to anything worth keeping.

Be specific: Let's go back to Ogilvy's classic. Do you think it would have been nearly as good with "This is one really quiet car" or "The clock is louder than the engine"? Without turning it into a laundry list

TABLE 9.2   Styles of Headlines

Style	Headline	Visual	Client
Question	Do you really need more proof that drinking impairs your judgment?	Plain girl morphing into a fashion model as it gets later in the evening.	MADD
Question	Ever see a grown man cry?	Broken bottle of whiskey on floor.	Crown Royal
How to	How to convert liters into cups.	Race car and racing trophies.	Acura
How to	How to write an obituary for your teenager.	[All-type ad.]	Partnership for a Drug-Free America
Quote	I told my dad I stopped raising hell and he called me a quitter.	Redneck-looking guy smoking a cigarette.	Winston
Quote	These tables are my voice and I'm about to holla at the world.	DJ scratching two turntables.	Mountain Dew Red

of specs and features, see if you can work some details into your headline. Brooks Brothers, quietly but very specifically, states the value of their brand (reprinting a pitch for a 1942 newspaper ad): "It pays to buy at Brooks Brothers." Consider the economic parallels between 1942 and 2009 and you'll see how timeless simplicity can be.

Rhyme, rhythm, alliteration: As with taglines, using rhyme, rhythm, and alliteration can make a headline more memorable. Some might say a rhyming headline is clever. Others may think the same headline is cheesy. If it's memorable and sells something, who cares? Rhythm usually employs connecting a few well-chosen short words such as "Coke is it." Alliteration, for those who can't remember English composition, combines two or more words with the same initial sound, such as "The joint is jumpin'" or "Every kiss begins with Kay."

Judicious use of puns and wordplay: Sometimes puns work. We did an ad for a luxury boat company that showed our product docked at a marina with many other fancy boats. Some of the other owners were checking out our client's product. The headline: "Pier Pressure." Cute? Stupid? You decide. This tip could also include wordplay and double meaning. As with puns, be careful.

- **Parallel construction:** This is just a fancy way to say you're combining phrases or sentences with similar key words to make a point. A few years ago, Florida tourism used the line, "When you need it bad, we've got it good." Now, consider the timely rhythm of these words from Crate & Barrel: "Oven-proof. Dishwasher-proof. 401(k)-proof." A student wrote an ad for Purell waterless hand cleaner, making the point that money is full of germs and other nasty stuff. Her headline: "Dirty money. Dirty hands."

- **Try it with a twist:** The headline is part of the concept, so give it a twist now and then. Another example from our luxury boat client: We showed the boat at a pier in front of a very nice house in an even nicer neighborhood. The owners of our boat were hosting a very fancy outdoor dinner party. The headline, "If your neighbors aren't impressed, move to a better neighborhood."

- **Be relevant:** Hot cultural trends and salient social issues matter greatly, and so does the health of the economy. Always consider what's happening around you. Stuart Elliott, the insightful advertising writer for *The New York Times,* suggests that financial institutions focus on the *S* words: strength, safety, stability, and security.[4]

Involve the product: Sometimes the package or logo can be an integral part of the headline. Then you really have some synergy between visuals and text if it's done right.

Image 9.5

A question headline from an era long ago when people were actually concerned about appearing literate. Today the headline might read, "RU OK 4 Nglish?"

Image 9.6

Here's a question headline you don't want anyone to ask. If they do, it's time to go to the Y.

FIGURE 9.1   *Creative Tree for Headlines*

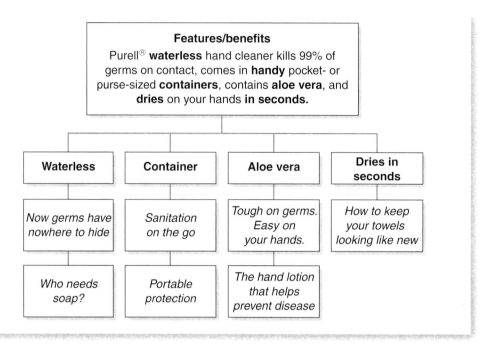

Understatement/overstatement: George Felton makes a good point in his book *Advertising: Concept and Copy* about headline/visual synergy and tone. "If your visual is wild and crazy or obviously excessive, then back off verbally. And vice versa. In other words, don't shout twice."[5]

Ineffective headlines

We can't tell you how to write the perfect headline. Unless it's an all-type ad, the headline usually doesn't stand alone. So the value of a headline is usually related to how well it interacts with the rest of the ad. The ultimate value of a headline depends on the expectations of the client and the results achieved. "Free donuts" may be the most effective headline to attract policemen, if that's your objective. Some headlines just scream, "Think again!" Try harder when you see a headline doing any of the following:

Words of Wisdom

"Make the novel familiar."[6]

—Douglas Atkin

- Asking a question that can't be answered (confusing).

- Asking a question that can be answered with a simple yes or no (no involvement).

- Being used as a caption. Captions describe rather than interact (no synergy with visuals and limited involvement).

- Relying on stupid puns ("stupid" defined as having absolutely no relation to the product or market).

- Using insulting, condescending, or patronizing language that annoys intelligent readers.

- Being clever for the sake of cleverness (trying to impress rather than persuade).

Image 9.7

Single-word headlines are seldom more effective than this one. In an era when advertisers would not risk saying anything perceived as negative, VW gave readers credit for reading deeper to discover the real meaning of this ad.

Image 9.8

Is the visual part of the headline or vice versa? Either way, it works with the subhead and pulls you into the body copy. It's also a good example of selecting the right prospect (this ad ran in a magazine targeting mature readers).

Image 9.9

Graphics in the headline: Nike gained a strong foothold in the golf market with simple yet powerful messages.

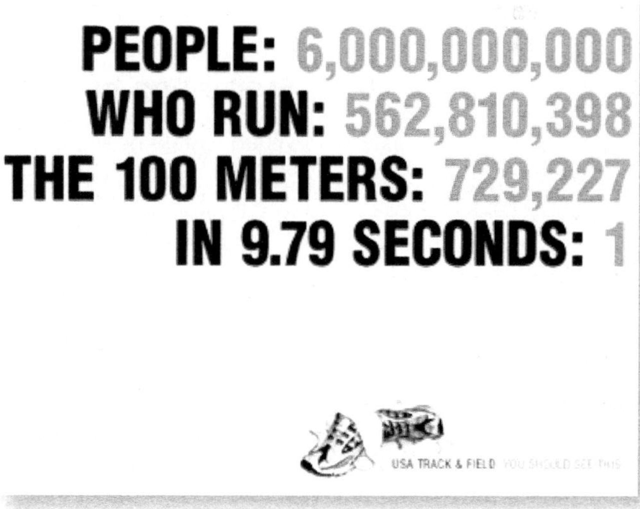

Image 9.10

The details are what made this student-designed ad interesting. When you run the numbers you see why the fastest person in the world is so special.

Sticks and stones may break my bones, but words will break my heart.

She's young, innocent, and defenseless. She values your opinion and hears everything you say. Your words have the power to make her day or break her heart.

Children who are emotionally abused often grow up with low self-esteem and chronic feelings of worthlessness, which may lead to teen pregnancy, substance abuse, or even suicide. Is that what you want for your little girl?

Get the help you need today, call 1-800-4-A-CHILD.

Show them they matter.
www.preventchildabuse.com

Image 9.11

This student took a familiar childhood rhyme and added a powerful message about child abuse.

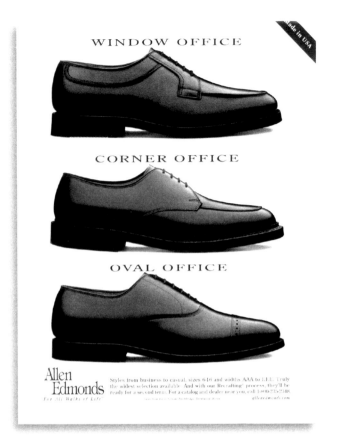

WINDOW OFFICE

CORNER OFFICE

OVAL OFFICE

Allen Edmonds
For All Walks of Life

Styles from business to casual, sizes 6-16 and widths AAA to EEE. Truly the widest selection available. And with our Recrafting process, they'll be ready for a second term. For a catalog and dealer near you, call 1-800-235-2348

allenedmonds.com

Image 9.12

This is one of a long-running series from Allen Edmonds that used parallel construction headlines and the slogan "For all walks of life."

Evaluating headlines

When writing headlines, you're faced with the same dilemma as with the overall concept. Do you write one that looks good in your portfolio or one that works hard at selling something? Once again, the answer is . . . that depends. Just as most people think they are experts on taglines, even more have an opinion on headlines. Some like straightforward news headlines since there's no mistaking the message. Others like obscure references that hook a select group and leave the rest scratching their heads. Still others think silly puns are the height of creativity, while others just groan.

While there are infinite degrees of cleverness and clarity, our advice is:

If you can't be clever, be clear.

In other words, if you can't come up with at least one different, twisted, unusual, or interesting headline, then say it straight and always keep in mind the visual is there to work with the headline, not to just sit above a caption.

Headline Checklist

Before you settle on one headline, run through the following guidelines. Your headline doesn't have to meet all these criteria, but it should cover some of them.

1. Let your headline sit for a while. Do you still love it the morning after? (Or do you slap your head and say, "What was I thinking?")

2. Does your headline work with the visual, or is it just a caption or, worse, completely irrelevant?

3. In your vision of the layout, does the headline look important? Is it readable? Does it have the proper proximity to the visual and body copy?

4. Can you do the "billboard test" and still have a concept that makes sense?

5. Does your headline appeal to the reader's self-interest?

6. Does your headline pull readers into the body copy?

7. Be honest. Is this the best you can do? Or can you start round two or three or four to come up with a list of great headlines?

8. Do not use a strong subhead to "explain" a weak headline. Use a strong headline, and you might not need a subhead. (Remember, less is more.)

9. Be careful with puns. There's a reason they're called the lowest form of comedy. Don't be cute just for the sake of cuteness. If a pun has a purpose, try it. Otherwise, find a more clever way to say it.

10. Think campaigns. How are you going to follow up that killer headline? Will your next five ads be just as good?

Image 9.13

Note the punctuation in the headline. While the FDA may argue that this is possibly the worst thing you could eat, the student who wrote this ad claims that a Hardee's Thickburger is both good *and* for you.

Words of Wisdom

"I've done as many as 19 drafts on a single piece of copy. I wrote 37 headlines for Sears Roebuck last week and I think I got three good enough to submit." [7]

—David Ogilvy

Subheads

As you would expect, the subhead is usually underneath the headline. Sometimes it immediately follows the headline, as if to say, "What we *really* mean is . . ." Other times subheads are used to separate long copy blocks or introduce new thoughts in an ad. In this context they are sometimes called "breakers."

Image 9.14

This headline is split between two photos, which form the whole picture. "Performance Art" takes on a different meaning when used in this treatment.

Don't waste any more time, money and energy traveling to meetings. With GoToMeeting you can hold unlimited online meetings with anyone, anywhere — right from your desk. Whether you need to present, demonstrate, collaborate or train, GoToMeeting makes it easy. Spend less time on the road and more time improving the way you do business. Do more and travel less with GoToMeeting.

Try GoToMeeting FREE for 30 days.

Start now! Visit GoToMeeting.com and use the promo code: ad

Image 9.15

Using parallel construction, this headline states a direct benefit and illustrates both ideas with a straightforward use of photography.

Image 9.16

How do you promote a clothing-optional resort in a tasteful way? By twisting the traditional meanings of button and suit.

Most of our guests wear one-button suits

Playa Naturel. 80km and 25 years south of Cancun. Do more with less.
www.playanaturel.com

Image 9.17

Sort of a pun. Sort of a twist. Sort of a double meaning. Sort of a waste of time, since the client rejected it.

The four main purposes of a subhead are:

- Clarify the headline.

- Reinforce the main idea stated in the headline.

- Break up large copy blocks.

- Lead you into the body copy.

Subhead traps

Too often subheads are used to "explain" the headline. You may feel the headline is too weak or the reader won't get it. So you add a straight line so there's no mistaking the benefit. Many times this is done to convince a skeptical client that your risky ad concept really is a serious selling effort. We don't like subheads used this way for two reasons: (a) Why write a weak headline and prop it up with a subhead? Write a strong headline in the first place; and (b) use as few words as possible to convey your message. Adding a subhead can more than double the copy clutter in an ad.

Another subhead trap: Don't use the subhead to introduce a new, separate idea from the headline. Going back to our Ogilvy headline, you don't want to follow that beautiful headline with a subhead that says, "What's more, the new Rolls-Royce offers the highest horsepower of any luxury car."

Image 9.18

The split headline in this student-designed ad positions the product. The visual conveys speed and power, resonating with guys who might be interested in "picking up girls," but the second part of the headline changes the meaning with "taking them to soccer practice."

Preheads

This is also called the overline. Whatever you call it, it precedes the headline. You can use preheads for a number of reasons, but the four most common are:

- Set up the headline.

- Define the audience.

- Identify the advertiser.

- Identify an ad in a series.

As with subheads, decide if the prehead is needed to explain the headline. If so, rethink the headline, and you may not need the prehead. In many cases, the prehead asks a question that the headline answers or starts a thought completed by the headline. In these cases, you could consider that prehead as an integral part of the headline.

Image 9.19

This irreverent headline/subhead combo is perfect for The Onion, *with a curious hook to start and an irreverent close.*

Why Have a Tagline?

We call them taglines, but you could also say they're slogans, signature lines, or theme lines. Usually, they are the catchphrases that appear after the logo in a print ad or at the end of the commercial, and, in most cases, they are very forgettable. However, if they're done right, taglines can be the most important element of a campaign. Some clients expect too much from a tagline. They don't want a little blurb to sneak under their logo. They demand a "statement" that (a) defines the company, (b) positions the product, (c) denigrates the competition, (d) reassures the stockholders, and (e) will be approved by the CEO's wife. The more objectives a tagline tries to achieve, the more generic it becomes. When a tagline becomes generic, you can put it under any logo with negligible effect. Too many taglines are written by committees and tested by management panels. They're cobbled together with a few key words that by themselves mean nothing but, when used in a composite slogan, become completely irrelevant. Before you start cranking out slogans, you have to ask the client, "What's the One Thing you want to say?" Do you want to convey a general attitude or tone? Do you want something specific about the products? Do you want something relating to your customers? Just what the heck do you want? George Felton sums it up pretty well in *Advertising: Concept and Copy:* "Slogans . . . had better do more than just be clever . . . they need to be smart."[8] The smart taglines stick with you years after they first appear. They become part of the popular culture and define their place in time as well as the brand.

According to *Advertising Age,* these are the top 10 slogans of the 20th century:

1. "A diamond is forever" (De Beers)

2. "Just do it" (Nike)

3. "The pause that refreshes" (Coca-Cola)

4. "Tastes great, less filling" (Miller Lite)

5. "We try harder" (Avis)

6. "Good to the last drop" (Maxwell House)

7. "Breakfast of champions" (Wheaties)

8. "Does she . . . or doesn't she?" (Clairol)

9. "When it rains it pours" (Morton Salt)

10. "Where's the beef?" (Wendy's)[9]

Ad Story

Get Mad . . . and Watch the Ideas Come
"A client once said to Leo Burnett (the man), 'If you're going to have a good idea, have it now.' Fear gets the gods of inspiration moving. Anger has always worked for me, too.

"A few years ago, Leo Burnett (the agency) was one step away from losing the Allstate insurance account. We'd had it for nearly 50 years. Twenty teams had tried and failed to come up with the answer. We had one last chance.

"Allstate was under intense competitive pressure. Direct sellers had turned car insurance into a commodity—'All insurance is the same,' they crowed, 'so buy the cheapest!' They were outspending Allstate by a huge margin. We had to take back the conversation. And the fact is, Allstate is different. They do things for their customers that other companies don't.

"It was Labor Day weekend when inspiration struck. I thought about those rival insurance companies. I thought about all the ways Allstate put people in Good Hands. Things those other companies didn't do. And I got mad. In a fit of anger, I started to write.

"Seven scripts later, I had a campaign. And three little words that made all the difference: 'That's Allstate's stand.' Because Allstate took real stands: 'You should never be alone.' 'Safe drivers cost everybody less. They should pay less.' 'Trouble never takes a holiday. Neither should your insurance.' 'Crime doesn't pay. Neither should you.' It wasn't a funny campaign, like some in the category. It was one true to the honest, straightforward brand character of Allstate.

"I still remember the hush that fell over the room after I finished presenting. The head client spoke first. She said, 'I love it . . . but do you have to say "That's Allstate's stand?"' I said, 'Yes, because then you won't water it down. You won't call something a stand when it isn't.'

"Casting the campaign was fun. As I was writing the scripts, I had Dennis Haysbert in mind. I'd loved his portrayal of President David Palmer in the TV series '24.' But most people didn't know him. So we had a casting session with other actors and [an] actress who'd played the President of the United States in film and on TV. After much discussion, I got my way. I've never thought of Dennis as a spokesperson, though. I call him Allstate's 'third-party advocate.' It's a subtle point, but it gives Allstate's work honesty and strength.

"Five years later, Leo Burnett and Allstate are going strong. The business is doing well; the campaign has been adapted to embrace home insurance, motorcycle insurance, teen driving, life insurance, retirement, sports sponsorships . . . and a host of other subjects. We celebrated that 50th anniversary together. Whew."[10]

—Jeanie Caggiano
Vice President, Executive Creative
Director, *Leo Burnett,* Chicago

The primary purpose of a tagline is to establish or reinforce the brand name. To do this, the tagline should do the following:

Provide continuity for a campaign: A tagline may be the only common component of a multimedia campaign. It can also be the link between campaigns with very different looks. A good tagline transcends changes in campaign strategy. No matter what BMW is doing with their ads, the cars are always "The Ultimate Driving Machines."

Crystallize the One Thing associated with the brand or product: Whether it's staking out a position or implying an abstract attitude, the slogan is an extension of the brand name. When you can mention a brand name and someone else

Small but tough. Polo.

Image 9.20

VW's Polo has been a hot seller in Europe and was launched in the United States with a decidedly American look. The tagline is short and simple, while the visual justifies the claim.

quotes the slogan, you know you've got something. Going back to concepts discussed in earlier chapters, the tagline can help foster *awareness* and *interest* of a brand or product. A few well-chosen words can define the brand, separate it from the competition, and anchor it in the reader/viewer's brain. Think of M&M's candies that "melt in your mouth, not in your hand." It's not only a statement of a real product benefit; nobody else can say this. A good tagline increases your creative freedom. When the message ends with "Only in a Jeep," you can have a lot more fun with the content.

How to Write More Effective Taglines

The following are a few tips and techniques for writing better taglines. Of course, not every tagline is going to possess all these traits (unless you find the successor to "Just do it"). These guidelines are offered to help you evaluate your taglines before you submit them to the client.

Keep it short and simple: VW came up with "Drivers wanted" a few years back because it stuck in the mind better than their older slogan, "It's not a car. It's a Volkswagen." After a decade of "Drivers" they came out with "Das Auto" (The Car), which may have taken German simplicity a little too far. Not to be outdone for brevity, Best Buy came up with "You, Happier." The goal is not to keep the word count to two or fewer or to make something so obscure you need another slogan to define it. However, when you develop a slogan, think of billboards—no more than six words. Three words is even better. As Shakespeare said, "Brevity is the soul of wit." Just make sure your witticism makes sense.

Think jingle: Even if you never put your tagline to music, picture it in a TV commercial. You can use the old tricks of rhythm, rhyme, and alliteration to make it more memorable. For example, no one over 40 can forget "Winston tastes good like a cigarette should," even though cigarette advertising on TV ended in 1971. A modern example: Kay Jewelers says, "Every kiss begins with Kay."

Try to differentiate the brand: Can you come up with a simple way to separate yourself from the competition? Visa used to say they're "Everywhere you want to be," implying that American Express and MasterCard were not. They followed that with "Life takes Visa," which not only gets the product's name in the slogan; it also implies that the card is universally accepted. Dodge used to say, "Grab life by the horns," which only made sense if it was paired with their Ram logo. They shortened it to "Grab life," which worked a little better with their other vehicles. The ideal slogan can't be used by any other brand. Altoids established themselves as the "Curiously Strong Mint" so well they could extend the tagline to other products such as the "Curiously Strong Sour."

If you have to be generic, go global: Many brands use what could be called generic slogans. They're positive and easy to remember, and they can be translated into most languages without changing their meanings. When they stand alone, these slogans could work for just about anyone. The difference is they're supported by millions of dollars of advertising and promotion. So if Joe's Burger Shack says, "I'm lovin' it," no one notices. When McDonald's does it, it becomes major marketing news. If you can remember the innocuous slogans for most mass-marketed package goods, it's only because they've been beaten into your brain through relentless advertising.

Play with words: A tagline can be more memorable if you take a common expression and twist it just enough to get attention. Chrysler used to promote their pre-owned cars as "Brand Spankin' Used." Years ago Panasonic promoted the ergonomics of their home electronics with "So advanced, it's simple." Sometimes you can give your slogan a double meaning. For example, a drug company targeted doctors with "Healthy concern for your practice," indicating that the drug company was successful and cared about their customers.

Don't confuse or mislead: In the effort to be creative, some writers forget that the rest of the world is not as clever as they are. An obscure one-word tagline could be misunderstood or, worse, ignored.

Justify your choices: Everyone is an expert on taglines. So when you submit a list to the client, make sure everyone knows the parameters you were given. Too often the rules change after you've received the initial game plan.

Image 9.21

A GM Hispanic ad campaign highlighted leadership in safety, innovation, and customer satisfaction. Unlike other mainstream campaigns targeted to Latinos, the corporate slogan changed to fit the market.

Image 9.22

Whether it's used as a headline or a tagline, the alliteration and the jingle in TV commercials makes "Every kiss begins with Kay" memorable.

Creating Taglines

Writing taglines is a lot like developing whole concepts. Start with the One Thing. Then say it straight. From there you can veer off in several directions, each with a list of possible slogans. Figure 9.2 illustrates a brief template for a business-to-business client, although this technique works for any product or service.

As you've probably noted, the majority of the taglines in Figure 9.2 stink. Most of the time, you'll start with a generic slogan, but as you keep working, you'll branch out. You can have as many branches as you'd like. Don't worry if some of your slogans don't fit a defined category—just keep writing.

FIGURE 9.2   *Creative Tree for Taglines*

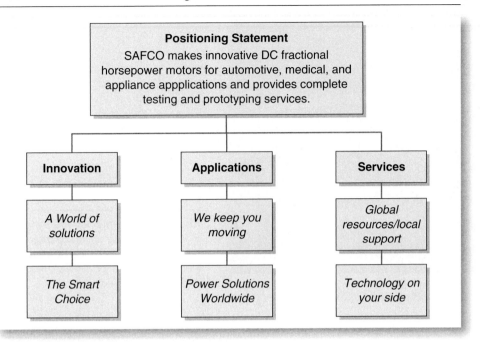

Don't start editing until you get a huge list. Then weed out the obvious stinkers. Keep refining your list until you have a group of taglines you can live with. So you might come up with something a little better, such as:

- The Power of Innovation

- Solutions in Motion

- We Power Your Ideas

OK, they're still not "Just do it," but don't stop trying. Keep sending out branches. You'll find one that works as long as it stays true to the values at the base of the tree.

Taglines Need Your Support

Even "Just do it" would not have made much sense if it had been launched in a campaign that highlighted the features and benefits of Nike shoes. It had to be paired with people dedicated to exercise. That synergy made it magic. That's why writing taglines can be so pointless. They're usually evaluated by a committee in a vacuum, without the benefit of massive ad support or even a connection to the campaign. Once a slogan becomes established, you can vary the images and copy in the ads, but they have to be there when that tagline is introduced. Once it's established in the consumer's mind, it becomes part of the brand, transcending the creative execution that may change from year to year.

Image 9.23

A modern take on the classic Rolls-Royce headline. In this case Hyundai states, "If the cabin were any quieter, you might begin to wonder where we hid all the books"—a much more engaging method than saying "it's as quiet as a library."

CARPE MOUNTAINUM.

AN AMERICAN R VOLUTION

colorado AVAILABLE 220-HP VORTEC™ I-5 WITH MORE HORSEPOWER THAN ANY V6* | EXCLUSIVE AUTOMATIC LOCKING | REAR DIFFERENTIAL* | SKID PLATE | EVERYTHING'S BIGGER IN THE ALL-NEW CHEVY™ COLORADO™ Z71*

Image 9.24

Chevy replaced their long-running "Like a Rock" tagline by declaring they were "An American Revolution." The new slogan was used for all Chevrolet truck and car advertising.

Who's Who?

Morris Hite may well be the most significant figure in the evolution of advertising in the Southwest. He grew TracyLocke from a small Dallas-based advertising agency into a communications empire that included the Southwest's largest advertising agency, one of the country's five largest marketing research companies, a major public relations company, and an agency for smaller clients. (See, you don't have to be a copywriter to offer words of wisdom.)

Founder of Ogilvy & Mather, **David Ogilvy** was, first and foremost, a copywriter. One of the pioneers of image advertising, Ogilvy also wrote two best sellers, *Confessions of an Advertising Man* and *Ogilvy on Advertising*. He was one of the most eloquent and influential voices in advertising and today is still one of the most quotable.

Keith Reinhard, now Chairman Emeritus of DDB Worldwide, is credited for giving birth to the Hamburglar and other residents of McDonaldland when he was a working copywriter. Other McDonald's classics penned by Reinhard include "You Deserve a Break Today" and "Two-all-beef-patties-special-sauce-lettuce-cheese-pickles-onions-on-a-sesame-seed-bun." He also created "Like a good neighbor, State Farm is there." Under his creative direction, his agency produced award-winning work for Volkswagen, Frito-Lay, Dell Computer, and many others.

Shirley Polykoff was a pioneer for women in advertising and outstanding creative talent. She started out in advertising as a teenager working for *Harper's Bazaar*. After a career in retail copywriting, she took over the Clairol account at Foote, Cone & Belding, where she penned the classic "Does she . . . or doesn't she?" Polykoff reached the position of executive vice president and creative director at FCB and left to found her own successful agency.

Exercises

1. Chocolate Coke

Here's the scenario: your team is on the Coca-Cola account at Leo Burnett. You are all gathered in the conference room for a major announcement. The client is ready to introduce a new product and wants to hear some campaign ideas to consider. Typically, this client will consider five ideas before deciding on one to move forward. Every teams is given the task to come up with five ideas each. As always, it's a very big deal to be the team that comes up with the chosen idea.

- The announcement: Coca-Cola has decided to add chocolate to its line of flavored Cokes, cherry and vanilla. However, the client (and the creative team) chokes on the name Chocolate Coke. It's your job to dream up a better name.

- Brainstorm a huge list of possible names. Together pick the five top names.

- Individually create a tagline for each name. Knowing what you do about the Coke brand and imagining the possibilities for Chocolate Coke, find the One Thing and then use the Creative Tree to move forward. Good luck.

Adapted from an exercise shared by Roy Winegar, PhD, Assistant Professor, Grand Valley State University.

2. Brainstorming Cubed

This time you need to enlist the help of your teacher. Tell him or her you need a cube—a very particular cube. It's a brainstorming cube. Like every cube, it will have six sides. In addition, this cube has one of the following written on each side: Describe it. Associate it. Compare it. Analyze it. Apply it. Argue for/against it.

- Pick a topic or product or service—say, hot tamales.

- Take the cube and toss it to a classmate. The first person that catches it looks at whichever side is facing up, reads it out loud, and then instantly responds with a word related to what they read. And example might be: "Associate it. Movies."

- Then the cube gets tossed to another person. "Describe it. Wrapped in corn husks." Another toss. "Compare it. Hotter than Skittles." It flies all over the room, sometimes to a repeat person but eventually to everyone in the class. As the thoughts/ideas are shouted out, persuade your teacher to write them on the board. It's very fast, and all ideas count.

- When you're done you'll have a long list on the board that you can then go back and sort through. Sometimes you'll find new angles. Sometimes you'll find patterns. Sometimes you'll find thoughts that can be combined. You almost always get a broader range of ideas.

- It's a quick technique that allows you to look at your topic from six different perspectives. That may reveal new strategic connections and the One Thing and will lead to the perfect campaign.

- Now, individually, write a headline or tagline related to each statement. Along the way, you just might find the right headline or tagline.

Adapted from an exercise shared by Sheri Broyles, PhD, Associate Professor, University of North Texas.

(Continued)

(Continued)

3. Energy Drink

This exercise is designed to help you see the synergy between copy and art/words and visuals.

- As a group brainstorm a list of emotions or feelings that you could experience from consuming a brand new energy drink.

- Now, split into two teams with a captain for each team.

- Discuss what will be more effective in communications . . . communicating with visuals or with words.

- One team will defend words and other visuals.

- Each team reviews the list of emotions and feelings, and independently selects the two emotions that feel the most marketable.

- The "words" team write a headline for each of their two emotions. The "visuals" team sketch out two simple visuals expressing the two emotions they chose.

- Now each team tries to guess the other team's pair of emotions. See if any of the headlines and visuals match-up.

- Finish with a discussion of the power of words and visuals and the importance of the synergy between headlines and visuals.

Adapted from an exercise shared by Mike Cissne, Group Leader, Production, Bader Rutter.

Notes

1. David Ogilvy, *Confessions of an Advertising Man* (New York: Ballantine Books, 1971), p. 92.

2. Morris Hite, *Adman: Morris Hite's Methods for Winning the Ad Game* (Dallas, TX: E-Heart Press, 1998), p. 33.

3. Quoted in Philip Ward Burton, *Advertising Copywriting* (Lincolnwood, IL: NTC Business Books, 1991), p. 54.

4. Stuart Elliott, "Ads That Soothe When Banks Are Failing," *The New York Times,* October 7, 2008, p. B10.

5. George Felton, *Advertising: Concept and Copy* (Englewood Cliffs, NJ: Prentice Hall, Inc., 1993), p. 93.

6. Douglas Atkin, *The Culting of Brands: When Consumers Become True Believers* (New York: Portfolio, 2004), p. 137.

7. Quoted in Denis Higgins, *The Art of Writing Advertising: Conversations With Masters of the Craft: William Bernbach, George Gribbin, Rosser Reeves, David Ogilvy, Leo Burnett* (New York: McGraw-Hill, 2003), p. 92.

8. George Felton, *Advertising: Concept and Copy* (New York: W. W. Norton, 2006), p. 99.

9. "Top 10 Slogans of the Century," *Advertising Age,* March 29, 1999, http://adage.com/century/slogans.html (accessed June 15, 2005).

10. Jeanie Caggiano, Ad Story: *Get Mad . . . and Watch the Ideas Come,* February 2009.

Chapter 10

Body Copy

As you've seen in many of the examples in previous chapters, not all ads have body copy or any copy. In fact, many people believe that readers won't read copy in ads and the best we can do is get them to remember a brand name. That may be true, but a good creative person needs to know how to write body copy.

Who Needs Body Copy?

You'll never know when you'll need it

Versatility is one of the keys to survival in the creative field, especially in a tight job market. You might write a cool tagline now and then, but what happens when the client wants a campaign with a series of 200-word spread ads? You should know how to write all varieties of copy well. If you can't write that well, you should at least be able to recognize and respond to good writing from others.

Ads aren't the only place you'll need copy

As we'll discuss a little later, there are many reasons to include copy in advertising. But there are so many other varieties of marketing communication where good writing skills are just as important:

Web content: An ad with one line of copy may drive a reader to a Web site that's chock full of copy. Writing copy for the Web has its special rules, but a good portion of it is traditional advertising writing. The objectives are the same as with print ads: grab readers, hold their attention, persuade them to consider your product, and tell them how to get it.

Collateral: Your ad may have only one line that says, "Send for a free brochure." Who's going to write that free brochure? Hundreds of millions of sell sheets, catalogs, brochures, flyers, spec sheets, magazine inserts, and other promotional items are printed every year. Somebody's got to write 'em all.

Words of Wisdom

"I have always believed that writing advertisements is the second most profitable form of writing. The first, of course, is ransom notes." [1]

—Phil Dusenberry

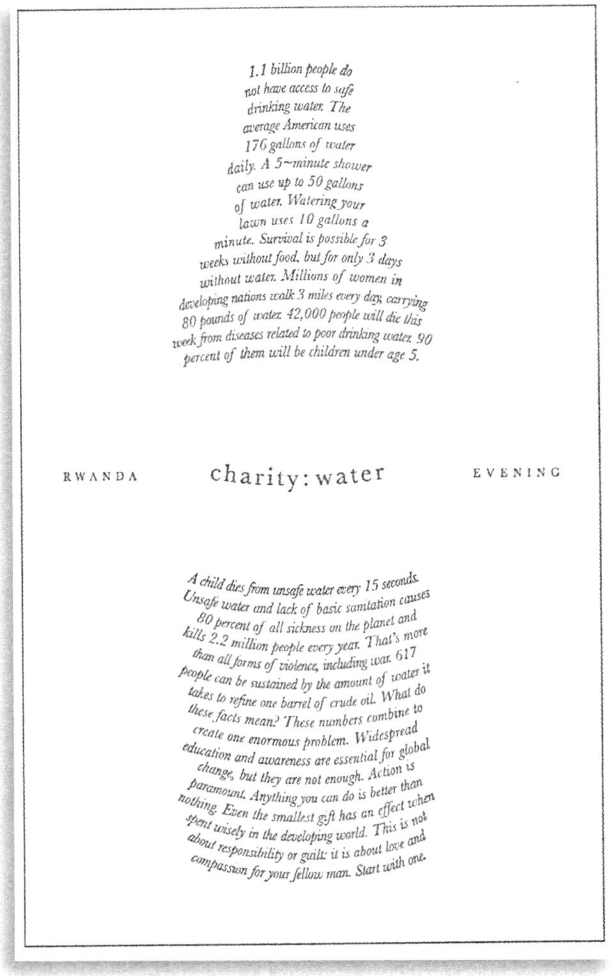
1.1 billion people do not have access to safe drinking water. The average American uses 176 gallons of water daily. A 5~minute shower can use up to 50 gallons of water. Watering your lawn uses 10 gallons a minute. Survival is possible for 3 weeks without food, but for only 3 days without water. Millions of women in developing nations walk 3 miles every day, carrying 80 pounds of water. 42,000 people will die this week from diseases related to poor drinking water. 90 percent of them will be children under age 5.
RWANDA
charity: water
EVENING
A child dies from unsafe water every 15 seconds. Unsafe water and lack of basic sanitation causes 80 percent of all sickness on the planet and kills 2.2 million people every year. That's more than all forms of violence, including war. 617 people can be sustained by the amount of water it takes to refine one barrel of crude oil. What do these facts mean? These numbers combine to create one enormous problem. Widespread education and awareness are essential for global change, but they are not enough. Action is paramount. Anything you can do is better than nothing. Even the smallest gift has an effect when spent wisely in the developing world. This is not about responsibility or guilt: it is about love and compassion for your fellow man. Start with one.

Image 10.1

What's missing? Here's a smart layout with compelling copy but no information on how to take action. While the use of copy to shape the One Thing is highly strategic, Charity Water can't afford this missed opportunity.

Direct mail: What makes you open a piece of junk mail? Somebody wrote something that caught your eye. Once you open it, you want to know more. Maybe it's a letter, a brochure, or some other piece of information. Somebody wrote that too.

Reports, plans books, proposals: Who says creative writing has to be limited to promotional material? Clients appreciate a well-written, crisply edited proposal or plans book. In fact, any manager would rather read something that quickly gets to the point and doesn't waste his or her valuable time. You can take entire courses on business writing, and judging by some documents we've read, not enough people have taken these courses. Using some of the writing skills we'll discuss here will help make all your business writing better, not just ad copy.

What you need to know... and use

No matter the length or content of the body copy, you should keep a few basic concepts in mind. These apply to advertising, collateral, business documents, and basically any commercial form of writing:

1. Don't write to impress—write to persuade.
2. What you say is more important than how you say it.
3. Remember the rules of English but don't feel forced to use them.
4. Write to the individual, not the masses.

Why do we need copy in ads?

Some ads just work better with copy. Here are a few reasons why:

Considered purchase: Whether it's an industrial flow control valve or a power drill for the homeowner, people want to know more about the product than its brand name. Go back to the foundations of the project and find out how the product features align with the wants and needs of the intended buyer. Prioritize them and string them together with style. That's body copy.

Differentiate products: Why should a reader believe a Hyundai Genesis is a better value than a BMW 3 Series? Because the headline says it is or because the copy details independent testing that shows the Hyundai Genesis is faster, corners better, and overall performs better than the more expensive import? Sometimes you have to lay out the facts to make your case.

Multiple features: We hammer that One Thing into your brain. But sometimes there's more than one thing to talk about. You may lead with the main point but then bring in other key benefits to build a more persuasive case for the product. If you don't have the luxury of producing single-feature ads, you may have to find a way to weave several key points into the copy.

Difficult, complicated or controversial subjects: If you want to change people's minds or have them do something difficult, a catchy slogan isn't enough. For example, a recent antidrug ad tells parents who smoked pot in their youth not to feel like hypocrites when they talk to their kids about drugs. That's much more effective than "Just say no."

The Case for Long Copy

Writing good long-copy ads (200 words or more) is a fast-dying art. Reason 1: It's assumed no one reads ads, so why bother? Reason 2: No one knows how to write long copy well enough to hold a reader's interest . . . so see reason one.

Images 10.2, 10.3

These ads for Medical City Cancer Centers offer hope through an empowering timeline of life, which reinforces their tagline: "Specialists. In life." The timeline comes to life as bullets threaded together by a visual intrinsically related to the story of each person, and that's what makes these testimonials sing.

Be honest. Even in textbooks that showcase the greatest ads ever written, do you actually read the copy? You probably don't even read the captions if they're more than five lines long. Before television shortened our attention span to 30 seconds and the Internet cut that to 2 seconds, magazine and newspaper ads had enough copy for a beginning, a middle, and an end. We could feature many wonderful classic ads that read like well-crafted short stories, so damn persuasive that even we want to run out and buy the product. But showing these great ads from another age won't be of much value if your creative solution is a three-word headline plus logo.

When we look at ads from the 1920s through the 1950s, we're amazed at the craftsmanship. The best ads had a rhythm and flow that sucked the readers in, held their attention, and, in the end, left them convinced that the right brand of baked beans or laundry soap could improve their lives. Can you imagine a 400-word ad today for any kind of commodity package good like detergent, cereal, coffee, cigarettes, or whisky?

People will read a long-copy ad if they have a reason. John Caples said, "Don't be afraid of long copy. If your ad is interesting, people will be hungry for all the copy you can give them. If the ad is dull, short copy won't save it."[2]

The key to writing copy that's read, long or short, is to involve the reader. If the ad holds no reason to read on, don't expect anyone to get past a headline or visual.

THERE'S BEEN A LOT OF TALK about the environment lately. But out on Chesapeake Bay, sailing around on a vintage skipjack, a group of school kids are learning that when it comes to the environment, actions speak louder than words.

Myrtha Allen, Environmental Sciences teacher at P.S. 405, Baltimore, explains, "Most of my kids are city born and bred. They live in apartments, they get their milk in cartons, their eggs in those styrofoam containers. They were about as interested in the environment as they are in homework." She smiles at a nearby eight-year-old. "And who can blame them? Some of them, like Jawan here, had never even seen a live fish before."

That's where the Chesapeake Bay Foundation stepped in. Since 1966, when it started in Annapolis, Maryland, with a rented fishing trawler and little else, the Foundation has taken more than 300,000 students out into the Bay to experience the environment first hand. And at the same time making them aware of how important their contribution is to the future of the planet.

Myrtha puts it simply. "To get these kids wanting to clean up the world, we've got to get their hands dirty."

And they do. They get very dirty.

"Oh yeah," chuckles Myrtha, "we do it all. Once we threw a net in just to see what we'd get. When we pulled it up, sure enough there were the milk cartons, the soda cans, the egg containers. And flapping around in the middle of it all was this big, cranky striped bass. You should've seen their faces.

"We took 20 little consumers out on a boat that day. We came back with 20 budding environmentalists."

At Toyota, we're proud that through the support we give to the Foundation more kids like Jawan will be able to experience our fragile environment first hand. And hopefully start playing an active part in preserving it.

Is the program working? "These kids are organizing neighborhood recycling drives, they're writing letters to Senators. Take a look at these posters some of my students have been doing.

The classroom walls are alive with crayon and pencil. Bright orange crabs. Smiling oysters. Families of ducks.

And one poster that stops everyone. It's of a smiling little boy holding hands with a big striped bass. And boldly scrawled above both their heads is one word: "Brothers".

And it's signed by Jawan. Age eight.

TOYOTA
INVESTING IN THE INDIVIDUAL

"IT WAS THE FIRST FISH Jawan had seen that WASN'T SURROUNDED by french fries."
MYRTHA ALLEN, Teacher

Image 10.4

One of a long series of corporate ads for Toyota. This one talked about Toyota's involvement in environmental education for children in Baltimore. It's a story that can't be told in 25 words or less.

The Story Continues...on the Web

Long copy isn't dead. A lot of it just moved to the Internet. The purpose of many ads is to drive readers to a Web site. There they can read to their hearts' content unlike having advertising that interrupts their magazine article. Or they can download and print the copy for future reference. Beyond print, the Internet can show video and animation, gather information, and do a lot of tricks you'd never get from a magazine ad. Plus it multiplies the impact of the message and, because the reader makes a conscious effort to contact the site, streamlines the awareness-to-action process. Remember IMC? This is a big part of it. We'll discuss writing for the Web in more detail in later chapters. The principles of writing good, readable print copy apply to the Web, with a few refinements:

1. As with newspaper editorial writing, remember who, what, where, when, and why in the lead paragraph. You may change the headline and lead paragraphs several times to keep Web content fresh, while the rest of the text remains the same.

2. As with newspaper editorials, there is a "top of the fold" space that viewers look to first. If you want higher readership, your Web content and ads should be toward the top of the Web page.

3. Keep it brief and easy to read, with bullets and callouts to relieve eye fatigue.

4. Don't use too many links in the text since they draw viewers away from your copy.

5. Make it easy to download and print. Many people would rather print copy and read it at their leisure than scroll down a computer screen.

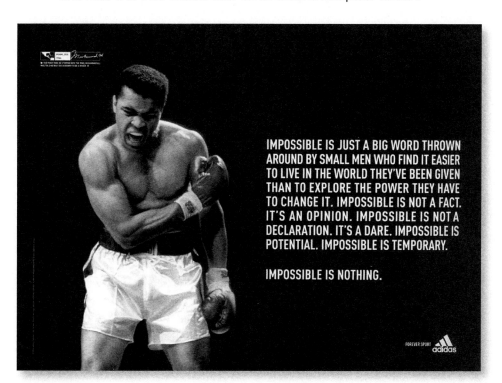

IMPOSSIBLE IS JUST A BIG WORD THROWN AROUND BY SMALL MEN WHO FIND IT EASIER TO LIVE IN THE WORLD THEY'VE BEEN GIVEN THAN TO EXPLORE THE POWER THEY HAVE TO CHANGE IT. IMPOSSIBLE IS NOT A FACT. IT'S AN OPINION. IMPOSSIBLE IS NOT A DECLARATION. IT'S A DARE. IMPOSSIBLE IS POTENTIAL. IMPOSSIBLE IS TEMPORARY.

IMPOSSIBLE IS NOTHING.

FOREVER SPORT adidas

Image 10.5

It's not a mistake that this copy is all caps; nor is the choice of the spokesperson accidental. Its powerfully persuasive start and rhythmic end pack a punch.

Ad Story

**YOU WERE BORN
A DAUGHTER.
YOU LOOKED UP TO
YOUR MOTHER.
YOU LOOKED UP TO
YOUR FATHER.**

**YOU LOOKED UP AT
EVERYONE.
YOU WANTED TO BE
A PRINCESS.
YOU THOUGHT YOU
WERE A PRINCESS.**

Eight Pages and No Product: Who Says Long Copy Doesn't Sell?

When they developed Nike's "Empathy" campaign for women, Janet Champ (copy) and Charlotte Moore (art) decided to ignore the research and simply "talk to women as human beings." The campaign won a Kelly Award, and the phones at Nike didn't stop ringing for months. Janet Champ told us: "We used only one model. All the others were real people from a casting house in Texas. We were tired of being hemmed in to two or four pages. It bothered us that the men got big budgets. We said if we're going to be stuck with print, let's do the longest ad we can. Charlotte had this idea—let's write a woman's life. So I wrote it too long and had to cut it in half. I took it to Nike and I got all choked up while reading it. Charlotte cried. Nike cried. Then they said, 'Can you do it on a run of the press (magazine stock)?' We said, 'No, absolutely not.' Finally, they said OK. It was a hard sell because of the length (eight pages) and no product. Everyone went crazy once it ran. There were 500,000 letters and calls to the agency and Nike. This man whose wife suffered from depression for years called and said he showed the ad to his wife and she cried and said, 'This is me.' And then she started to run again."[4]

—Janet Champ
Former Creative Director, *Wieden + Kennedy,* Portland

Writing Structure

Types of copy

Knowing the various types of ad copy will never be as important as knowing how to write a good sentence. However, it can be useful to recognize several copy styles and know when to use them.

The story: This is also called "traditional" copy and features three main components: a beginning, a middle, and an end. Usually the beginning establishes the theme, makes a promise, plays off the headline, and in general sets up the ad. The middle is typically the sales pitch, with reasons why you should consider the product or service. The end is the summary and call to action. It wraps up the selling argument and encourages the reader to do something. A well-crafted story does not have to be a long-copy ad. But it should flow smoothly . . . as if you were telling a story that has a point.

Bullet points: Many clients will say, "No one has time to read copy. Just list the key points." In many cases, this is just fine, especially if you can't think of One Thing to say and need to list a lot of features. Usually, the points are prioritized by the importance of selling features, with the most important always going first. Too many times, the writer and client can't decide what's important, so they list everything and hope the reader will find something he or she likes.

You'll see a lot of bullet-point copy in retail newspaper ads, business-to-business magazines, and direct mail. This technique has sort of a "down and dirty" look, so it's usually not appropriate for a high-quality or brand image promotion. In addition, a long list of short bullet points takes up more real estate than a few well-written sentences in paragraph format. So if saving space is your only justification for using bullet points, measure carefully and reconsider.

One technique that can be very effective is a mix of traditional sentences and bullet points. The bullets highlight key points, and when done correctly, these draw the reader's eye to the most important selling messages.

One liner: Sometimes the headline is the only copy in the ad. Other times the headline and visual work together to convey the main message, and a single copy line adds additional information. If you don't have to explain a lot about the product, need to direct readers to a Web site for more detailed information, or just want to promote a brand image, one liners (or no copy at all) work just fine.

Writing Style

Advertising is not English

In other classes, you were told to write essays and reports with an assigned number of words, paragraphs, or pages. These were graded for spelling, composition, vocabulary, and comprehension. Your teachers were looking not for tight, get-right-to-the-point persuasion but rather for how you could expand a one-sentence idea into a four-page paper.

In advertising classes and in the real world, your writing will be evaluated on how well you communicate. Period. Using real words. In the way real people talk. Your writing must attract a jaded reader and hook him or her in the brain. You are appealing to a consumer's wants and needs. Not to teachers who get paid to grade papers by the pound. As Shakespeare said, brevity is the soul of wit. Good advertising is both witty and brief. Now, this doesn't mean you can completely ignore grammar and spelling. A copywriter can dress like a bum, but you can't write sloppily. Even though you may shatter a few rules of English grammar, the copy should be tight, easy to read, and clearly understood. Your copy style should be tailored to the target audience and the product. Remember tone? That should guide your style of writing. So an ad for a brand of chewing gum can be hip and informal, while a brochure for a million-dollar yacht should be more formal and elegant.

Persuade, don't impress

When it comes to ad copy, you don't have to impress readers with how many words you know. Or even with how much you know about the product. Instead, you have to persuade them your product meets their wants and needs. And you don't have a lot of time or space to do it.

Image 10.6

Body copy doesn't always have to be in nice, neat blocks. In this ad, Pur outlines the cost savings of filtered tap water versus bottled water, all within a single drop.

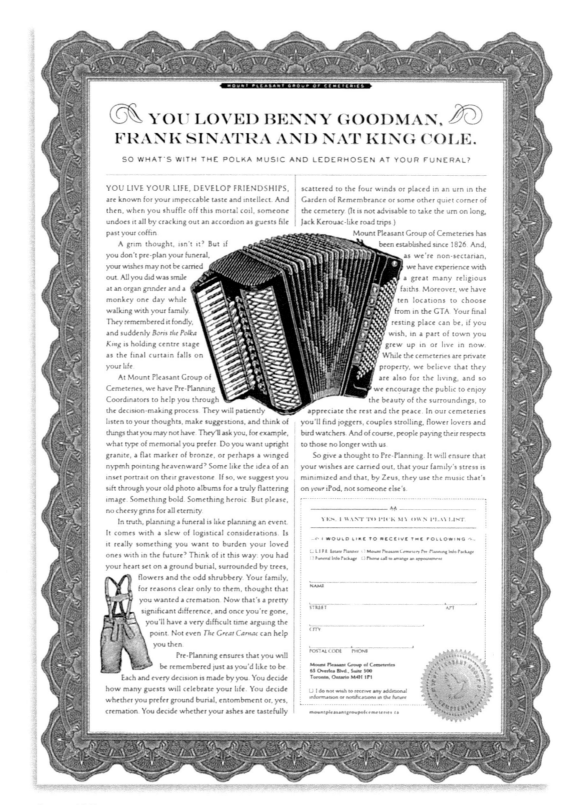

YOU LOVED BENNY GOODMAN, FRANK SINATRA AND NAT KING COLE.

SO WHAT'S WITH THE POLKA MUSIC AND LEDERHOSEN AT YOUR FUNERAL?

YOU LIVE YOUR LIFE, DEVELOP FRIENDSHIPS, are known for your impeccable taste and intellect. And then, when you shuffle off this mortal coil, someone undoes it all by cracking out an accordion as guests file past your coffin.

A grim thought, isn't it? But if you don't pre-plan your funeral, your wishes may not be carried out. All you did was smile at an organ grinder and a monkey one day while walking with your family. They remembered it fondly, and suddenly *Boris the Polka King* is holding centre stage as the final curtain falls on your life.

At Mount Pleasant Group of Cemeteries, we have Pre-Planning Coordinators to help you through the decision-making process. They will patiently listen to your thoughts, make suggestions, and think of things that you may not have. They'll ask you, for example, what type of memorial you prefer. Do you want upright granite, a flat marker of bronze, or perhaps a winged nymph pointing heavenward? Some like the idea of an inset portrait on their gravestone. If so, we suggest you sift through your old photo albums for a truly flattering image. Something bold. Something heroic. But please, no cheesy grins for all eternity.

In truth, planning a funeral is like planning an event. It comes with a slew of logistical considerations. Is it really something you want to burden your loved ones with in the future? Think of it this way: you had your heart set on a ground burial, surrounded by trees, flowers and the odd shrubbery. Your family, for reasons clear only to them, thought that you wanted a cremation. Now that's a pretty significant difference, and once you're gone, you'll have a very difficult time arguing the point. Not even *The Great Carnac* can help you then.

Pre-Planning ensures that you will be remembered just as you'd like to be. Each and every decision is made by you. You decide how many guests will celebrate your life. You decide whether you prefer ground burial, entombment or, yes, cremation. You decide whether your ashes are tastefully scattered to the four winds or placed in an urn in the Garden of Remembrance or some other quiet corner of the cemetery. (It is not advisable to take the urn on long, Jack Kerouac-like road trips.)

Mount Pleasant Group of Cemeteries has been established since 1826. And, as we're non-sectarian, we have experience with a great many religious faiths. Moreover, we have ten locations to choose from in the GTA. Your final resting place can be, if you wish, in a part of town you grew up in or live in now. While the cemeteries are private property, we believe that they are also for the living, and so we encourage the public to enjoy the beauty of the surroundings, to appreciate the rest and the peace. In our cemeteries you'll find joggers, couples strolling, flower lovers and bird watchers. And of course, people paying their respects to those no longer with us.

So give a thought to Pre-Planning. It will ensure that your wishes are carried out, that your family's stress is minimized and that, by Zeus, they use the music that's on *your* iPod, not someone else's.

Image 10.7

This ad targeting mature readers is the perfect place for long copy. Here you can see how each paragraph focuses on a specific benefit as it draws readers in, building credibility, and the ad ends with a call to action.

A common error many novice writers make is to show the client how much they know about the product, especially for new products or new clients. You should make people believe how good the product is, not how smart you are. Some ads don't say, "Buy me"; they say, "Look how I can repackage what the clients told me so I can show them I was listening." That's OK for the first draft. But on the next round, take out the meat axe and start hacking away.

When you are given a Creative Brief or write a copy platform, don't forget to keep looking for the "so whats." Find out what's really important to the consumer; then see if the client's priorities mesh.

The "Seven Deadly Sins" of Copywriting

A lot of teachers have told you how to write. Now we're telling you how to write better—by pointing out some common mistakes and how to correct them. We call these the Seven Deadly Sins. When you see them in your writing, make a brief confession and do penance by rewriting. Even experienced writers commit these sins. As with other transgressions, you can't feel guilty until you know it's a sin.

The Seven Deadly Sins are:

1. Advertising-ese

2. Bad taste

3. Deadwood

4. Generic benefits

5. Laundry lists

6. Poor grammar

7. Wimpy words

Let's explore each of these sins in detail and discuss ways to avoid them.

Advertising-ese: Don't confuse using proven selling words with the mindless clichés in some advertising. We've grown up with advertising jargon, so it's natural to write ads that way. Read your copy out loud. If it sounds like it should be on QVC, rewrite it.

IT HAS A SAFETY FEATURE FOR MOST EVERYTHING EXCEPT MONTEZUMA'S REVENGE.

That's because Jeep Grand Cherokee is well prepared for possible hazards. Thanks in part to the collaboration of some of the most advanced safety systems ever engineered into a sport utility.

For starters, there's its potent 4.7 litre Power Tech V8* engine and exceptional anti-lock braking system, both designed to help deliver you from danger posthaste.

Next are the features that keep things a safe distance from you: high ground clearance, power locks, and, for off-road use, steel skid plates.* Not to mention the preserving powers of crumple zones and dual air bags,** should you find yourself up against something more formidable than a nasty little microbe.

And, most important, with a really rugged Quadra-Coil™ suspension and Quadra-Drive,™* our most advanced four-wheel drive system ever, Jeep Grand Cherokee enables you to foil a victory party for peril practically any place—provided you don't stray far from its protective parameters or steel-reinforced cabin.

So, in addition to not drinking the water, we strongly recommend you contact us online at www.jeep.com or call us at 1-800-925-JEEP.

THERE'S ONLY ONE

*Optional. **Always use seat belts. Remember a backseat is the safest place for children. Jeep is a registered trademark of DaimlerChrysler.

Image 10.8

Jeep has had a long history of creating clever, interesting, and informative ads. Many used the classic beginning-middle-end style. This ad begins with a slight trace of humor in the headline; pays off that headline with the first line of copy; goes on to support that main idea with an artful weaving of features and benefits; and closes to tie up the main idea and include a call to action.

The best money can buy. You've seen the rest, now try the best. Isn't that amazing? Don't delay, call today. One call does it all. Nobody else offers this kind of quality at such a low price. Hurry, these deals won't last forever! Unique. New and improved. Exclusive. State-of-the-art. Incredible. More for your money. You deserve the best. Get it now! But wait, there's more . . .

. . . the list goes on and on.

In some cases, advertising-ese includes unsubstantiated claims or boasts of being the best without providing detail to back it up. If you can't prove it, don't say it, because you've just lost all your credibility.

Advertising-ese also includes trite punctuation, especially the dreaded exclamation point. If you have to add ! to a headline or even a line of copy, you're shouting that you can't think of anything clever or memorable. You used to see phrases like:

It's just wonderful! The all new 1965 Oldsmobile Vista Cruiser with the new improved smooth-as-silk Strato-Glide transmission!

Bad taste: Sexist, racist, insensitive, offensive, and vulgar language. In this age of political correctness, people can find hidden meanings in the most innocent messages. When you look at some of the ads from the 1930s and '40s, it's amazing how African Americans were portrayed. In the 1950s and 1960s, women were shown as mindless neat freaks, more concerned with whiter shirts than careers. Today, writers who would never use stereotyped racial or sexist language think nothing of using sexual puns, vulgar language, and scatological humor. If you are appealing to a general audience, be careful what you say and how you say it. If you are going for an edgy concept that appeals to a very select group who won't be offended by your bad taste, go for it and accept the consequences.

Deadwood: This is one of the most common sins committed by beginning writers. They say the same thing several different ways, time after time, in a very redundant fashion that wastes time and space, over and over again, ad infinitum. Say what you mean. Then tighten it up. Look for ways to eliminate unnecessary words and phrases. Don't overstate the obvious. Don't include a description when a visual will work better. This has been stressed by English composition teachers since grade school, but somehow, ad students forget it.

Original: Wamco engineers have developed several new ways to help original equipment manufacturers make products that are accepted better by their customers, which, in turn, makes them more profitable.

Better: Wamco makes your products more profitable.

Generic benefits: Also known as "weasel words," these benefits are so vague they could apply to almost anybody and anything. You may have attached a benefit to a feature, but have you gone far enough? Keep asking, "So what?" and you'll eliminate generic benefits. Always lead with the strongest benefit. Readers may not get to it if you bury it at the end of the ad.

Laundry lists: This sin usually involves grouping features with no benefits, and all have equal value. It's hard to find the "big idea." This is a crutch used by some writers who don't know much about the product, so they throw all its features into the copy and string them together with no relation to each other or connection to a benefit. The temptation is to cram as many copy points as possible into an ad to let the client think you know the product. For example:

> *This sleek powerboat features a powerful fuel-injected engine, a two-tone gel coat finish, a tandem trailer, removable carpeting, lots of cup holders, an in-dash CD player, and a 5-year warranty. Who could ask for more in a family runabout?*

Poor grammar: You should make your copy easy to read, and sometimes that means using the proper mechanics of English, such as when to end a sentence and when to use commas, dashes, colons, and other punctuation. You should understand sentence structure, such as the need for a subject and a verb and how to use prepositions and conjunctions and phrases. Given that, don't feel compelled to follow every rule of English composition. While you should not try to impress readers with your brilliance, you don't want them to think you are an illiterate slob.

Speaking of punctuation, as we mentioned earlier, don't overuse the exclamation point! Also, don't overuse ellipses . . . they break up the flow and usually indicate you haven't figured out a good transition between sentences. Use commas only when it's necessary to provide a pause or improve the readability. Some writers (David Ogilvy included) don't like to use periods in headlines, even if it's a complete sentence. Others believe a period adds deliberate emphasis. As long as your copy reads well, punctuation is usually a matter of personal choice.

Wimpy words: This category covers a lot of territory. Certain words rob copy of its vitality. Writing in passive voice also weakens copy. Beginning a sentence with a prepositional phrase or subordinate clause also dilutes the power.

Some examples:

- Usually you should never start a sentence with **There**.

  Bad: There are a lot of reasons why people visit their friendly Toyota dealer. First of all there's the large selection they have.
  Better: People visit their Toyota dealer for a lot of reasons: First, they offer the largest selection . . .

- **That** is overused. Try reading it out loud, with and without *that*, and see what sounds better.

- **Be** verbs. "To be or not to be" is great for Shakespeare but not advertising copy. Derivatives of *to be* include *is*, *are*, *was*, *were*, and *being*.

  Bad: If you *have been* considering purchasing a luxury sport utility, then you *are* in luck.
  Better: Interested in a luxury sport utility? Lucky you.

- **Passive voice**: Your copy should take action rather than being acted upon (even that tip reads awkwardly). Examples:

  Bad: Why do you think Sony computers *were chosen* by design engineers *who have held* senior positions in this industry?
  Better: Why the industry's top design engineers picked Sony.

- **Lead with phrases and clauses**: Get right to the point. Don't put a phrase or clause in its path. Also, don't string a lot of phrases together in the same sentence. Short, simple declarative sentences work best. For example:

  Bad: After shopping *for your family, on the way* home, stop in *for a cool* refreshing DQ Mister Misty.
  Better: DQ Mister Misty: a refreshing treat after a long day of shopping.

Make a copy of the following table, cut it out, and keep it handy when you're writing copy. It's also handy when reviewing other people's work.

TABLE 10.1   Seven Deadly Sins of Copy

The Seven Deadly Sins of Copywriting and How to Correct Them	
1. Advertising-ese	Write the way people talk, eliminate clichés and useless phrases, and keep it conversational (read it out loud).
2. Bad taste	Watch for sexist, racist, or offensive language and symbols. If it feels wrong, it probably is.
3. Deadwood	Weed out weak, redundant, unnecessary words and phrases. Keep the flow of thought moving.
4. Generic benefits	Provide consumer benefits in terms they understand. Appeal to their lives. Lead with the strongest benefit. Is one benefit so strong that it is the central truth or One Thing about this product?
5. Laundry lists	Don't list features without reference to what they mean to the consumer. Weave benefits into the ad, appealing to the consumer's point of view.
6. Poor grammar	Watch for errors in spelling, punctuation, and verb tense. Know the rules and when to break the rules. Use fragments if it improves readability.
7. Wimpy words	Use power words, active voice, and short, simple sentences. If it doesn't feel strong, it's not.

Power Writing

We discussed what not to do. Now we'll offer some recommendations that will help make any ad read easier and communicate more effectively.

Mix short and long sentences: Sometimes short sentences work best, but you don't have to make every sentence three words. Mix up short and long sentences. Use the short ones for the sales message or, if you'd like, use the long sentence for the setup and the short one for the "punch line."

Use simple words if you can: If you're writing a technical brochure for orthopedic surgeons, you're not going to talk about the "shin bone." But in most consumer work, simple language usually communicates best. Remember you are writing to persuade, not to impress readers with your vocabulary. Again, we refer to the venerable John Caples: "Simple words are powerful words. Even the best educated people don't resent simple words. But they're the words many people understand. Write to your barber or mechanic . . ."[7] Caples found a simple word change had an immediate impact on response rates.

1. **Write the way people talk:** Most people use contractions and speak in sentence fragments. Try to write copy as if you're talking to a friend. Read your copy out loud. Does it sound like a normal person talking or an announcer from a 1960s game show?

2. **Match the copy style to the product tone:** More sophisticated products require more formal approaches (you'll never see "Yo. Check out Rolls-Royce. We got yer luxury right here!"). Copy for technical products should indicate some level of technical competence in the copy. But for the vast majority of consumer products, an informal, conversational style works best.

3. **Active verbs and positive attitude:** Don't tiptoe into a benefit. Get right to the point. Use active voice and show excitement for the product. You can't do this with every sentence, but try to make an effort to activate your writing.

4. **Be specific:** "A flat-faced, bug-eyed, pig-snorting Boston terrier" conveys a stronger image than "dog." Rather than using "soon," say "today." Instead of "It's been stated by many physicians . . .," write "Doctors say . . ."

5. **Parallel construction:** As with taglines and headlines, you can use parallel construction in ad body copy. But use it judiciously and only to emphasize a point. Otherwise, it can become annoying or something even worse—poetry.

Words of Wisdom

"Fine writing? Do you want masterpieces? Or do you want to see the goddamned sales curves stop moving down and start moving up? What do you want?" [6]

—Rosser Reeves

6. **Alliteration, rhythm, and rhyme:** These techniques can spice up body copy. But use them carefully. You can emphasize key points, but you don't want your text to look like a string of slogans or a Dr. Seuss book. (So, you do not like rhyming text today? Try it and you may, I say.)

7. **Tighten it up:** The old rule is if you want 100 words, start with 200. As opposed to most good things in life, shorter is better. Find a way to say things in fewer words. Don't waste your reader's time. This is very important, so to say it in two words, "Write tight."

8. **Write out loud:** Read your print copy out loud. Does it sound as good as it reads? If you need inspiration, read some of the great speeches of all time—fireside chats by Franklin Roosevelt, Winston Churchill's messages during World War II, Kennedy's inaugural, Martin Luther King's "I Have a Dream" speech, and Ronald Reagan's tribute to the Columbia astronauts. No matter how you feel about politics, these speeches were powerfully written. They featured simple eloquence, memorable catchphrases, and vivid imagery. Most of all, they resonated in the hearts of the listener long after they were delivered.

Checklist for Better Copy

After you've written what you think is your final draft, use this checklist. You might find that you're not done writing.

- **Strong opening line (pull through):** Is the first line good enough to be a headline? It's got to pull the reader through. Readers take the path of least resistance—make it easy for them.

- **Appeal to the consumer's point of view:** Why do I want to buy this product or service? Appeal to the reader's self-interest—what's in it for him or her? Remember the "so whats." Is the style appropriate for the audience? *Tell me about my yard, not your grass seed.*

- **Clear central idea (the One Thing):** After reading your ad, will the reader be left with the one main idea you want to convey? Does your copy provide mixed messages? Go back to your copy platform to check.

- **Strongest sales point first:** Lead with the strongest selling point. The reader may not get to it if you bury it.

- **Strong supporting information:** Is the information persuasive and presented in a logical order? Does it support the main idea?

For a change, we'd like to talk about *your* air bags.

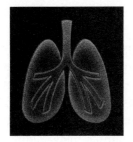

Take a deep breath. Relax. Get comfortable. You are about to read some good news.

Recently, Honda brought its advanced Low-Emission Vehicle (LEV) technology to everyone in America. All fifty states. Voluntarily.

It arrived in the form of the all-new 1998 Accord and the Civic. Both offer engines which meet California's strict Low-Emission Vehicle standard. But now you can buy one not just in California, but in Michigan. Texas. Ohio. Georgia. Wherever you live.

Both cars meet a 70-percent-lower emission standard for smog-contributing non-methane organic gases than is required by the most stringent federal standard. With no performance sacrifice or cost penalty.

Plus, in California and specific states throughout the Northeast, we're now offering our new Accord Ultra-Low Emission Vehicle (ULEV). It's the first auto certified by the California Air Resources Board as a ULEV, making it the cleanest gasoline-powered production car sold in the U.S. Ever.

That means, based on last year's sales figures, more than 60 percent of all new Accords and Civics, some 450,000 cars, will now be more environmentally friendly.

Historically, Honda has continually been a leader in fuel-efficiency and low-emission technology. Because we always think about more than the products we make. We think about the people who use them, and the world in which they live.

Which, in the end, helps us all breathe a little easier.

HONDA
Thinking.

Image 10.9

This is what we mean by power writing. Notice the mix of long and short sentences, the use of specific information, the conversational style, and the smooth flow from beginning to end.

- **Easy reading:** Is the message clear? Does it say it in as few words as possible and as many words as necessary? Even the most intelligent people appreciate simple language. People will read long copy if they are interested in the subject.

- **Power writing:** Can you use active voice rather than passive? Do you start any sentences with "There are"? Ruthlessly weed out unnecessary words. Get rid of the deadwood. "Avoid clichés like the plague." Strip away the ad jargon and "me too" phrases.

- **Call to action:** What do you want the reader to do? Where can he or she get more information? Where can readers buy the product? For well-known, widely distributed consumer products it may not be necessary. But for retail it's mandatory. For technical products and other considered purchases, you need to establish a connection that may require several more contacts. The ad is merely a conduit to more meaningful communication.

You're not done yet

You've just written a modern masterpiece of ad copy. You've avoided all the Deadly Sins. It's passed the checklist with flying colors. So what's next? Honest evaluation.

Give it a rest: The best advice we can give any creative person is "**Write hot. Edit cold.**" In other words, if you're on a roll, keep going. Don't worry about word count, style, or even content. Write what's on your mind. Then put it away. Watch TV. Go jogging. Do anything but think about your ad. After a decent interval, look at your copy. Most people think, "Jeez, that's awful. What was I thinking?" So start the process again, this time with more focus and insight.

Adjust your work habits: We all have times when we're most creative. Unfortunately, it's usually not during the typical 9-to-5 workday. That's why it's important to write hot and edit cold. When you get an idea, jot it down no matter where you are. If you feel like writing 1,000 words at 2 a.m., that's great. E-mail it to work and edit as long as you can stay awake.

Get help: Most good writers are excellent proofreaders—of someone else's work. They are usually criminally sloppy when it comes to their own writing. For proper editing, you need diligent, objective, and independent proofreaders. Don't rely on a computer spell checker. *You may have the write spelling butt the wrong meaning.*

Mark it up: Whether you're editing another writer's or your own work, document the problems or change them. This requires printing a hard copy and scribbling comments just like your great-grandparents did. We've included a selection of editing marks in the Appendix. Use these when you're proofing your copy.

Don't stop: We can't think of a single project that we couldn't do better the second or third time (including this book). If you have the luxury of time, keep improving your copy. Replace weak words. Cut out the deadwood. Say it better with fewer words. Keep polishing that copy 'til it shines.

Who's Who?

Charles Browder, influential chairman of BBDO, one of the leading ad agencies in the world, is noted for stating, "The good ideas are all hammered out in agony by individuals, not spewed out by groups."[9] Browder also gained some notoriety in the early 1960s by firing Ronald Reagan from his role as spokesman for BBDO client General Electric, which helped propel Reagan into a new career—politics.

Janet Champ started her career in advertising as the 15th employee, the receptionist, at Wieden + Kennedy. But Champ had a dream and the talent and passion to back it up. Over her 15 years at W + K, she worked on several accounts, including Nike, Coca-Cola, Microsoft, Neutrogena, and every women's brand that happened to show up. For 7 years she, along with her partner Charlotte Moore, created the influential (and, at that time, groundbreaking) Nike "Women's Fitness Campaign," receiving numerous awards and recognition, including Cannes, One Show Best of Shows, National ADDYs, and two consecutive Kelly Awards for best national print campaign (making her the only writer in the history of the Kellys to do so). She was also recognized by the *National Women's Law Review,* the National Woman's Health Board, and the Office of the U.S. Surgeon General for the TV spot "If You Let Me Play." She was also named *Adweek* Copywriter of the Year and has the painful distinction of having been sued by the surviving Beatles for the use of their song "Revolution" in the first TV spot she ever worked on. Since 1999, she has been a freelance copywriter "trying to do good, instead of evil."

As copywriter and cofounder of the Ally & Gargano agency, **Jim Durfee** was one of the leaders of the Creative Revolution. A&G's philosophy was that advertising is a product, not a service. "A product," Durfee said, "is something that is molded, produced, thought out and set out before the person: 'We have made this for you, we think this will help.' A service is hat-in-hand and through the side door. It was a completely different attitude toward what an agency was and what an agency made."[10]

Ed McCabe has profoundly influenced the field of advertising. For more than 4 decades, his ads broke new ground for such clients as Volvo and Perdue chicken. Many of today's most creative advertising professionals follow his innovative teachings and examples. He cofounded Scali, McCabe, Sloves, Inc., and helped build the company into the 10th-largest ad agency network in the world. For 10 years after leaving Scali, McCabe, Sloves, he was CEO of McCabe & Co. At the age of 34, he was inducted into the Copywriters Hall of Fame, the youngest to be so honored.

Exercises

1. Branded Surprise

Do you remember a time when you were surprised by a brand?

- Share a story about a time when you or someone you know was surprised by a brand. The surprise could have come at any point in life. The surprise can be good and bad . . . just look at the element of surprise and the emotions behind it.

- Now get ready to write. If the surprise happens with the brand, be ready to spin it into body copy. If it's not, do the *twist* and see if you can make lemons out of lemonade. Remember the old VW ad: *Lemon?* Something not so good sold a lot of cars. Focusing on the emotion behind the surprise, write 150 words of copy to express the experience. Think beginning, middle, and end as you tell your story.

- Now trade stories with a partner who will use the Seven Deadly Sins to edit hot.

- Return the edited copy to your partner and rewrite your own story. Add a headline and visual and they've got a storyline ad.

- Share the ads as a class and be prepared to discuss the strategic strength of your branded story and consider if it has legs.

2. Consumer Packaged Goods

We've always figured that if you can write copy for a consumer packaged good you can write for anything. After all, shampoo is shampoo is shampoo—until you read the ads.

- Pick a brand; we like Excedrin Migraine. Now talk your teacher into providing a creative brief so that you're all working from the same strategic document.

- Develop three taglines and be ready to share, and defend, your favorite.

- Make a list of the tags on the board, everyone sharing their best tagline. Then, across the top, write the tips for effective headlines (Chapter 9). Use this as a matrix to discuss the merits of each tagline. Get it down to the strategically strongest two or three—then vote on the winning tagline.

- Now everybody develops their own ad with a headline, a visual, and 75–100 words of copy—each ad using the new tagline.

- Present your ad and discuss the rationale for your copy choices. Your classmates will critique your work using the *Checklist for Better Copy*. It's very interesting to see how the creative varies and yet how each approach fits with the tagline.

3. Editing the Pros

This will help you edit cold—taking something from good to great.

- Find a long-copy ad—one with copy that's good but not great. An ad with multiple components—subhead, captions, and bullets—is preferable. We recommend talking your teacher into finding the ad, and having he or she write up the copy as a copy sheet, so you're all working with the same copy—but you don't know what it looks like.

- As a group decide who the target audience is. And sketch out a consumer profile.

- By the end of class rewrite the copy and rough out a pencil sketch to show copy placement.

- Then share your copy edits, along with the pencil sketch.

- Once everyone has shared, ask your teacher to share the original ad. Imagine the discussion that will lead to.

- This can be spun a different direction focusing on design. In this case take an ad that's light on copy, but the copy is very well written. Working from the same two documents (copy sheet and profile) comp up a layout using the existing copy.

Notes

1. Quoted in Eric Clark, *The Want Makers: Inside the World of Advertising* (New York: Penguin Books, 1988), p. 56.

2. John Caples (*Wall Street Journal* ad), 1978.

3. Designers and Art Directors Association of the United Kingdom, *The Copy Book* (Hove, UK: RotoVision SA, 2001), p. 120.

4. Janet Champ, Ad Story: *Eight Pages and No Product: Who Says Long Copy Doesn't Sell?,* 2005.

5. Quoted in James Simpson, *Contemporary Quotation*s (Binghamton, NY: Vail-Ballou Press, 1964), p. 83.

6. Quoted in Denis Higgins, *The Art of Writing Advertising: Conversations With Masters of the Craft* (Lincolnwood, IL: NTC Business Books, 1990), p. 118.

7. John Caples (*Wall Street Journal* ad), 1978.

8. Quoted in Higgins, *The Art of Writing Advertising*, p. 83.

9. Quote from the Brainy Quote Web site, http://www.brainyquote.com/quotes/authors/c/charles_browder.html (accessed June 27, 2005).

10. Quoted in Randall Rothenberg, "The Advertising Century," *Advertising Age,* March 29, 1999, http://www.adage.com/century/Rothenberg.html (accessed June 27, 2005).

Chapter 11

Print

We're using print to start our section on writing for each of the major media. In this chapter we cover magazines, newspapers, collateral, and out-of-home. Let's begin with magazines.

Magazines

A magazine ad is an ideal palette for applying all the creative strategies and tactics we've discussed in previous chapters. Magazines also present a lot of creative opportunities based on the variety of sizes, shapes, and multiple-page combinations. Finally, a magazine ad is a perfect size and shape for your portfolio—small enough to fit anywhere, large enough for long copy and to make a design statement.

Why magazines?

From a creative standpoint, magazines offer many advantages. Specifically:

- **Magazines are selective.** Some magazines are devoted to very narrow interests, such as water gardens or old Porsches. Many general-interest publications print special editions based on region, occupation, or income.

- **In most cases, the printing quality is much better than in any other medium.** Four-color ads really pop. And when you run inserts, the sky's the limit for the number of inks and varnishes.

- **Magazines usually last longer than other media.** Weekly, monthly, and quarterly publications get passed around and reread. Your ads are seen longer and more often by more people.

- **Magazines can add prestige.** Publications such as *Architectural Digest* reach an upscale market. So if you're selling expensive cars, jewelry, or real estate, upscale magazines are the perfect choice.

- **Many magazines offer value-added services to advertisers.** For example, many business publications have "bingo cards" in the back where a reader can circle a number to get literature. Others offer advertisers their lists for direct mail or market research databases.

- **Magazines give you a lot of design flexibility.** Whether you use a series of fractional pages, multipage inserts, advertorials, or a series of single-page ads, magazines give creative people and media directors a lot of options.

- **Magazines are integrated with the Internet.** Most major magazines also have Web sites, which opens all kinds of promotional and cross-promotional opportunities for print and online advertisers.

Why not?

Here are a few reasons magazines may not be the ideal place for your ads:

- Even though magazines have a higher pass-along rate and hang around a little longer than other media, they still get dumped in the garbage, and all those ads are gone for good.

- Magazines are a relatively expensive way to get information. Many people just click on the online versions of their favorite publications to get feature articles or news reports.

- Even weekly magazines can't stay current in this all-news-all-the-time world. Closing times may be 2 months for some publications, so your ad may be hopelessly out-of-date by the time it runs.

- Magazines can be very expensive for advertisers. Sure, you get the CPM (cost per thousand) you pay for, but at $250,000 a pop in some magazines, you'd better have a killer ad.

- The more popular the publication, the more competition you have from other ads. It's easy to get lost in the clutter of the top-selling consumer magazines.

Magazine campaigns

Magazines and campaigns seem made for each other. You can have a campaign within a single issue with multiple insertions. The periodic nature of magazines also fits many campaign strategies. Since readership of various magazines transcends demographics, it's natural to run ads in several magazines to maximize impact. Magazines also fit well as part of an integrated marketing campaign. Here are just a few examples:

- Include a music CD or an interactive CD-ROM as an insert in a magazine.

- Use cross-promotion with a compatible brand to cosponsor a contest, sweepstakes, or special offer.

- Run a series of short-copy ads that direct readers to a Web site for more detailed information.

- Use tear-out mini inserts that include coupons.

- If they will fit within a magazine, include product samples in your insert.

Where to find the best magazine ads

The Magazine Publishers of America present the Kelly Awards for the best magazine advertising each year. Winning a Kelly is a major accomplishment, and all the top creative shops compete. When asked what it takes to win a Kelly Award, Mal MacDougall, executive creative director at Bodden Partners, gave the following advice:

> **Keep it simple. Don't try to be crazy. Don't try to go to your computer and think you can do something off the wall. Do something within a very narrow strategy. The narrower the better. The strategy is a very short sentence—the soul of the brand you're trying to talk about. Simplicity is what's going to work. You cannot win a Kelly Award with a complicated message. Get to know who is really reading that magazine. Decide who you really want to talk to. Narrow it down to a tiny few people. Then you know exactly who is reading this golf magazine, fishing magazine, fashion magazine, or gardening magazine. Make your message simple and clear and aim it right at them.**[3]

Image 11.1

A simple statement reminds viewers of what they love about Oreos, while the juxtaposition of size works to introduce Mini Oreos.

Image 11.2

Nudity isn't just about sex! Evergreen Travel uses a visual metaphor to express how their fares are so low you and your family can travel anywhere. Bet their ads would stand out in the travel section.

Newspapers

What's black and white and read all over? Not necessarily newspapers. Today they use almost as much color as magazines. Read all over? Not anymore. Readership has dropped off drastically, especially in people under 35. Still, in terms of advertising dollars spent, newspapers are a major force, especially when ads are packaged with both the print and online versions of the paper.

Image 11.3

Smart marketers are always looking for ways to engage their customers. M&M's provided a way for customers to personalize their candy in time for Valentine's Day. Readers of the magazine ad were directed to a landing page with all the details.

Image 11.4

Variable printing allows advertisers to personalize messages in magazine ads. In this case, the name of the subscriber appears in an ad promoting Oprah's Big Give series.

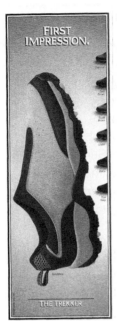

Image 11.5

Magazines are great for creative media buys such as this use of facing fractional pages. Note the parallel construction in the two headlines.

Why newspapers?

From a creative standpoint, newspapers offer many advantages:

- **Local:** They fill in small niches so you can pinpoint advertising in a city or suburban area.

- **Timely:** Ads can be changed within hours of appearance; they can promote short-term events.

- **Widespread in their coverage** (although readership is declining).

- **Controlled by the readers:** They can scan, skip, or plod through paper (allows for long-copy ads).

- **Well suited for co-op opportunities:** National advertisers develop ads and help pay for them.

- **Specialized:** They include supplements and special-interest sections (sports, features, etc.).

- **Believable:** They offer news and sports first; entertainment is secondary.

- **Convenient:** Papers can be taken anywhere—trains, restaurants, bathrooms.

- **Large size:** A newspaper page offers a huge canvas for your ad. A full-page magazine ad is only a fraction of the size of a full-page newspaper ad.

Image 11.6

Never heard of REV'd magazine? It was created as part of the "Hammer & Coop" campaign for Mini. A multipage segment that looked like a real magazine was added to the back of real car magazines.

WE FIRED OUR FACT-CHECKERS
AND PASSED THE SAVINGS ON TO YOU.

the ONION

· SUBSCRIBE ·

Image 11.7

Newspapers have been looking for ways to cut costs, even "America's Finest News Source." The tongue-in-cheek headline is even funnier when the subhead reinforces the "benefit."

Why not?

Here are a few reasons newspapers may not be the ideal place for your ads:

- **Short life span:** The flip side of timeliness. Yesterday's newspaper is, well, yesterday's news.

- **Hasty reading:** Other than Sunday morning, most people don't take the time to read the paper. Many people spend more time with the crossword puzzle than with the news.

- **Poor reproduction:** Printing quality has improved greatly, but a color ad in newsprint can't match the quality in a glossy magazine. Inserts let you control quality, but they can be expensive.

Newspaper readership trends

Current trends indicate newspapers are skipping a generation. Young adults are turning away from the news media their parents and grandparents relied on for information about their neighborhood, city, region, and world. The trend started 30 years ago but has accelerated since the late 1990s. It's not that people don't want news. It's just that they'd rather get it instantly on the Internet or cable news networks . . . without having to buy a paper.

Retail advertising

About $4 out of every $5 spent in newspapers goes to retail advertising. Retail is also called "local" advertising; however, with national chains running traditional-looking retail ads in national newspapers like *USA Today,* it doesn't seem proper to call them local.

Retail is different from other advertising in the following ways:

- **Urgent:** Consumers act on it quickly ("Buy me today or you miss your chance"). It works quickly or not at all.

- **Price oriented:** Most national magazines do not feature price; most retail newspaper ads do.

- **The cheaper the merchandise, the more elements in the ad:** Tiffany's does not have 24 different items with prices in their ads like Wal-Mart.

- **The store personality is very important:** What is the personality—bargain prices (Wal-Mart), service (Nordstrom), reliable (Sears), long established (Jewel-Osco), or classy (Lord & Taylor)? Remember, the merchandise can be the same at every store, so making the store image different is the key.

Words of Wisdom

"There's no better place for a young writer than in retail advertising. You have to write ad after ad, and meet deadlines that force you to be fast. And every ad is judged on the basis of sales—period." [5]

—Tom McElligott

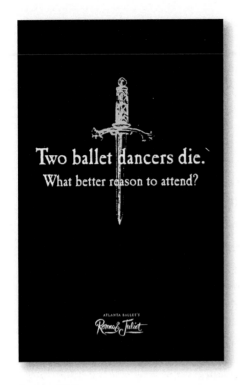

Image 11.8

Newspapers are made for black-and-white ads, but they don't have to be boring. Ballet lovers are going to go to this event anyway, so why not attract some new blood?

Image 11.9

This ad celebrated the birthday of the Minnesota Zoo. Note the simple idea and use of white space. Get the point?

The biggest challenge in designing retail advertising is organizing the various elements. You may have two, four, or a dozen different products featured in an ad. How do you arrange them in an attractive layout that stresses the brand, price, and store personality? When it comes to writing the copy, consider the following guidelines:

1. **Tailor the copy to the customer:** Your tone should be in keeping with the price of the products, the clientele of the store, and the types of products.

2. **Be brief:** Just the facts.

3. **Use direct benefits if you can:** Mention features if you must.

National newspaper ads

Most national newspaper ads are like magazine ads. However, if it's a daily paper you can change the message every day if necessary. For large retailers with multiple outlets, you obviously can't list every store location, but you can convey a store's personality.

National newspapers are also ideal for corporate image, public service, and open-letter advertising. In fact, national newspapers are great vehicles for any message you want to convey quickly to a large audience.

National inserts

When you want the best color reproduction or really want to make a spectacular splash, you can produce full-page (or larger) inserts. *USA Today* has included some huge inserts. One for a hotel chain in Florida folded out to 20 × 48 inches.

Sometimes advertisers insert whole sections in newspapers. Many readers pull out these inserts and keep them like brochures.

Newspapers and campaigns

Newspaper advertising can fit very well into an overall campaign strategy. You can maintain continuity with other creative elements; plus you have the flexibility to make rapid adjustments. For example, you may want to use TV and magazines to establish an image for a product but use newspapers to promote its price or guide readers to local retail stores. Many tourism accounts show beautiful images of their destinations in color magazine ads and run price promotions in small black-and-white ads in the Sunday travel sections of local newspapers.

Image 11.11

This large-format insert in a newspaper showcased a wide assortment of products in a fresh way, typical for Target's more upscale positioning. Note the reference to "wants and needs."

Making your newspaper ads work better

The guidelines for writing good newspaper ads are basically the same as for other media. But note a few special rules for retail:

- Establish a store character: A store is also a brand.

- Use a simple layout: Sometimes fine detail is lost in newsprint.

- Use a dominant element if you can.

- Let white space work for you (or negative space if your ad is in color).

- State the price or range of prices (especially for retail).

- Specify branded merchandise (especially for retail).

- Urge your readers to buy now (especially for retail).

Collateral

Collateral is a big catchall category that includes printed material used for personal selling, handouts, and sometimes direct mail. The materials can be as elaborate as a coffee-table book featuring the illustrated history of a company or as cheesy as a black-and-white single-page flyer stuck under your windshield.

Collateral includes, but is not limited to, the following items:

- Product brochures

- Corporate image brochures

- Catalogs

- Sell sheets

- Capabilities brochures

- Personal selling kits

- Trade-show handouts

- Annual and quarterly reports

While virtually every consumer product uses some kind of collateral, much of it is done by a design firm or collateral agency other than the (advertising) agency of record. However, in most cases, business-to-business collateral is integrated into a total communication program developed by one agency or design firm. When you're writing collateral pieces, especially multipage brochures or a series of pieces, keep the following tips in mind:

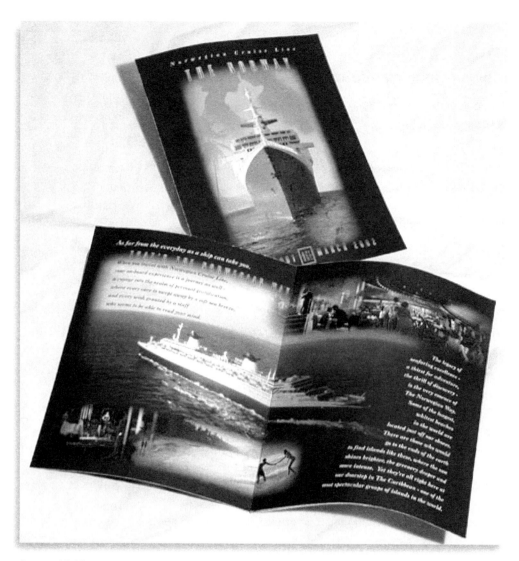

Image 11.12

- **Have a theme** and carry that theme throughout the brochure, whether it's a graphic or a text theme (or both).

- **Think of the brochure as a campaign**—each major element has to work by itself and collectively with other parts of the brochure.

- **Appeal to wants and needs of the readers.** To do this you have to know and understand the intended target audience.

- **Think visually.** Even technical pieces need good, attention-getting graphics.

- **Pay attention to typography,** especially for copy-intensive pieces.

- **Stretch your thinking.** Consider gatefolds, pockets, inserts, die cuts, windows, and other creative devices to liven up the design.

- **Consider printing limitations when doing your layout.** Don't forget that in most cases you have to think in terms of four-page units (unless you have one or more gatefold pages).

There are no other rules for collateral, except following good design and copywriting practices. Other than budget, there are no restrictions on paper stock, number of colors, binding technique, or paper size. Many businesses have drastically cut back on printed literature. Instead, they put their literature on their Web sites as PDF documents so customers can download them. This not only saves a lot of money in printing costs, but there's no inventory and you can make changes whenever you want. If printing quality is not an issue and you don't need a salesperson to walk a prospect through the literature, it makes a lot of sense.

Out-of-Home Media

We used to call this outdoor advertising. But what do you call signs inside an airport terminal, posters in a subway station, or three-dimensional displays in a shopping mall? So we're using the term *out-of-home* to cover all advertising that's seen outside the home but is not in the point-of-sale category. That's not a nice, neat definition, but bear with us. We think this will make sense by the end of the chapter.

Even more complicated is the category called "nontraditional media." As media once considered nontraditional have become mainstream, more variations have emerged, especially those driven by technology. In this chapter we'll discuss the role of sales promotion, guerrilla marketing, and word-of-mouth and hybrid marketing under the banner of nontraditional media, and then you can decide what it all means.

Why out-of-home?

From a creative standpoint, out-of-home offers many advantages. Specifically, out-of-home is:

- **Flexible:** The location, timing, structure, and dimension of the concept give you a lot of options.

- **A high-impact medium:** Nothing gives you a bigger canvas.

- **Exclusive:** You can select a specific location.

- **Economical:** Low cost per impression.

- **Great for establishing brand image** and building rapid awareness.

Image 11.13

Now that's a big bill. Three-dimensional billboards gain attention and, in this instance, provide a benefit to bank customers.

Image 11.14

This outdoor board demonstrates the product benefit perfectly and caused a lot of buzz. Notice the brand name neatly tucked within the roll of tape. Sometimes you just don't need a headline.

- **Ideal for promoting package goods.**

- **Effective for reinforcing existing brands.**

- **Is always on display.**

- **Fun:** Because it combines selling with entertainment.

- **Good for your portfolio:** Because it instantly conveys a concept.

Why not?

- You usually can't change the creative quickly.

- In most cases, you can't provide detail.

- You have to tell the whole story in about 5 seconds or less for billboards.

- Your message may be on display 24/7, but you're paying for off-peak times too.

- In most cases, you're limited to certain urban areas/country roads.

- People hate the idea of billboards, because most of them are ugly and stupid (we mean the billboards).

Posters and bulletins (aka billboards)

People in the outdoor advertising business don't talk about "billboards." The two main types of outdoor displays are the *painted bulletin* and the *outdoor poster.* The difference is the way they are displayed—posters use sheets of preprinted paper glued to backboards, and bulletins traditionally have used hand-painted images. Today, painted bulletins have given way to Superflex vinyl-coated fabric that gives them almost magazine-like quality. For simplicity's sake, we'll use the layperson's term *billboards.*

Image 11.15

A strong message like this doesn't really need a visual. The headline does it all.

Posting companies offer a variety of sizes, usually described in poster terms, such as 36-sheet, 30-sheet, 24-sheet, and 8-sheet.

For layout purposes, all you have to know is that billboards are very wide and not very tall. So if you're using an 8.5- × 11-inch sheet of paper and your design is 10 inches wide, it should be about 4.5 inches high to have a 2.5-to-1 ratio. The reason we mention this here is that too many students treat billboards like magazine ads. When you start thinking about how they are different, it opens up a lot more creative opportunities. Which means they are much better suited to show a hot dog than a wedding cake.

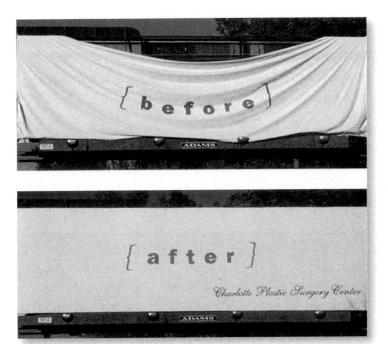

Image 11.16

A fixed location offers creative opportunities. The first board with the saggy "before" captures attention. When it's replaced by a taut "after" and the advertiser's name, it all makes sense . . . and gets people talking.

Image 11.17

Ski resorts know something about white space. The snowboarder on this 3-D board really caught some air.

Beyond the dimensions, billboards are available in several different formats or combinations of formats:

- **Standard static boards:** Your basic poster or bulletin that fits within the limits of the sign's borders.

- **Extensions:** Part of your image violates the boundaries of the board.

Image 11.18

With outdoor advertising, as with real estate, the secret is location, location, location. Who would not notice this sign?

- **Motion boards:** These can be motorized images on a static board with sliding panels that reveal a totally different message, usually another advertiser.

- **Illuminated boards:** The board can be lighted for night viewing or, more dramatically, to include neon, moving lights, and selective spot lighting.

- **Digital boards:** These high-definition boards project a very bright, crisp image. However, these are tremendously more expensive than traditional boards, so time on the board is usually sold by the second. Some cities regulate the time of the display, requiring longer display times so there is less distraction to drivers.

- **Three-dimensional boards:** You can add dimensional objects to and around the board, such as a car crashing through the middle, people sitting on the top edge, or parts of the poster removed to reveal the backing framework.

Digital and interactive out-of-home media

Digital technology has taken out-of-home advertising to new levels, allowing much more interactivity between consumers and the ads. Motion-activated displays, such as those patented by MonsterVision, can be displayed in store windows, in airport and train terminals, at trade shows, and basically anywhere people congregate. These interactive displays, some as big as 30 feet long, are activated by the motion of people who can manipulate and

Ad Story

What's Hot and What's Not?
"At Lápiz we believe that controversy is a good thing. Usually, work that gets noticed and debated works harder for the brand. Not that we do it intentionally, but sometimes it happens as a consequence.

"A few years ago, we were hired by Labatt USA to re-launch their Tecate beer brand. First we listened to consumers, who basically told us that the can was so ugly and old-fashioned that they wouldn't be caught dead holding one.

"Instead of suggesting a package redesign (which, at best, would have made it as cool as hundreds of other brands), we decided to be proud of our nasty appearance and authenticity, and give the product some attitude. For example, one bathroom board read: 'You think I'm ugly? Look in the mirror.' The success of the campaign was spectacular.

"About a year later, the client decided to launch Tecate in a longneck. It wasn't a big launch, just some billboards. True to the Tecate sense of humor, the billboard featured a big, ice-cold bottle, and the headline: 'Finally, a cold Latina.'

"It was one of my least favorite pieces since we had started working on the account. Right or wrong, I see plays on words as a lazy, inferior form of copywriting. Still, I let it go to the client, probably because we were running out of time and I hadn't seen anything better. The piece was approved and produced.

"A few days later, I'm watching the evening news at home and there it is, our billboard! In front of it, angry women being interviewed. I keep watching. Feminist groups all over the country are protesting against it, doing all sorts of crazy things, short of burning the billboards. I change the channel. There it is, again. Next morning, it's in the radio talk shows, it's in the papers, it's everywhere.

"I'm thinking, why are we being treated like chauvinist monsters? We do think Latinas are hot, so what? Even Latinas think Latinas are hot, and they're proud of it. I know it—my wife is Brazilian!

"The client is totally cool about it but, understandably, takes the boards down. Peace is back.

"When the reports come in, sales went up an average of 8% nationally. In New York alone, sales went up 40%. Not bad. So this is how a small and obscure Mexican brand became the third largest-selling imported beer in America."[8]

—Laurence Klinger
Senior Vice President,
Chief Creative Officer, *Lápiz*, Chicago

Images 11.19, 11.20

Not your usual bus shelter, and that's the brilliance of it. Science World *took its show on the road with a series of bus shelters each demonstrating a funky science fact, while creating buzz. Suddenly science wasn't so boring.*

change the images on display. For example, if a person approaches, the display of a puppy will do different tricks, depending on the activity of the viewer. They can even be placed on a floor, and the images will change as people walk over the display. These displays can be quite expensive, so many advertisers use them to promote special events, launch a new brand, or introduce a new ad campaign.

Transit

Transit advertising also has its own special terminology. To make it simple, think of transit as advertising that goes on the outside or inside of things that move and at the places where you wait for things that move. Examples of transit advertising include:

- Inside and outside bus cards
- Outside bus murals
- Bus shelters and benches
- Kiosks
- Train, bus, and subway stations
- Airports
- Mobile billboards: car, truck, and trailer ads

Words of Wisdom

"Billboards are most effective if you can say these two magic words: 'Next Exit.' If you can't, they work best as a reminder of your other marketing." [9]

—Jay Conrad Levinson

Posters

Posters can be a creative person's best bet to pad a portfolio and win awards. Technically, all you have to do is print one, post it somewhere, and *voilà,* you've produced a real-world advertisement, seen by someone other than your roommate.

Out-of-home campaigns

Out-of-home advertising is usually used as a secondary medium. Billboards and posters are great reminders of a slogan, a logo, a package, or another aspect of a total campaign. Keep the two key aspects of campaign continuity in mind when using out-of-home. Can you extend the message by using out-of-home, and can you repeat the theme created for out-of-home?

When you are developing concepts for a campaign, you might want to go with out-of-home first. Nothing crystallizes a concept like a billboard. If you can communicate that One Thing with one billboard, you've got something you can build on.

Tips and techniques

The following recommendations are based on the collective wisdom of outdoor advertising professionals and our personal experience. They're not hard-and-fast rules but factors you should consider when you're creating out-of-home advertising:

- **Be telegraphic.** The rule of thumb for billboards is nine words or fewer, with the emphasis on fewer. Some say six words is the limit. Keep in mind that someone driving by has about 5 seconds to get it.

- **Think big.** You've got an ad that can be seen from 500 feet away. The images and the type should be huge.

- **Go for a strong visual/verbal connection.** Think metaphors and visual puzzles. Many times you don't even need copy.

- **Stick with one main idea.** Above all, keep it simple!

- **Take advantage of location.** A sign on the side or back of a bus can be different from a static billboard because it's constantly in motion. The message on a billboard can be very local.

- **Use all caps for short headlines and uppercase/lowercase for longer heads.** Using all caps makes long copy harder to read.

- **Use short words when possible.** They're easier to read and you can get more on a billboard.

- **Use bold colors, not pastels.** You're trying to attract attention. That's why you see so many yellows and reds in billboards. Even white space draws attention, as long as it surrounds a bold color.

- **Use few elements.** Remember, keep it simple!

- **Use product package instead of words.** Show the Coke bottle or can, not the word *Coca-Cola.*

Who's Who?

Howard Gossage influenced a generation of copywriters with innovative and often unconventional approaches to marketing communications. He began his copywriting career at age 36 in San Francisco. Success soon followed with award-winning work for Land Rover, Paul Masson wines, Rainier Ale, Eagle shirts, and Qantas airlines.

Tom McElligott and creative partner Pat Fallon started out with a freelance business called Lunch Hour. After winning several awards, the pair launched their own shop in 1981. They quickly recruited art director Nancy Rice and account executive Fred Senn, and the legendary Fallon McElligott Rice was born. Thanks to award-winning creative and rapid acquisition of blue-chip accounts, such as US West, FMR was named Ad Agency of the Year just 3 years after its founding. A short time later, Rice left, and McElligott jumped ship when Fallon sold a majority share to Scali, McCabe, Sloves, an Ogilvy & Mather subsidiary.

Helen Lansdowne Resor provided the creative spark in the early days of J. Walter Thompson. As the first female copywriter to write and plan national advertising, she opened the door for many women in advertising as she was constantly creating new ways to attract readers. She brought a woman's point of view to advertising, addressing clients' conventions as she managed and supervised two thirds of the business in the JWT New York and Boston offices. She was a revolutionary inventor of a new style in advertising. Among her many achievements is one of the greatest slogans of all time, for Woodbury soap— "The skin you love to touch."

Nancy Rice was a founding partner in the fabled Fallon McElligott Rice agency. Shortly after its founding, FMR began a meteoric rise in creative recognition and account growth, including Agency of the Year honors. Rice worked on such groundbreaking campaigns as *Rolling Stone* ("Perception/Reality") and Coleman. She later joined DDB Needham Chicago as senior vice president and group creative director. Working with numerous high-profile clients from Anheuser-Busch to General Mills, Rice's group has garnered an extensive list of awards, including gold and silver medals in the One Show, CLIOs, and ATHENAs. She was the first woman elected to the Advertising Hall of Fame.

Helayne Spivak now runs a consulting company (HRS Consulting) and is still considered one of the most accomplished leaders in the ad business. She has run some of the world's top creative departments: At Young & Rubicam, she was chief creative officer; at J. Walter Thompson, she was worldwide creative director. She has won nearly every major honor the industry offers, including numerous CLIO Awards and the Gold Award at the Cannes Advertising Festival.

Exercises

1. Branded Shopping

Doing some ethnographic homework to understand consumers can be insightful for every creative. Let's get you started.

- Pick a branded product available at a local retail venue: Toyota Prius, Crest toothpaste, Apple MacBook Pro, Hoover vacuum cleaners, Lancôme cosmetics, and so on. Be sure that at least two or three of you choose the same brand.

- Conduct some initial secondary research on the brand, learning as much as you can about your brand. Write a consumer profile together.

- Now, head off to observe consumers in the retail environment and observe at least 10 shoppers interacting with the product and potentially its competitive set. To access the retail environment and shoppers' experiences within that environment consider the following questions. What is the retail environment like? How does it feel, look, and sound? What is the sales staff like? How long do consumers spend in the retail environment? How many competing brands do they also interact with? Do they shop alone—if not, who were they with, and how did they interact? How long do they spend with the brand? What were their physical responses?

- Taking your new found ethnographic knowledge, individually concept three print ads with the objective of increasing traffic.

- Share your ads with your team and discuss how your ethnographic research in the retail environment influenced your creative.

2. Retail Roulette

This is an exercise that will help you understand retail and the competitive set.

- Choose one particular retail client and discuss the overall competitive set, and the target audience. Brainstorm a list of 50 adjectives that might apply to the category generally. (We suggest your teacher put each word on individual note cards and save them for next semester).

- In class post the names of your retail brand along with its main competitors. Have your teacher hold up each word, while you shout out which brand it fits. Create a stack of word cards by each brand. Where there is obvious debate toss out the word card.

- Using each stack of adjectives, work in groups to create a profile of each brand.

- Now take the adjectives for each brand and use them as a seedbed for generating a plethora of headlines.

- Now pick your favorite headline—the one you think is strategically strongest. Write copy for a newspaper ad, dropping it into a comped layout with a visual.

- Share the ads with your group and watch the brief come to life.

Adapted from an exercise shared by Sue Northey, Cramer-Krasselt.

Notes

1. Quote from the CLIO Awards Web site, http://www.clioawards.com/html/wsj.riney.html (accessed December 20, 2004).

2. Quote from the CLIO Awards Web site, http://www.clioawards.com/html/wsj/chiat.html (accessed December 20, 2004).

3. Quoted in "Advertising & PIB: Kelly Awards," Magazine Publishers of America Web site, http://www.magazine.org/advertising_and_pib/kelly_awards/winners_and_finalists (accessed June 28, 2005).

4. Quote from the CLIO Awards Web site, http://www.clioawards.com/html/wsj.spivak.html (accessed January 10, 2005).

5. Quote from the CLIO Awards Web site, http://www.clioawards.com/html/wsj/mcelligott/html (accessed December 20, 2004).

6. Quote from the CLIO Awards Web site, http://www.clioawards.com/html/wsj/spivak/html (accessed January 10, 2005).

7. Quoted in Luke Sullivan, *Hey Whipple, Squeeze This: A Guide to Creating Great Ads* (New York: John Wiley, 1998), p. 82.

8. Laurence Klinger, Ad Story: *What's Hot and What's Not?,* February 2009.

9. Jay Conrad Levinson, *Guerilla Marketing Attack* (Boston: Houghton Mifflin, 1989), p. 109.

10. Sullivan, *Hey Whipple, Squeeze This*, p. 80.

Chapter 12

Electronic Media

Radio

Copywriters who work in radio today face many new challenges, the biggest one being *people don't listen.* You need to find a way to break out of the audio wallpaper that radio has become. From a copywriting standpoint, radio presents a perfect opportunity for you to flex creative muscles in totally new ways. You're using words, music, and sound instead of pictures. When you're the writer/producer, the radio commercial is your baby, and the art director can't save your lame idea with a great layout.

Why radio?

For advertisers and the people who write the ads, radio offers many unique advantages:

- It's everywhere, and it's free. There's nothing to buy (other than a radio) and no effort to find programming.

- You can stimulate immediate action. And you know if your spots are successful.

- It supports local retailers and national brands. You can combine national campaign themes to support local stores.

- It features segmented markets. You can personalize your messages. Radio has become a very personal medium, so you can tailor specific messages to reach specific demographics.

- Radio personalities sell. Well-known voices have built-in credibility with key listener demographics.

- It offers creative opportunities. It's the ultimate creative challenge to create visuals with music, voice, and sound effects.

- Digital technology, such as podcasts, provides radio programming on demand.

Image 12.1

Miller High Life's campaign to offer a reasonably priced beer was extended to include a series of "1 second" spots aired on Super Bowl Sunday. The gimmick was to reduce outrageous advertising costs and pass the savings to the consumer.

Why not?

- Radio is usually a background medium. People seek out magazines and newspapers, buy them, and keep them. Selecting a radio station is a completely different process. In many cases, people switch stations just to avoid commercials.

- It's hard to control listenership. While you can select station demographics, you can't be sure anyone's listening.

- It can have high production costs. The expenses of talent, music, production studios, and residuals (the fees you pay the talent each time a spot runs) can really add up.

- It's not good for providing product information—you need other media to give consumers details.

- It imposes time constraints. How much can you really say in 15, 30, or 60 seconds?

- Satellite radio is virtually commercial free.

Creative challenges and opportunities

In most cases, the copywriter plays a big role in production. In smaller shops, he or she may be the sole decision maker for production—the person who selects the talent, music, sound effects, and production studio. As writer/producer, you supervise the recording and editing sessions, making sure everything matches your vision.

It takes talent to cast talent

As Luke Sullivan says: "Casting is everything. In radio, the voice-over you choose is the star, the wardrobe, the set design, everything all rolled into one. It's the most important decision you make during production."[2]

Where to start: When you're a beginning writer, the list of people who can and will help you is rather limited. Let's see: There's you, your roommate, your significant other, and the crazy guy who works the late shift at the Quickie Mart. Not much of a choice, is it? Just for timing and testing purposes, any voice will do. But before you actually record the spot, think carefully about talent. Perhaps you can work with other beginning writers who are really into broadcast—people who work at the campus radio station or broadcast students. Check out your school's drama department. Those trained actors could be natural voice-over talents. If you're looking for the proverbial man on the street, take your recorder down the street and find him. The point is not to take the easy way out and record your friends the night before a radio assignment is due.

In the real world, when you work for a shop that's able to pay talent, your possibilities open up considerably. If you're not familiar with specific voice talent, you can get demos online from talent agencies. Most voice talents are capable of many different styles, so listen carefully. If you're looking for multiple voices,

TABLE 12.1 *Creative Techniques and Their Applications*

Technique	Variations/Applications
Straight announcer	Serious news style
	Humorous read
	Distinctive accent
	Voice modification (fast or slow)
Dialogue/interview	Two or more characters (slice of life)
	Announcer-consumer interaction
	Authority figure/consumer
Dramatization	Mini play
	Reenactment
	News/historical event
	Outrageous situation (comedy)
Testimonial/case history	First-person testimonial
	Story about person's experience
	Celebrity endorsement
Music dominant	Full jingle—original music
	Jingle with "donut" for voice segment
	Popular music
	Adapted popular music—new lyrics
Combinations	Any of the above so that one component is not dominant

you don't have to select them from the same agency or even have them work face-to-face, thanks to the beauty of digital editing.

When you pick your talent, depending on the budget, you may want to hold an audition, especially if you have to sell the client. Many voice talents will do free auditions with your copy. You don't even have to be there. You'll listen to a phone patch, and they'll send you the MP3 via e-mail. It's a great way for a lot of people to listen to a lot of voices. (Beware of selecting talent by committee, though.)

Spend some time considering the voice talent. Even if you just need a straight announcer, there are many styles. Some sound "authoritative"; others are warm and friendly, with "a smile in their voice." The casting of character talent is especially critical. Be very specific about the voice tone, inflection, accent, and timing. You might need to write casting specs to help the talent agent find the perfect voice. Keep a file of voices you'd like to use for future

Example: Dialogue/Interview

This "man on the street" interview by Mal Sharpe takes a deadly topic and makes it fun.

CLIENT: Forest Hills Mortuary
TITLE: "Detroit"

SHARPE: Where are you from, by the way?

MAN: Detroit, Michigan.

SHARPE: You're from Detroit. You're living here now?

MAN: No, I've only been here one day.

SHARPE: Do you realize that the Forest Lawn mortuaries are within your reach financially?

MAN: Forest Lawn mortuaries?

SHARPE: What's wrong?

MAN: What do I want to do with that? I'm from Detroit.

SHARPE: You can go back to Detroit and tell all the people that last year at Forest Lawn, almost one third of all the mortuary arrangements cost under six hundred dollars. Detroit wants to hear that.

MAN: I don't know why Detroit would want to hear that.

SHARPE: What else do they have to listen to?

MAN: What does Forest Lawn mean to Detroit?

SHARPE: What does Detroit mean to Forest Lawn?

MAN: Nothing.

SHARPE: But you are excited to learn that—

MAN: No I'm not. I'm from Detroit. I come here on vacation. Why would I want to learn about mortuary services? You're the first person out here who's talked to me, and now you talk to me about mortuary services.

SHARPE: You want to know about mortuary services. That's why you came out to

Los Angeles.

MAN: No, no, I come out to forget about death. I come out here to live a little.

SHARPE: Yeah, well, I can understand that, being from Detroit. It is exciting to know, though, that last year at Forest Lawn almost one third of all the mortuary arrangements did cost under six hundred dollars. That is exciting, right?

MAN: Not to me it isn't.

SHARPE: Why?

MAN: I'm from Detroit.

---

commercials. However, don't lock yourself into the voice *du jour*—you know, the guy who's suddenly doing every commercial on the air. No matter how great you think your commercial is, it will start to sound like all the others.

TIMING IS EVERYTHING

Beginning writers (and clients who fancy themselves as broadcast writers) sometimes have a hard time with the immutable time constraints of radio. They write beautiful 45-second spots and can't cut them down to 30s. Or they pack in a lot of useless filler to stretch them to 60s. How to make your creativity fit? One way is count the words. If you have a 60-second straight announcer commercial, you should have between 130 and 160 words. As you approach that 160-word limit, your announcer is likely to talk faster, so the whole spot seems frantic and poorly planned. A 30-second announcer spot should be between 60 and 75 words. The announcer will thank you if your word count runs a little on the short side.

The best way to make your spot fit is to time it! Get a stopwatch (don't try to use your wristwatch) and read the commercial the way you'd like it delivered, leaving room for music and/or sound effects that will take time. If you time out at 60 seconds, it's too long—because 9 times out of 10, you'll read it faster than a professional. Try to give the announcer and producer a few precious seconds to play with.

IS THIS FUNNY? (COMEDY IN COMMERCIALS)

Few topics are less humorous than a dissertation on comedy. If you are naturally funny, you don't have to be told how to make people laugh. If you're not gifted with a funny bone, chances are no textbook can tell you how to use humor effectively. However, most people can appreciate humor in advertising, even if they can't deliver it. After toiling to write a funny commercial, you may find that drama or music may be a better way to go. Or you may discover that you have a gift. You'll never know until you try. So, what's funny? Comedienne Carol Burnett said, "Comedy is tragedy plus time."[4] Most comedic situations are about pain or the threat of pain—physical or mental. That pain can be as obvious as dropping a piano on a person's head or as subtle as a mildly embarrassing situation.

Rejection is one of our most powerful psychological fears. So being exposed as stupid, uncaring, socially inept, weak, uncool, or just different can be very painful. And even a threat of rejection brings that pain to the forefront. But it's only funny when it happens to someone else, and then you need some distance in time or space to minimize the tragic effect.

The following commercial is for a local sporting goods retailer in Michigan. This spot proves you don't have to be a big chain with a huge production budget to produce an award-winning commercial. It's also a good example of using pain as a comedic device.

Example: Pain as Comedy

CLIENT: Gordo's Snowboard Store
TITLE: "Snow Down the Crack"

MUSIC: GENTLE GUITAR INSTRUMENTAL

IN AND UNDER

MEDIC: As a ski patrol emergency medic I've seen it all. And the thing that I encounter the most, year after year, is snow down the crack. This occurs when a snowboarder is sitting in the snow trying to get in or out of their bindings. In this position, snow easily gets in the back side of their pants, and in a matter of seconds, they get snow down the crack. Oftentimes, a victim, unable to bear the pain, will scream out, "I've got snow down my crack." It's so frustrating because there's nothing you can do. You just have to wait it out and hope for the best. The good news is, it's completely avoidable . . . by simply going to Gordo's Snowboard Store in the Maple Hill Mall in Kalamazoo. You can buy external high-back step-in bindings for only a hundred and forty nine dollars. So call Gordo at three-four-nine-eighty-three-twenty-eight, and see what he can do for you this winter. And bring an end to the senseless pain of snow down the crack.

When you're writing radio, first listen to a lot of commercials. Then, think about what makes them funny. We did, and we found some common threads in hundreds of funny radio commercials:

Be outrageous. While radio is theater of the mind, it can also be theater of the absurd. Stan Freberg was a master of using radio to turn the absurd into memorable commercials. To demonstrate the power of radio, one of his spots conjured up images of draining Lake Michigan and filling it with the world's largest ice cream sundae. The helicopter bringing in the giant cherry was the perfect way to top off the commercial.

Do something unexpected. Remember the "twist" in Chapter 6? That's what we're talking about here. You introduce a topic, sound effect, or musical cue and then take the listener in an unexpected direction. You can also take a seemingly straight commercial out of the ordinary with twisted copy. The deeper you get into it, the more it twists. Avoid the trap of giving away so much that the listener is ahead of the twist. Sometimes the gimmick is too obvious. It's as if you're saying, "Here's the joke . . . get ready . . . here it is . . . the joke is coming . . . and bingo, here's the punch line you already knew."

Use detail. The combination of sound effects, music, and voice can provide a rich visual image. Radio can't provide detailed information about the product itself, but used the right way, details can make a commercial funnier and more memorable.

Combine extreme situations with realistic dialogue. Some of the funniest commercials feature the most outrageous situations but use downplayed dialogue. Some of the most annoying commercials are just the opposite. The casting, timing, unscripted expressions, overlapping of lines, and subtle sound effects combine to make an outstandingly well-produced and funny spot. There is no way to convey this spot in print. You have to hear it to appreciate it.

Again, think about the commercials you find funny. Then analyze them for their structure. Chances are they will fit one of these three formulas. But keep in mind, it's not the formula that makes it funny; it's the content. Don't write a commercial to fit a formula. Instead, consider whether using some of the techniques in the formulas would make your commercial any better. If not, forget the formulas. As Luke Sullivan says, "Being funny isn't enough, you must have an idea."[5] Above all, you have to be honest with yourself. If you're not funny, face it and move on. Most people aren't funny, and those who are funny might be a little screwed up in other parts of their lives. If, after all your introspection, you find that your sense of humor just doesn't come out in your commercials, try a new tactic.

A word or two about dialogue

Some writers forget how real people actually talk. In their effort to cram the client's name and as many features and benefits as they can into 60 seconds, they turn ordinary folks into aliens from Planet Schlock. Here are the three biggest problems with radio dialogue:

PROBLEM: CONSUMERS BECOMING SALESPEOPLE

You've heard commercials where neighbors, friends, spouses, or whoever launch into spirited and highly detailed conversations about laundry detergent, motor oil, or feminine protection products. It usually starts with one person stating a problem. The other person comes up with a solution with lots of reasons why it's so great. The first person is instantly convinced and relieved that the problem is finally solved.

Solution: *Use the announcer for the sales pitch.* Let the characters talk like real people and let the announcer do the heavy lifting. People expect an announcer to deliver a sales message, whether it comes at the end or separates the dialogue.

Solution: *Use an "authority" figure.* This can be a sales clerk, a doctor, a teacher, or anyone who is expected to know more about the product than the consumer. While the authority may be better suited to pitch the product, you still need to keep the conversation real.

PROBLEM: STILTED LANGUAGE

Even if characters don't become salespeople, many radio commercial conversations sound awfully fake. In reality, people interrupt, step on each other's lines, slur words, say "uhh" and "umm," and are generally pretty inarticulate.

Solution: *Write the way people talk and allow for ad-libs.* If you listen closely to some of the best dialogue commercials, you'll notice people hesitate, overlap each other's lines, use contractions and sentence fragments, and, in general, talk the way real people talk. To do this right, you need the right talent and the flexibility to let them ad-lib. Give the talent the general premise and have them improvise as they rehearse. The announcer can be as polished and articulate as you like, but keep him or her out of the conversation, especially for dialogue. Read both parts yourself or have someone else read with you. If it sounds phony, keep trying until it sounds natural.

PROBLEM: GAPS IN CONVERSATION

Slight pauses between lines ruin many dialogue commercials. In real conversations, most people don't wait a beat before answering a question or responding in a conversation. Sometimes they take a dramatic pause, but more often they start answering while the other person is finishing so that words overlap. Dialogue should not be a tennis match.

Solution: *Compress.* Whether you do it in the actual recording or in editing, look for ways to close the gaps. That does not mean you want the spot to be one breathless run-on sentence, but go for good natural flow—in other words, the way real people talk.

The following spot does a good job with natural-sounding dialogue and separates the sales message from the conversation.

Example: Realistic Dialogue

CLIENT: Minnesota Department of Health
TITLE: "Classified Ad"

SFX: PHONE RINGS

CLERK: Good afternoon, classified ads.

EXEC: Ummm. I wanted to put an ad in the paper.

CLERK: What would you like your ad to say?

EXEC: I want it to read—lost—tobacco executive's soul.

CLERK: (PAUSE) What?

EXEC: Uh. I've lost my soul.

CLERK: What will the rest of the ad say? Just give me the general—

EXEC: The general gist of it is—I'm a corporate tobacco executive and responsible for promotions like giving free cigarettes away to kids during recess in other countries—stuff like that.

CLERK: Oh my goodness.

EXEC: I'm sorry. I missed what you said there.

CLERK: I just—the idea of somebody giving away free cigarettes at recess—it almost knocked me off my chair.

EXEC: Yeah, so I guess you can understand why I feel emptiness inside.

CLERK: Uh-huh. So are you planning on staying with the company?

EXEC: Well, yeah, I mean, it pays really well.

ANNCR: Corporate tobacco knows that if they don't get you hooked before age 18 they probably never will.

Give me a jingle

As we discussed in Chapter 8, music can tie a whole campaign together with one catchy jingle. Some copywriters hate jingles even more than the people who have to listen to them. Luke Sullivan advises not to resort to using a jingle.[6] But as Jewler and Drewniany note: "Not everyone agrees with that. . . . A catchy jingle can make a lasting impression in our minds. For example, there's a good chance you can sing the lyrics to 'Oh I wish I were an Oscar Mayer wiener'"[7] (at least if you're over 30). Most original music is not all that memorable, or if it is, it's remembered for being annoying. Maybe that's why you hear so many recycled popular songs in commercials today. As Bruce Bendinger notes, "One of the best ways to connect with a target is by playing the music he or she was listening to at about the age of 14."[8]

It's all about resonance.

Tips and techniques

- If you forget every other tip, remember this: *Keep it simple.* One main idea per commercial. Preferably one main idea per campaign.

- **Get to the point early and stick with it.**

- **Identify SFX creatively; don't label them.** For example, if you use a thunderstorm effect, don't have a character say, "Uh-oh. Looks like we're having a thunderstorm." Use something like "Looks like we're stuck inside all day."

- **Use music to evoke a place or mood.** For example, mariachi music in the background says you're in Mexico so the announcer doesn't have to.

- **Repeat the client's name.** Some people say you should do this at least three times, more if it's retail. We don't have a magic formula, but if you do repeat the brand or store name several times, make sure it flows naturally and isn't forced.

- **Capture attention early.** The first 5 seconds are critical, whether it's drama, comedy, or music.

- **Use voices to create visuals.** For example, an old lady with a soft, kind voice is a loving grandma. The same voice that's harsh is a witch. Remember the importance of casting specs.

- **Make sure your copy is tailored to the market.** A hip-hop music bed is not going to work on a classic hits station.

- **Avoid using numbers,** especially long phone numbers and street addresses. Instead, feature the Web site where all that information is available.

- **Help your announcer.** Keep the copy a little shorter and watch for hard-to-pronounce words and awkward phrasing. Listen to the announcer if he or she has suggestions for making it sound better.

- **Write the whole spot and read it out loud** before you decide it's not going to work.

Television

Television offers the glamour of show business plus the impact to make or break a brand virtually overnight. Creating a major TV ad campaign not only lets millions of people see your work, it may also shape pop culture for years. As Luke Sullivan says, "Great print can make you famous. Great TV makes you rich."[10] No other medium does a better job of delivering those three motivators— Fame, Fortune, and Fun.

In this digital age, some people wonder if new technology will kill television. In many ways, it's similar to the same fears the movie studios had when television was new. The answer is online content will not replace television. Television will adapt just as the motion picture industry did. Broadcast and cable TV will become more seamless with the Internet. In fact, Nielsen research shows the network's own Web sites are the most popular destinations for viewers when they watch streaming television on the Internet. Television today offers more content from more broadcasters and cable networks, all mashed together and offered in a rapidly growing number of outlets that are manipulated by the viewer. With DVR and 24/7 online viewing capability, "must see" TV will never again describe one night on one network.

Words of Wisdom

"Quick, do something good on radio before someone catches on and makes it as difficult as it is everywhere else." [11]

—Ed McCabe

Image 12.2

Problem: A stain on a shirt talks louder than the interviewee. Solution: Tide to Go, a handy little stick that removes stains. This Super Bowl spot drove millions to the Web site where they could "be the stain" and even submit their own talking stain commercials.

Why television?

In addition to the above considerations, television offers other creative advantages:

- **Impact:** With the exception of the Internet, no other medium does a better job of combining sight and sound.

- **Universal access:** Almost everyone has a TV. Most American homes have three or more sets. TV is the great disseminator of pop culture.

- **Huge audience:** Hundreds of millions of people watch the Super Bowl each year. But even the lowest-rated late-night show attracts millions of viewers.

- **Segmentation (programming, time of day, cable/satellite):** Specialized programming makes it easier to deliver highly targeted commercials.

- **Integrated marketing:** TV is ideal to promote a promotional campaign.

- **It's perfect for cross-promotion:** With advancing technology, TV and the Internet are becoming a seamless entertainment and information medium.

- **More ways to view content:** You can watch your favorite program on DVDs, on your desktop or notebook computer, or on your iPod or BlackBerry.

Why not?

- **Time limits:** Except for some cable channels and infomercials, you are limited to 10-, 15-, 30-, 60-, and 120-second messages. While it's easier to show and tell on TV than on radio, you still have to make every second count.

- **High cost:** Some Web sites offer cheap TV commercial production for as low as $1,299 a spot, but according to the American Association of Advertising Agencies (AAAA), the average production cost is more than $330,000, with director's fees alone averaging more than $21,000.[12] The cost of airtime is subject to the laws of supply and demand, rising and falling on economic trends.

- **TV commercials are the most intrusive form of advertising:** We all say we hate commercial interruptions. It's when people go to the bathroom, get a snack, or just groan about "another stupid commercial."

- **Technology might stifle creativity:** Some people spend a lot of money on TiVo just to avoid commercials. Programs shown online present new challenges to advertisers used to the standard 30-second format.

How to solve those special problems

Concepting. Really study the commercials you see. What makes them funny? Why do you remember them? Then analyze them—how do they handle transitions between scenes, camera angles, lighting, sound effects, music, titles—everything that makes a commercial great? The rest of this chapter offers some ways you can analyze commercials and, we hope, use that information to create your own great commercials.

You may have to limit your concepts to spots you can shoot and produce. You probably can't visit or even simulate some exotic location, indoor shoots present problems without proper lighting, you're not going to have blue-screen or other computer-generated effects, and you're not going to get a movie star for your spot. Be realistic about what you can accomplish if you're planning to actually produce the spot.

Conveying your concept. Computers can help you produce professional-looking print ads. They can also help you put together a good-looking storyboard.

Stock photos and scanned images work well in storyboards. If you're showing a progression of scenes using the same characters, you'll probably need to shoot your own still photography. Whether you use photos or marker renderings (hand-drawn art), make sure your storyboard captures the key frames to convey the concept of the commercial.

Postproduction. Since the advent of camcorders, shooting a commercial has not been the problem. The trick has been editing. Now with Final Cut Pro, Premiere, and other video editing software, it's easier than ever to make your own commercials. It still takes time, talent, and experience to know how to do it right. Make sure you have the patience to review every frame of your commercial until you get it right. The temptation is to say, "It's good enough!" but it usually never is. Also keep in mind even the slickest production can't save a weak concept.

Showing it. If you have a great TV commercial, you can post it on YouTube and provide links so everyone can applaud your masterpiece. You can also mix in your print and radio samples to make a multimedia portfolio. If you don't have produced spots, you can put storyboards in your book, but they have to be as good as your print work.

Technology and trends that affect the creative process

New technology is changing TV as we know it. Some of these technological advances will also change the way you will develop commercials.

Image 12.3

Why tell someone about all the cool apps on an iPhone when you can show them? Apple's simple commercials are pure product demonstration, the oldest technique in the business, but highly effective for the newest technology.

Image 12.4

In a campaign for Volkswagen, Brooke Shields expresses her concerns about yuppie parents who were having children just so they'd have an excuse to buy a Routan minivan. She implored couples to have "babies for love, not German engineering."

Consumer-generated content: Got a camcorder, digital camera, and cell phone that takes video? You can be a commercial producer. In this YouTube generation, the quality of the image takes a back seat to the content. In fact, if your commercial or video looks too slick, you lose your credibility. Consumer-generated content is used by many marketers to generate buy-in from customers, drive traffic to their Web sites, and, if they're lucky, create a mainstream media buzz on traditional television.

Video on demand: Sites like YouTube, MSN Video, Hulu, and others provide TV shows, Webisodes, commercials, viral videos, and just about anything else that can be captured digitally. Unlike broadcast TV, no one will sit still for 10 minutes of commercials in a 30-minute program online. That's why sites usually limit their commercials to the beginning of the program. It's the price you pay for watching a free program.

More devices: TV is moving in two directions at once. Flat-panel digital screens keep getting bigger, brighter, and more affordable. Simultaneously, programming is being downloaded on the tiny screens in iPods and smart phones, the so-called "Third Screens" that increasingly serve as entertainment outlets. A few years ago, the TV set was seen as a future display device for computers. That may still be happening, but the digital revolution has made the iPhone screen the new way to display TV programs. The challenge is to find a way for content providers to make a buck advertising in this digital age.

Web-only studios: Online programming created by Web-only studios such as Sony's C-Spot might provide strong competition to traditional broadcast and cable networks with new original content not available on traditional TV.

Addressability: Addressable advertising lets marketers custom-target different creative content to various audiences, which in turn allows them to make ads more specific to the wants and needs of the viewers. Interactivity will allow viewers to respond to these highly targeted ads to select longer-format commercials, to access retailers, and to order directly while watching TV.

How to show your concept

You have several ways to convey your concept for a TV commercial. The one you use depends on the stage of development and the conceptual ability of the person approving it.

SCRIPT

This is the most basic and often the only method you need to show your concept. It's written in the same way as a radio script, except there is a column on the left for VIDEO that lines up with the AUDIO column on the right. As with radio, the directions and effects are in CAPS.

STORYBOARD

For more detail, you can create a storyboard, with pictures of key scenes from beginning to end. The audio and video directions are under each frame. A storyboard can be sketched by hand or created with photography. Storyboards really help the producer, director of photography, and postproduction crew, as well as the client, understand the spot.

KEY FRAME

This should be the most memorable scene of a commercial. It may be the "punch line" or "payoff frame" in the spot. Think of the single image that a newspaper or magazine might use to describe a TV commercial, and you'll know what we mean.

SCENARIO

This is a brief description of the commercial concept. Typically, it starts with an introduction such as "We open on a. . . ." The scenario can describe scenes in more detail and can also work in marketing and creative strategies.

Image 12.5

Pepsi's "Refresh Anthem," which debuted at the 2009 Super Bowl, resonated with baby boomers and Gen Y by using vignettes of youth activities from both generations. Dylan's "Forever Young" is the soundtrack, which was covered by Will.i.am later in the spot.

Styles of commercials

Describing different kinds of commercials won't make you creative. However, if you start to analyze the various styles of commercials, you'll see a pattern. You may begin to understand why they are moving, funny, or hard selling. A lot of the styles blend together, so you may have a celebrity in a problem/solution format or a vignette with a strong musical theme. We offer the following list of styles not as formulas but rather to help you watch and then create commercials with a critical eye and ear.

Slice of life (problem/solution): In the so-called Golden Age of Television, many commercials featured a slice of life (which was more often a parallel universe) in which a frustrated housewife couldn't solve some kind of cleaning problem. A helpful neighbor, announcer, or cartoon character told her about the advertised product, and like magic, her problems were over. Today's commercials (except for most infomercials) are not quite that cheesy, but they're still using problem/solution formats.

Demonstration: It didn't take advertisers long to figure out that TV is a natural to show a product being used. Especially one that moves. Demonstrations have also been very effective in showing what a product can do. One of the best demonstrations was a wordless commercial for Cheer that showed a funny little guy putting a dirty napkin into a clear bowl of cold water, adding Cheer, swirling it all around, and pulling out a clean napkin. The following are various types of demonstrations:

- Straight product in use

- Torture test

- Comparison to competitor

- Before and after

- Whimsical demonstration—exaggerated situation

Spokesperson (testimonial): You don't have to be famous to pitch a product, although if you do it right, you might become famous, like Subway's Jared. Some brands are associated with a single character, created just to promote that brand, such as the Maytag repairman, played by several different actors over 3 decades. Whether it's the CEO or an actor, some companies use the same person to represent them on TV. Richard Branson is the personification of Virgin airlines, records, cell phones, and whatever else he's selling today. Vacuum cleaner innovator James Dyson is the perfect spokesperson to hype his own products.

Celebrity: This is perhaps the oldest technique in television advertising, borrowed from decades of use in print and radio. Whether it's a sports figure, cartoon character, or movie star, a celebrity can gain immediate attention and shine some of his or her limelight on the product. As we discussed previously, make sure the celebrity has some logical connection with the product, even if it's indirect. For example, several years ago, country singer Willie Nelson did commercials for H&R Block. What's the connection? Years ago Willie had some problems with the IRS. A good tax preparer could have helped him stay out of trouble with the feds.

Image 12.6

Doritos has earned a lot of great publicity by soliciting commercials from ordinary consumers. This spot (which cost a few thousand bucks to produce) was number one in USA Today's Ad Meter *competition. The spot featured a guy using a snow globe to break into the snack vending machine to score some Doritos for lunch.*

Story line: This may be a mini movie, with beginning, middle, and end. Budweiser has produced a series of popular brand-reinforcing commercials featuring their iconic Clydesdales. For example, in one spot a Clydesdale briefly meets a circus horse and chases across the country to find her, and at the end the two run away presumably to be happy ever after.

Vignettes: These are usually made from a series of short clips that are strung together, usually with a strong musical track to hold them all together. Vignettes can be used to show different people using the same product or a variety of products with the same brand. A good example of using vignettes is the global "I'm lovin' it" campaign for McDonald's. The initial spots showed a wide variety of ages and races. An example of different products for the same brand would be some Honda corporate spots that show cars, lawnmowers, motorcycles, generators, and all the other products that Honda makes.

Musical: It's hard to separate music as a category, since it's so integral to commercials today. However, we'll consider this as a unique type when music is the dominant factor of the commercial. For example, Pepsi's commercial using Bob Dylan's "Forever Young" did a nice job of tying together youth culture from two generations.

Humor in TV

The commercials people remember most seem to be the funny ones. Probably 9 out of the top 10 Super Bowl spots each year are meant to be funny. As with radio, don't start out to create a funny television spot. You may have a good joke, but it's not a commercial unless it sells something. Luke Sullivan offers some excellent advice for writers who want to make their mark with humorous TV spots: "Don't set out to be funny. Set out to be interesting. I find it interesting that the Clios had a category called Best Use of Humor. And curiously, no Best Use of Seriousness."[14]

What makes it funny?

Some of the funniest commercials include at least some of the following elements:

- **The unexpected:** Throw in a surprise ending, a twist, a zinger, or something they don't see coming. Many times that unexpected ending involves pain—physical or mental.

- **Pain/risk of pain:** The old formula of tragedy plus time works for TV even better than for radio because you can show it as well as tell it.

- **Exaggeration:** Making things extremely bigger, smaller, faster, or slower than expected can be humorous. So can giving animals human traits or vice versa. Extreme behavior can be funny too.

What makes it good?

You need more than a funny situation to make a good commercial. Many humorous ideas fall flat because of poor production. The best humorous commercials need all four of the following:

- **Good direction:** The writer and director need to know when to use a wide shot, when to zoom in, how many scenes to use, and all the other intangibles that make a good spot great.

- **Attention to detail:** Do the sets look real? Are little kids dressed like real children? Are the props accurate for the time frame depicted? Little things mean a lot, and they show.

- **Talent/acting:** This is perhaps the most critical element. The same qualities that make a great comic actor different from a clown apply to commercials. Remember that with TV you can show subtle expressions and nuances in close-ups. You don't need the broad gestures of a stand-up comic or stage actor.

- **Editing:** Well-executed postproduction makes a huge difference. The timing and transition of scenes can turn a "cute" concept into a truly funny commercial.

Tips and techniques

Aside from the general advice for humorous spots listed above, the following tips apply to nearly all commercials. These are offered as rules of thumb and not as hard-and-fast guidelines you must follow. However, experience shows that you can have a lot better results if you heed most of them when you are critiquing commercials.

- **Get immediate attention.** The first 3 to 10 seconds are critical. Make the first couple of seconds visually interesting.

- **Stick with one main idea.** Keep it simple. Don't try cramming more than 2–3 scenes per 10 seconds or more than 10 scenes per 30. If you're using vignettes, you might need a lot more.

- **Think about brand awareness.** Show the product and involve characters with it.

- **Use titles to reinforce key points.** But don't use so many that the viewer feels like he or she is reading the commercial.

- **Think visually.** Consider how you want to move within a scene, transition between scenes, and change scenes.

Words of Wisdom

"The best advertising comes out of a sense of humor and perspective about life and a realistic perspective on the importance of the product in our lives." [15]

—Jeff Goodby

- **Don't forget synergy.** Don't show what you're saying or say what you're showing.

- **Audio is still important.** Use music/SFX to describe place or mood.

- **Make every word count—count every word.** The rule of thumb is about 60 words for a 30-second spot. That's less than radio.

Ad Story

Thinking on Your Feet While Working in a Vacuum

Jeff Ericksen has served as a copywriter and creative director at some of the biggest agencies in the Midwest. In this story he tells how to turn a potential disaster into a great commercial:

"Insurance is boring. Therefore, insurance advertising must be even worse. Not so. In creating a television campaign for Travel Guard Insurance, we had the benefit of working with an incredibly insightful client who knew that when all others zig, you have to zag. They also understood that not having a huge media budget, their 1 campaign would have to do the work of 10. They wanted to stand out. Cool. In doing research for the project we came across a number of very odd but real claims travelers had filed. This led us to the platform and copy line, 'For the things you can't imagine when traveling, there's Travel Guard Insurance.' With this as our starting point, we created even more bizarre scenarios in which Travel Guard could save a vacationer's day. One approved commercial had airport baggage handlers trying on people's clothes and 'borrowing' items like toothbrushes to highlight baggage protection.

"Another spot featured a couple on a romantic bike ride in Italy. When the man's eye wanders to another woman, he ends up sailing over some bushes, showing the need for emergency medical coverage. But it's the third one that proved to be most interesting.

"Here's the concept: A guy is using one of those vacuum packing systems to get ready for a trip. He notices the device's superior sucking power, so he decides to put it down his pants. Cut to him doubled up on the floor as the paramedics come to take him away, thus showing the need for trip cancellation coverage. Funny . . . sure. Not a chance in hell it'll get approved . . . wrong. The client loved it. Sold. Now the real fun begins. Two days before the shoot, the director and I are in the hotel bar talking about some last-minute issues when we get a call. The vacuum spot has to die. Did some VP get cold feet? Were the People for the Ethical Treatment of Penises planning a boycott? Nope. It turns out legal discovered the underwriters of the insurance policy would not cover any self-inflicted wounds. So now what?

"With locations picked, talent chosen, schedules made, and crew hired, there was a lot set in stone and paid for. Never willing to give up, we looked at the hand we were dealt. We have a guy, a bedroom location, and a vacuum packer. Now here's where the lesson lies. It seems the most successful people in advertising are the ones who can think on their feet, see opportunity in the face of disaster, and always believe there's a solution.

"In the end we created a spot where a wife was packing for a vacation while a lazy husband lies on a bed eating cheese puffs. Noticing the man with crumbs on his chest, the wife starts to vacuum them off. Unfortunately for him, yet hilarious for us, the hose gets stuck on his nipple, nearly ripping it off. The spot ends with the man in the hospital with a protective cone over his nipple, foolishly eating cheese puffs again, afraid his wife will notice. Spot airs. Sales rise. Client is happy. All is right with the world."[16]

—Jeff Ericksen
Founder and Instructor,
Ms Coffmansen's Portfolio Finishing School,
Milwaukee

- **Give the viewers some credit.** Let them complete the creative equation.

- **Don't overexplain.** They'll remember it better, too.

- **Keep conversation real.** Dialogue should be natural, not forced. Let the announcer be the salesperson, if you have to have one.

- **Don't save it all for the ending.** A commercial should be entertaining through the whole spot. Don't have a sloppy buildup to a punch line.

- **Think in campaigns.** Make your commercial compatible with, but not identical to, the other elements. It should not be a video version of the print ad. Think in terms of extending a concept without repeating the same idea in subsequent spots.

- **Study great commercials.** Look for style, camera angles, editing techniques, and so on. Understand what makes them great.

Checklist for your TV commercial

When you've finished your script or storyboard, let it rest, if you can. Then come back to it and check the following:

- Does the video tell the story without audio, and how well?

- Did you specify all the necessary directions? Could a director take your script and produce the spot?

Image 12.7

Even though they're an online insurance company, Progressive.com in their TV commercials features a rather quirky clerk to check out customers as if they were buying insurance in a retail store. Love her or hate her, she is memorable.

Image 12.8

Budweiser has consistently featured their Clydesdale brand icons in Super Bowl commercials. This one told the love story between a Clydesdale and a circus pony named Daisy.

- Do the audio and video complement each other, and are they correctly timed for each other?

- Are there too many scenes (can some be omitted)? Do you need more scenes?

- Have you identified the product well?

- Does your script win attention quickly and promise an honest benefit?

- Have you provided a strong visualization of the One Thing that will linger in the viewer's memory?

- Could a competitive brand be substituted easily and fit well?

- Is it believable?

- Are you proud to say you wrote it?[17]

Image 12.9

Dentyne twists technology by showing the original meaning; in this case, whispering a secret is "voicemail." Other spots showed a romantic kiss as "the original instant message."

Ad Story

The Word That Won the Super Bowl
"Castrol Edge was a new synthetic motor oil, going head to head against the world's market leader. And challenger brands have to do extreme things to win. So Castrol chose the Super Bowl, the world's biggest media venue, to launch Edge. They had a compelling claim: New Edge had eight times better wear protection than the market leader. We needed just one more thing to make the launch a hit. Monkeys.

"You can follow all the conventional strategic rules and still fail in the Super Bowl. Sure, you made a perfectly nice little spot, but it wasn't a Super Bowl spot. The kind that gets talked about.

The kind that gets in the top ten of *USA Today's* [Ad Meter]. Our client expected to be among the top ten most-liked commercials. Not an unreasonable request when airtime costs $3 million.

"There were a lot of crazy ideas thrown around. But the creative guys kept returning to monkeys for a simple, smart reason: Everybody likes monkeys. One hundred million people of all stripes and persuasions watch the Super Bowl. You gotta go broad.

"Yet using monkeys was not without risk. Had America seen one too many monkey spots in the Super Bowl? The creative team had an answer. Grease monkeys.

"You now have two of the cardinal rules of Super Bowl strategy: Go broad and go high concept—the idea that these monkeys actually work on your car. They have real skills.

"But the creative team pushed it further up the concept ladder. What if grease monkeys actually existed and made you their king when you bought new Castrol Edge?

"Wow. The rare double high concept—by making the consumer king, the grease monkeys also elevate his stature as protector of the family car. Castrol puts Dad on the pedestal.

"And then there's the final piece of the Super Bowl matrix. Humor. What we had was amusing. It was double high concept. It was memorable. It fit the brand and the product. By virtue of monkeys, there was some guarantee of humor, but was it enough? Was it Super Bowl worthy?

"We scripted and shot several endings but then something beyond unexpected happened. The monkey, who was sitting on the actor's lap, kissed him on the lips. And the actor actually kissed him back. Now we had our funny Super Bowl Ending. It made it into the [Ad Meter] top ten.

"There were smart strategic calls at every step of the way and a monkey who brought us a final bit of dumb luck.

"Strategy, luck and monkeys."[18]

—David Fowler,
Executive Creative Director,
Ogilvy, New York

Presenting your TV commercial

OK, your spot meets all the requirements in the checklist. Now you're ready to show it to the boss. It's not a print ad that you can just hand in. You have to sell it. The following is a pretty good procedure for presenting a TV commercial, especially to a small group.

- If it's a stand-alone concept, review the creative strategy and state the One Thing you want to convey.

- State your main creative theme for the commercial.

- Describe main elements—music, effects, actors.

- Walk through the video portion; describe what's happening.

- Hit the key visual points, with emphasis on the key frame.

- Once the visual path is established, go back and read the copy.

- Summarize the action in a brief scenario.

Image 12.10

Demonstrations don't always have to be literal depictions of the product in use. In the UPS "White Board" TV campaign, Andy Azula (the agency's creative director) used simple drawings to explain the company's services to B2B customers.

Image 12.11

The classic storyboard is still the simplest way to show how audio and visual work together in a TV commercial.

Who's Who?

Stan Freberg fathered "abnormal" or comic advertising in the late 1950s through the 1970s. His spoofs of Madison Avenue on his CBS radio show convinced Howard Gossage to use Freberg's warped sense of humor for real commercials. His ads "that don't take themselves so damn seriously" won awards and sold Contadina tomato paste, Pacific Airlines, Chun King foods, Jeno's pizza, Sunsweet prunes, and Heinz Great American soups. Freberg established and exploited advertising's fun potential.[20]

Dick Orkin first broke into radio with syndicated comedy serials such as "Chicken Man" and "The Tooth Fairy." With his distinctive voice and off-the-wall sense of humor, it wasn't long before Orkin was in high demand to write and produce comedy radio spots. Through his partnership with Bert Berdis, Orkin won scores of awards for his radio commercials. Later, he cofounded the Famous Radio Ranch in Hollywood. In 2002, Orkin was inducted into the National Association of Broadcasters Radio Hall of Fame.

Lee Clow was the art director and creative force behind some of the most influential advertising of his generation. His work for Chiat\Day and later TBWA\Chiat\Day includes the famous Apple "1984" spot as well as the Taco Bell Chihuahua, Nike's "Air Jordan," and the Energizer Bunny. Dan Wieden of Wieden + Kennedy, another creative giant of the modern era, described Clow this way: "Lee Clow's heart has been pumping this sorry industry full of inspiration for longer than most its practitioners have been alive. He is the real thing. He is indefatigable. I hate him."[21]

Cliff Freeman has used outside-the-box creative vision to build recognition and brand awareness. His agency's unique approach attracted the general media coverage that transformed advertising into popular icons. Freeman gained fame with the still-popular Mounds/Almond Joy candy bars ("Sometimes you feel like a nut . . . sometimes you don't") and Wendy's "Where's the Beef?" campaigns. His own agency, opened in 1987, brought forth Little Caesars' "Pizza! Pizza!" Freeman's distinctive work has brought him numerous major awards along with "most remembered" and "most popular" honors.[22]

Hal Riney achieved creative excellence by getting people to like his clients. His work for Saturn cars, Bartles & Jaymes, President Reagan, and others celebrated a unique American spirit that was confident yet at times self-effacing. While working at the San Francisco office of Ogilvy & Mather, he was part of the First Tuesday team, which created ads for Ronald Reagan's reelection effort. In 1986, he took over the office, renaming it Hal Riney & Partners, and went on to mastermind GM's Saturn introduction with dazzling success.

Exercises

1. Sketching in Words

This will help you get outside the demographic cube and into the psychographic menagerie and closer to radio, TV, and digital production.

- Create a character sketch of someone you know—as if you were describing a character in a movie or novel.

- Next introduce this person and your relationship to this person in one short paragraph.

- Now describe the following in great, juicy detail:

  o Physical appearance: gender, age, body type, hair, eyes, facial features, dress, posture, movements, mannerisms, speech . . .

  o Background: education, religion, family, childhood experiences, financial situation, profession, marital status, other relationships, habits, surroundings/environment, health . . .

  o Personality: distinctive traits, self-image, yearnings/dreams, fears/apprehensions, sense of humor, code of ethics, attitude . . .

  o Other details: hobbies, skills, favorite foods, colors, books, music, art, and so on . . .

- Now get together and evaluate your work focusing on the following: Did the writer create a person that that feels real? Does the person have depth? If an actor were going to play the role of this person, would the actor have enough insight to justly portray him or her?

Adapted from an exercise shared by Kimberly Selber, PhD, Associate Professor, University of Texas–Pan American.

2. Audio Hunting Expedition

Let's see how sound can inspire you.

- Working in pairs choose one brand—a brand that is a big part of your everyday life.

- Get ready to go exploring. Hunt down audio recordings of sounds connected with your brand.

- Then record 10 people expressing their affection for the brand—anything goes.

- Now do some secondary research on their brand. Consider if anything you found out about the brand matches the audio images you've collected.

- Inspired by your audio hunting expedition and grounded in secondary research, sketch out a quick 30-second radio spot.

- If you're really adventurous, record your spot it using some of the footage you've collected. Use your own voice-over or find a brave and willing friend (preferably from the drama department!).

Notes

1. Dick Orkin, president of the Radio Ranch in Los Angeles, California, in an audio clip (track 19) available at the Radio Marketing Bureau's Web site page advertising the CD *Radio Renaissance,* http://www.rmb.ca/asp/creative-radiorenaissance.asp (accessed July 5, 2005).

2. Luke Sullivan, *Hey Whipple, Squeeze This: A Guide to Creating Great Ads* (New York: John Wiley, 1998), p. 142.

3. Ibid, p. 145.

4. Quoted in A. Jerome Jewler and Bonnie L. Drewniany, *Creative Strategy in Advertising,* 7th ed. (Belmont, CA: Wadsworth, 2001), p. 168.

5. Sullivan, *Hey Whipple, Squeeze This,* p. 132.

6. Ibid, p. 139.

7. Jewler and Drewniany, *Creative Strategy in Advertising,* p. 160.

8. Bruce Bendinger, *The Copy Workshop Workbook* (Chicago: Copy Workshop, 2002), p. 279.

9. Quoted in Jewler and Drewniany, *Creative Strategy in Advertising,* p. 168.

10. Ibid, p. 103.

11. Quoted in Sullivan, *Hey Whipple, Squeeze This,* p. 139.

12. See the AAAA Web site at http://www.aaaa.org.

13. David Ogilvy, *Ogilvy on Advertising* (New York: Random House, 1985), p. 111.

14. Sullivan, *Hey Whipple, Squeeze This,* p. 56.

15. "Jeff Goodby's Creative Rules," from *Advertising Age,* January 29, 2001, available on the Center for Interactive Advertising Web site, http://www.ciadvertising.org/student_account/spring_02/adv382j/eoff/ultimategoodby/creative.html (accessed July 6, 2005).

16. Jeff Ericksen, Ad Story: *Thinking on Your Feet While Working in a Vacuum,* September 2005.

17. Phillip Ward Burton, *Advertising Copywriting* (Lincolnwood, IL: NTC Business Books, 1991), p. 258.

18. David Fowler, Mark Davis, and Stephen Winston, Ad Story: *The Word That Won the Super Bowl,* February 2009.

19. David Ogilvy, *Confessions of an Advertising Man* (New York: Ballantine, 1971), p. 70.

20. See *Advertising Age*'s "Web Version of the 1999 'Advertising Century' Report," 1999, http://www.adage.com/century (accessed July 5, 2005).

21. Quoted in Karen Lee, "The Lowdown on Lee Clow: Advertising's Chief Creative Maven of the Last Quarter Century," 2000, available on the Center for Interactive Advertising Web site, http://www.ciadvertising.org/student_account/fall_00/adv382j/klee/Lee_Clow/Lee_Clow.htm (accessed July 6, 2005).

22. "Cliff Freeman," in "Top 100 People of the Century," *Advertising Age,* March 29, 1999, http://www.adage.com/century/people098.html (accessed July 6, 2005).

Digital

Predicting the Digital Future

In the first edition of this book, the digital world was changing so rapidly the best we could do was state all we knew about the Internet, knowing that much of it would be obsolete when the book was finally printed. Now that we are so much smarter, with this edition, we would like to list what we know for sure about the future of the digital world.

Words of Wisdom

"Ten years ago we thought of the Internet in terms of technology and not as medium. Today, we're in the media business where we use technical people to quantify it." [1]

—Steve Moss

That's it. Nada. Because as fast as the advertising world catches up with new technology, all the rules change. In the first edition we made some predictions—some of which have come true, and some of which are still to come. But much more has happened that no one could have predicted. Who could have anticipated the impact of YouTube, MySpace, or Twitter? Who knew that BlackBerry and iPhone would help create a Third Screen Revolution in marketing communications? Who was talking about viral seeding, mashups, and hybrid marketing as part of their mainstream campaigns? More important, who knows how technology and creativity will merge to create the *next* big thing in the digital world?

In this chapter, we will examine some trends and technology as they apply to the creative end of our business, although it's almost impossible to separate the message from the medium. As you'll see, when it comes to digital, it applies to so many topics in this book—promotions, broadcast, business-to-business, campaigns . . . just about everything we see and touch nowadays. Our challenge with this chapter is to not get too bogged down in *how* things work. If we do, it becomes a regurgitation of geek-speak reference articles. Instead, we will gloss over the technical jargon and try to deal with how to make all that left-brain stuff merge with right-brain creativity.

Why the Internet?

In addition to the statistics listed above, the Internet is desirable for a creative person for several reasons:

- **It's always on.** It provides entertainment and information 24/7, anywhere in the world.

- **It's personal.** Perhaps the most personal medium ever.

- **It's dynamic.** The use of video and audio plus print generates more impact. 3G and Wi-Fi speed the delivery of streaming video and other rich media to cell phones and laptops.

- **It's a Web.** Links provide easy access to marketing partners for co-op and cross-promotion opportunities and integration with other media.

- **It's scalable.** In other words, you can expand the content and capabilities of a Web site in ways unimaginable in any other medium.

- **It fits into a campaign.** You can make a Web site the flagship of your campaign and promote it with other media.

- **It's a data mine.** Whether visitors provide data consciously or you get it under the radar, you know who's visiting your site.

- **Almost everyone is connected.** The digital gap is closing fast. The Internet will continue to be more accessible through laptops, cell phones, and wireless desktop devices.

Why not?

Most of the following drawbacks will be solved in the near future through better technology. But right now, the Internet is not the final solution.

- You need a computer or a cell phone . . . with all the connectivity issues ranging from signal strength to battery drain.

- Attention spans are shrinking. People don't want to wait for rich media to load. That means you have to grab attention in a few seconds and hold it.

- You are limited to the size of a computer screen. No matter how it's displayed, you still can't touch and feel it.

Web 2.0

Around 2004, online gurus began to talk about a new way to look at the Internet and started calling it Web 2.0. It wasn't so much about new technology as it was about new ways to use it. Developers began using the Web as a platform that allowed for the creation of social networking, video sharing, blogs, wikis, and folksonomies that have generated unprecedented levels of participation among and between communities of users. Web 2.0 has become a marketing revolution that takes advantage of much of the Web technology that has existed for years. Web 1.0 was about developing a link between the marketer and the individual user. Web 2.0 is about helping users connect with each other. As broadband, Wi-Fi, and 3G technology became more widespread, a critical mass of Web users formed online communities connected by computers and mobile devices. Successful online marketing concepts such as MySpace, Facebook, YouTube, Flickr, and Twitter have connected millions and must continue to evolve to retain the loyalty of an increasingly fickle and tech-savvy generation.

Web 2.0 sites typically include some of the following features, which Andrew McAfee calls SLATES:

1. **S**earch: the ease of finding information through key word search, which makes the platform valuable.

2. **L**inks: guides to important pieces of information. The best pages are the most frequently linked to.

3. **A**uthoring: the ability to create constantly updating content over a platform that is shifted from being the creation of a few to being the constantly updated, interlinked work. In wikis, the content is iterative in the sense that people undo and redo each other's work. In blogs, content is cumulative in that posts and comments of individuals are accumulated over time.

4. **T**ags: categorization of content by creating tags that are simple, one-word descriptions to facilitate searching and avoid rigid, premade categories.

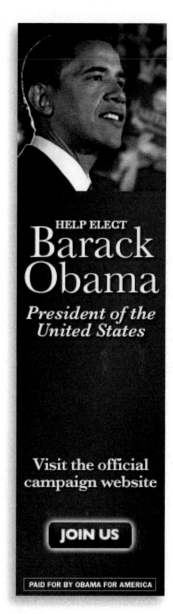

HELP ELECT
Barack Obama
President of the United States

Visit the official campaign website

JOIN US

PAID FOR BY OBAMA FOR AMERICA

Image 13.1

The Obama campaign used Internet advertising such as this banner ad and other online marketing techniques to reach younger, more affluent, and technologically savvy voters.

5. **E**xtensions: automating some of the work and pattern matching by using algorithms (e.g., amazon.com recommendations).

6. **S**ignals: the use of RSS (Really Simple Syndication) technology to notify users of any changes in the content by sending e-mails to them.[2]

Web Site Design

As a copywriter you may be involved in Web site design in several ways, ranging from developing a total site to writing a headline for a banner ad. As art director, you may have to develop a design for whole sites down to fourth- or fifth-level pages or landing pages that instantly capture the user's attention. Whatever your role, you need to have a big idea for the site. What's the One Thing that people will take away from looking at your landing page or Web site? Beyond that, you need to know if your ideas are practical and affordable. Your role in Web site development begins with your understanding the client's wants and needs as well as those of the customers. What does the client want to accomplish? Do they want an e-commerce component? Is this site only for information? Do they have opportunities to include consumer-generated videos, blogs, or interactive games?

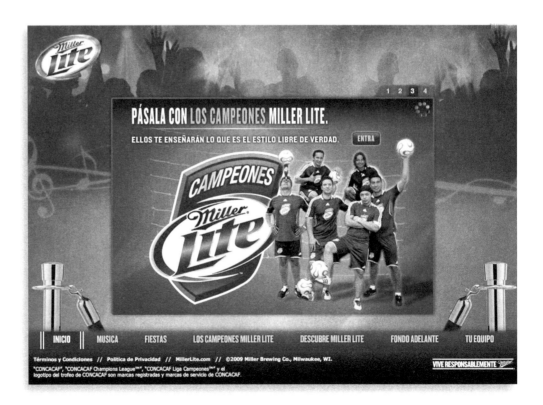

Image 13.2

Miller Lite Latino, part of the main Miller Lite site, is not only in Spanish; it also embraces Hispanic culture and along the way it's simple and easy to navigate.

When you are creating a Web site, there are only three main things you need to do:

1. **Get them to come**
2. **Get them to stay**
3. **Get them to come back**

Do all three, and your Web site will be successful.

Get Them to Come

If your Web site is the hub of your marketing communication program, the goal is to have a lot of spokes and make sure they're well connected. Your traditional print, out-of-home, direct mail, and broadcast should all point to your site. Here are some tips for using online tactics to increase traffic:

1. Always feature the URL in your traditional advertising. If you don't have an easy-to-remember URL, get one.

2. Create one or several landing pages with unique URLs rather than forcing the user to wade through all the information in a complicated or hard-to-navigate corporate site.

3. Get serious about Search Engine Optimization. If you can't develop the key word in your organic content, work with an expert in optimization.
   (a) Put your most important and descriptive key word first and include popular key word in the title tag.
   (b) Don't repeat your key word, or it will look like spam.
   (c) Avoid doing the whole site in Flash. Flash is not searchable.
   (d) Use 25 words or less for key word.
   (e) The more social networks you join, the more Google mentions you'll have.

4. Sometimes you have to invest in a sponsored search, buy key word, and bid up your rankings on search engines. Most legitimate marketers buy words associated with their brand or product category. Others buy words that casual surfers are looking for to get their messages moved to the top of search lists.

5. Develop an e-mail program that gets read and stimulates action. Give recipients the means to respond immediately or a way to opt out.

6. Make sure your banner ads and text links go exactly where they should. Too many hot leads end up getting lost.

Internet advertising

Banner ads have been the staple of Internet advertising. The most common size is 468 × 60 pixels, and they usually appear at the top of a commercial Web page.

Image 13.3

Dove's Campaign for Real Beauty did more than show how ordinary women could feel comfortable posing in their underwear. This Web site also contained information on spreading the message with workshops, reports on self-esteem, and information about the Dove Self-Esteem Fund. It's become the hub of movement.

They are priced on a cost per thousand (CPM) page basis. Prices vary based on targeted sites and whether the banners are static or pop-up. According to Bruce Morris: "Banners are not terribly good for generating traffic but have a powerful branding effect. Matching site content to banner ad subjects can certainly increase their power."[3] Rich media banners go beyond the ordinary banner ad to add drop-down boxes, sound-on mouse-overs, animated bits, and even interactive games. Rich media banners and badges provide advertisers with ways to present additional content and interaction within traditional ad sizes. According to studies, they can also lead to significant increases in response, brand perception, and recall.

Get Them to Stay

OK, now you've got them hooked. How do you keep them on the line and get them into the boat? Like any other advertising message, you have to provide something that interests the user. Remember wants and needs? The person who clicks on your Web site has to be convinced in a matter of seconds that it's worth his or her time to take a longer look. Janine Carlson, marketing director at ESI International, points out the greatest challenge facing online marketers: "You can't be satisfied with getting a reaction. You have to spark an interaction. One is simply a split-second exchange with your audience. The other opens the door for an ongoing relationship. And that should be the goal for anyone working in advertising or marketing."[4]

The following are some ways to keep viewers engaged.

Portals

The personal portal is the interface to all the back-end services that the user needs most often. Many of these sites have names that begin with the word *my,* such as "My Yahoo" or "My eBay." The purpose is to give visitors the ability to customize the content they see and how it is displayed. If you produce a lot of new content regularly, a portal model may be a great way to serve the needs of a number of diverse Web audiences. Portals operate on the traditional Web 1.0 server model, using a "salad bar" style with content presented side-by-side without overlaps.[5]

Mashups

Mashups differ from portals in that they rely on newer, loosely defined Web 2.0 technology. Applications provided from many different sources are combined and sent to the server or client. Instead of discrete boxes of information, mashups are "melting pots" of content, combined in arbitrary arrangements. For example, a real estate Web site may want to include Google Maps to show the location of a property. But if the house for sale is in Aspen, for example, the site may also want to have local ski conditions, a blog by local ski bums, a list of trendy new bars, and an interactive photo gallery of the neighborhood. Mashups are a key component of integrating business and data services.[6] They allow business Web sites to provide the personalized information their potential customers desire. Once more, it's all about satisfaction of wants and needs.

Interactive entertainment

People don't watch television to see commercials. And they don't visit Web sites to see your ads. But unlike TV, which is limited when it comes to merging products into programming, the Web is wide open to innovative entertainment options.

Interactive programs have been around for a few years with increasing levels of technological sophistication. They can be contests, polls, and games that are directly tied to a brand or ad campaign. Or they can be destination sites with sponsors. Regardless of the brand tie-ins, the goal is to keep people on the site.

Burger King's "Subservient Chicken," which promoted TenderCrisp chicken sandwiches within the "have it your way" brand message, was a huge interactive entertainment and brand-building hit, keeping viewers on the site for an astounding average of 5 minutes and 44 seconds. Just as important, the viral buzz from viewers sending the link to friends generated more than 7 million impressions.[7] CareerBuilder created "Monk-e-mail," which was integrated with their TV campaign about employees forced to work with chimps. Their site allowed viewers to select various images of chimps; customize them with hats, clothing, and other accessories; and make them talk in a number of voices and accents. The fun part was you could make them say anything you typed or you

Image 13.4

Burger King set out to conduct the ultimate taste test— comparing Big Macs to Whoppers in remote areas of the globe that had never seen a hamburger, let alone Golden Arches or the King. The Whopper Virgins Web site featured a richly produced video that looked like a network documentary.

could record your own voice. As with the Subservient Chicken, the potential of the viral buzz multiplied the effectiveness of this campaign. In fact, Monk-e-mail was voted into the Viral Hall of Fame.

Online video and Webisodes

As part of Burger King's "Whopper Virgins" campaign (where people in remote locations around the world tried eating a Whopper for the first time), they created a "documentary" film for the Whopper Virgins Web site. The premise was for people who had never even heard of hamburgers to compare the Whopper to the McDonald's Big Mac in a totally unbiased taste test. While it got people talking, ad critic Barbara Lippert commented, "Attention-getting, yes. Diabolically clever, uh-huh. But it's advertising, and there's nothing honest about it."[8]

Suave and Sprint collaborated to develop "In the Motherhood: For Moms, By Moms, About Moms." The Web site featured a series of 5- to 7-minute Webisodes showing funny situations with three main characters. In addition to watching the produced videos, viewers were encouraged to send in their own scripts. The winner would be used for a new episode. The site also included a social network component where moms could share stories with each other. It also included recipes and games. Viewers could also click on buttons for Suave and Sprint. The success of the online programming convinced ABC to pick up the concept for their prime-time lineup, further blurring the lines between the Internet and television.

Blogs

If blogs are handled properly, they can keep the viewer engaged long enough to read some of the entries and maybe long enough to participate. Weblogs started as a grassroots movement where ordinary people could share their thoughts, pictures, videos, and other personal information, from vacation photos to deep philosophical dialogues. The key to the popularity of blogs is their impromptu, unstructured, bottom-up nature. When the spirit of consumer-generated blogs is co-opted by marketers, the results are often disastrous for a brand. Many companies, in their attempt to promote a trendy brand, lost all credibility by heavy-handed attempts to invade the blogosphere with poorly designed campaigns. A survey released in 2008 by Forrester Research noted that only 16% of people trust what they read on corporate blogs, ranking it below message posts and direct mail. Social networking from brands provided the second least trusted source of information.[9] For example, a few years ago Dr. Pepper showered teen bloggers with gifts and tried to instruct them on how to blog about the new Raging Cow beverage. The plot backfired, with a well-publicized boycott and global media covering the debacle.

More recently, Beck's beer introduced the "Daily Different" blog using British comedian Darius Davies to serve as the voice of the brand. To promote the site, Davies created a "Daily Different Facebook" page as well as a channel on YouTube. The results? Adrants.com welcomed the new site with the headline

"Beck's Launches Blog. Does Everything Wrong."
Angusgastle.com outed Davies as working for an ad
agency.[10] The most successful corporate-sponsored blogs
make no attempt to be covert. Bottom line: If you're using
blogs in a commercial site, keep it totally transparent.

Don't forget basic Web design

If your Web site is not well designed and easy to read, it
doesn't matter how clever you are. People will not stay.
Here are some considerations for making the content of
your Web sites more engaging.

- **Think campaigns.** Your pages have to work
  individually and cumulatively. Make sure your design
  has the same look and feel throughout the Web site,
  even though many pages will have different functions.
  Most designers start with the most complicated page.
  If you can make that work, the simpler pages will be
  easier to lay out.

- **Design at different levels.** Your site map is usually
  headed by the home page, which should set the tone
  for the whole site. Then the first-level, pages are used
  to hold content for the main sections. Each of these
  first-level pages has buttons or links to second-level
  pages, which in turn may have links to third-level
  pages, and on it goes. Your first-level and subsequent
  pages should have the same look and feel as the
  home page, even though they have different functions.
  This does not mean they have to look exactly the
  same, but consider font size, colors, graphic style, and
  all the other design elements that hold together a campaign.

- **Prioritize.** To paraphrase Howard Gossage, people read
  what interests them, and sometimes it's a Web site. But
  there is a limit to what they are willing to read, and Web site
  visitors have short attention spans. There's just too much to
  see on any given site, so it's natural to jump around. It's
  critical to put the most important information up front and
  display it prominently. For example, if e-commerce is an
  important marketing activity, make sure the casual visitor is
  directed to that section of the site.

Image 13.5

*Suave and Sprint cosponsored a site that combined
product advertising, social networks, online videos, and
high levels of interactivity. The "In the Motherhood" site
showcased a series of 5- to 7-minute videos starring Jenny
McCarthy, Leah Remini, and Chelsea Handler as three
moms in funny situations. Blogs, reader polls, child care
tips, and product promotions filled out the site and kept
viewers engaged after the video was viewed. The site led
to approval of an ABC series based on the characters.*

Image 13.6

*Burger King created an interactive site that allowed visitors to
"Simpsonize" themselves by converting their photo into a
Matt Groening–style cartoon. The site was launched to coincide
with* The Simpsons Movie.

- **Don't forget the navigation.** Think about how a visitor finds his or her way around your Web site. *Primary navigation* on a home page directs visitors to the major sections or first-level pages. *Secondary navigation* directs visitors to content inside a specific section. *Universal navigation* is on all pages—for example, links to the home page, "search," or "contact us."

- **Keep it simple.** Besides overdesigning a Web site from a graphic standpoint, you can also overdo the technology. Too much movement is annoying and pulls readers away from the text. Don't use technology for its own sake. Instead, try this concentration strategy: Focus on what you want to accomplish, not how cool you can make it. A Web page template is basically a table—a grid. The navigation sections can go anywhere on the page, and the main content can be anything that fits in the window.

Writing the content

While most of the basic writing guidelines we've presented in previous chapters apply, writing copy for Web sites also has its own set of rules. First of all, people do not like to read online—mainly because it's harder to read a screen than the printed page. Instead, they scan copy, much the same way they look at full-size newspapers. Bold headlines and pictures catch their eye and may draw them into the copy for more detail. In many cases, visitors print pages to read later rather than wade through a lot of text on-screen. Here are a few tips for writing Web site content that people will want to read:

- **Call out important words.** Use boldface and/or color to highlight important words. But don't overdo it. You still want to make it easy to read.

- **Use subheads to break up major copy blocks.** Since people scan rather than read, make sure your subheads have some meaning related to the body copy. Don't be so cute with your subheads that visitors miss the point of your content.

- **Keep it simple.** Stick with one main idea per copy block or paragraph. Don't introduce too many new ideas per section. In some ways a text-heavy Web site is like a bad PowerPoint presentation—too much copy on too few slides.

- **Convert paragraphs to bullet points.** This is especially critical if you have several key features and/or benefits. Make it easy to see the key copy points.

- **Limit your text links.** The beauty of the Web is the ability to navigate within and to other sites. However, too many links interrupt your message. You don't want to hook readers and then lose them to another topic or even another Web site, which may take them to yet another destination.

- **Lead with the main message and then drill down.** This is the inverted pyramid style of journalistic writing. You state your main message up front and gradually add more detail to support that message. Many times, the opening paragraph will be enough to hook the readers or at least get them to download the whole message.

Words of Wisdom

"The Web is a process, not a project. It's a living and breathing thing that requires a commitment. The Web affects all marketing communications and operations of a business." [11]

—Dan Early

- **Keep it short.** The rule of thumb is to use half as many words as you would for a comparable print piece. As we mentioned, people read text on-screen much more slowly than they read print.

- **Avoid scrolling.** If at all possible, try to keep a short block of text within the visible window, so readers don't have to scroll down. Since people don't like to read online, they really hate to take any special effort to read even more text.

Get Them to Come Back

Keep it fresh

No matter how engaging you make your site, people won't stay there forever. So how do you get them back? The most obvious way is to continually update your content. You wouldn't buy a 2-week-old *USA Today* to check the news. So why should someone come back to an out-of-date Web site? This applies to adding new videos, updating blog entries, showing new photos . . . anything that gives people a reason to come back.

Image 13.7

Networks also have their own Web sites to feature their top programs. Some work, some don't. Somewhere in this crowded layout are banner ads for Weight Watchers and Target. Is it working?

Image 13.8

Hulu (and other sites) brings television programs and other video content to your computer, iPod, or cell phone screen. Usually programming is interrupted briefly by a short commercial, but usually not as often as with broadcast programming.

The tactics mentioned in the "Get Them to Come" section should also be applied and reapplied to keep giving people reasons to come back. So use e-mail, online ads, and traditional media to invite people to check out what's new at your site.

Using widgets to keep traffic flowing

Widgets are great for providing a steady stream of new information, such as weather, stock prices, or even the time. If they're tied to a specific brand, you have to revisit a Web site to check them out. When Harley-Davidson wanted to promote the annual Sturgis Bike Week motorcycle rally, they developed a Google gadget offering a live feed from the streets of Sturgis and interviews with bike designers. The widgets were promoted on biking blogs and Web sites. In a week's time, over 25,000 users downloaded the widget to keep tabs on the daily happenings in Sturgis.[13]

Viral Marketing

How many times a day do you receive an e-mail asking you to look at something really cool? Sometimes it's a photo, but more often it's a video. More and more, it's a link to YouTube or some other site. Marketers have been trying to tap into the growing trend of sharing pictures or videos or telling others about them. If they can foster product or brand awareness via unsolicited testimonials, they not only multiply their media dollars; they also benefit from more effective communication. As the cliché says, word of mouth remains the most effective form of advertising. Another word for it is viral marketing. One person "infects" several people, who spread the contagion to others, until it's an epidemic of messages.

Image 13.9

PETA, no stranger to controversy, knew NBC would never run their "Veggie Love" ads during the Super Bowl (the spots featured scenes of women simulating sex with vegetables). However, they "earned" millions in advertising value by creating a buzz on the Web and in mainstream media.

Principles of Beach Relaxation

"We were working with Cramer-Krasselt, who had defined the Corona brand as living at the beach—a perfectly relaxing first person beach. But how do you translate the brand's quirky headlines into something authentically digital? We knew we needed to remain authentic to the brand *and* the medium. Most beer brands have played out the gags and party thing with scantily clad women—and that wasn't the Corona identity anyway. Our first thought was that Corona owned relaxation and escape. Totally integral to the brand. So what if we created the most relaxing Website in the world?

"We created *Principles of Beach Relaxation,* a Web site where you didn't actually have to do anything, which kept us true to the brand. There's just this perfect beach and there's the bottle of Corona—that iconic visual. And because of the context of how people look at Web sites—they're often at work, in their office—it became an instant escape. The act of navigation wasn't even necessary. They could visit the Web site and have instant escapes—a trip to that relaxing Corona beach in the middle of their day. We created a lot of things to do, but still you don't have to do anything to enjoy the site. All the activities conformed to the *Principles of Beach Relaxation* as if you were sitting in the beach chair drawing in the sand or squeezing a lime into the bottle or lying back and playing with the cloud or blowing in the bottle to make different sounds. The interesting part was taking all the assumptions about a Web site, and what's it supposed to do, and turning them on their ear."[14]

—Michael Lebowitz
Founder and CEO, *Big Spaceship,*
New York

The things that make viral marketing so popular—randomness and lack of structure—are the things mainstream marketers hate. That's why smart marketers created *viral seeding agencies* to ensure placement of brand-promoting videos on a wide variety of blogs and Web sites. However, consumer resistance has led to widely unpredictable results as marketers try to control the viral buzz. For example, "Dove Evolution" was uploaded to YouTube, and it took off like wildfire, drawing over 2.5 million viewers. It was an instant viral hit. Several parodies made the rounds, which further enhanced the buzz for the original. On the flip side, lingerie maker Agent Provocateur promoted a slick film by Hollywood director Mike Figgis that featured 7 minutes of supermodel Kate Moss in her underwear. Who could resist? Apparently a lot of people, since it was viewed only 75,000 times in its first 3 months.[15]

Brian Morrissey writes on Adweek.com, "There is still some debate over what constitutes a true viral campaign. As some feel it's one that happens organically, not planned out like a regular ad push." Christian Dietrich, head of the gaming unit at Tribal DDB, said smart creative that speaks to an audience will win out, and a low-key approach is often better to achieve grassroots appeal. "There's too much risk of it coming across as false or commercial."[16]

Social Networks

A sense of belonging is one of the basic needs we discussed in Chapter 2. Now Web 2.0 technology has made it possible for almost everyone to belong to some kind of online community where people share interests or activities. They can also involve people who are interested in exploring the activities of others or telling others about their interests.

Some social networks sell advertising. However, many mainstream marketers have not had great success breaking into social networks, despite the popularity of the sites. By nature, social networks have a "closed community" feeling, and many users don't want advertisers to be one of "us." Also, ads are intrusive. If you want to share your passion with fellow community members, you don't want to be interrupted or spied upon.

Canadian blogger Kate Trgovac, a self-described "marketer, mystery and legend," says social media are about passion. To be a better marketer, for your client or for your organization, you need to get in touch with your passion. She goes on to offer nine easy steps to engage with your passion and learn about social media tools, starting with the easiest and increasing to the most difficult.

Image 13.10

Brides.com tapped the potential of social networks with marketing on MySpace, Facebook, and YouTube and downloadable "wedding widgets."

Image 13.11

Tide to Go had a very clever integrated campaign on TV and the Web; however, some people drew the line when they invaded Facebook. Corporate involvement in social networks is sometimes resented by the very target audiences advertisers want most.

1. Comment on a blog or a podcast (but *not* a marketing one!). If you're looking for an online community, check out **Technorati.com**.

2. Participate in a folksonomy (aka "tag something"). For example, you can bookmark articles on the Web and use various tags that will pass them along to a much wider community. Two popular social bookmarking services are **Delicious** (**delicious.com**) and **ma.gnolia.com.**

3. Upload a photo to a group on **Flickr**. One photo may have a lot of interest for a number of diverse groups.

4. Write a review—for books, movies, music, customer service experiences, whatever.

5. Upload a video to **YouTube. Answerbag** has a video tutorial on how to upload your video. **Lifehacker.com** shows you how to upload direct from your mobile.

6. Join and participate in a social network (in addition to Facebook). **Mashable.com** is one.

7. Write (or edit) a **Wikipedia** entry. Write about your passion. Wikipedia has entries on starting or editing pages.

8. Participate in a mashup. Find ways to combine tagging, photo sharing, geo targeting, and other applications with your passion.

9. Show off your expertise and create a Squidoo lens. **Squidoo.com** is a social media venue that gives authors a platform for really specific interests and lets them hook into popular commercial services like Flickr, eBay, and Amazon.[17]

Internet and the Third Screen

The penetration of WAP (Wireless Application Protocol) devices such as smart phones, PDAs (Personal Digital Assistants), and MIDs (Mobile Internet Devices) has broken down traditional barriers to the Internet, allowing new opportunities for online marketing. However, the mobile online experience is far different from that on desktop or notebook computer screens. Use of rich media banners is limited to the capabilities of the device and the network. Even if you could access everything available on the Web, the screen is smaller, which reduces the impact of downloaded videos, TV programs, and games and static graphic content. Given the limitations of the Third Screen, mobile seems a better application for direct marketing, especially when the users opt to receive information on their cell phones. The use of mobile for really impactful online advertising is the equivalent of watching TV through the wrong end of a set of binoculars.

Where to Find the Best Online Marketing

You can choose from dozens of sites that recognize the "best" interactive work in various categories. Any awards for last year's work will probably be hopelessly out-of-date. A better idea is to just keep using the Internet. You'll see exciting new stuff all the time. The rules keep changing. The creative just keeps getting better. Bookmark what you like and keep surfing.

Note: We have made every effort to provide information about online communications that is as up-to-date as possible. However, the Internet is a moving target. Technology advances at a rapid rate, and, with it, marketing challenges and opportunities change radically. This is what we know at the time of publishing. Much of it may already be obsolete, and if we do a third edition in the future, it may be introduced with *two* blank pages.

Who's Who?

Steven Chen is the cofounder and chief technology officer of the popular video sharing Web site YouTube. Born in Taiwan, Chen attended high school in the Chicago area and graduated from the University of Illinois at Urbana-Champaign. He was one of PayPal's early employees, where he met Chad Hurley and Jawed Karim. In 2005, the three founded YouTube. Chen was named by Business 2.0 as one of "The 50 people who matter now" in business.[18] On October 16, 2006, Chen and Hurley sold YouTube to Google, Inc., for $1.65 billion.

Jack Dorsey, best known as the creator of Twitter, was a computer prodigy at age 14 when he developed Web-based dispatch routing software for taxis. Dorsey, Biz Stone, and Evan Williams cofounded Twitter, Inc., after taking all of 2 weeks to develop the prototype. As chief executive officer, Dorsey saw the startup through two rounds of funding by the venture capitalists that back the company. In October 2008 Williams took over the role of CEO, and Dorsey became chairman of the board.

Tara Lamberson leveraged her experience with Walt Disney Co., Fox Television, and EarthLink to become vice president of marketing at MindComet, a digital solution agency. The range of services include social networks, podcasting, blogs, viral seeding, e-mail marketing, iPhone development, and brand monitoring for blue-chip clients such as General Motors, Disney, AOL, and Tyco. She received a bachelor's degree in media arts and design from James Madison University and coauthored the book *Understanding Y: Inside the Minds of Millennials.*

Mark Zuckerberg dropped out of Harvard . . . and created one of the hottest social networks in the business, Facebook. His first attempt to create an online student directory based on students' attractiveness landed him in hot water with the administration. His second try made him a Silicon Valley wheeler and dealer. Selling banner ads to make money, Facebook connects people with one another. Originally, Zuckerberg fretted over the $85 a month it cost to run. As of this writing, Facebook has raised millions from Silicon Valley names like PayPal founder Peter Thiel and Accel Partners.

Exercises

1. It's a Quirky World Out There

It's time to take advantage of just how quirky you really are.

- Think of something that's really quirky about yourself, something that sets you apart. Do you collect comic books? Are you the only unicyclist on campus? Have you been a closet juggler since middle school? Are you the only one that you know who has lived through five surgeries before age 18? Do you have four toes? We guarantee there will be some quirky people in your class!

- List all the benefits of having your quirk. Have some fun with this. After all, this is advertising.

- Next, write a 200- to 250-word story, along with a headline, expressing your quirkiness in vivid detail.

- Now it's time to reveal your quirk or remain anonymous. Hop on blogger.com and create a blog that tells the world about your own unique quirk. That's right; create a blog dedicated to your very own quirkiness. You might even want to follow some of the tips in this chapter.

- Once you're done, track your blog for three weeks and keep blogging. Track how many posts you have each day. Are there patterns? Who is posting? What kinds of things do they have to say? At the end of three weeks make a list of all the branded opportunities that could be leveraged by people who share their particular quirkiness. You just might be surprised by how many others share your unique eccentricity.

- Share your findings with the class. Yes, you will have to reveal your quirkiness, at least to the class. If you like your blog keep it—expand it. If not, game over.

2. Digital Transference

This one will help you see the importance of consistency across all media.

- Find a long-copy ad for a B2B brand.

- Dissect the copy into a series of benefits and prioritize them based on the key message within the ad.

- Now go online and search for your brand to see if the benefits in the ad match up to the brand's Web presence. If not, have them choose one of two options: (a) rewrite the ad to fit the digital brand presence or (b) rewrite the Web content to fit the ad. The goal is to create seamless branded transference and make suggestions for visual consistence.

- Now that you have created a consistent print and Internet presence for your brand, suggest two other tactical opportunities that would be consistent with the revised brand voice.

3. **Virtual Artifact Room**

This exercise is all about brand environmentalism. And, you may need to talk your teacher into finding a place for you to play!

- Have students pick a product. Any product.

- Conduct enough secondary research so you are familiar with the target and as a class draft a consumer profile.

- Now, take your ethnographic feet on the road to find objects: toys, food, music, products, photos, clothing . . . anything and everything that your consumer might have in his or her world. Gather it together into one place, an artifact room.

- Spend time in the artifact room and get to know what objects the consumer holds near and dear. See what you can learn about the consumer's lifestyle from these objects. Compare how you "see" the consumer with how their classmates "see" the consumer.

- Now get out a pencil or pen or laptop and start writing. Begin by having revising the consumer profile. Next write a short story—then another, and another, and another—about their consumer. These are the foundation for the branded story.

- Next cluster the objects in the artifact room and consider how they can make the artifact room come to life digitally. How can they make all the objects, and what they symbolize, available to their target virtually? Is it a Web site, a blog, wallpaper, an application, or perhaps an alter ego? Do they arrive via a podcast, a text, or a gadget? Maybe you can engage the consumer in contributing to the artifact room. Maybe your brand is the next to be "Simpsonized."

- Finally mock up your concept and share it with the class. If you want to, and are tech savvy, go live.

Notes

1. Steve Moss, senior sales director, national field sales, MSN; remarks made during the panel discussion "On-Line Advertising: Turn Virtual Exposure Into Real Results," American Advertising Federation National Conference, Dallas, TX, June 14, 2004.

2. Andrew McAfee, "Enterprise 2.0: The Dawn of Emergent Collaboration," *MIT Sloan Management Review 47,* no. 3 (2006), pp. 21–28.

3. Bruce Morris, "Internet Ad Types," *Web Developer's Journal,* April 22, 1999, http://www.webdevelopersjournal .com/columns/types_of_ads.html (accessed July 8, 2005).

4. Quoted in A. Jerome Jewler and Bonnie Drewniany, *Creative Strategy in Advertising,* 7th ed. (Belmont, CA: Wadsworth, 2001), p. 221.

5. Mashup (Web application hybrid), Wikipedia, http://en.wikipedia.org/wiki/Mashup_(web_application_hybrid) (accessed December 20, 2008).

6. Ibid.

7. Quoted on the Crispin Porter + Bogusky Web site, "Burger King Subservient Chicken," http://www.cpbgroup .com/awards/subservientchicken.html (accessed December 21, 2008).

8. Barbara Lippert, "Carnivoral Knowledge: Burger King defiles its 'Whopper Virgins' with a tasteless new campaign from Crispin," December 8, 2008, http://www.adweek.com/aw/content_display/creative/critique/ e3ie8946cda1b3f6da2ca92ebf1b5c68935 (accessed December 21, 2008).

9. Quoted in Kenneth Hein, "Beck's Tries Something 'Different': Blogging," *Brandweek,* December 10, 2008, http://www.brandweek.com/bw/content_display/news-and-features/digital/e3i6b23edbb3085dfe3444ccc48d26966d2 (accessed December 12, 2008).

10. Ibid.

11. Dan Early, president, Ascedia, Inc., "Interactive Marketing Overview," lecture presented at Marquette University, Milwaukee, WI, November 6, 2003.

12. King Hill, principal marketing strategist, DigiKnow, Inc.; remarks made during the panel discussion "On-Line Advertising: Turn Virtual Exposure into Real Results," American Advertising Federation National Conference, Dallas, TX, June 14, 2004.

13. Brian Quinton, "Widgets? They're Easy," *Direct* magazine, January, 2008, p. 35.

14. Michael Lebowitz, Ad Story: *Principles of Beach Relaxation,* February 2009.

15. Quoted in Brian Morrissey, "Clients Try to Manipulate 'Unpredictable' Viral Buzz," Adweek.com, March 19, 2007, http://www.adweek.com/aw/esearch/article_display.jsp?vnu_content_id=1003559592 (accessed December 21, 2008).

16. Brian Morrissey, "Clients Try to Manipulate 'Unpredictable' Viral Buzz."

17. Kate Trgovac, "9 Easy, Social Media Steps to Get Beyond Fear & Laziness in Marketing," My Name Is Kate Web site, 2007, http://www.mynameiskate.ca/2007/06fear-and-lazine.html (accessed December 20, 2008).

18. Business 2.0 Management Staff, "The 50 people who matter now," CNN Money Web site, July 21, 2006, http://money.cnn.com/2006/06/21/technology/50whomatter.biz2/ (accessed January 6, 2009).

Chapter 14

Direct Marketing

Direct Marketing Defined

Even seasoned marketing professionals sometimes confuse all the terms relating to direct marketing. Some call it direct response. Some only think of direct mail. Others think door-to-door selling is its main component. For this text we'll use a definition created by Bob Stone and Ron Jacobs that covers all direct transactions.

> *Direct Marketing is the interactive use of advertising media, to stimulate an (immediate) behavior modification in such a way that this behavior can be tracked, recorded, analyzed, and stored on a database for future retrieval and use.*[1]

In short, direct marketing is *interactive*, stimulates an *immediate response*, and is *measurable*.

According to the Direct Marketing Association (DMA), the three purposes of direct marketing are to:

- Solicit a direct order

- Generate a lead

- Drive store traffic[2]

In addition, we would add that direct marketing should also:

- Generate a measurable response

- Grow the long-term value of a relationship between the marketer and customer

Why direct marketing?

From a creative standpoint, direct marketing, whether it's direct mail, e-mail, telemarketing, or personal selling, offers many benefits.

Words of Wisdom

"Testing is the kernel of direct marketing. The truth is that every major direct marketing business that succeeds does so largely by testing—or a run of exceptional luck." [3]

—Drayton Bird

255

- **It's specific.** With good data, an advertiser can zero in on specific demographics and lifestyles to create a more powerful message.

- **It talks to the individual**—It's as close as you can get to one-on-one marketing.

- **It can be high impact.** If you correctly tap those wants and needs, you provide something of real value to the recipient.

- **It can be localized.** A mailer for a nationally advertised brand can include the names and addresses of local retailers.

- **It can generate sales where there are no stores.** In other words, it generates a direct response, whether it's mail order or online.

- **It can help gather information.** Given the right incentives, many people send back snail mail or online surveys.

- **It can be used to encourage trials of new products.** Samples and discount coupons help launch many new products.

- **It delivers instant results.** You know almost immediately if your mailing is successful, based on direct sales, phone orders, hits on a Web site, return of reply cards, or other measurement methods.

- **It can be used as part of an integrated marketing program.** For example, sending direct mail fulfills requests for information in a magazine ad; you can direct people to a Web site for more detailed and interactive messages.

Why not?

- Your direct marketing program is only as good as your mailing list (garbage in, garbage out).

- People hate it: It's unwanted, mistrusted, and, in some cases, feared.

- It's often misdirected or undelivered: Most companies screen snail mail, eliminating the junk before it gets to the addressee. Junk mail filters screen out what they consider spam.

- It's difficult to create economical and effective direct mail that doesn't look like junk mail. It's expensive to create high-impact e-mails that people actually want to open.

- It's costly: The cost per thousand for snail mail is very high in most cases. Elaborate print pieces and three-dimensional mailers can be very expensive to produce, and postage prices keep climbing.

The Components of All Direct Marketing

No matter if you're developing mail, e-mail, telemarketing, or interactive TV or selling door-to-door, every direct marketing effort contains these three elements:

1. **The List (or Media):** Simply put, this is who you are talking to. As we'll say repeatedly, the value of the direct marketing effort is only as good as the list.

2. **The Offer:** The offer is a promise of a reward. Is it a limited time discount? Bonus product? Something they can't buy in a store? A new product with an incredible competitive advantage? Why should the recipient be interested?

3. **The Creative:** How do you show it/how do you tell the story? What will get their attention, generate their interest, and flame their desire, and most of all, what will get them to act—and act now? The bulk of this chapter will focus on these tactics.

Database marketing: using the list

We can't stress this enough: The most creative concept ever devised is no good if it goes to the wrong person. The better the list, the more on-target your creative message will be.

The more you know, the more personal the message. Some of the information you might need to develop your message is listed below. The importance of these categories will vary depending on the type of product, marketing situation, price points, buying cycle, and other variables.

You may wonder when you pick up a stack of junk mail or when your inbox fills up with urgent requests about Nigerian bank accounts, "How did they get *my* name?" If you're a direct marketer, you will *never* have an accurate, up-to-date mailing list. Ever. But you can try to make it as accurate as possible so the names on your list better match the profile of the people you want to reach. Rather than go through the intricacies of database management, we will assume you will employ the tips and techniques we offer below *after* you have secured information about your intended direct marketing recipients.

Customer Relationship Management (CRM)

Customer relationship management tracks and organizes the interaction between the advertiser and current and potential customers. CRM usually refers to the software used to manage customer relationships, but it's just as important for the marketer to really understand the customer's wants and needs, as well as knowing who they are and when they buy. CRM is a key component of campaign management. It coordinates operational and analytical functions to target groups from a database, send e-mails or snail mail and track the results, and store and analyze the data. Successful CRM is a convergence of traditional direct marketing, database marketing, and online marketing. So what does all this have to do with the creative component? The key is to know the wants and needs of the target audience, because without that, there's not much of a relationship to measure.

Direct Mail

Direct mail (often derisively referred to as snail mail) may not have the speed and immediacy of e-mail, but it's the best way to put an advertising message in the hands of a potential customer. Unlike other forms of print media, it has no competing messages (advertisers or editorial) attached to it. Direct marketing not only invites; it also provides recipients with the means to take real, measurable, physical action.

Several categories of direct mail formats are available. The choice depends on the budget (production and postage), content, type of product, purchase cycle, and response mechanism.

Image 14.1

This letter package really did contain an X-ray, which turned out to be an invitation to see the hospital's expanded facilities.

Envelope mailers (letter package)

Anything you put into an envelope applies. It may be as simple as a letter or as elaborate as a 10-piece multicomponent mailer. Keep in mind that every component has a purpose, even the envelope itself. The basic components can include a letter, a brochure, and a reply device, such as a prepaid reply card. You want the outer envelope to say, "Open me." You can do this several ways:

- **Teaser copy:** It could be a special offer or some twist on the message. For example, one envelope for a Florida resort said, "Open carefully: contains white sand, dolphins, seashells and coconut palms."

- **Blind envelopes:** These are usually standard-sized envelopes that suggest normal business or personal correspondence rather than direct mail advertising.

- **Stamps:** These can be used rather than a meter stamp to make it look more like personal mail.

- **Official envelopes:** These look like government correspondence, a check, or a telegram. While you might get some immediate attention with these, you're more likely to annoy people by deceiving them.

- **Personalized copy:** Sometimes this is effective; other times it may offend people who wonder, "How do they know so much about me?"

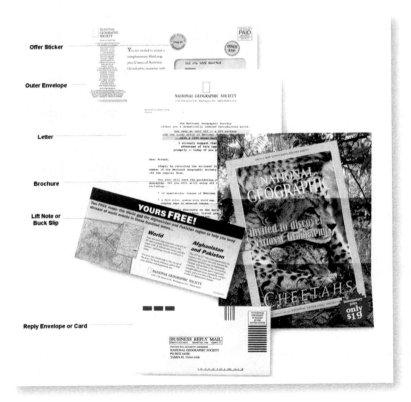

Image 14.2

The anatomy of an order solicitation letter package. A lot more can be involved than just a letter and an envelope. Each component plays a key role in getting the recipient to return the reply card, pick up the phone, or log onto the Web site. It's like having a mini campaign in every envelope.

Flat self-mailers

A self-mailer contains the mailing address on some part of the piece itself rather than on an envelope. Some traditionalists don't like self-mailers. They claim letter package will always out-pull a self-mailer. A letter is more personal, while a self-mailer shouts, "I'm an ad!" However, a well-designed self-mailer can be cost efficient and effective from a creative standpoint. Types of self-mailers include:

- Postcards
- Folded mailers—one fold, two folds, and multifolds
- Brochures and pamphlets
- Newsletters

Dimensional mailers

Some of the most innovative (and expensive) direct mailers are three dimensional.
Basically, they can be anything that can be mailed or shipped. Many times the box will include a separate item, sometimes called a *gadget*. This may be a sample, a premium item that might have some use, or something totally off-the-wall that makes a selling point. The limits to 3-D mailers are governed only by your imagination and your budget.

The fine art of writing a cover letter

A cover letter is an introduction, a sales pitch, and a proposal for further action all in one. Cover letters are typically one-page documents and, in most cases, have a beginning, a middle, and an end—usually an introduction saying who you are and why you're writing, followed by a sales pitch for what you have to offer, and then a closing in which you propose steps for further action. These three components often amount to three or four paragraphs, but there are no ironclad rules about how to break up the information. Philip Ward-Burton offers some good advice for cover letter writers in *Advertising Copywriting*.[4] We've paraphrased a few of his suggestions:

Image 14.3

Direct marketing involves the list, the offer, and the message. In this postcard, the offer is a 10-pack of LIVESTRONG wrist bands. The creative is a DVD attached to the card that has a personal message from Lance Armstrong.

COVER LETTER OUTLINE: 7 STEPS

1. Promise a benefit in the headline or first paragraph—lead with your strongest sales point.

2. Enlarge on your most important benefit.

3. Tell the reader what he or she is going to get.

4. Back your statements with proof and endorsements (testimonials).

5. Tell the reader what's lost if he or she doesn't act.

6. Rephrase the benefits in your closing offer.

7. Incite action—set a time limit ("Buy now").

COVER LETTER STYLE: 7 STEPS

1. Start with short opening paragraph—four lines or shorter.

2. No paragraph should be longer than eight lines.

3. Vary the length of paragraphs.

4. Use deep indents and center bullet points.

5. Close with a two- to three-line summary.

6. Don't forget the envelope (teaser).

7. Don't forget a follow-up letter—reinforce the message/refine your data mining.

Customization and variable printing

We've been saying that you must know the wants and needs of the consumer, and technology today allows you to know more and more every year. Sophisticated database software not only provides spot-on identification but also matches it to very specific information about that recipient. So the message can be personalized using variable printing techniques to deliver unique messages. However, just because you can personalize a mailing doesn't mean you have to.

It can be annoying for consumers to receive mailings from a company that pretends to know them, especially if they make the appeal too personal. Grant Johnson of Johnson Direct LLC offers this advice: "Let the target audience define how it wants to be marketed to and via what channels, then test various offers and messaging platforms based on that date to gauge results."[5]

He offers examples of marketers who are exploiting the personal relevance of their brands and why they are successful:

- Starbucks. How I want *my* coffee is different from the way *you* want yours.

- Harley-Davidson. How I customize *my* bike is different from the way *you* do it.

- Apple. The music on *my* iPod is different from that on *yours*.

Is personalization a bad thing? No. But we need to let our customers and prospects tell us how to proceed.[6]

Image 14.4

Direct mail allows for the inclusion of many pieces that work individually and collectively to encourage an immediate response.

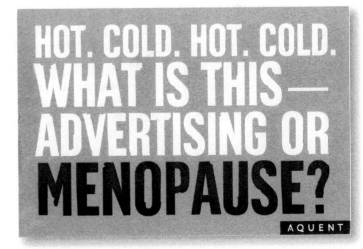

Image 14.5

Jumbo postcards are an economical way to get your message out. Treat them like billboards on the front and provide more detail on the back. They're great for integrated campaigns or a series of mailers.

TABLE 14.1   Cover Letter Example

Dear Jack:	Personalize with name and other information.
Here's how you can keep your Sea Ray 230 looking showroom fresh—above and below the waterline.	Promise a benefit up front.
During the boating season, you work hard to keep your Sea Ray 230 looking shipshape. But when you haul it out in the fall, you know you're facing many long hours of scrubbing that green slime off the bottom. It won't come off with a pressure washer. And don't think about using harsh acid cleaners on your fiberglass hull.	Enlarge on that benefit.
Here's a better way.	Vary the length of sentences and paragraphs.
New **BoteBrite** hull cleaner cuts through that grungy bottom grime to restore your boat's original color and shine. Without hard scrubbing. Without abrasives. Without dangerous acids.	Tell the reader what's lost if he or she doesn't act.
Just spray **BoteBrite** on the bottom of the boat—wait 15 minutes—and rinse with a garden hose. That's all there is to it!	
BoteBrite is a unique detergent that dissolves organic stains from algae and dirty water.	Use deep indents and bullet points to call out key features/benefits.
BoteBrite will not damage fiberglass, plastic, metal, or your driveway when used as directed.	
BoteBrite is easy to apply and even easier to clean up.	
BoteBrite has been approved by the industry's leading manufacturers, including Sea Ray. It's safe, easy to use, and effective against tough bottom stains.	Back your statement with proof or testimonials.
We hate to admit this boating season is coming to an end. After you pull out for the season, will you spend a weekend scrubbing and breathing chemical fumes? Or spraying on **BoteBrite** and rinsing off a whole season of crud in just minutes?	Tell the reader what he or she is going to get.
For a limited time, we're offering a **Buy 2–Get 1 Free** deal on **BoteBrite**. Just bring the attached coupon to any **BoteBrite** retailer before September 30 and get a free 16-oz. bottle of **BoteBrite** when you buy two 16-oz. or larger sizes.	Incite action.
When it's time to clean your boat this fall, take it easy. Use new **BoteBrite** for fast, safe, and effective bottom cleaning.	Close with a benefit summary.

E-mail

E-mail represents the best and worst of what direct marketing is all about. On the plus side, e-mail is great for customer retention and relationship management, especially if the recipient has opted in to the campaign. E-mail also has been effective in viral seeding to gain attention and interest among new customers. The downside—one word: spam. Spamming and its evil cousin phishing (using legitimate-looking e-mails to scam people) have poisoned the perception of e-mail. As a result, sophisticated mail filters screen out many legitimate e-mails and even quite a few that people might actually want to read. Because spam has the potential to harm your computer and potentially suck money out of your bank account, many people fear it more than ordinary junk snail mail. However, there are ways to take advantage of e-mail's benefits and reach recipients who actually want to see your message. One technique is to use *rich mail* that allows graphics,

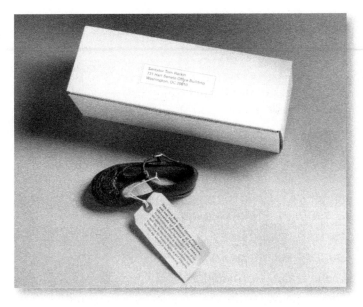

Image 14.6

This student-designed 3-D mailer was sent to members of Congress, urging them to vote for anti–land mine legislation. The box contained a single small shoe that was formerly worn by a child whose leg had been blown off by a land mine.

video, and audio to be included in the e-mail message. When you open up a rich e-mail, your e-mail client automatically calls up your Internet connection and launches an HTML page in your browser. E-mail clients that are offline will invite you to click on the link when you have your Internet connection open again. If your e-mail client does not support graphics, you will receive the e-mail in text only. Most HTML pages instantly appear as complete with the visuals and don't require the added, and often annoying, step of downloading the graphics. As with the most successful e-mail marketers, give recipients the opportunity to opt out by having a "please remove me from your list" reply.

Here are a few tips for getting a better response from your e-mail messages.

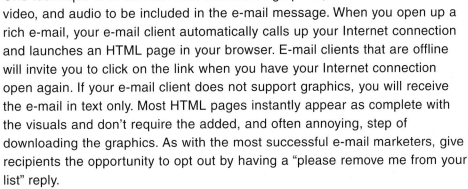

"If you can't figure out what makes a great letter, advertising isn't for you. After all, direct mail is one of the purest forms of advertising." [7]

—Lee Kovel

- The e-mail FROM line should show someone the readers will trust. If it's for a customer, be sure to put the company's name in the FROM line. For example, "FROM: Briggs & Stratton Customer Service Department."

- You should treat the SUBJECT line like envelope teaser copy. You have to give the prospect some reason to open the e-mail. For example, "SUBJECT: Try the New Update for Your Macromedia Project."

- Your first paragraph or two should contain a mini version of your whole e-mail. So instead of carefully spreading out your AIDA (Attention, Interest, Desire, and Action), you should try to get all these elements in early. Online users have little patience in general, and they need to understand your whole offer fast.

Words of Wisdom

"Historically, clients came to us thinking they wanted us to work on their direct marketing. Now we get involved in their work from a strategic standpoint and we see what makes sense—direct, promotion, experiential—providing them the broad range of services." [8]

—Howard Draft

- Avoid using "hard-sell" techniques. These tend to produce poor results.

- Readers on the Internet expect to see information on the benefits and how to order, but the tone must remain helpful. If it's too slick, your e-mail will be trashed.

- *Always* remember to include a Web-based response form. Many online users prefer to keep the entire transaction online.

- Premiums and sweepstakes work great online. You have the opportunity online to animate your premiums in action or even make them interactive.

- Avoid the word *free* in the SUBJECT line. *Free* is too blatantly promotional a word for people to bother opening your e-mail. Besides, many online users now employ spam filters that work to screen out messages with *free* in the SUBJECT line.

- Try to make your headline different from your SUBJECT line. Your best benefit up front usually does the trick. Injecting a news feel and some self-interest doesn't hurt either.

- *Always* include an opt-out statement! The only thing more powerful than goodwill toward your company is ill will.

Ad Story

What the Buck Were We Thinking? The Joys and Pains of E-mail Marketing

Johnathan Crawford is founder and CEO of DataDog Interactive Marketing, a Milwaukee-based firm that provides integrated marketing programs for retailers, member organizations, and the B2B industry sector. Crawford is a 25-year veteran of the advertising and marketing business with a background in radio, outdoor, print, and e-marketing. Some of his client biggies have included The Sharper Image, Burger King, and Tyson Chicken. He told us this story:

"I was working for a Chicago firm that developed mail marketing programs for a variety of national companies. The e-mail medium was still somewhat young and there was a lot of learning to do, but we were ahead of the curve in many areas. One of those areas was using data to determine the content of the email. A small portion of the data and email addresses we had collected for a client were from a promotion called 'Buck Head' (a suburb of Atlanta), and this was an insignificant issue until our data linking went haywire. Due to a variety of reasons, we accidentally sent 50,000 e-mail messages to people addressed with 'Dear Buck Head' (instead of Dear First Name). We realized this mistake approximately

7 seconds after clicking the 'send' button. Talk about panic. Once you click 'send,' it's all over, done, it's 'out the door.' If it's wrong, you're basically stuck with the results. Well, 50,000 people were addressed as 'Buck Head,' and because that sounds very close to an expletive some of us periodically use, that had an impact. Some people complained, others were amused. The client wasn't amused, but we were able to quickly send out a short apology e-mail making light of our mistake and explaining how it happened."[9]

—Johnathan Crawford
President, *DataDog Interactive Marketing*, Milwaukee

- Shorter is better. If some of your prospects require more information before they make purchasing decisions, include a click-through to an expanded version of your e-mail.

- Consider viral marketing techniques. Prospects can pass your messages on to others they think would be interested.

Although we've touched on these tactics in previous chapters, there are several areas where digital technology is used for direct marketing. Among them are:

- **E-letters:** More formal than e-mails, in many cases e-letters are used as attachments to an e-mail introduction.

- **E-cards:** These are the equivalent of a postcard delivered electronically; however, unlike the mailed kind, it will have active links to a landing page and may even have video or Flash animation.

- **Webinars:** Many business-to-business Web sites feature online seminars for customers or potential customers. While the seminar is sent to what the advertiser hopes is a large group, the interaction between the presenter and recipient is one-to-one.

- **Podcasts:** If the listener can customize the play list or select from a list of programs, it becomes a personal form of communication even though it's "radio on the Internet."

- **Blogs:** They facilitate one-on-one communication, even though millions may read the two-way conversations.

- **Subscription services:** Using RSS (Really Simple Syndication), you can reverse the flow from your computer to check for updates on blogs and news sources and instead have updates from your favorite sites sent to you. To make it work, you need to subscribe to a reader such as Google Reader or My Yahoo. Then you visit your favorite sites and click on the RSS logo to make the connection to your reader. Updates will be sent to you as they happen rather than you searching for new stuff.

PURLs: Where Direct Mail Interfaces With the Internet

PURL (Personalized URL) is a landing page created for one person. Actually it could be one of hundreds of Web page templates that allow for placement of an individual's name and information derived from a database that is relevant to that person. An example of a PURL would be John R. Smith.TravelAdventures.com. When John Smith clicks on the

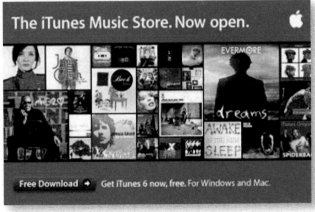

Image 14.7

While some recipients can't receive or don't want to receive more advertising in their inbox, HTML e-mails allow marketers to create more impact than regular messages. If recipients have opted into a permission-based marketing program, they will welcome the added content.

Say hello to iPhone. Today.

Find an Apple Store near you.

Image 14.8

Smart phones such as the Apple iPhone have opened up new opportunities for direct communication to consumers.

link, he goes to a customized Travel Adventures landing page that may have a headline reading, "Hey, John Smith. Looking for a New Adventure?" Copy on the page would use his name and weave in some information such as hiking, photography, and white-water rafting, based on data compiled for this person. John is given the opportunity to request a brochure, chat with a travel consultant, look at a blog of like-minded adventurers, and, of course, book travel online. All the time he is providing information to Travel Adventures, which is recording the information, analyzing it, and preparing future contact with John, including more mailers, e-mail blasts, and possibly telemarketing.

Step 1: Print PURLs (Personalized URLs) on each direct mail piece. Include personalized copy.

Step 2: Recipient clicks on the PURL, which leads him or her to a personalized landing page built specifically to support the direct mail piece.

Step 3: The personalized landing page provides information and captures the viewer's activity for additional follow-up and lead generation in real time. Reports can be generated later to display response rates, visitor patterns, and more detailed lead information.

Mobile: The Third Screen

First screen—TV; second—computer; third—your cell phone. Marketing on mobile phones has been around since the early 2000s in Europe and Japan and now is gaining rapidly in North America. Still, compared to traditional online marketing, it's a tiny business. In 2006, spending on mobile advertising was only $871 million, but some marketers forecast that annual expenditure will reach $11.4 billion by 2011. Other analysts predict the market will be as big as $20 billion by then.[11] Unlike traditional e-mail over the Internet, carriers can set their own guidelines for mobile advertising, reducing the incidence of mobile spam. The Mobile Marketing Association provides a set of guidelines and standards for the recommended format of ads, presentation, and metrics. Mobile marketing is different from most other kinds of direct marketing communication because the consumer typically controls the flow of information—-the user often initiates contact with the advertiser and must give the advertiser permission to contact him or her.

A major portion of mobile advertising takes the form of text messages. But telecom firms are delivering a fast-growing array of rich media ads to

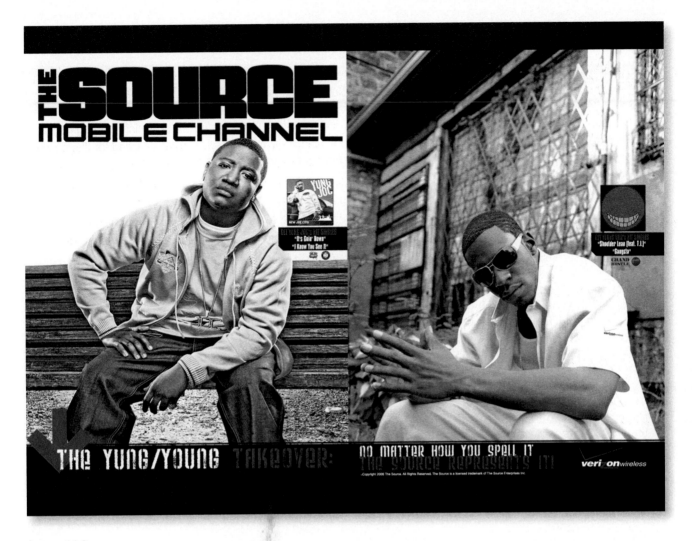

Image 14.9

The Source magazine, aimed at a young urban audience, also created an online presence like so many other publications. But they also ventured into the fast-growing mobile market to reach their audience.

handsets that include video clips, Web pages, and music and games. For example, BP gas stations wanted to promote the fact they offered great-quality coffee and fresh food for folks on the go. Nokia Ad Business and i-movo devised a promotion that invited customers to enter competitions to win navigation systems and cash prizes across a myriad of channels. In return, every entrant was sent a voucher by text message for a free coffee. McDonald's used a mobile campaign to announce the return of their McRib sandwich. McDonald's spread the word with ads that invited consumers to text "MCRIB" to 69937, and they would get free stuff like McRib ringtones and wallpapers. (You'd think McRib fans would rather have a sandwich.) Myxer, a hypertargeting ad service, designed the program that allowed McDonald's to narrow the demographic by gender, age, music genre, and mobile preferences.As a result, 65% of the people reached were in the highly coveted 15- to 28-years range.[12]

Who's Who?

At the time of this writing, **Howard Draft** is CEO of the 10th largest agency in the United States, Draftfcb. His rise to the top began at a 13-person Chicago shop that specialized in direct response advertising. When that agency partnered with the much larger Ted Bates Worldwide agency, Draft moved to New York and set up a direct marketing branch that was soon billing more than his old shop. By the mid-1990s, Draft owned the agency, now called Draft Direct, which grew to $600 million in billings. In 2003, he merged with FCB, one of the best known agencies in the world, to form Draftfcb, now billing over $3 billion.[13]

As worldwide creative director of Ogilvy & Mather Direct, **Drayton Bird** was a key to the success of the world's largest direct marketing agency. He went on to found what became the United Kingdom's largest direct marketing agency. With more than 40 years of experience in direct marketing and advertising, Bird wrote and published *Commonsense Direct Marketing, How to Write Sales Letters That Sell,* and *Marketing Insights and Outrages*—all best sellers. He also writes regular columns for marketing/advertising publications in the United Kingdom, the United States, Malaysia, India, and Europe.

Often called the father of direct response advertising, **John Caples** was one of the most influential copywriters of all time. He spent a lifetime researching the most effective methods of advertising. His direct approach for writing headlines cut through the clutter and grabbed the readers, pulling them into the ad. Caples penned one of the most famous headlines ever written: "They laughed when I sat down at the piano, but when I started to play!"

Exercises

1. Right Cause–Right Brand

The focus of this exercise is to help you understand the importance of using the "right" cause to appeal to the "right" target market in cause-related marketing—in short, how to link to the right cause to the right brand.

- Pick one or two brands popular among a specific demographic group. In terms of age range, we suggest 18–24 or 15–34 as most consumers make decisions about which causes they will support early in their lives.

- Interview five people in each demographic group. Focus on finding out (a) what causes are important to them, and (b) what people, things, events and/or places they are passionate about. Narrow down the responses to two major causes per demographic group.

- Then study the cause-related marketing practices used by the brands identified in the first step.

- Now compare whether there is any congruence between the causes identified by each demographic group and the causes affiliated with their favorite brands or if there are any perfect partnerships waiting to happen. Use the things they are passionate about to as you select partnerships.

Adapted from an exercise shared by Kwangmi Ko Kim, PhD, Associate Professor, Towson University.

2. Visual Word Associations

This exercise is designed to demonstrate the visual power of word associations.

- Think of a brand. Let's say: FedEx. Begin by generating a benefits list.

- Pick the top three benefits and find the key words associated with each.

- Now go to visualthesaurus.com and type in each key word. (It's free the first time, and then it will cost you, but not much. We think it's worth it and it's great for headline generation too.) You will see a graphic clustering of associated words. Talk about proximity! For example, with *dependable* the clusters are (a) good, safe, and secure; (b) honest, reliable, and true; and (c) steady-going and rock-steady.

- Use your three benefits and associated words to create three concepting approaches. Generate three layouts that visually express each of the three concepts.

3. Passionate for a Cause

Letting your passion show is a great way to engage the target audience, and with direct marketing engagement is paramount.

- Choose a nonprofit or a social cause that you are passionate about such as: the American Red Cross, Greenpeace, Big Brothers Big Sisters, breast cancer awareness, or a host of other great causes.

- Create a print ad with headline, body copy, visual, and tagline. As this is part of a direct campaign, you should be sure to pay special attention to the call to action.

- Now, consider the strategically ideal direct medium in order to reach your target audience. Next execute your direct tactic.

- Present your direct tactic and your print ad and sell the class on why your two-part campaign has the potential to be extended—why it has legs. Provide a rationale for why, even with just these two tactics, your call to action will be heard and responded to. Sell the class on the strategy. After all, this is a cause they are passionate about.

Notes

1. Bob Stone and Ron Jacobs, *Successful Direct Marketing Methods*, 7th ed. (New York: McGraw-Hill, 2001), p. 5.

2. Direct Marketing Association, "Findings and Analysis from the DMA 2001–2002 Economic Impact Report" (press release), June 10, 2002, http://www.the-dma.org/cgi/disppressrelease?article=339 (accessed June 30, 2005).

3. Drayton Bird, *Commonsense Direct Marketing,* 3rd ed. (Lincolnwood, IL: NTC Business Books, 1994).

4. Philip Ward-Burton, *Advertising Copywriting* (Lincolnwood, IL: NTC Business Books, 1991), p. 163.

5. Quoted in Maxine Paetro, *How to Put Your Book Together and Get a Job in Advertising* (Chicago: The Copy Workshop, 2001), p. 189.

6. Grant Johnson, "Hey, (Your Name Here)! When does personalization go too far?" DIRECT magazine, February 2008, p. 20.

7. Quoted in William F. Arens, Michael F. Weigold, and Christian Arens, *Contemporary Advertising* (New York: McGraw-Hill Higher Education, 2009), p. 584.

8. Ibid.

9. Johnathan Crawford, Ad Story: *What the Buck Were We Thinking? The Joys and Pains of E-mail Marketing,* September 2005.

10. Connie O'Kane, "Direct Mail with Promotional Products," *Imprint* (publication of the Advertising Specialty Institute), available on Printable Promotions Web site, http://www.printablepromotions.com/Articles/DirectMail.htm (accessed June 30, 2005).

11. Mobile Advertising, The Economist.com, October 4, 2007, http://www.economist.com/displaystory.cfm?st (accessed December 5, 2008).

12. Elaine Wong, "McDonald's Launches Mobile Promotion for the McRib," *Brandweek* Web site, October 28, 2008, www.brandweek.com/bw/content_display/news-and-features/promotion/e3ic75447be81df667c7cbdbe 1fc2c89a3e (accessed December 28, 2008).

13. Arens, Weigold, and Arens, *Contemporary Advertising,* p. 584.

Chapter

15

Beyond Media

So far just about everything described in the book has been applied to measured media. However, a big part of the marketing communication spectrum includes tools that are difficult to measure. They're even hard to define. So many of them blend together that you can't put them in nice neat categories.

Sales Promotion

Promotion is one of the Four Ps of marketing. In its strictest definition, all marketing communication is a form of promotion. However, in this text we'll call it *sales promotion* and define it as an activity that stimulates purchases by adding a *short-term additional value* to a product or service. In other words, the advertiser is bribing you to buy something quickly. That bribe may be as basic as a discount or as lofty as a donation to a worthy charity. Too many students think of promotion as nothing more than a boring discount coupon, two-for-one sales, and free merchandise when you buy something. But when you explore all the facets of promotion, you'll understand why it's one of the hottest fields in marketing, and when marketers cut traditional advertising in tough times, their dollars often shift to sales promotions.

Most (but not all) sales promotions have specific short-term goals. They are designed to produce results quickly. Once the promotion is over, sales can slip, sometimes prompting an unending chain of new sales promotions.

In some professions, sales promotions are still rare—you probably won't see a plastic surgeon advertising a free tummy tuck with every nose job. However, the use of sales promotion is increasing, even in the service sector. Many marketers have seen diminishing returns from their traditional advertising efforts. Sales promotions, for both trade and consumer, give their sales that extra boost. This is especially common in the cutthroat world of package goods, where the only perceived differences between products are in their promotions. Traditionally, three fourths of the total marketing communication budget for package goods goes to trade and consumer promotion, while the rest goes to traditional advertising.[1]

Sales promotion is actually more of a product than an advertising medium. To be successful, promotions must be promoted, usually by traditional media, such as television, magazines, and newspapers, as well as by Web sites and other so-called nontraditional media.

Words of Wisdom

"Most clients are corporate people protecting their own mortgages. They mistakenly see ideas as a risk rather than advancement in their careers." [1]

—Paul Arden

271

Why sales promotion?

For a copywriter, sales promotion offers many advantages, especially when it's integrated into a total campaign. Some of these advantages are as follows:

- **It's fast.** Sales promotion accelerates the selling process and maximizes sales volume.

- **It can cover the whole distribution channel.** Targeted promotions reach wholesalers, retailers, and consumers.

- **It can help retain customer loyalty.** Promotions provide a way to stay in touch with current customers and to give them incentives for continuing their relationship with a brand or business.

- **It can increase early adoption.** You provide an incentive for a customer to try a product for the first time. With the proliferation of new brands, incentives shorten the path from awareness to action.

- **It's measurable.** In most cases sales promotion is designed for short-term sales increases, not long-term brand image. You get results (or lack of results) almost immediately.

- **It supports retailers.** The growth of *account-specific marketing,* or *comarketing,* requires customized sales promotion programs for retail chains. For example, Sony might offer a promotional program just for Best Buy stores.

- **It fits the consumer's expectations.** On the plus side, consumers are receptive to promotions. On the minus side . . . that's coming later.

- **It fits into an integrated marketing campaign.** To be successful, most promotion needs to be promoted by traditional media.

Why not?

For each of the major advantages, there is a flip side:

- Because of their short-term, price-oriented nature, most sales promotions do not help build long-term brand equity.

- Although incentives can help retain customer loyalty, they can also encourage brand switching. If a brand has no perceived advantage, the consumer will base the purchase on price (or added value).

- Retailers are demanding more, and they are getting it. So in addition to slotting allowances, retailers are demanding more generous account-specific marketing programs that often include expensive sales promotion programs.

- Customers not only respond to promotions; they expect them. Automakers would love to get out of the endless chain of rebates, discounts, and other incentives. But when one offers them, the others follow suit until the whole industry suffers.

- Most promotions can't stand alone. So the advertiser has to weigh the short-term increase in sales against the cost of the incentive and the cost to advertise it. Sometimes an advertiser will settle for breaking even or even a small loss if it means retaining a retail account or gaining market share. For example, automakers may offer very generous year-end deals just to say they're the number-one seller in the rest of their advertising.

Images 15.1, 15.2

Banner ads are linked to landing pages that provide a lot more detail. This one invites people to enter a contest to own the Oscar Mayer Weinermobile for a day.

Consumer sales promotions

With the exception of long-term PR tactics such as sponsorships, most consumer sales promotion is considered to be *non–franchise building*. Promotions are intended to jump-start sales and do almost nothing to build brand image. Another purpose is to gather information (give us the data, and we'll give you a prize). Either way, the ultimate goal is to stimulate action. Examples of sales promotions include the following:

Contests/games: The consumer actively participates in some way by writing an essay, taking a quiz, or engaging in some other mental activity that would not challenge a first grader's intellect. In return for providing some marketing data, you have a one-in-a-gazillion chance to win something.

Sweepstakes: These involve chance more than contests do. Just enter and you may already be a winner. Sometimes you don't have to do anything except wait for your prize. The laws governing contests and sweepstakes vary from state to state. A few years ago, Pepsi announced a chance to win a billion dollars. Although no purchase was necessary, you can bet the winner probably bought some Pepsi along the way.

Product giveaways: Buy the product and you might get the next one free. Fast food restaurants and soft drinks use this quite a bit. You have to buy something first, but you have a better chance of winning.

Samples: You can get them in the mail, in magazine inserts, or from little old ladies in the supermarket. You can give away more than pills, perfumes, and fabric softener sheets. A few years ago AOL gave away millions and millions of CD-ROMs in every imaginable way.

Paper coupons: Essentially these are little slips of paper that ensure a discount. They are distributed in a number of ways: traditionally, in magazine and newspaper ads; in freestanding inserts (FSI) in newspapers; in direct mail packs (such as Valpak); and online, in a form that consumers print at home.

Digital coupons: Anyone who's bought anything online probably knows about discount codes that can significantly reduce the price. Downloadable online coupons have been around for a while too and act basically the same way as traditional paper coupons. Location-based technology allows for delivery of coupons via mobile phones, the Internet, or in-store devices when a shopper enters a specific section of a store. In the future we may see displays with personal chef avatars or holograms that create tonight's menu with the generation of an automatic shopping list for the ingredients, naturally available at that store. Social networks based on shopping preferences will build demand and drive sales, combining online coupons with store locations and conversations with others in the shopping community.

Discounts: These are temporary price reductions. *Temporary* is the key word, because a permanent price reduction creates no urgency to buy.

Bonus packs: The consumer gets more of a product at the regular price. For example, detergent boxes may be bundled in a buy-one-get-one-free promotion. Bonus packs provide more value to the consumer. However, if the consumer is already a loyal customer, there is no incremental value to the manufacturer.

Rebates: Consumers are offered money back if they mail receipts and packaging to the producer. This requires more effort, and the seller bets that a large percentage of people will not bother. If they do, they have to provide information for the seller's database. Many times, prices listed contain "after rebate" in the fine print.

Premiums (merchandise): Instead of money back, the consumer gets stuff. It can be as simple as the toy in a Happy Meal (marginally harder to digest than the food) or as elaborate as thousands of dollars in water toys with the purchase of a new boat. Premiums can also be intangible items, such as frequent-flier points.

Loyalty programs: These reward customers for continuing to purchase the same brand of a product or service. Airline frequent-flier plans are the most obvious form of loyalty programs. But retailers such as grocers, discount stores, and electronics stores, where customers shop frequently, also use loyalty programs. Many consumer package goods companies have frequency programs that award points for purchases. The points can be redeemed for gifts, such as merchandise, or for discounts.

Cross-promotion: Some products just seem to complement each other. If so, they can work together to multiply their promotional dollars. For example, a cookie company may offer coupons for milk. Other times the lead brand in a promotional campaign will bring in partners. For example, BMW's test-drive program to raise money for breast cancer also included Harman Kardon and Michelin, which are used in BMW cars. Pepsi has teamed with Apple to promote free iTunes with the purchase of Pepsi.

Trade sales promotions

If you're a manufacturer, how do you motivate your sales staff, move product through distributors, and encourage retailers to stock your brands? Trade sales promotion is used for business-to-business products and for wholesale transactions for consumer goods. Some trade sales promotions include the following:

Financial incentives: Lower interest rates, reduced freight costs, price discounts, and extended payments can encourage retailers to stock up on products. Some of these include slotting allowances to provide shelf space, buying allowances to reduce the introductory price, and promotional allowances for short-term promotions. These allowances are usually meant to be passed on to the consumer, but some retailers pocket the savings and charge full retail prices, which does not help to move the product. To counter this, some package goods companies have dropped their everyday prices and cut back on trade allowances. Push money—also known as "spiffs"—can be an extra commission paid to a sales force, wholesaler, or retailer.

Trade contests: Salespeople, wholesalers, and retailers receive rewards for increasing their sales. The more you sell, the more you get. These often involve travel incentives, such as a trip for two to Hawaii or tickets to a major sporting event.

Sales support: The manufacturer provides displays, posters, counter cards, signage, and other point-of-sale items. Products sell better with attractive displays, which are often accompanied by price deals. The manufacturer may also provide special promotional literature for the dealer to hand out.

Training programs: The manufacturer trains the distributor or dealer employees in selling the product.

Trade shows: Manufacturers display their products, salespeople meet and greet potential customers, distributors and wholesalers check out new lines, and everybody sees what the competition is up to. Trade shows can be small regional events with nothing more than a few 10-by-10-foot booths or major

Image 15.3

McDonald's engaged European consumers with this interactive push puzzle to promote their coffee. The theme: "Sort your head out."

extravaganzas such as the Consumer Electronics Show, which generates worldwide coverage. Some manufacturers spend millions every year on trade shows—for elaborate booths, celebrity talent, high-profile events, extravagant banquets, contests, and handouts. Trade shows provide a lot of opportunity for creative people. Dozens of details require creative planning: the booth design itself; displays, posters, handout literature; event planning, preshow promotion, and premium selection; audio and video displays; and more. In a way, a trade show booth is a campaign in itself, with components that work individually and cumulatively to convey a single message.

Cooperative advertising: Basically, the manufacturer helps the retailer pay for advertising its products. Sometimes the ads are provided, and all the retailer has to do is slap a logo and address on the bottom. In many cases, the co-op ad is similar to the national brand advertising done by the manufacturer. Other times, the manufacturer provides images and copy that the retailers use to build their own ads. If you ever have to produce co-op ads, always keep the intended media in mind. For example, don't try to convert an elaborate four-color magazine ad into a black-and-white co-op ad for a local newspaper.

Like consumer sales promotions, trade promotions usually have to be supported with some form of marketing communications, usually print advertising, direct mail, and the Internet.

Promotional strategy and tactics

Promotional strategy stems from marketing objectives. For example:

- Get 20% of Brand X users to try Brand Y within 3 months.

- Get 40% of current Brand Z users to increase purchases from 5 to 10 packages per month within 6 months.

- Expand distribution for Brand A from 40% to 80% in all X-Mart chain stores within 1 year.

You need to first have a clear idea of what the client wants to accomplish before you create a promotional program.

COMPONENTS OF THE PROMOTION

Assuming you know the client's objectives, you need to follow these steps:

1. **Think campaigns.** If the promotion is part of a total campaign, make sure your sales promotion will fit the way the product is positioned in the market, the brand image, the target audience, and how it is sold.

2. **Develop a promotional theme.** It's like a tagline. Use some of the guidelines for taglines in Chapter 9.

3. **Consider the incentive.** What will you offer that adds value to the product or service and encourages quick sales? As with the theme, you have to consider the target audience and brand image. For example, a free trunk full of frozen pizzas may get a prospect into a Hyundai dealer, but it probably won't motivate a potential Audi customer.

4. **Promote the promotion.** Once you have determined the theme and the incentive, how do you let people know? Your marketing of the promotion also depends on the target audience and brand image. Using multiple media, such as the Internet and print, provides for more interaction and greater involvement with the product.

TIPS AND TECHNIQUES FOR PROMOTION

- Use a memorable theme.

- Relate to the product attributes (brand image).

- Keep it simple.

- Make the benefit (reward) clear.

Image 15.4

*Target promoted their commitment to local communities with a series
of public relations advertisements. In this ad, they promoted support
of local schools.*

Promotional Public Relations

The term *public relations* covers any nonpaid
information from a third party that mentions an
identified product or service. It's also called *earned
media,* since the placement of a story depends on
convincing an editor to run it rather than just
sending in an insertion order. There are many
kinds of PR, and we're not going to address them
here. Instead, we'll focus on the publicity aspect of
PR and how it applies to promotion and Integrated
Marketing Communications. Examples include
event sponsorship, donations to causes, charitable
foundations, and other good things companies do
that deserve positive mention. PR can also be
used to announce a sales promotion activity.

A dedicated public relations practitioner
would probably be outraged to see PR relegated
to a subhead in a discussion of promotions. We
do not mean to dismiss the value of public
relations. In fact, we believe PR should be the
foundation of most marketing communications
plans. In this context, however, we will discuss
public relations in terms of creative strategy, with
special emphasis on how public relations can fit
into a promotional campaign.

Good deeds get good press, even if you have to buy it

One function of public relations is getting credit
for the good things your company does. So, many
promotional PR efforts concentrate on charitable
acts. For example, your promotion could be about
donating money to research against diseases
such as breast cancer, supporting national parks, building local playgrounds, and
cleaning up river walks. In addition to doing the good deed, you need to promote
it through publicity releases and editorial contacts as well as traditional and
nontraditional media. Marketers can't always be assured they will earn space in
a publication or TV news story. So they produce ads and commercials touting
their good deeds.

Public relations advertising uses traditional advertising messages to promote
the good deeds of a company. For example, companies may run TV ads stating
that they'll donate a percentage of the purchase price to a charity. Or, as was the
case with a pharmaceutical manufacturer, they may announce available support
plans if patients can't afford the drugs.

Event Marketing and Sponsorships

Event marketing and sponsorships are specialized forms of promotion that link a company or brand to a specific event or a themed activity. Event marketing and sponsorship are sort of like public relations because they can be long-term goodwill efforts that can enhance brand image. Marketers often participate in event marketing by attaching their brand to a sporting event, concert, fair, or festival. In event sponsorship, a brand or company name usually precedes the name of the particular event. Examples include the following:

- Corona presents Kenny Chesney in concert

- The FedEx Orange Bowl

Event marketing has become very popular in recent years for several reasons:

- It creates experiences for consumers and associates a company's brand with certain lifestyles and activities.

- It provides opportunities to distribute samples as well as information about a marketer's product or service or to let consumers actually experience the product.

- It gives marketers access to large numbers of consumers at a relatively low cost and can be effective as a grassroots marketing program.[2]

Cross-media event promotion can be very effective cross-culturally too. Tecate beer launched a promotion centered on Mexican Independence Day that touted three major boxing matches in Houston, Las Vegas, and Los Angeles. Special events and promos surrounding the event included key restaurant and bar accounts, ticket giveaways via local radio partners, thematic point-of-purchase displays, mail-in rebates for HBO pay-per-view events, and autograph sessions with local boxers.[3]

Product Placement

Some companies specialize in placing their clients' products on game shows as prizes. Others concentrate on getting their clients into movies and TV shows. For example, in *E.T.: The Extra Terrestrial* the hero was lured with Reese's Pieces because M&M's would not pay for product placement. Short-term sales of

Reese's Pieces skyrocketed. In *Quantum of Solace,* James Bond and other characters used many Sony products including VAIO laptops, Sony Ericsson cell phones and GPS units, BRAVIA televisions, and a Cyber-shot to take photos. This is in addition to OMEGA watches, Heineken beer, Coca-Cola, Aston Martin, and other Ford cars, which played prominent roles. In fact, the $79 million spent on product placements, brand integration, and promotional tie-ins set a new record for Bond movies.[4] So when you see a character reach for a box of Cheerios, drink a Coors, or drive a new Honda, it's no coincidence. Product placement, also called *embedded marketing*, is negotiated with the producers and, as we noted above, can run into tens of millions of dollars for a single film or television program.

Even though product placement enhances brand awareness, it still can't match traditional ads for effectiveness. According to MediaPost, 52% of viewers would buy a product after watching the commercial for it versus only 23% after product placement. Consumers are more likely to recall brands in traditional ads than through product placement.[5]

Ad Story

Coke "Brand Managers" Score a Zero and Win Big

"Diet colas have always tasted odd at best, and, well, a bit like turpentine in the worst cases. So the idea that a drink with no calories could actually taste like regular Coke would surely be met with skepticism by consumers. Rather than simply announce to people that Coke Zero tasted like Coke, we started thinking about how to prove it. We asked ourselves what sort of things might really happen if Coke Zero successfully replicated the taste of Coke.

"One thing that struck us was how fractious big corporations like the Coca-Cola Company are, and how individual parts of the company actually compete with one another for resources and prestige. If the Coke Zero brand team really had knocked off the taste of Coke, how would the guys who work on the Coke brand feel about it? Enter 'Brand Managers,' a campaign built around two Coke executives who are incensed that Coke Zero has stolen their taste and simply repackaged it in a different can. We hired two actors to play 'Matt Anderson and Phil Rose,' fictitious Coke Brand Managers bent on stopping Coke Zero. Matt and Phil then invited real attorneys to help them sue Coke Zero, even though it was part of their own company.

"The responses, which ranged from amusement to dismay to outright derision, were all captured on hidden camera and cut into 30 TV spots, as well as longer Web films. As these hapless characters endured the slings and arrows of agitated attorneys, the public fell in love with them, and in effect they became spokesmen (or anti-spokesmen) for the real Coke taste of Coke Zero.

"For phase two, we leveraged the Brand Managers as intellectual property, creating a series of commercials chronicling their daily struggle to stop Coke Zero from tasting like Coke. The Brand Managers showed up across sports properties like NASCAR, the NCAA Final Four, and of course the Super Bowl, where they attempted to prevent Pittsburgh Steeler Troy Polamalu from enjoying a Zero with disastrous results. And they starred in eight separate 4-minute segments on the Jimmy Kimmel show, crossing the line between advertising and content, and as always, proving inadvertently that Coke Zero tastes a whole lot like Coke."[6]

—David Schiff
Associate Creative Director, *Crispin Porter + Bogusky,* Boulder

In-Game Advertising

In-game advertising (IGA) uses computer and video games as a medium to deliver brand messages, logos, and products in use within games as a way to offset development costs for increasingly sophisticated graphics. Advertisers see in-game advertising as a direct path to the coveted 18–34 demographic, which is becoming increasingly hard to reach with traditional media. Early games feature static displays such as billboards in the background or logos on stadium scoreboards. With ad revenues increasing rapidly, IGA has become big business—big enough to merit the attention of Nielsen Media Research (GamePlay Metrics) to measure ratings of ad messages inside games. As online gaming grew, advertisers could develop dynamic ads that change the messages depending on who is playing the game, where it's played, and when, since ad messages do not have to be hard coded into the game. In October 2008, billboard ads featuring Barack Obama appeared in the game *Burnout Paradise*, which was first released in January of that year. Electronic Arts, the game's publisher, confirmed that the Obama campaign paid for the advertisements, marking the first time that a U.S. presidential candidate has bought in-game advertising.[7]

While game marketers and advertisers like the potential of IGA, what about gamers? Some gamers may see in-game ads as another way for the corporate world to invade their world. However, a study by Nielsen and IGA Worldwide showed that 82% of consumers did not object to in-game ads and 61% expressed a more favorable view of the advertiser after they played.[8]

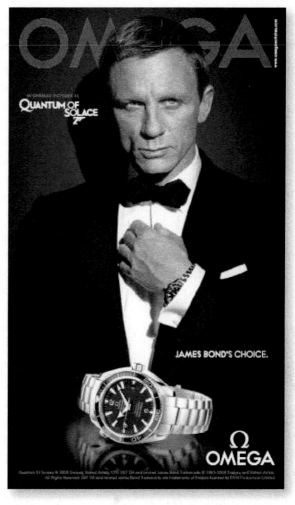

Image 15.5

No matter who plays 007, he always sports an OMEGA watch, or whatever brand paid the most money. Bond movies usually top the list of high-profile placements, but products appear in almost every television show or motion picture out today.

Hybrid Marketing

Hybrid marketing takes product placement one step further and integrates it into commercials before, during, and after the program as well as the programming itself. Hybrid ads include customized ads, branded promotions, vignettes, interstitial, and micro-series where sponsor messaging is combined with program or entertainment content.[9] Some examples include a customized 40-second hybrid ad sponsored by CoverGirl cosmetics on *America's Next Top Model* to announce the Meet the Model Sweepstakes; T-Mobile sponsored a 35-second custom ad on the American Music Awards to encourage viewers to text message their votes from a T-Mobile phone or go to abc.com to vote; during broadcasts of Major League Baseball on TBS, Ernie Johnson appeared in a 15-second commercial sponsored by BlackBerry to encourage viewers to send questions to his phone and to check out his blog on MLB.com; and a 70-second

custom commercial on Bravo's *Project Runway* promoted a contest to win a $10,000 shopping spree on Bluefly.com when viewers voted on the models. Participants could also receive a Bravo ringtone and wallpaper by texting their vote. Or they could have voted on bravotv.com.

Hybrid ads are often placed before episodes of programs telling the viewers to visit the sponsors' Web sites and buy products that will appear throughout the episode. Media critic David Hauslaib comments, "Hybrid commercials work regardless of what field you're in. So Toyota, Keebler Cookies, and Travelocity can enjoy the same bump from their symbiotic show relationship as any other product, as long as they can somehow make their item correlate with the show in people's minds."[10]

Guerrilla Marketing

In the 1980s, the term *guerrilla marketing* came to represent a number of nontraditional MarCom tactics used to gain awareness without spending a lot of money (at least not as much as for traditional TV advertising). Some exhibitive advertising has been called a guerrilla tactic—because it's relatively low cost—but it gets people talking and the media to cover it to get even more people talking.

Other guerrilla tactics involve a number of weapons to multiply the coverage. The campaign for Aflac is a prime example. Their duck icon was supported with a relatively modest $45 million ad budget. But the behind-the-scenes effort multiplied the impact. In 4 years, awareness of the company grew from 12% to more than 90%. The following blurb from *The Wall Street Journal* describes how it works: "Creating a breakout ad character is in some measure a matter of luck and circumstances, but Aflac lowered its odds considerably by supplementing its

Image 15.6

Mr. Clean is beyond tough. He not only cleans; he stops traffic.

Image 15.7

The Greenville Literacy Project wanted folks to donate books, so they took over a high-traffic spot downtown—the main parking garage. It created a lot of buzz, and books poured in.

Image 15.8

How much better does it get when the very product a company makes holds up the corporate headquarters? A great example of branding synergy that creates buzz.

TV ads with a well-orchestrated, behind-the-scenes guerrilla public relations campaign. Instead of simply buying lots of TV ads, a team of four ad and marketing executives are focused on getting the duck on TV at no cost to Aflac."[12] Some of their actions have included handing out plush duck toys to people on the outdoor set of the *Today* show, sponsoring a water tank for synchronized swimmers on David Letterman's show, getting coverage on CNBC (which ran the commercials for free as part of a news story), and lobbying consumers to vote for the duck in a Yahoo/*USA Today* poll on favorite ad icons.

When it comes to out-of-home, using guerrilla tactics can be very effective. Keep in mind that by its nature, guerrilla marketing is meant to provide big results for less money than traditional media. The goal is to generate a buzz—word of mouth (either in person or through viral channels) and earned media coverage that generates far more coverage than you can afford with traditional advertising.

Image 15.9

Here's a visual metaphor writ large. And it's not accidental the bench is placed beside a lawn.

Image 15.10

When all else fails, take your brand on vacation. Skippy decided that one place to find young moms was at the beach. So they partnered with resorts and had sand rollers created with the Skippy logo. They spread fun, goodwill, and a branded message.

Image 15.11

These sheep didn't stay bundled in their own fluffy blankets for long. When Dutch commuters saw their beloved sheep grazing in blankets promoting hotels, there was an outcry. Obviously someone underestimated Dutch sentimentality.

Once again, the point of using these tactics is not to saturate a mass market. It's to get people talking about your brand. So it's important to make sure the creativity does not overshadow the brand message. You don't want people to remember the gimmick but not the advertiser.

Word-of-Mouth Marketing

How many times have you heard "the best advertising is word of mouth"? Today's it's more than a tired cliché, because new technology is creating a whole new word-of-mouth (WOM) category. Word of mouth is simply the act of consumers providing information to other consumers. Sometimes it's an honest appraisal. Sometimes the buzz is manipulated. When WOM can be manipulated, accelerated, and multiplied exponentially, you can make the case that it's a legitimate form of advertising. In fact, when it's managed to deliver a defined result, it's called Word of Mouth Marketing (WOMM).

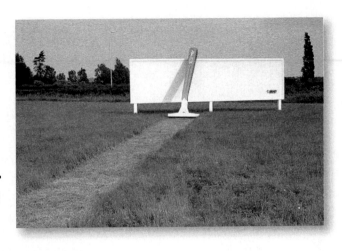

Image 15.12

Not only does this Bic razor catch your eye; it also does double duty as a lawnmower. Three-dimensional extended boards attract motorists and also generate a buzz in traditional media.

Why is WOMM so important? Research shows that when a person is happy with a product or service, she tells 3 people. When she's unhappy, she tells 11.[13] Don't you want as many people as possible telling 3 friends about your wonderful product? Now, what if you could multiply the number of people talking about you a thousand fold? When people naturally become advocates of a product because they are satisfied customers, it's called organic word of mouth. When marketers launch campaigns to accelerate WOM, that is when it becomes WOMM; "influencers" spread the message. The key to successful WOMM is not how many consumers you please but rather how many influencers you reach to spread the message. Viral seeding agencies will place your cool product-oriented video on hundreds, if not thousands, of Web sites, blogs, and social sites. The advantage of online WOMM is that your message does not fade after a one-on-one conversation. It keeps multiplying, even if at a decelerating rate. Your guerrilla marketing efforts may be picked up by mainstream news media and online news sources where millions will see it, comment on it, download it, and send it to their friends. Your provocative billboard, poster, or exhibitive advertising will be photographed by cell phones and sent to dozens of people, who in turn will send it to dozens more, and so on. As long as we're tossing out old clichés, with properly managed WOMM, one picture is worth a thousand downloads . . . more likely, a thousand times a thousand. Another thing to remember about WOMM is that the influencers, those people you recruit to spread your message, are influenced by traditional media to generate more buzz. They'll see a story on CNN, watch the video on YouTube, or get an e-mail that will accelerate their dissemination of your WOM message. When WOMM is discussed, other terms get thrown around like *buzz marketing*. It's simply another way to get people talking, hopefully in a positive tone. As we discuss in other chapters, be very careful about trying to manage a viral buzz. If it's perceived as too heavy-handed,

Words of Wisdom

"Word of mouth is the best medium of all." [14]

—Bill Bernbach

Image 15.13

How strong is 3M Security Glass? Strong enough to protect thousands of dollars at a bus stop. The tone of this display almost dares someone to try to bust through.

Image 15.14

Who wouldn't notice this wall mural for Nationwide insurance? However, will they remember the fictional Coops Paint or the Nationwide brand?

dishonest, or manipulative, it will definitely generate a buzz, but not the kind you want. Remember those 11 people who hear negative news?

Whether you call it WOMM or buzz or whatever, one of its real powers is to create and sustain a brand. Where would Harley-Davidson be without a small but rabid gang of brand evangelists in black leather jackets? Ben & Jerry's would be just another ice cream if people didn't talk about their support for worthy causes. Macintosh might just have been another futile experiment in operating system development if dedicated art directors, designers, and other right-brainers didn't spread the word within and between agencies and studios.

No matter how many success stories you dig out, the value of word of mouth as a marketing tool will remain anecdotal until more accurate metrics are developed. BzzAgent, a Boston-based word-of-mouth marketing agency, fixed the value of one conversation at about 50 cents.[15] But, as of this writing, the Word of Mouth Marketing Association has yet to settle on a standardized ROI (return on investment). David Bank, an analyst for RBC Capital Markets, commented, "I might think I'm paying X amount for a CPM [cost per thousand]. But if virality is 30 times that, I'm paying so much less."[16]

Image 15.15

Giant crop circle ads promoting McDonald's coffee and Papa John's pizza mysteriously appeared in Midwestern fields. Whether they were the work of aliens or agencies, they generated a lot a buzz (at least until harvest time).

Who's Who?

Jay Conrad Levinson is the author of a wildly successful series of books about "guerrilla marketing" tactics. He cites many examples of unconventional marketing and communications programs that generated spectacular results. Typically, these guerrilla tactics use existing marketing communication tools, such as direct mail or outdoor, but in highly targeted, very creative ways.

Cliff Marks is the creator of "premovie" showings in theaters. His CineMedia company pioneered the introduction of high-quality advertising content on the big screen. Marks and his company introduced The 2wenty, a digital prefeature program that included traditional 30-second spots and longer-format ads. While some moviegoers don't appreciate the intrusion of commercials, most accept the advertising, especially the slick longer-format spots that are different from typical TV advertising.

Exercises

1. Brand Sensing

We think using all your senses to there fullest will only enhance your strategic and creative work. Here's one way to get started.

- Make a grid on the board with seven columns. In the first column make a list of big brands such as Aflac, Apple, Birkenstock, BMW, Chevrolet, Coke, Dell, ESPN, FedEx, *GQ,* Kashi, Marlboro, Motorola, NBC, Nicorette, Nokia, Starbucks, State Farm, UPS, Wii . . .

- Across the top row, above the next five columns list one of the five senses. In each of the next five columns note how one might experience each brand based on the five senses. How does Brand X look, feel, taste, sound, and smell? Leave the final column blank.

- Now, discuss each brand and list how consumers might experience the brand with each of their senses.

- After completing the entire brand list, return to the first brand, review the sensory aspects. Consider what already exists for them to experience and where there are sensorial opportunities? In the last column list nontraditional options inspired by the sensory list.

- Continue down the list and see how the senses can lead you to see options you might never have thought of before.

2. Unusual Matches

Some times opportunities to reach consumers are found in unexpected places. Here's one way to dig deep to find those places—with your teacher help.

- Before coming to class generate a long list of highly unexpected touch points—those nontraditional places you might never have thought of finding an advertising message. *Unexpected* is the key word. Push the envelope.

- Your teacher will have predetermined list of brands, the same number of brands as students, and will have the brand names in a hat.

- Reach in and select a brand.

- Quickly, relying only on your personal knowledge and/or experience with the brand, write a positioning statement.

- Now, go around the room with each of you presenting the positioning for your brand along with a brief description of the target audience.

- After each of you present, discuss ideas about which touch points might fit with each brand using your lists of unexpected touch points.

- Keep a running list of brands—listing each touch point.

- At the end, see which touch points have the most brands associated with them and discuss why that might be.

Notes

1. Paul Arden, *It's Not How Good You Are, It's How Good You Want to Be* (London: Phaidon, 2003), p. 30.

2. George E. Belch and Michael A. Belch, "Sales Promotion," in *Advertising and Promotion: An Integrated Marketing Perspective,* 6th ed. (New York: McGraw-Hill, 2003), pp. 510–561.

3. Della de Lafuente, "Tecate Punches Up Marketing for Boxing Events," *Brandweek* Web site, August 15, 2008, www.brandweek.com/bw/content_display/news-and-features/shopper/e3i59d687c2e454352e46418143086e31dd (accessed December 28, 2008).

4. Internet Movie Database, accessed December 15, 2008.

5. FIND/SVP & Media Post.com, accessed December 15, 2008.

6. David Schiff, Ad Story: *Coke "Brand Managers" Score a Zero and Win Big,* February 2009.

7. Brendan Sinclair, "Obama Campaigns in Burnout, 17 Other Games," GameSpot Web site, October 14, 2008, http://www.gamespot.com/news/6199379.html (accessed January 5, 2009).

8. Ernest Cavalli, "Study: 82 Percent of Consumers Accept In-Game Ads, "Game|Life Web site, June 17, 2008, http://blog.wired.com/games/2008/06/study-82-percen.html (accessed January 5, 2009).

9. "10 Most-Recalled New 'Hybrid' Ads: Oct./Nov. 2008," Nielsen Wire Web site, December 10, 2008, http://blog.nielsen.com/nielsenwire/consumer/10-most-recalled-new-hybrid-ads-octnov-2008/ (accessed December, 20, 2008).

10. David Hauslaib, "Hybrid Ads: The Only Commercials That Are Still Worth the Cash," www.already.com, October 24, 2008, http://www.jossip.com/hybrid-ads-the-only-commercials-worth-the-cash (assessed December 20, 2008).

11. Jay Conrad Levinson, *Guerilla Marketing Attack* (Boston: Mariner Books, 1989), p. 146.

12. "Aflac Duck's Paddle to Stardom: Creativity on the Cheap," *The Wall Street Journal,* July 30, 2004, p. B1.

13. Jeff Lyon, "Viral Marketing," *Chicago Tribune Magazine,* August 5, 2007, p. 6.

14. Bill Bernbach, *Bill Bernbach Said . . .* (New York: DDB Needham Worldwide, 1989), p. 15.

15. Todd Wasserman, "Is Talk Cheap? How Cheap?" *Brandweek* Web site, June 29, 2008, http://www.brandweek.com/bw/content_display/news-and-features/crm/e3i3a6a726c3dd89a14be65cf4e81526914 (accessed December 28, 2008).

16. Ibid.

Chapter 16

Business-to-Business

B2B: Challenges and Opportunities

Some beginning copywriters dread business-to-business (B2B) assignments. The products aren't fun. The target audience is deadly serious. You're mostly stuck with trade magazines and collateral pieces. Many creative directors tell their team, "There are no boring products, only boring advertising." But many times, you don't know enough about a product to make it interesting. Too often even the clients don't know why anyone should buy their products. So they settle for a sterile recitation of facts and figures. While it doesn't take a rocket scientist to figure out beer, soap, or toilet paper, you have to know something about your subject as well as the customer when you're creating business advertising.

While creating good B2B concepts can be a challenge, it also presents a great opportunity, especially for entry-level writers. Rather than being stuck with a small piece of the account, you're more likely to work on a whole campaign. You might be able to work out a whole integrated plan that uses a lot of fun promotional and Web components in addition to print ads and collateral. You can probably work in some cool guerrilla marketing ideas. Some clients love that, since they think they're getting more for their money. In *Hey Whipple, Squeeze This,* Luke Sullivan praises B2B: "Trade ads are just as important to your client's economy as its consumer work, and they're usually a better gig than a consumer campaign."[1]

Why B2B is different

- The customer is buying products with his or her company's money.

- Traditionally, the copy has been more factual and less emotional than what's usually found in consumer advertising.

- In general, the emphasis is on generating immediate response rather than on long-term brand building.

- Ad budgets are usually much smaller than with mass-appeal consumer products, restricting many creative options.

Words of Wisdom

"It's . . . likely your trade assignment will have a cleaner playing field than a mass-market ad. There's a built-in villain: the other guy's product." [2]

—Luke Sullivan

Paper you can trust.

Productolith by STORAENSO

Image 16.1

In the past, B2B advertisers might have listed the specs or featured testimonials. But here, they're asking printers to take a leap of faith to demonstrate their paper's strength.

- Most business products are not sold retail, which means they are sold either direct to buyers or through dealers or distributors.

Why B2B is the same

- Business customers still have wants and needs—saving money, success, self-esteem. Sure, they want facts, but ultimately it's about making more money and feeling good about it.

- The copy and design principles discussed in previous chapters apply to business readers, maybe even more than they do with some consumer products.

- The Internet is just as important, and in some cases even more important, as a communication source and as part of an Integrated Marketing Communications campaign.

- Branding for business products and services is becoming hugely important, especially as companies merge and change affiliations. Sometimes the brand name is the only constant.

- Even though the numbers of business customers may be smaller, using traditional mass media such as television, radio, outdoor, and newspapers may be an effective way to reach them.

- Companies do not buy products and services. People do.

Don't Forget Those Wants and Needs

A salesperson who just got rejected by a heartless purchasing agent may disagree, but business buyers are human. They may use economic rationales, but they still have wants and needs similar to those of other consumers. For example:

- An office manager responds to a direct mailer from an office supply store that offers free delivery. This saves her time so she can get more work done; she can save her company money, which makes her look good to the boss, which might mean she gets a raise. All of which satisfies her needs.

- A factory manager sees an ad for a robot that stacks boxes on pallets in minutes, saving valuable time and labor. This will save his company a lot of money, making him look good, which may mean a promotion and more money. (Starting to see a pattern?)

- A doctor reads a brochure, sees a medical journal ad, and checks a Web site for a new blood-thinning drug. She gets more information from a sales rep, including research reports. She prescribes the drug, not because she'll make more money, but because her need is to help her patients. Sometimes business is about more than making money.

Most of this chapter will deal with trade advertising, which is generally aimed at businesspeople who buy products or services sold direct or through dealers, wholesalers, or retailers—for example, sump pumps sold to plumbers; bathroom fixtures for schools; lumber for housing contractors; engines for jet planes; and a million other products we all take for granted. Besides trade, there are two other B2B specialties:

Agricultural advertising: another animal

Agricultural advertising requires a special approach. Farmers are consumers who buy industrial products—tractors, buildings, seed, chemicals, and the like. They ride boom and bust cycles that would make the most daring stockbrokers nauseous. When you talk to a typical farmer, he will always complain about the weather, the government, the markets, and whatever else is bugging him today. But for the most part he wouldn't trade his career choice for any city job. Some of the hottest creative shops have taken on ag clients and won a ton of awards. Someday you just might work on an ag account, so here are a few tips:

- Many successful farmers are college-educated businesspeople and should be treated as such, not as bib-overall-wearing hicks. Appeal to their business sense, not to the nostalgia of a small family farm that disappeared years ago.

- Farmers are extremely sensitive to detail and very concerned about being up-to-date. Show a 10-year-old tractor, a CRT computer monitor, or an out-of-date satellite dish in your ad, and you've killed your sales message.

- You can have fun with the product, but never mock the farmer's country, family, profession, or lifestyle.

- Be careful with claims. If anyone recognizes BS, it's a farmer.

This will give you a rough idea of Bear Brand quality.

Now you can offer a quality line of sandpaper, a Norton line, even to price-conscious customers. So if you're thinking of adding an economy sandpaper to your premium Norton line, just keep these Bear facts in mind. Bear Brand sandpaper from Norton costs up to 30–40% less than other popular brands, so you can pass on the savings and still satisfy your customers with good quality. Bear Brand is available in most popular grits and sizes and in retail and contractor packaging. For more information about Bear Brand products call 800-524-2110.

NORTON

Image 16.2

This insert for Norton's Bear Brand sandpaper is actually printed on a sheet of sandpaper. It not only gains attention; it also provides a product sample.

Professional advertising

Not that we don't think other businesspeople are pros as to what they do, but in this context *professional* applies to teachers, engineers, lawyers, accountants, doctors, dentists, architects, and other people who have specialized careers that usually require advanced education and training. Professionals read journals that are often the official publications of their profession, such as the *Journal of the American Medical Association.* Professionals operate under a code of ethics, so journals that allow advertising frown on wild, unsubstantiated ad claims; unauthorized use of a product; or any image that would denigrate their field. That's why so many professional journal ads play it safe and don't risk offending their readers. Other publications that appeal to professionals may be given a little more creative latitude, but remember; These professionals worked hard to get where they are, and it's not something to trivialize with silly advertising.

Business-to-Business and Campaigns

Many B2B marketers have discovered that magazines may not be the primary method to reach their customers. Using Integrated Marketing Communications for B2B makes sense because customers are easier to define and locate. All the IMC components listed in Chapter 2 apply to business-to-business. Because the number of key customers is sometimes very small, you may be able to create expensive high-impact communication tools that generate higher response rates.

As with consumer advertising, you need to think of how many different ways you can reach a customer. Do you go for a few high-impact "rifle shots" or use a lot of different marketing tools? Here are some examples:

- A Japanese engine manufacturer wanted potential customers to recognize their commitment to the U.S. market. So they sent a large box to the nation's top industrial engine buyers. On the box lid was the slogan, "Take Power Trip." Inside was a high-quality garment bag embroidered with the company logo. In the pocket of the bag were vouchers for two plane tickets to the company's North American headquarters in California. Also enclosed were a cover letter from the U.S. general manager, product literature, and a corporate brochure. Each mailing cost about $200, but when compared to millions of dollars in engine sales, it was very economical. Just as important, salespeople from the engine company called potential customers after the big boxes arrived. You can be sure the prospects remembered the mailer, which made it much easier for the sales force.

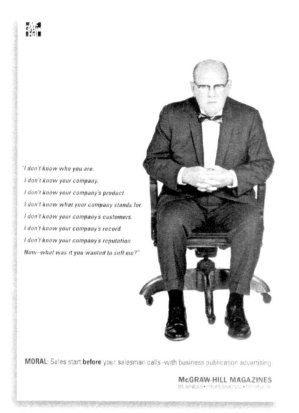

I don't know who you are.
I don't know your company.
I don't know your company's product.
I don't know what your company stands for.
I don't know your company's customers.
I don't know your company's record.
I don't know your company's reputation.
Now—what was it you wanted to sell me?"

MORAL: Sales start before your salesman calls—with business publication advertising.

McGRAW-HILL MAGAZINES
BUSINESS • PROFESSIONAL • TECHNICAL

Image 16.3

Many years ago, magazine publisher McGraw-Hill made the case for business-to-business advertising. The grumpy little man in the chair may not represent typical buyers today, but they still want answers to the questions in the headline.

• A manufacturer of construction equipment launched a new line of telescopic material handlers. They used print ads but also produced a series of sell sheets, full-line brochures, head-to-head comparisons with other brands, a walk-around guide to help salespeople sell the machine, a feature/benefit video, an operational video showing applications and attachments, an interactive multimedia program to show potential customers, a co-op advertising kit, a dealer sales kit, point-of-sale displays for dealers, a complete trade PR program on CD-ROM, and oversize posters and motorized displays for trade shows. The company's dealers had the tools they needed to sell to their contractor customers, who were also very familiar with the new products after seeing the ads and direct mailers.

• A marketer of veterinary products launched a line of products to help vets treat ear problems in dogs. They produced a magazine insert that folded out to form a poster for the vet's exam rooms. They ran spread and single-page ads in professional journals. The company offered audiocassettes about building a clinic's business by using these new products. A direct mail kit included a 100-page technical guide. They provided handouts for clinic customers and even ran ads in consumer publications to encourage dog owners to visit their vets.

Image 16.4

GHX helps health care facilities save money on equipment and supplies. So the concept of applying defibrillator paddles to the hospital resonates with hospital CEOs.

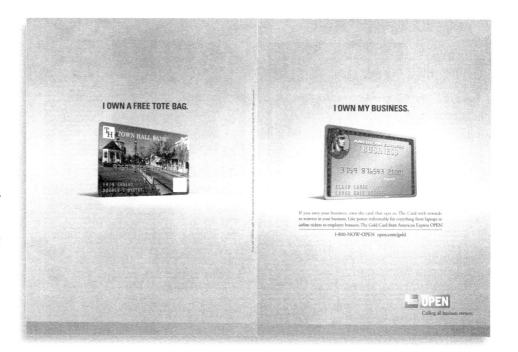

Image 16.5

As part of an integrated marketing campaign, American Express compares ordinary consumer credit cards with their cards for business owners. The American Express Gold Card tells the world you're a big shot—especially if you pick up the check. The headline: "I own a free tote bag/I own my business."

Image 16.6

Looking for the image of "overconfidence"? You might consider this one or something a little less cheeky from the Corbis library.

Here's one way to sum up the use of IMC for business-to-business campaigns: Imagine that in order to get a sale, you have to open a big iron door. Run a few magazine ads, and you're throwing pebbles at that door. Use all the integrated marketing tools at your disposal, and you've got a big boulder that'll knock that door wide open.

Online Marketing Tools for B2B

Many B2B clients adopted the Internet long before consumer brands did. Whether it's used strictly for information or for direct selling, the Internet provides B2B marketers with tremendous advantages over "traditional" media, including the following:

- Provides more detailed information than you can fit in an ad.

- Shows streaming video, animation, and interactive media.

- When used as part of an integrated personalized direct mail program using PURLs, it can build customer relationships faster than with traditional methods.

- Includes links to co-op partners and/or affiliated companies.

- Provides updated product information such as spec sheets, catalogs, parts forms, and troubleshooting guides that can be downloaded.

- Delivers company news; announces new promotions and special offers.

- Sets up merchant accounts for direct sales.

- Identifies dealers, shows their locations, and provides links to their sites. Widgets such as Google Maps can be integrated into the site for more impact.

- Tracks inquiries, builds databases, and establishes Customer Relationship Management (CRM) programs.

When building a B2B site, don't forget the three things you need to accomplish—get them to come, get them to stay, and get them to come back. When you want to drive customers to your site, trade ads, direct mail, articles in trade publications, banner ads on other sites, and all the other tactics used in B2C marketing apply. As far as keeping them there, the focus should be on education, motivation, and generating action, not entertainment. Even if viewers feel like playing games, watching videos, and reading blogs, chances are their bosses would rather see them downloading specs, comparing prices, and saving time on the Web. When you want to get them to come back, it's the same as with consumer sites—keep the content fresh and let them know you have a new product or service worth checking out. Businesspeople are looking for updated sites that offer a wide range of Web-based tools for sales leads, direct mail marketing, telemarketing, and customer relationship marketing. RSS (Really Simple Syndication) technology is a proactive way to send news to subscribing businesspeople.

Ad Story

For B2B Shippers, It's All There in Brown and White

The challenge for UPS has always been how to turn one of the world's most respected companies into one of the world's most respected brands. The Martin Agency began the process by redefining the UPS brand with their distinctive "What can brown do for you?" campaign. The client challenged the agency to accelerate the process. The problem: how to find a simple way to clearly explain the business solutions UPS provides—such as international shipping, delivery intercept, and operational logistics. They had to make the message simple, relevant, and motivating. In an *Adweek* interview, Senior Vice President and Creative Director Andy Azula stated, "The challenge was to let the world know what they did beyond delivering a package from point A to point B. The truth is, even the stuff that happens between A and B is pretty amazing."[4]

As the creative group brainstormed, Andy captured the best ideas on a whiteboard. Somewhere in the process of recording ideas, THE idea was born. Let's show these concepts on a whiteboard in a form so simple that anyone can understand them.

The team shot demo videos of Andy at the whiteboard, standing in for the talent who would be hired if the concepts sold. The client loved the idea and showed Andy's clips to focus groups, who kept coming back with "we really liked the guy with the long hair who can't act." So instead of hiring actors, Andy appeared in a dozen or so simple but very effective commercials. In just one take, he used his brown marker and eraser to quickly and cleverly diagram UPS advantages for B2B customers. Every spot featured the expected marker squeaks but also a nice little surprise ending, such as the addition of an inflatable gorilla for a grand opening promotion or cherry blossoms added to the sketch of Washington, DC.

Making the complex simple—in a clever and engaging way—has been a hallmark of The Martin Agency's creative process. More importantly, the "Whiteboard" campaign helped UPS increase revenue and recognition as the number-one supply chain management service.

—Michele Barker
Corporate Communications Manager,
The Martin Agency, Richmond

LinkedIn: Facebook for businesspeople?

In 2003, a business-oriented social network called LinkedIn was launched. As of this writing, over 30 million people have registered around the world, representing over 150 industries.[5] LinkedIn gives registered users the opportunity to interact with other businesspeople, called connections, whom they know and trust. The searchable LinkedIn Groups feature allows users to establish new business relationships by joining alumni, industry, or professional and other relevant groups. In 2008, a mobile version of the site was launched along with LinkedIn DirectAds, a form of sponsored advertising.

Image 16.7

Microsoft asked corporate executives to discuss how their business gets done, touching on the role of enterprise software—in this example, it's Katie Bayne, CMO of Coca-Cola. The TV spots use an entertaining mix of real audio and lively animated effects. The campaign also extends to print and online executions. The tagline: "Because it's everybody's business."

Who's Who?

Reid Hoffman is best known as the founder of LinkedIn, a social network used primarily for business connections and job searching. After working at Apple Computer and Fujitsu, Hoffman cofounded his first company, SocialNet.com. While at SocialNet, Hoffman was instrumental in the creation of PayPal before he went on to found LinkedIn. He has been called the "most connected man in all of Silicon Valley." He has personally mentored many of the Web 2.0 CEOs and invented the term for his people as the new "Second Generation Web Entrepreneurs."[6]

Harry Jacobs exploded the myth that great advertising could only be done in New York. Under Jacobs's leadership, The Martin Agency in Charlotte, Virginia, became a creative powerhouse for consumer as well as agricultural and other business-to-business products. Today, the agency works on national and international accounts such as Coke, Hanes, Mercedes-Benz, Seiko, UPS, and Wrangler, to name a few. The Martin Agency has also been an incubator for the nation's top creative talent, developing creative directors who achieved acclaim at Wieden + Kennedy, Wells Rich Greene, Fallon, DDB, and Chiat\Day. Upon retirement from The Martin Agency, Jacobs was a founding board member of one of the top creative schools in the country, the Adcenter at Virginia Commonwealth University.

Exercises

1. Spinning B2C to B2B

This exercise is all about finding the One Thing, linking it to strategy and moving seamlessly from B2C to B2B.

- Everyone brings in an example of a campaign for a major consumer packaged good or service brand with at least three ads. Online options, such as adsoftheworld.com, are great because you can download the ads.

- As a class, select one campaign for which the brand would have strong B2B opportunities.

- Write a Copy Platform or Creative Brief, based on the concept in the B2C ads. The trick is to make the strategy, evolving out of the B2C ads, equally relevant to B2B consumers. End with one sentence describing the overarching concept in the campaign—the One Thing.

- Now concept an ad that is consistent with the brand but solves the problem of moving the brand through the B2B marketplace.

- Present the ads and share your rationale. It's great way to see a wide range of strategic interpretations.

2. Who's Your Target?

This is a great exercise to show how brand messaging shifts depending upon the audience. But you'll need to work with your teacher to make it happen.

- Pick a classic service brand such as FedEx.

- Write a positioning statement and create a short list of features and services.

- This is where your teacher comes in. Before class he or she will go to the library and pick up as many B2B publications as there are students. The magazines will represent a broad range of industries. The mystery magazines will arrive in class tucked in their own envelope.

- You will randomly select an envelope. The publication inside represents the target audience you are going to try to reach, pitching FedEx's services. Your ad will run in the same magazine.

- Write copy, with 150–200 words, for a print ad to run in your magazine. Consider the visuals that will accompany it and make notes on them. Comp up the ad.

- If you're really daring, execute one other strategically conceived tactic based on what they learned about that industry.

- Present your work. You will be amazed at how different each approach will be, thus demonstrating the importance of understanding your B2B audience—or any audience for that matter.

Notes

1. Luke Sullivan, *Hey Whipple, Squeeze This: A Guide to Creating Great Ads* (New York: John Wiley, 1998), p. 83.

2. Ibid.

3. Seth Godin, *Purple Cow: Transform Your Business by Being Remarkable* (New York: Penguin, 2002), p. 87.

4. Andy Azula, quoted by Richard Williamson, *Adweek*, March 19, 2007.

5. "What is LinkedIn?" LinkedIn Web site, http://www.linkedin.com/static?key=company_info&trk=hb_ft_abtli (accessed December 24, 2008).

6. Reid Hoffman, Wikipedia, http://en.wikipedia.org/wiki/Reid_Hoffman (accessed December 23, 2008).

Chapter 17

Survival Guide

How to Break Into This Business—and Stay There

We designed this book as a "how to" guide to help you develop better creative work. Now we'd like to share some of our personal insights about how to break into the business. We've also gathered some gems from some of the top names in our business, our fellow teachers, and creative recruiters to help you survive and thrive in the creative jungle. Gary Goldsmith, a former chief creative officer at Lowe/USA, sums it up nicely: "They [students] are entering a business where the staffing is leaner and deadlines shorter than ever before. A business that has less and less time for the necessary teaching and mentoring that is required more than ever before. . . . The more those of us in teaching and in the business can do to increase their chances, the better."[1]

Talent. Persistence. Luck. Talent is the key, but you need the persistence to keep trying to get that one interview, the one that lands you your first job. And you need a lot of luck to come out ahead of all the other persistent people who are just as talented. Nancy Vonk and Janet Kestin, co–creative directors at Ogilvy in Toronto, have been committed to mentoring junior creatives for a long time. Along the way they launched a Web site dedicated to mentoring creatives—ihaveanidea.org. That led to a best-selling *Adweek* book, *Pick Me: Breaking Into Advertising and Staying There.*

This is a tough business, which you've probably figured out by now. But as Ellen Steinberg, vice president and group creative director at McKinney in Durham, said, quoting Tom Hanks in *A League of Their Own,* "There's no crying in baseball!" There's no crying in advertising. It's business.[2]

How to Build Your Portfolio

The time to start building your portfolio is about 3 years before you need one. Like now. Then take the advice of Joyce King Thomas, chief creative officer at McCann, New York: "Show your book every 6 months and never stop working on it."[4] How many items should be in your portfolio? Every creative director may have a different answer.

Words of Wisdom

"Do not covet your ideas. Give away everything you know, and more will come back to you." [3]

—Paul Arden

The following is a compilation from dozens of creative professionals who have suffered through reviews of thousands of bad portfolios:

Inside a junior copywriter's portfolio

- **Hard assignments** like consumer package goods where the only real difference is the quality of the advertising. As one creative director said, "Show me something I never would have thought of."

- **Complete campaigns** from multiple product categories with a combination of print, outdoor, nontraditional, Web, TV, and radio. Make sure it all looks like a campaign. Show your unique creative perspective and in the process make yourself an asset that their agency can't live without.

- **Print ads** that clearly show concepting ability and always show a series. Demonstrate that you can extend your ideas.

- **Billboards** or **posters** that demonstrate exceptional creative and strategic thinking.

- **Long-copy ads** or **brochures** that show you actually can write copy.

- Overall, demonstrate that you are **great** at **concepts** and trainable as a writer and be ready to explain the strategy behind every piece in your book.

Inside a junior art director's or designer's portfolio

- **Logos** and **brand identity projects** including several examples across different product categories.

- **Complete campaigns** from multiple product categories with a combination of print, out-of-home, nontraditional, and Web. Make sure it all looks like a campaign. Show your unique creative perspective and in the process make yourself an asset that their agency can't live without. Pay special attention to the layout, typography, and color.

- **Print ads** that clearly show concepting ability and always show a series. Demonstrate that you can extend your ideas.

- **Billboards** or **posters** that demonstrate exceptional creative and strategic thinking.

- **Brochures** or other collateral pieces that show you actually can lay out different kinds of marketing tools.

- Overall, demonstrate that you have **good design sense** and superior concepting ability, you know design software, and you can be trained to create great-looking stuff. In short: Ideas. Ideas. Ideas.

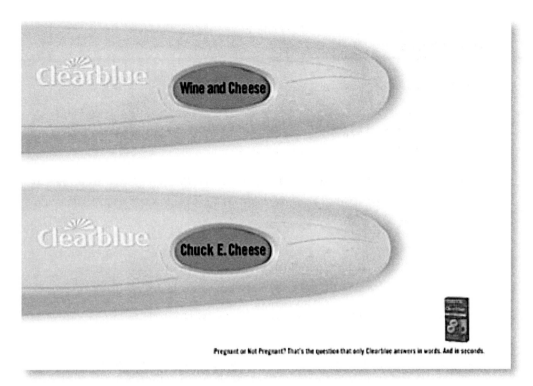

Image 17.1

Pregnant or not pregnant? Rather than providing the obvious answer, this student-designed ad uses parallel construction to show the implications of both conditions.

What *not* to put in your book

- Anything that is predictable—ads for hot sauce, condoms, animal shelters. . . . If the product calls for an obvious approach, don't bother putting it in your book.

- Ads for brands with well-known advertising—do you really think you have a better TV commercial than Bud Light or Apple?

- Too much television—put your TV on your Web site. If nothing else it's an opportunity to drive them to your site. The truth is most entry-level people won't touch TV for a few years.

- Radio scripts—your book should be a fast-moving visual delight. Scripts slow it down or interrupt the flow; besides, you've got them posted on your Web site.

- Creative Briefs, Creative Strategy Statements, and Consumer Profiles— it's assumed you know this. But be ready to verbally demonstrate your strategic brilliance.

Words of Wisdom

"I have seen no difference whatsoever between the ability of male and female creatives. I see the difference in work styles, but no difference in ability." [6]

—Jeanie Caggiano

Image 17.2

This student portrayed a traditional symbol of Judaism in a monumental way. Many students put public service ads in their book, so it's worth your time to create something truly different.

- Sentimental favorites—don't include a sample just because your ad ran in the school paper or your poster design was used by the Ad Club. A good concept that never saw the light of day is a much better option.

- Too much stuff—half a dozen great samples are better than 20 or 30 mediocre ones. Interviewers don't have a lot of time. They can spot great ideas instantly. Always think "campaigns."

Maxine Paetro has written the ultimate book on portfolios—*How to Put Your Book Together and Get a Job in Advertising.* It's chock full of great advice from the author and some of the top names in the creative field. One of her portfolio strategies is to build a "killer sandwich." We've taken that basic idea and offer our own recipe:

- First entry in your book—the very best thing you've ever done. If you could put one thing in the book, this would be it.

- The last thing in your book—the second best thing you've ever done. Something so good it took a coin toss to move it to the back.

- Everything in between—first, think "campaigns" and be sure most of them have a nontraditional execution. Second, have examples across multiple product categories. You don't need a lot, but all of it needs to kick butt.

Why put the best at the beginning and end? Psychologists say people remember the first and last thing they see (the theory of primacy and recency).

How should you format your book?

If you can actually show your work in a one-on-one meeting, nothing beats a hands-on portfolio. However, it's expensive, and you will want to leave something

It's a jungle up there.

REMINGTON
Nose-Hair Clipper

Image 17.3

Keep it simple—the student who designed this billboard gets it! The concept of symmetry between a headline and a graphic is also clearly demonstrated.

behind. So it makes sense to prepare a few mini books. You can do more than one at a time, or you can customize them for each interview. The latter is best, but it's also the most time consuming. Mini books can be created at an office supply store or through an online service like Shutterfly. Don't forget the "killer sandwich" approach, and only put the best stuff in your mini book. Have your work on a CD or DVD, and if the creative recruiter prefers electronic, he or she will let you know. Just remember the book always comes first. You can also e-mail samples of your work by attaching JPEGs or building an instant-loading HTML e-mail page. But we don't recommend this unless the recruiter or HR people request it. Chances are it will end up in the junk mail folder. Your best bet is putting your work on your own Web site or posting it on sites dedicated to showing student work. If you can segment your work into categories, you have the opportunity to show more variety—your best six print ads, your best 10 photographs, your best three videos, and your best five logo designs. It's up to the person looking at the site. Of course, when you build a Web site, you have to get someone to look at it. So whether it's through snail mail, e-mail, a telephone call, or other means, you have to promote your own site.

How to Write Your Cover Letter

Your résumé tells the basic facts of your academic and work career and, as we mentioned, probably should not be the place for wild flights of fancy. However, your cover letter can be the one place to demonstrate your writing ability and creativity. As with a cover letter for a product or service, you can follow the basic structure we described in Chapter 14. Except *you* are the product. What can you say about yourself that will get attention, stimulate interest, create a desire to know more about you, and ultimately generate action—an interview? One letter for an applicant started with "I knew I'd be the right person for this job when the toilet fell on my head." That got our attention! The letter went on

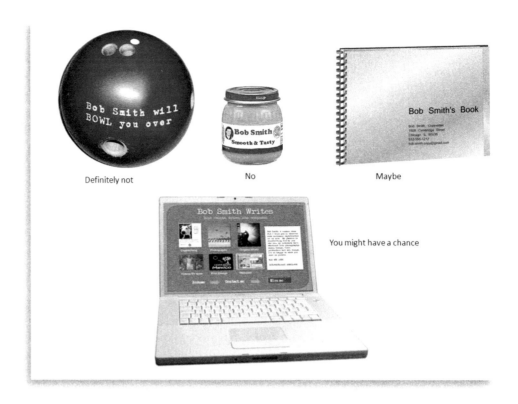

Image 17.4

Cheesy gimmicks probably won't get you an interview. A great mini book and a cool Web site might.

to describe how an accident at Home Depot convinced the applicant that he should pursue a career in advertising instead of in a big box store. You can find hundreds of Web sites that will help you craft a cover letter. Your college career office will also help you with this. Most of them give you a formula for a pure vanilla letter. So before you take the easy way out, think about the wants and needs of the customer—your potential employer. How do you meet those wants and needs? What do you bring to the table? Then figure out a creative yet professional way to present the features and benefits of the world's most unique product—you.

How to Write Your Résumé

Most creative directors or others who hire creative people demand a résumé from applicants. Too many aspiring creatives assume that this is the time to demonstrate all the creativity they can muster. So they put their names on bowling balls, bananas, toilet paper rolls, and a million other objects, in the hope that their unique résumé package will pull them out of the pack. The truth is no one wants to file a bowling ball, keep a banana in a drawer, or forward toilet paper to human resources. As cute as these gimmicks are, they usually won't help and, in most cases, will put you at the bottom of the pile.

Ad Story

Interviewing Monster Mom

Jennifer Randolph, senior vice president at Saatchi & Saatchi, has seen thousands of résumés and interviewed hundreds of applicants. Sometimes, she's forced to ask, "Are you interviewing for the job . . . or is your mom?"

"There is an interesting phenomenon occurring in business that seems to be endemic to the 'millennial' generation and that is the advocacy of parents on behalf of their children. I can't tell you how many times I've received phone calls or had parents forward résumés to my attention on behalf of their children.

"While attending a recent career fair I actually had a parent come to my booth on behalf of her child who was unable to attend the fair, due to another commitment. This mom researched sources within all the companies and set herself up as an advocate for her child's virtues with the goal of securing a summer internship opportunity.

"I think the most egregious story tops that one. A parent forwarded her daughter's resume through our Web site for our summer internship program. As luck would have it, we had a cancellation and actually had an extra seat available. I subsequently conducted an interview and hired this student. All students were told that they would receive an offer via e-mail and once we received confirmation of their participation, a formal letter would be forwarded laying out the details in order to prepare them for 'day one' of the internship program. This particular student's mother e-mailed me every 3 days to remind me that her daughter had not received a formal letter and to make me aware that my company was her first choice. Mom also called to confirm salary, inquired about the safety of the office location, and if that wasn't enough, she also arrived on the first day of the program to ensure that the company was providing all the relevant information needed for her child's successful internship.

"I can't tell you how counter-productive this type of behavior is, especially when clear direction has been provided and I am coordinating a high volume of activity at the same time. We secretly labeled her 'monster mom.'

"When a child has had so much hand holding, it makes us wonder how he or she is going to survive in the real world of work. We wonder if this person will be capable of making competent and confident decisions about where to work and what they want to do in life. Will he or she be paralyzed by fear of making mistakes? That kind of fear can cripple a career.

"Buyer beware! We had enough information to know that this would be a high-maintenance student and she was. She was very needy, desiring constant feedback and positive reinforcement. Our staff anxiously counted down the days until she would leave and we would NEVER have to see her again. We vowed never to make that mistake again! Would you believe that her mother actually called this year to see if there was another internship opportunity for her daughter? I don't have to write here what I told her.

"One caveat—if you want a job . . . do us a favor . . . call yourself and leave Mom at home!"[7]

—Jennifer Randolph
Senior Vice President, Director,
Saatchi & Saatchi, New York

Here's what the vast majority of creative executives who hire entry-level writers and art directors are looking for, in approximately this order:

- Your name, address, phone number(s), and e-mail address at the top.

- Your career experience and how it relates to the job for which you are applying. The key here is insight. Don't give a laundry list of tasks; show them what you've learned. We think this is so important, we want to show you a couple of examples from one of our students who turned tasks into *insights* and landed a lot of interviews.

TOUR GUIDE, MARQUETTE UNIVERSITY

- Brand ambassador for Marquette University (task)

- *Learned how to read people* (insight)

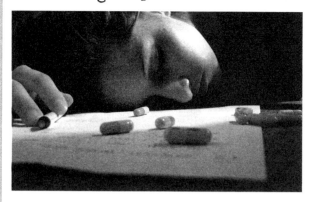

It's easier writing that goodbye letter than being the person who finds it.

Take your life, and you take away a piece of the lives from everyone you leave behind.

You may not think you're important. But others do.

Learn to live... Not for just yourself,

but for all the people who care about you.

Call us at I.800.SUICIDE. We're here to help.

HOPELINE

Image 17.5

This student was not afraid to tackle a serious subject in her portfolio.

ART CLUB EXECUTIVE, MARQUETTE UNIVERSITY

- Organized and promoted Student Fine Art Night at the Haggerty Art Museum (task)

- *Recognized that creativity takes courage* (insight)

- Accomplishments or achievements related to your work experience that might be relevant to the job or internship.

- Your education—where you went to school, your major, relevant courses, or special programs such as study abroad.

- Sorry to tell you, but your GPA, fraternity or sorority membership, and athletic achievements aren't likely to wow them. So only add them if you have room on one page, but be ready to talk about them.

- Keep it clean, easy to read, and simply designed. Designers may be able to show off a little, but applicants for writing jobs should stick to a basic design. Remember, the résumé is for identifying you. The portfolio and cover letter are for pulling you out of the pack.

What *not* to include

- A picture of yourself. The truth is some places will automatically toss your résumé due to nondiscrimination in hiring practices. Besides, they can always access your Facebook, MySpace, or LinkedIn page if they really want to see what you look like.

- Typos. One misspelled word or faulty punctuation will automatically send you to the bottom of the pile or to the circular file.

- References. You can put those with the cover letter. Hardly anyone checks references until you're much further along in the interview process. Besides, for entry-level positions, very few employers care if your professors or summer job boss liked you.

How to Get That Entry-Level Job

What agencies are looking for in entry-level creatives

CORE COMPETENCIES

- Digital. Digital. Digital. Understand the content of the digital world and the software that supports it.

- For art directors, mastery of QuarkXPress, Adobe InDesign, Adobe Photoshop, and Adobe Illustrator is useful.

- For copywriters, a working knowledge of those programs is essential. For writers, mastery of Word, WordPerfect, or other word-processing software and Excel gives you an advantage.

- Find, assemble, and organize background research.

- Understanding of agency structure, agency-client relationships, and the traditions of the advertising business.

- Understanding of basic marketing principles and key advertising terms.

- Mastery of the English language, including correct grammar and spelling.

CREATIVE SKILLS

- Ideas. Ideas. Ideas. And having the ability to explain them.

- Combine headlines and graphics into a single idea.

- Connect reader/viewer/listener with advertiser.

- Create campaigns with elements that work independently and collectively.

- Present ideas with confidence and enthusiasm.

- Ability to accept criticism and use it to improve.

PROFESSIONAL SKILLS

- Present. Present. Present. Be able to sell your ideas, as well as those of your teammates.

- Leadership ability, including being a team player.

- Willingness to learn about clients' businesses.

- Strong work ethic and the willingness to check a bad attitude at the door.

- Confidence without arrogance.

Image 17.6

Simplicity is a fantastic idea, and that's what makes this ad work. The copy tells a story that deserves an exclamation point, and that's exactly what Nano provides. This student work won silver at the Milwaukee 100. As good as it is, the copywriter headed off to portfolio school, because good sometimes is just not good enough.

How to survive as an entry-level creative

OK, you're in. Now the hard part starts. If you're lucky, you've had a few internships. If you're really lucky, you were a sponge, picking up survival tips along the way. In this age of entitlement, keep in mind that very few advertising students get their dream job.

And fewer still keep it for very long. Jean Grow and Sheri Broyles, of the University of North Texas, talked to some of the top creatives across the United States and Canada. Here's some of what they learned:[8]

SURVIVAL TIPS FOR EVERYONE

- Be a sponge.
- Don't have an attitude unless it's a good one.
- Have guts and balls.
- Don't be arrogant.
- Nothing matters but the quality of your work.
- Do more than you're asked to do.
- Know the digital landscape.
- Challenge the status quo.
- Be nice to everyone. Advertising's a small industry.
- Be a squeaky wheel. Speak up.
- Have a sense of humor.
- Be brave.
- Be yourself. Don't try to sound like everyone else.
- Ask questions and observe your environment.
- Don't say no to any assignment.
- Keep your head down and get the work done.
- Understand brands and consumers, and never ignore the client.
- Hang around with account planners and others at the agency, not just creatives.
- Be aggressive about your career. Always be looking for your next move.
- Keep your eyes on the prize and you'll always be in demand.
- Let your work be the great equalizer.
- Learn to present your work.
- Find a mentor.

What every junior woman creative needs to know

There are a lot more men than women in creative departments— a lot. It ranges from 75%–80% depending upon who you talk to.[10] In addition, in the last 10 years we have noticed a shift in the enrollment of advertising courses where we teach.

Without detailed research, we could safely say at least 65%–70% of our advertising students are female, maybe even more. Again, it raises the question: Why do men outnumber women by such wide margins in creative departments?

Knowing these dynamics, we thought it valuable to offer some advice for young female creatives trying to break into this business. The tips come from women at the top of their game, from CEOs to creative directors. They include Jeanie Caggiano, Leo Burnett; Nina DiSesa, McCann; Kara Goodrich, BBDO New York; Susan Hoffman, Wieden + Kennedy; Karen Howe, Due North; Margaret Johnson, Goodby, Silverstein & Partners; Janet Kestin, Ogilvy & Mather; Maureen Shirreff, Ogilvy & Mather; Ellen Steinberg, McKinney Silver; Linda Kaplan Thaler, Kaplan Thaler Group; Nancy Vonk, Ogilvy & Mather; and Linda Yu, Lowe Roche. Here's to "making yourself known."

JUNIOR WOMEN'S SURVIVAL GUIDE

- Take risks.

- Hang in there.

- Don't limit yourself.

- When a man gets a compliment, he says, "Thank you." Learn those two words.

- Don't be a girly girl.

- Use your instincts about women as consumers.

- Don't allow yourself to be pigeonholed in the Pink Ghetto ("women's" products).

- Don't ignore sexism if it exists. Confront it. It won't go away on its own.

- Use your emotional buttons to persuade.

- Learn from men—don't resent them.

- Don't let yourself be intimidated.

- Look for mentors and network—especially with other women.

- Work really hard while you don't have kids.

- Enjoy the guys and if you can't stand the heat, get out of the kitchen.

- Make your book so good no one notices you're a woman.[12]

How to Talk the Talk

Here are a few basic acronyms you can throw around and look like a genius. While you may get people to nod knowingly when you sprinkle these into your conversations, we suggest that you understand what they mean before you have to explain them in a client meeting.

Words of Wisdom

"It's important to be surrounded by really great people at the beginning of your career. It really sets you up for success." [11]

—Judy John

AAAA (known as the "4As")—American Association of Advertising Agencies

ABC—Audit Bureau of Circulations

AIDA—Attention, Interest, Desire, and Action

ANA—Association of National Advertisers

AQH—Average Quarter Hour audience

B2C—Business-to-Consumer, as opposed to B2B (business-to-business)

BDI—Brand Development Index

CDI—Category Development Index

CMS—Content Management System

CMYK—Cyan Magenta Yellow Black (Black is represented as K so it's not confused with Blue)

CPG—Consumer Package Goods

CPM—Cost Per Thousand (M stands for the Latin word for "thousand")

CPP—Cost Per Point

CRM—Customer Retention (or Relationship) Management

CTR—Click-Through Rate

DMA—Designated Market Areas (not to be confused with the DMA, which stands for Direct Marketing Association)

DVE—Digital Video Effects

FSI—Free-Standing Insert

GRP—Gross Rating Point

HD—High Definition

HTML—Hypertext Markup Language

HUT—Households Using Television

IGA—In-Game Advertising

IMC—Integrated Marketing Communications

ITV—Interactive TV

LTCV or LTV—Lifetime Customer Value

MIS—Marketing Information System

PLA—Program-Length Advertisement (infomercial)

PM—Push Money (also known as "spiff")

PMS—Pantone Matching System

POP—Point of Purchase (also called POS—Point of Sale)

PURL—Personalized Uniform Resource Locator (personalized domain name)

RFM—Recency, Frequency, Monetary

RGB—Red Green Blue

ROP—Run of Paper or Run on Press

ROS—Run of Station

RSS—Really Simple Syndication

SAU—Standard Advertising Unit

SEM—Search Engine Marketing

SEO—Search Engine Optimization

SRDS—Standard Rate and Date Service

SWOT analysis—Strengths, Weaknesses, Opportunities, Threats

TAP—Total Audience Plan

TVHH—Television Households

UPC—Universal Product Code

USP—Unique Selling Proposition (or sometimes Unique Story Proposition)

VALS—Values and Lifestyle System

VNR—Video News Release

VO—Voice-Over

How to Sell Your Work

In Chapter 1, we said one of the creative person's roles is selling his or her ideas to the client. You could opt to just slide your ideas under the client's door and run away, hoping the client will like them. However, in selling your ideas, you're also selling yourself, ensuring gainful employment, and building some very valuable self-esteem. People learn a fear of public speaking in kindergarten. Most people, even gifted public speakers, never get over that naked fear of standing in front of an audience. The difference is that gifted public speakers have the ability to channel that fear into positive energy.

At the risk of sounding like an ad for Toastmasters: The ability to present your ideas in public is a skill you'll use all your life, whether you're an advertising executive or just offering a toast at a wedding. While you may dread presenting your work to your peers or outside reviewers, without solid presentation skills your best idea will die before it even gets past your creative director.

Here are 10 tips offered to students competing in the National Student Advertising Competition sponsored each year by the American Advertising Federation. While they apply to a high-level formal new-business pitch, most of the tips work for informal presentations as well.

1. **Start with an idea.** Tell how that idea relates to your strategy and tactical recommendations. Keep using that idea throughout your presentation, and come back to it at the end. Tell 'em what you're gonna tell 'em, sell 'em, and then tell 'em what you told 'em.

2. **If you have a theme, use it early and often.** Weave it through your presentation. If you use a stunt or a gimmick, make sure it fits. It should complement your theme and recommendations. Don't use a gimmick just to be different; rather, focus on the theme.

3. **Remember, the first minutes of your presentation are critical.** This is when you set the tone of your presentation. The introduction grabs attention. It should instantly engage the audience.

4. **Your insight of the target audience will drive your presentation.** It's very simple—who are you talking to/what will you tell them/how will you deliver the message/how do you know it will work?

5. **Don't memorize.** Know your material and speak from the heart, not from memory. And above all, don't read from note cards. If you need note cards, sneak a peek before you begin speaking.

6. **Eye contact is important.** Use "eye bursts," where you look at an individual audience member for 2 to 3 seconds at a time. Find the "head nodders"—people who are listening and agreeing with you. (These should be your nonpresenting teammates.) They'll give you confidence.

7. **Aim for a tone that's confident but humble.** In other words, be confident and enthusiastic but also self-effacing when necessary. Don't come across as a know-it-all. Refer to your research as the basis for your opinions rather than your superior intelligence. Don't be afraid to use a little humor, if it can be naturally worked into the presentation. You should not be deadly earnest or too flippant.

8. **Don't be a slave to your graphics or technology.** PowerPoint slides or Flash programs should highlight your verbal presentation, not replace it. Don't read from your slides, and keep them simple. If you have a lot to say, use more slides. Never apologize for poor-quality visuals, video or audio, and so on. All the reviewers will hear is that you didn't care enough to give it your best effort.

Words of Wisdom

"At the end of a presentation, it's not your brilliant strategy or clever ideas that win the business. It really depends on whether the client thinks you're the kind of people they want to hang around with." [14]

—John Melamed

9. **Get technical help to set up.** If you're not confident of your technical ability, make sure you have someone who is an expert at setting up the equipment.

10. **Ask for the business.** You're not there to just entertain them. You're there to land the business—or win the competition.

How to make it memorable

You have to find the right blend of entertainment and serious business information. Here are some methods others have used to open up their presentations:

Tell a story. Every brand has a story. Every consumer has a profile. Every marketer has an inspiration. Discover the story behind the product and the people who buy it—or need to buy it—and use it to open your presentation.

Ask a question. One winning presentation opened with "Your house is burning down. Your family is safe, but you only have time to get one possession from your house. What would it be?" Or more generically, "What's the most important thing in your life?"

Start with a video. If you use a video, it should be short and crisply edited, with a clear message. Remember, this sets the tone for the whole presentation.

Make a series of statements. Each team member states an opinion or a misconception about the client or their products. Follow with "That's what people told us . . . and this is how we plan to change their minds."

Bring your target audience to life. A day in the life. "Let me introduce you to . . . [name of people]." Or some other compelling way to draw the audience in.

How to handle questions

Sometimes the outcome of a presentation depends more on how you defend your work than on the quality of the work itself. Here are a few tips for dealing with questions. Remember, how you answer is just as important as what you say.

Each question is an opportunity. Don't take it as a criticism of your effort. Sometimes reviewers just want to see how you defend your work. If you get too defensive, vague, or impatient, your attitude may turn them off. (They are much more sensitive to this than you may realize.)

Answer the question! You should be able to explain calmly and confidently why you did what you did. Don't be a politician. (If you can't defend what you did, then you made the wrong decisions.) Prepare for them. Try to come up with the toughest possible questions.

Words of Wisdom

"Don't give a speech. Put on a show." [15]

—Paul Arden

Pay attention to your tone of voice. Just like your physical motions, your tone of voice says a lot about you. Be sure to answer questions in a strong, consistent tone. Don't act offended, impatient, or flustered.

Avoid wavering. Talking too softly, mumbling, or speaking too quickly won't win them over.

You are too close to your work. That's why it's hard for you to understand why someone doesn't get it. Think about the early phases of your planning. What questions did you ask yourselves? Why did you do things that way? Those are some of the questions others will also have.

Get an outsider's opinion. Have them review your book and presentation and invite their questions and comments. Don't be surprised if people are not as crazy about your ideas as you are. Encourage constructive criticism. It's good practice for handling reviewers.

How to think on your feet

Take a deep breath. Think for a second and then begin to answer. This will help calm your nerves and will give you the opportunity to "look before you leap" when it comes to answering important questions.

Repeat the question. You can always ask the client or reviewer to clarify a part of it. This gives you and your teammates more time to think about an answer.

Finish your answer. Don't taper off and leave a question unanswered. Your teammates will instinctively jump in to finish your sentence and try to bail you out.

Don't act surprised. If a question comes out of left field, try to retain your composure because it may seem very logical to the reviewer. For example, if someone asks you why you didn't do something, you could say, "We looked into that, but our research indicated that some other approaches would work better" or "We studied a lot of ways to do this and found this was the most cost-efficient way to achieve our objectives."

Forget "That's a good question." That's code for "We never thought of that and don't have the answer."

Don't change the subject. Think for a second and then answer the question to the best of your ability. If you sense the reviewer is not satisfied, simply ask, "Did I answer your question?"

Don't argue. Don't cave in. You had reasons for making these decisions. The reviewers don't necessarily disagree, but they want to see how you defend your work.

Words of Wisdom

"The secret is to keep listening to that wee, small voice—and don't ever be afraid of getting your hands dirty." [16]

—Leo Burnett

How to Get That Next Great Job

Young creative people often ask about job hopping. They're worried that changing jobs too many times will limit their future employability. In many industries that's a concern. But in the ad business, jumping from agency to agency is the norm. However, honor any commitments you've made and try to stay at least 1 or 2 years before you start looking. Just don't burn any bridges when you leave; you might have the opportunity to come back to a former employer in a few years for even more money. Advertising is a small world, and the "get along" factor is almost as important as talent. In the end, you will be judged on how well coworkers, bosses, and especially clients like you. That may very well determine how much you're really worth.

How to Get More Information

We've compiled a list of trade publications and creative magazines, books, and Web sites that will help you understand more about the creative side of the business. This is only the beginning of a lifetime of learning.

Trade publications and creative magazines

- *Advertising Age*—for decades *Ad Age* has been *the* authoritative voice of the industry. If you read one magazine about advertising, this is it.

- *Adweek*—edited for ad agency executives with the inside stories on creativity, client/agency relationships, and successful global advertising strategies.

- *Brandweek*—covers marketer/retailer relationships, media strategies, agency/client relationships, and global marketing plus news briefs, trends, campaigns, promotions, and new products.

- *CMYK*—where aspiring creatives showcase their talents and where creative directors recruit students and recent graduates.

- *Communication Arts*—calls itself the world's most inspiring magazine, and who can argue with that, given that it's the first book nearly every creative looks to for ideas in concepts, design, and copywriting excellence for virtually every phase of our business?

- *Creativity*—a monthly magazine, published by *Ad Age,* covering all things creative in advertising and design.

Books

History

A History of Advertising by Stéphane Pincas & Mark Loiseau

Ad Women by Juliann Sivulka

Ogilvy on Advertising by David Ogilvy

Soap, Sex, and Cigarettes by Juliann Sivulka

Marketing & strategy

The Brand Bubble by John Gerzema & Ed Lebar

The Brand Gap by Marty Neumeier

Brand Portfolio Strategy by David Aaker

Obsessive Branding Disorder by Lucas Conley

Positioning: The Battle for Your Mind by Al Ries & Jack Trout

Purple Cow: Transform Your Business by Being Remarkable by Seth Godin

Media influence

Groundswell by Charlene Li & Josh Bernoff

Grown Up Digital by Don Tapscott

Here Comes Everybody by Clay Shirky

The Way We'll Be by John Zogby

The basics

Design, Form, and Chaos by Paul Rand

Eats, Shoots & Leaves by Lynne Truss

Idea Industry by Brett Robbs & Deborah Morrison

Perfect Pitch by Jon Steel

Creative thinking

Brand Sense by Martin Lindstrom

Hey Whipple, Squeeze This: A Guide to Creating Great Advertising by Luke Sullivan

The Do-It-Yourself Lobotomy by Tom Monahan

Unstuck by Keith Yamashita & Sandra Spataro

A Whole New Mind by Daniel Pink

Controlling your career

How to Put Your Book Together and Get a Job in Advertising by Maxine Paetro

Pick Me by Nancy Vonk and Janet Kestin

Radical Careering by Sally Hogshead

Seducing the Boys Club by Nina DiSesa

The Adventures of Johnny Bunko by Daniel Pink

Web sites

Creative inspiration
creativegeneralist.blogspot.com
creativity-online.com
copychief.com
edwardtufte.com
howdesign.com
theslot.com
wga.org

Brand strategy
apg.org.uk
brandrepublic.com
brandtags.net
garethkay.typepad.com
marketingpower.com
marketingsherpa.com
pinkair.com
russelldavis.typepad.com
sethgodin.com

Portfolio schools
braincomsa.com
creativecircus.com
miamiadschool.com
portfoliocenter.com
brandcenter.vcu.edu

Career planning
fastcompany.com
ihaveanidea.org
jobbound.com
radicalcareering.com

Get smart
changethis.com
russelldavies.typepad.com
darmano.typepad.com/logic_emotion
freakonomics.blogs.nytimes.com
socialmediatoday.com/SMC
ted.com
trendwatching.com
visualthesaurus.com

Who's Who?

For the most part, we've featured advertising superstars who have achieved fame over lengthy careers. In this section, we'd like you to meet some inspiring young entrepreneurs who could be destined for any number of future Who's Who lists.

The idea: To create a mobile ordering system where customers order and pay for take-out meals from restaurants on their cell phones.

The entrepreneur: Noah Glass

His age: 25

The launch place: New York

The launch date: 2005

The link: gomobo.com

The story: Before Noah Glass finished his political science degree at Yale, he had already worked at Shutterfly, Amnesty International, and Braun Consulting and had been accepted by Harvard Business School. He deferred admission to pursue an opportunity at Endeavor, a nonprofit organization supporting high-growth entrepreneurs in developing countries. After interviewing more than 150 entrepreneurs in South Africa, the entrepreneurial bug bit Glass too. Glass found inspiration in the long lines for coffee in his hometown of New York City and invented Mobo. The service alerts users with text messages when their meals are ready. Restaurants that use the service report an upsurge in business, since it saves them time and gets people in and out faster, reducing lines. Restaurants pay Mobo 10% of each sale generated through the service. Glass has plans for growth, but as of this writing, his business was booming in NYC with 2007 revenues topping $1.8 million.[17]

The idea: To be a professional brainstormer, using ethnographic research techniques to harness creativity and insight from diverse young minds to solve companies' problems.

The entrepreneur: Anand Chhatpar

His age: 24

The launch place: Madison, WI

The launch date: 2004

The link: www.brainreactions.com

The story: As a student at the University of Wisconsin–Madison, Anand Chhatpar saw a diverse student population with lots of ideas and in need of money. Chhatpar had recently interned at Pitney Bowes' renowned Advanced Concepts and Technology Center, where he learned techniques in ethnographic research and prototyping. He recognized that if he could harness the creativity and insight of a diverse group of people, he might be able to use their insights to solve business problems. From this idea BrainReactions was born, and so was a pool of professional brainstormers who create new product features, crack new market segments, and develop customer-service improvements for clients. The company's first client, Bank of America, was referred to BrainReactions by Chhatpar's former Pitney Bowes boss. BrainReactions now counts Intuit, the Peace Corps, Procter & Gamble, Pitney Bowes, and Quantum Learning Network as clients. BrainReactions has since expanded to offer Idea Generation Workshops that assist organizations in promoting new thinking. Talk about a right-brain business model! He's now onto his second startup and holds six patents, with one pending. His core belief is that innovative ideas come from fresh minds and new perspectives.[18]

The idea: To help Hispanic job seekers in metro New York develop job search tools and connect with employers on a Spanish-language Web site.

The entrepreneur: Eli Portnoy

His age: 25

The launch place: New York

The launch date: 2005

The link: www.buenachamba.com

The story: *Hola*, Employment! A Mexican native educated at the University of Pennsylvania, Eli Portnoy left a job as a business analyst with Deloitte Consulting to launch BuenaChamba.com. The English version is LatinoHire.com. The site aims to advertise jobs in predominantly Hispanic neighborhoods in New York and New Jersey. Leveraging Hispanic social networks, Portnoy also publishes a weekly newspaper with the ads and circulates it to churches and community centers. "The combination of Web and print helps take into account cultural and economic limitations, such as lack of Internet access. Job ads submitted to the site in English can be automatically translated into Spanish. The site continues to grow, and, says Portnoy, "If the basic concept of your business is to help people, the business will succeed."[19]

Words of Wisdom

The following was written by Charles Hall, an African American copywriter, film director, and now professor at the Virginia Commonwealth University Brandcenter. While some of it applies specifically to people of color, it's good advice for anyone starting out:

to the blacks browns reds and yellows periwinkles teals and fuchsias

if you want to be in advertising, there is one thing to remember.

don't be afraid.

of hard work, rejection, racism, responsibility, sexism.

don't be afraid of being the only one in the room.

don't be afraid to ask questions. find answers. listen. hear. trust.

don't be afraid to follow. don't be afraid to lead.

don't be afraid to learn. to grow. to mature. to change.

don't be afraid to try. to fail. to try again. fail again. try again and fail again.

don't be afraid to ask for help.

don't be afraid to be smart. clever. witty. funky. hard. street. elegant. beautiful. you.

don't be afraid to be fired.

don't be afraid when you hear the word nigger.

don't be afraid to remind them that right after the black jokes come the jewish jokes the polish jokes and the fat jokes.

don't be afraid to master the craft. to master the game.

don't be afraid when they don't understand your accent, dialect, or slang. your heroes, your sex symbols. your style. your music. your people. your culture. your you.

don't be afraid to take criticism.

don't be afraid to be wrong. to be right.

don't be afraid to speak your mind. stand up for what you believe and pay the consequences.

don't be afraid to be a team player.

don't be afraid to be the peon. the rookie. the junior. the helper. the pair of hands. the intern. the student.

don't be afraid to not be the victim. don't be afraid to not take it personally. don't be afraid to call a spade a spade.

don't be afraid to have a personality. an opinion. a point of view. a perspective. an objective. a positive attitude.

don't be afraid of those who are threatened by your presence. or feel you don't belong. or those who need you to fail for them to succeed.

don't be afraid to understand the difference between racism and insecurity. between racism and power. between sexism and chauvinism.

don't be afraid to forgive. to apologize. to be humble.

don't be afraid to surrender. to win. to lose. to fight.

don't be afraid of titles, awards. salaries. egos. offices. windows. ponytails. clothes. jewelry. degrees. backgrounds. lifestyles. cars. beach houses.

don't be afraid to compete.

don't be afraid of not being popular.

don't be afraid to work weekends. holidays. birthdays. sick days. personal days.

don't be afraid to work twice as hard. twice as long. twice as good.

don't be afraid to get more out of this business than this business ever intended on giving.

p.s. and under no circumstances whatsoever are you to be intimidated. because some will try.[20]

Exercises

With these final exercises we wish you well on your professional journey.

1. Creative Think Tank

- Find a group of fellow creatives and have a dedicated meeting time every week.

- Carve out two or three hours each week dedicated to going on a creative hunting expedition. Be committed to coming away with at least three new creative concepts, ideas, or campaigns that rock your world.

- Now use your weekly meeting as a creative think tank. Share the new ideas you find and critique each other's work. And if you can find a place dedicated to this process, leave things behind. Create an artifact room.

- Chances are you'll become friends and allies for life.

2. Improving on Schedule

- Find an industry mentor, someone you trust and who will be brutally honest.

- Make a commitment to seeing them regularly. No excuses.

- Show them new and revised work every time you meet. Listen to them. Trust them.

- One day, return the favor.

3. Do Nothing

- Do nothing related to advertising for an entire day.

- Do this with regularity, even if infrequently.

- Rest and replenish your creative spirit.

Notes

1. Quoted in Maxine Paetro, *How to Put Your Book Together and Get a Job in Advertising* (Chicago: Copy Workshop, 2002), p. 152.

2. Ellen Steinberg, interviewed by authors, May 2007.

3. Paul Arden, *It's Not How Good You Are, It's How Good You Want to Be* (London: Phaidon, 2003), p. 30.

4. Joyce King Thomas, interviewed by authors, June 2007.

5. Quoted in Paetro, *How to Put Your Book Together and Get a Job in Advertising,* pp. 185–186.

6. Jeanie Caggiano, interviewed by authors, July 2007.

7. Jennifer Randolph, Ad Story: *Interviewing Monster Mom,* February 2009.

8. Interview series, April–June 2007.

9. Susan Treacy, interviewed by authors, July 2007.

10. Sheri J. Broyles and Jean M. Grow, "Creative Women in Advertising Agencies: Why So Few 'Babes in Boyland,'" *Journal of Consumer Marketing,* 15, no. 1 (2008)*,* pp. 4–6.

11. Judy John, interviewed by authors, July 2007.

12. Interview series, April–June 2007.

13. Phil Dusenberry, *Then We Set His Hair on Fire* (New York: Penguin, 2005), p. 132.

14. John Melamed, presentation, Marquette University, Milwaukee, WI, February 10, 2004.

15. Arden, *It's Not How Good You Are,* p. 68.

16. Leo Burnett, "Keep Listening to That Wee, Small Voice," talk to the Chicago Copywriters Club, October 4, 1960.

17. Nick Leiber, "The Winners: Best Entrepreneurs Under 25," *BusinessWeek,* November 15, 2006, http://www.businessweek.com/smallbiz/content/nov2006/sb20061115_008589.htm?chan=smallbiz_special+report+—+best+entrepreneurs+under+25_best+entrepreneurs+under+25 (accessed January 3, 2009).

18. Stacy Perman, "Entrepreneurs: Cream of the Young Crop," *BusinessWeek,* October 31, 2005, http://images.businessweek.com/ss/05/10/young_entrepreneur/source/1.htm (accessed December 20, 2008).

19. Perman, "Entrepreneurs: Cream of the Young Crop."

20. Quoted in Paetro, *How to Put Your Book Together and Get a Job in Advertising*, p. 156.

Copy Platform (Creative Strategy Statement)

Product (Service) _____

The Product (or Service)

A. Primary features/benefits in order of importance (remember "so whats?")

Feature	Benefit
1. _____	1. _____
2. _____	2. _____
3. _____	3. _____
4. _____	4. _____

B. Exclusive or unique product (service) attributes

_____

C. Can product claims be substantiated?

_____

D. Parent company name important? _____ Why?

_____

E. Brand value: High status _____ Low status _____ No brand image _____

The Consumer

A. Demographics (age, sex, education, income, occupation, geographic distribution)

_____

_____

_____

B. Psychographics (lifestyle, attitude, personality traits, buying patterns)

_____

_____

_____

C. Needs fulfilled by buying this product or service

_____

_____

_____

The Marketplace

A. Major competitors/rank in market/market share

1. _____ / _____ / _____
2. _____ / _____ / _____
3. _____ / _____ / _____

B. Competitive advantage/disadvantage of product (service)

Competitor   Our advantage (disadvantage)

_____   _____

_____   _____

_____   _____

C. Position of product (service) in market

Parity product (no perceived competitive advantage) _____

_____

New product category (first of its kind) _____

_____

Significant improvement over similar products _____

_____

D. Pricing position (compared to competition)

Premium priced _____ Comparably priced _____ Low priced _____

Creative Strategy

A. The "One Thing": If you could say one thing about this product or service:

_____

_____

B. Significant facts or statistics about product, consumer, or market

_____

_____

_____

Copyediting and Proofreading Symbols

Begin paragraph	¶ Years ago we invested in a small Seattle-based coffee…
Set in italics	Isn't it <u>interesting</u> how the English countryside… (ital)
Set in caps	Try the hotpockets. they're breathtaking. (cap)
Set in lowercase	Is it an Evil Petting Zoo? (lc)
Insert period, comma	No, Mr. Powers, I expect you to…. ⊙ /
Insert question mark	Why won't you die ?
Insert apostrophe	It got weird, didn't it?
Insert hyphen	Do you like your quasi futuristic outfits?
Insert quotes	When a problem comes along, you must zip it.
Put in space	Are they angry seabass? #
Close up	Crikey! I've lost my mojo.
Set in boldface	I'm from Holland. Isn't <u>that</u> weird? (bf)
Insert word	He kind of looks like baby. a
Delete word	No, this is me in a nutshell.
Delete and close up	Moove over rover. This chick is taking over.
Leave as it was	A <u>trillion</u> is more than a billion… stet
Transpose	I call it the Parsons Allen Project. (tr)
Spell out word	Who does number ② work for? (sp)
Copy on next page	more
End of copy	### or —30—

Radio Production Terms

AFTRA: American Federation of Television and Radio Artists, one of the two main unions for voice talent.

ANNCR: Announcer.

Board: Electronic control panel for recording, mixing, and editing.

Boom mike: Microphone on long extension, over announcer's head.

Buyout: Total payment to talent for one-time use, as opposed to residual payments.

Cans: Slang for announcer's headphones.

Compression: Electronic removal of dead air between words.

DAT: Digital audiotape.

Dead air: No sound between words or sound effects.

Demo: Demonstration recording for reviewing or auditioning, not meant for airing.

Donut: Nonvocal musical segment or sound effect that allows an announcer to read copy over it.

Double donut: Usually a commercial with a musical intro, an announcer segment, a musical middle, an announcer segment, and a musical close.

Fade: Gradually reduce (fade out) or increase (fade up) volume.

Flight: Time frame during which a commercial runs.

In: Introduce music or effect.

Out: Music or effect is deleted abruptly.

Nonlinear: Segments recorded out of sequence and assembled digitally.

P&W: Pension and Welfare, additional payments made to SAG/AFTRA talent.

PD: Public domain (music with no royalty fees, as in classical music).

Phone patch: Review of recording over phone lines instead of in the studio.

Punch in: Insert rerecorded segment into commercial to replace a segment.

Quarter track: Analog recording tape with four channels (two each direction).

Residual: Payment made to talent after the initial run of the commercial.

Reverb: Reverberation, an echolike effect.

SAG: Screen Actors Guild, one of the two main unions for voice talent.

Sample: Digital recording and re-creation of music or sound effect.

Segue: Gradually lead into a new segment of a commercial.

SFX: Sound effects.

Slice of life: Simulated real-world situation, usually using dialogue.

Spot: Commercial.

Spot market: A local media buy rather than network.

Stage whisper: Whisper that's loud enough to be easily heard and understood.

Stinger: Musical effect to provide emphasis, usually at the end of a jingle.

Swell: Expansion of copy to fit a specific segment (e.g., translation of English to Spanish usually accounts for a 20% swell due to the increase in words).

Tag: End of a commercial, usually with the name of store locations, hours, or other information.

Take: Reading of a segment of copy at one time; each reading is a take. Most commercials involve several takes.

Talent: Announcer, actors, singers, or musicians in a commercial.

Talk back: The button an engineer or producer uses to communicate with talent in an isolated booth.

Under: Reduce the volume of music or an effect so you can hear the announcer.

Up: Raise the volume of music or an effect.

Voice of God: Conversation with someone "off-camera," usually with an effect such as an echo.

White noise: Undefined noise such as static.

TV and Video Production Terms

Accelerated montage: Sequence edited into progressively shorter shots to create a mood of tension and excitement.

Ambient light: Natural light surrounding the subject, usually understood to be soft.

Aspect ratio: Ratio of the width to the height of the film or television image. The formerly standard Academy aperture is 1.33:1. Wide-screen ratios vary. In Europe 1.66:1 is most common; in the United States, 1.85:1. Anamorphic processes such as CinemaScope and Panavision are even wider, 2.00:1 to 2.55:1.

Asynchronous sound: Sound that does not operate in unison with the image, sound belonging to a particular scene that is heard while the images of the previous scene are still on-screen, or sound from a previous scene that continues over a following scene. *Also* diegetic sound whose source cannot be seen on screen or sound unintentionally out of sync with the image track.

Backlighting: Main source of light is behind the subject, silhouetting it, and directed toward the camera.

Bird's-eye shot: Wide shot taken from high above the action. Also called *overhead shot.*

Blue screen or **green screen** or **chroma-key:** Shooting a subject in front of a blue or green background so the image can be superimposed over another background. The camera can be adjusted not to pick up blue or green, so, in effect, you have a blocked-out image on a clear background.

Boom: Traveling arm for suspending a microphone above the actors and outside the frame. See also **crane**.

Bridge: Passage linking two scenes either by continuing music across the transition or by beginning the sound (including dialogue or music) of the next scene over images of the previous scene. Also called *sound advance.*

Bridging shot: Shot used to cover a jump in time or place or other discontinuous changes.

Continuity editing: Technique whereby shots are arranged in sequence to create the illusion of a credible chronological narrative. Often contrasted with **montage editing**.

Crane: Mechanical arm used to move a camera through space above the ground or to position it in the air. A *crane shot* allows the camera to vary distance, angle, and height. Also called *boom shot.*

Crosscutting: Intermingling the shots of two or more scenes to suggest *parallel action.*

Cutaway: Shot inserted in a scene to show action at another location, usually brief; most often used to cover breaks in the main take, as in television and documentary interviews. Also used to provide comment on the action (e.g., by cutting away from scenes of explicit sex or extreme violence).

Day for night: Practice of using filters to shoot night scenes during the day.

Depth of field: Range of distances from the camera at which the subject is acceptably sharp.

Detail shot: Usually more magnified than a close-up; shot of a hand, an eye, a mouth, or a subject of similar detail.

Drive-by shot: View of a person, an object, or a place from a camera located on a moving vehicle as it passes by.

Dub: To rerecord dialogue in a language other than the original or record dialogue in a specially equipped studio after the film has been shot.

Dupe: To print a duplicate negative from a positive print or print a duplicate reversal print; also the term for a print made in this manner.

Establishing shot: Generally a long shot that shows the audience the general location of the scene that follows, often providing essential information and orienting the viewer.

Fast motion (or **accelerated motion**): Film is shot at less than 24 frames per second (i.e., the camera is undercranked) so that when it is projected at the normal speed actions appear to move much faster; often useful for comic effect.

Final cut: Film in its final state, as opposed to **rough cut**.

Flash forward: Scene or shots of future time. See **flashback**.

Flash frame: Shot of only a few frames in duration, sometimes a single frame, which can just barely be perceived by the audience.

Flashback: Scene or sequence (sometimes an entire film) inserted into a scene in "present" time that deals with the past.

Focus pull: Pull focus during a shot in order to follow a subject as it moves away from or toward the camera.

Follow shot: Tracking shot or zoom that follows the subject as it moves.

Frame: Any single image on the film. Also refers to the size and shape of the image on the film or on the screen when projected or to the compositional unit of film design.

Freeze frame: Freeze shot achieved by printing a single frame many times in succession to give the illusion of a still photograph when projected.

FX: Effects.

Gaffer: Chief electrician, responsible to the director of photography; responsible for all major electrical installations on the set, including lighting and power.

High key: Type of lighting arrangement in which the *key light* is very bright, often producing shadows.

Intercutting: See **parallel editing**.

Jump cut: Cut in which two shots of the same subject in sequence are taken from only slightly varied camera positions. (Do not confuse with **match cut**.)

Key light: Main light on a subject. Usually placed at a 45-degree angle to the camera-subject axis.

Mask: Shield placed in front of the camera lens to change the shape of the image. Often used in POV (point-of-view) shots (e.g., looking through binoculars or a keyhole).

Master shot: Long take of an entire scene, generally a relatively long shot that facilitates assembly of component closer shots and details. Because the editor can always fall back on the master shot, it is also called a *cover shot.*

Match cut: Cut in which the two shots are linked by visual, aural, or metaphorical parallelism. Famous example: At the end of *North by Northwest,* Cary Grant pulls Eva Marie Saint up the side of Mount Rushmore; match cut to Grant pulling her up to a Pullman bunk. (Do not confuse with **jump cut**.)

Montage editing: Technique of arranging shots in sequence to create connotations and associations rather than a standard chronologically unfolding narrative. See also **continuity editing**.

Parallel action (or parallel montage): Narrative device in which two scenes are observed in parallel through *crosscutting.*

Parallel editing: Narrative construction that crosscuts between two or more lines of action that are supposed to be occurring simultaneously. Usually restricted to particular sequences in a film, *crosscutting* can also occur between lines of action that are thematically related rather than simultaneous.

Postproduction: Increasingly complex stage in the production of a film that takes place after shooting has been completed; involves editing, addition of titles, creation of special effects, and final sound track, including dubbing and mixing.

Preproduction: Phase of film production following the securing of financial backing but preceding shooting; includes work on the script, casting, hiring crews, finding locations, constructing sets, drawing up schedules, arranging catering, and so on.

Reaction shot: Shot that cuts away from the main scene or speaker in order to show a character's reaction to it.

Rough cut: First assembly of a film, prepared by the editor from the selected takes, which are joined in the order planned in the script. Finer points of timing and montage are left to a later stage.

Shooting ratio: Ratio between film actually exposed in the camera during shooting to film used in the final cut. A shooting ratio of 10 to 1 or more is not uncommon.

Soft focus: Filters, Vaseline, or specially constructed lenses soften the delineation of lines and points, usually to create a romantic effect.

Subjective camera: Style that allows the viewer to observe events from either the point of view of a character or the persona of the author.

Sweep in (or **wipe in**): Frame-by-frame revelation from blackout of complete image.

Sweep out (or **wipe out**): Opposite of **sweep in**.

Swish pan (or **flick pan, zip pan, whip pan**): Pan in which the intervening scene moves past too quickly to be observed; approximates psychologically the action of the human eye as it moves from one subject to another.

Synchronous sound: Sound whose source is visible in the frame of the image or whose source is understandable from the context of the image (e.g., source music).

Tracking shot (or **traveling shot**): Generally, any shot in which the camera moves from one point to another sideways, in, or out. The camera can be handheld or mounted on a set of wheels that move on tracks or on a rubber-tired dolly.

Wild sound: Sound recorded separately from images.

Tom Altstiel is creative director and partner at Prom Krog Altstiel, Inc. (PKA), a Milwaukee-area marketing communications agency. He has been a copywriter and creative director at several Chicago- and Milwaukee-area agencies, working on accounts for consumer, business-to-business, and agricultural clients. He earned a master's degree in advertising at the University of Illinois–Urbana-Champaign and has been teaching at Marquette University as an adjunct instructor since 1999. In 2003 he received the Dean's Recognition Award for Outstanding Part-Time Faculty, and in 2004 he advised the Marquette team at the NSAC finals in Dallas. He is also an adjunct professor at Concordia University Wisconsin, teaching undergraduate and MBA marketing classes.

Jean Grow is associate professor in the Department of Advertising and Public Relations at Marquette University. She earned her PhD from the University of Wisconsin–Madison and her BFA from the School of the Art Institute of Chicago. She has won numerous teaching awards including the Dean's Award for Teaching Excellence in 2007. Grow remains active in the industry as a branding consultant with a focus on gender and semiotics. Prior to moving to Wisconsin, she worked in Chicago as an artists' representative; her agency clients included DDB Needham, Foote Cone & Belding, J. Walter Thompson, and Leo Burnett.